The Author

P. Sargant Florence was born in 1890, and educated at Rugby and at Gonville and Caius College, Cambridge, where he gained first class honours in Economics. He went as Garth Fellow to Columbia University, New York, and after research in industrial fatigue during the First World War, he became University Lecturer in Economics at Cambridge. From 1929 to 1955 he was Professor of Commerce at the University of Birmingham, where he is now Emeritus Professor. Since then he has held visiting Professorships at Johns Hopkins University and the University of Rhode Island. He was Chairman of the Greater Birmingham Employment Committee from 1957 to 1963, and Consultant to the Jordan Development Board from 1960 to 1961. He is the author of numerous books on Economics and the allied Social Sciences.

THE LOGIC
OF BRITISH AND AMERICAN INDUSTRY

The Logic
of British and American Industry

A REALISTIC ANALYSIS OF ECONOMIC STRUCTURE
AND GOVERNMENT

by

P. SARGANT FLORENCE

M.A.(Cambridge), Ph.D., Hon. L.H.D.(Columbia),
Hon. D.Soc.Sc.(Birm.), (Hon.) C.B.E.
Emeritus Professor, Faculty of Commerce and Social Science,
University of Birmingham

LONDON
ROUTLEDGE & KEGAN PAUL

46188

First published 1953
by Routledge & Kegan Paul Ltd
Broadway House, 68-74 Carter Lane
London, EC4V 5EL

Printed in Great Britain
by C. Tinling & Co. Ltd
London and Prescot

Second edition 1961
Third edition 1972
© *P. Sargant Florence* 1953, 1961, 1972

ISBN 0 7100 7155 8

PREFACE TO THE FIRST EDITION

SINCE my *Logic of Industrial Organization,* on which this present book is partly based, appeared in 1933, facts have changed and so have the records of the facts. In particular, data collected by the British census of production are now presented in a way that facilitates comparison with America in many structural features, such as the size or location of factories and the degree of concentration of an industry in a few hands. My own research into official records of English joint stock companies also permits comparison of large-scale industrial government in both countries. This book deals with the more persistent structure of a country's industry, and it is not necessary for its thesis, except where changes are discussed, to have the very latest news. But it is good at last to have a solid and firmly constructed foundation of fact on which to build, officially recorded for both countries.

In the search for the underlying logic of industrial organization the possibilities of such measured comparison justifies the focus on Britain and America implied in the title of this book. The sub-title indicates that though realistic and not an exercise in abstract economic theory, this work is not merely descriptive.

My realistic form of analysis has been developed over a long period and I am forced to refer for details to earlier works at many points. To save space, and spare the reader boredom, I have omitted repetition of the titles of the chief books involved and have been content to give dates only, thus:

Florence, 1929, stands for my *Statistical Method in Economics and Political Science.*

Florence, 1933, stands for my *Logic of Industrial Organization.*

Florence, 1948, stands for my *Investment, Location and Size of Plant.*

Other abbreviations for sources, hallowed in this case by common usage, are:

T.N.E.C. = Temporary National Economic Committee of the U.S. Congress 1939–41.

N.R.C. = National Resources Committee, which was followed by the

N.R.P.B. = National Resources Planning Board, in issuing reports from 1937–1943 on the U.S. economy.

H.M.S.O. = Her Majesty's Stationery Office, London.

I have also been content to use 'Britain' rather than the more legal, if not legalistic, 'Great Britain'. England and English have been used when appropriate, as of English public schools and of English joint stock companies for companies registered in London not Edinburgh.

My most grateful thanks for reading through my manuscripts are due to Mr George M. Lawrence, Senior Research Fellow, 1951–2, and Dr Michael Beesley, Lecturer in Commerce, both in the Faculty of Commerce and Social Science at the University of Birmingham. Many alterations were made at their suggestion. On special points most useful advice was also given me by Dr Frank H. Hahn, Mr W. M. Gorman and Miss Jean Melville. But final responsibility for sins of omission and commission rests with me.

I must also express my gratitude to Miss Marie C. Nutter for help in proof-reading and indexing, and to my secretary, Miss Rachel Lee, for so accurately and patiently typing tables and text.

P. S. F.

February 1953

PREFACE TO THE THIRD EDITION

THE preface to the second edition published in 1961 brought up to date (as far as they were published) the facts of British and American industry. In the present, third, edition I have incorporated the most recently published changes in British and American industry into the text, mainly Chapter I § 4 dealing with the size of industrial plants and firms (the section is completely rewritten) and Chapter III § 7 dealing with the detection of monopolistic conditions. To Chapter II, headed 'Logic and Fact of Industrial Structure', I have added a new section (§ 7) developing and summing up one important element in the logic that seems to explain much of the earlier and the later facts.

Some more should perhaps be said about the word 'logic' that appears in the heading of Chapter II as well as the title of the whole book. The book is not intended to be merely descriptive but to trace trends in the facts and the connection between trends, and to attempt explanations of trends and connections once they are traced. My predecessor in the Birmingham chair, Sir William Ashley, used always to urge the importance in teaching and in practice of trying to discover the *rationale* of business policies and organization. This is roughly speaking what I mean by 'logic'. Rational or logical organization and behaviour may be defined as the most economical means of obtaining any aim under given circumstances. In economic activities the aim is usually the maximum output or income from given resources, but not necessarily so. Aims may be not just monetary or physical but educational, or relating to health, amenity and sociability, and all these aims have more or have less logical means of being attained. In the course of observing existing or past forms of industrial organization and behaviour such as the location of factories, the division of labour and the formation of conglomerate firms, many instances of illogic can be discovered, due to lack of thought, pursuing out-of-date traditions, lack of adaptation to new circumstances, or due to a conflict of aims. But strands of logic can also be found, otherwise the organization would hardly be surviving, and on the whole raising standards of living.

In my definition of logic the last words 'under given circumstances' are no idle embellishment. Ever since my first edition I have stressed the logic typified by the observation (p. 14) that the 'manufactures with a horse-power or capitalization per worker ten times that of many others will not organize or behave the same way as the others'. This logic has affinity with Marx's dictum in his *Poverty of Philosophy* that 'the hand-mill gives you a society with the feudal lord; the steam mill, society with the industrial capitalist' and it is surprising that this affinity was missed in the (mainly critical) introduction to the Russian translation of my first edition. But Marx's so-called material or economic interpretation of history is too narrowly technological to account for all the large differences between the organization of differently circumstanced industries at any one time; and in the present edition I have developed my interpretation, especially in Chapter II § 7, under the heading of the ergological thesis. The purpose of coining this adjective, my only lapse, I believe, into jargon, is that more usual words such as 'technological' do not combine all the important circumstances of the type of work, the circumstances of demand, with those of supply. It is not just more or less mechanical horse-power or differences in other technical factors, or types of material used that counts, but also different sorts of markets: producers, consumers, governments, mass demand, bespoke, repair work, export and so on. Industries differ widely in markets as they do in technique, structure and government and care has been taken to enter in the index all particular industries named in the text.

Wider still than markets are the types of society for which the work of any industry caters. The present book is confined to two highly developed countries. Comparison between developed countries is illuminating not only directly but also in showing how far ergological development is similar in such countries, industry by industry, regardless of differences in resources, climate and social or political institutions and attitudes. The comparison (across the board) of countries, developed and underdeveloped, is discussed in my *Economics and Sociology of Industry*. In that work the earlier and later chapters (I, II, VI, VII, VIII) dealt with development and mobility and the special problems—largely sociological and methodological—of underdeveloped economies (not treated in this present work) but the structure and government of developed industry were covered in less detail.

A new edition can bring the facts up to date and can test how far trends noticed earlier have continued. But it also enables the author to see his work in greater perspective with relation to the work of others. A distinctive mark of my 'logic', I now feel, is the association of structure, which my first chapter openly announces as my 'approach', with economic behaviour. And much of my last chapters is devoted to assessing the likely economic performance of the different forms of industrial government, private or public, and of the different types of business leader brought forward by the past, or the existing, structure of societies. Rereading contemporary work, particularly in America, I am struck by the separate consideration (I am tempted to say segregation) in the leading textbooks of the structure of business organizations such as the company or corporation or the trade or labour union on the one hand and the behaviour of these organizations on the other. Behaviour or performance is treated by economic texts without reference to the very different types of behaving structures. These structures are often quite elaborately described, in separate chapters on 'organization', but without reference to how different organizations seem to behave. This segregation becomes a *reductio ad absurdum* when motivation is discussed without reference to the kinds of person or bodies of persons supposed to be moved. The founders of economics practised no such mistaken[1] segregation and some recent works,

---

[1] Adam Smith discourses in detail what trades he thought the joint stock company's characteristic behaviour would allow it to perform successfully. Maintaining that 'the preventive check to population prevails in a considerable degree', Malthus (Essays, 1803, Book II Ch. 8) treats the various social classes of his day—gentlemen, tradesmen and farmers, labourers and domestic servants separately, as being placed in very different circumstances. See my *Overpopulation*, Kegan Paul, 1926. More recently Alfred Marshall in his *Principles of Economics* (Book VI, VII § 6) has carried on Adam Smith's discussion 'Joint stock companies are hampered by internal frictions and *conflicts of interest* between shareholders and debenture holders, between ordinary and preferred shareholders, and between all these and the directors, and by the need for an elaborate system of checks and counterchecks. They seldom have the enterprise, the energy, the unity of purpose and the quickness of action of a private business. But these disadvantages are of relatively small

not textbooks, by economists, have continued their tradition.[1]

Among the recent works integrating structure and behaviour of which I have given instances, there is one right at the centre of my field written, in fact, by American economists about the British economy. In *Britain's Economic Prospects*[2] I find sharpened many of the points which I stressed in my first edition. Instances are the linking of British industrial performance with the recruitment of managers from the peculiar social institution of the so-called public school, the preference of university graduates for the civil service and professions rather than business, and the importance of the family firm. The lack, till recently, of Schools of Business Management is also integrated with British economic behaviour and performance.

The measurable similarities and differences between the American and the British economic systems are discussed in the several chapters dealing with the matter to which these comparisons are relevant. For the benefit of readers mainly interested in the comparisons, without the analysis or logic, we may refer to the main passages giving the chapter, section and page where they are set forth.

I § 1 pp. 5–6 and Table IA. The structure of economic activity.

I § 2 p. 15 and Table Ic. Agreement in relative horse-power per worker in corresponding industries.

I § 4 Table IF, pp. 28-9. Size of plant and firm and localization in corresponding industries and Table IG. Agreement in size of plants in corresponding industries.

---

[1] British and American instances since the publication of my first edition are J. H. Dunning, *American Investment in British Manufacturing Industry*, Allen & Unwin, 1958; C. F. Carter and B. R. Williams, *Investment in Innovation*, Oxford University Press, 1958 and *Science in Industry*, Oxford University Press, 1959; Edith Penrose, *Theory of the Growth of the Firm*, Blackwell, 1959; J. S. Bain, *Industrial Organization*, Wiley, 1968; R. Evely and I. M. D. Little, *Concentration in British Industry*, Cambridge University Press, 1960; M. Gort, *Diversification and Integration in American Industry*, Princeton University Press and Oxford University Press, 1962; A. D. H. Kaplan, J. B. Dirlam and R. F. Lanzillotti, *Pricing and Big Business*, Brookings Institution, 1967; P. E. Hart (ed.), *Studies in Profit, Business Saving and Investment in the U.K., 1920–62*, Allen & Unwin, Vol. 1, 1965, Vol. 2, 1968. On the particular question of the effect, if any, of changes in the structure of capitalist firms upon behaviour which I discussed in 1953, see especially two books published in 1964, Robin Marris, *The Economics of Managerial Capitalism*, Macmillan, and O. E. W. Williamson, *The Economics of Discretionary Behaviour: Managerial Objectives in a Theory of the Firm*, Prentice Hall.

[2] Edited by Professor R. E. Caves, Allen & Unwin, 1968.

---

importance in some trades. They are seldom willing to sacrifice their reputation for the sake of a temporary gain; they are not inclined to *drive such extremely hard bargains* with their employees as will make their service unpopular.'

A*

PREFACE TO THE THIRD EDITION

For help in preparing this third edition I wish to thank my secretary, Mrs Rita Lowe, and for proof-reading, Miss Diane Trevis.

P.S.F.
October 1971

CONTENTS

I. THE STRUCTURAL APPROACH

CONTENTS

II. LOGIC AND FACT OF INDUSTRIAL STRUCTURE

III. THE RELATIONS OF INDUSTRY AND CONSUMER

CONTENTS

CONTENTS

CONTENTS

XV

CONTENTS

MAIN TABLES

xvii

MAIN TABLES

CHAPTER I

THE STRUCTURAL APPROACH

§ 1. THE QUESTION 'WHO?' AS A REALISTIC STARTING POINT

INDUSTRIAL problems in America and Britain today appear from so many angles, at so many levels and in so many directions that their pursuit without a regular path will soon become lost in details. In this book the pathway is the logic, based on the technical characteristics of different industries, which underlies the varying but often measurable surface features of industrial structure and government. If we are actually to measure these features—and not just to argue from abstract and possibly unreal assumptions—there are several ways of approach. The approach adopted here begins with the visible social structures, the factories and the firms, and the bodies of persons of which they are constituted, and observes the pattern and behaviour of these specific structures accurately before beginning to speak of patterns and behaviour, models, or functions in the abstract. The nature and need of this approach must be explained a little further.

This book is written, partly at least, as a protest against the increasingly abstract quality of studies in the economics of the industrial firm; and to show, constructively, that the alternative is not necessarily a 'mere' description of industrial organization. The attitude may be *realistic* and *analytical* together, by starting with the real facts of some analysed structure.

Structure is a word easily slipped in, and slipped into, and we hear and read constantly of wage-structure, capital-structure, class-structure, age-structure, as well as anatomical structure and even the 'structure of the novel'. Diverse as they may appear, these usages have something important in common. Each refers to some systematic and comprehensive arrangement, as it exists at a given moment, of the different parts, or members, comprising a whole. The age-structure gives the number or proportions of all persons in a whole population systematically grouped by successive age-ranges; anatomical structure, the system of organs of which a body, or organism, is composed. The parts may be qualitatively different items—organs like the heart, liver, kidneys, or in social science the different organizations or bodies of persons that form sub-groups of a constitution; or may be quantities of similar items, e.g. individual persons constituting a comprehensive whole, but differing in one character such as age.[1]

[1] Various important references of 'structure' in industry are illustrated by tables

1

The *Concise Oxford Dictionary* stresses the qualitative as well as the comprehensive aspect in its definition of structure as the 'manner in which a building or organism or other complete whole is constructed, supporting framework or whole *of the essential parts of something*', and it is useful to discriminate between analysis of parts necessary to keep the whole going and of the inessential. Here, the structural approach often leads into functional analysis. One of the reasons for selecting certain parts of a structure as starting points is the importance of their functional relations. The industrial firm, for instance, is an important structure because governmental functions or relations occur between its sub-structures, employers and employed. The word 'relations' has rightly come into use precisely because it points to function as a relation between measurable structures such as groups of persons.

Structural analysis . . . indicates the persons and groups of persons within a society whose inter-relations are to be measured. It brings to light the sub-societies, within that society acting as 'parties' in its procedure and transactions. . . . *Apart* from some specific social structure that is taken as the standpoint, the use of distinctions such as [external] transactions and [internal] procedure is not merely meaningless but confusing. Hence the importance of a consistent preliminary structural analysis.[1]

Its probable importance functionally is not, however, the only test of an essential structural part; there are the more physical tests of persistence in time and frequency in space—characteristics that may be said to constitute a pattern.[2] The structural approach looks for the more permanent, persistent, features, not to the temporary fluctuations, accidents or aberrations. Economists, for instance, speak of structural as against seasonal or cyclical unemployment to refer to men thrown out of work owing to a permanent rather than a temporary difference in demands. And the structural approach to society starts with bodies

---

[1] Florence, 1929, pp. 359, 360.
[2] The word pattern has recently been applied rather promiscuously. To be useful it should be reserved for structures whose main features appear repeatedly, like the pattern of a wallpaper.

---

appearing early in this book. Table IA, a summary of the population census, is a purely quantitative study, giving the proportion of all individual workers in sectors of industry, constituting the total of British and American industry. Table IB presents a qualitative structure, not involving sub-groups, in which the main technical processes or divisions of labour are arranged systematically to show their position at any one time in the total framework of the productive sequence. A structure involving sub-groups is presented by the lower rows of Table ID, naming firms and plants in the British electrical industry in a particular year. Finally, Table IK, again summarizing a census, gives the relative importance of firms and plants of various size-grades in British and American industries and presents a structure involving a quantitative measure in the number of persons employed.

of men observed as assembling together frequently and regularly (church congregations, public house clientele, factory staffs, boards of directors) without any previous presumptions about their actual function.

In adopting a 'structural', and particularly a social structural, approach this book will start, then, with a comprehensive arrangement of concrete, persistently observable social groupings, not with abstract functions. It will start with the question Who? before How? or Why? Systematic and comprehensive treatment will avoid (and be a tacit criticism of) theories that explain (often, no doubt, brilliantly) some corner of the field, but fall down as soon as the author is reminded of events in other parts of the field—events which, comparing decade with decade rather than year with year, may well be found the more persistent and pervasive features.

Though, to the unsophisticated reader, it may seem the obvious approach, this setting out from the actual observable persons and groups of persons who constitute an industry is normally rejected by economists in favour of a 'functional' approach. Economists even when purporting to deal with the structure of industry (for instance E. A. G. Robinson in his *Structure of Competitive Industry*) are inclined to discuss the optimum size or scale not of actual structures but of functions such as managing, marketing, financing, risk-taking and risk-bearing. The result of starting out with this abstraction of characteristics—like the smile without the Cheshire cat—is that readers (and often the authors themselves) are not always sure what is the body, the size or scale of which is being discussed. Functions (conveniently denoted by 'ing' endings) may refer either to the internal relations, mechanism, procedure or interacting of the members, parts or sub-structures within a whole structure like the sharing in the legislating, administering and judging within a state government; or may refer to the external relations, transactions or activities of the whole government structure within a larger structure, i.e. relations of state-government to its people or to the outside world.[1] But this interacting and transacting cannot be said to have a size or scale till we know who is interacting and transacting.

In industry the essential social structures or sub-structures are the factory or plant, the firm and the association or combination of firms. The size of each of them can be measured. But how can the size— optimum or not—of the 'function' or 'factor' of industrial management

---

[1] Under trade union 'Function' (Part II of their *Industrial Democracy*) Sidney and Beatrice Webb consider, for instance, both the internal relations of the union with its members in mutual insurance and 'progression within the trade', and the external relations of the union to other structures such as collective bargaining with the employers, or influencing the state government (more or less efficiently) for specific objectives or policies such as a standard rates of wage and a normal day.

be measured if the author is not sure whether he is writing or thinking about managing a plant, a firm or a combine?

Besides varying in size, the plants of different industries vary, with important consequences, in their location; and both firms and plants vary, again with important consequences, in their degree of specialization or integration. These variables are all related in some degree. If organizations (firms or plants) of any given size specialize in one or a few products or processes, output will be on a larger scale than if they integrate many products or processes. This *large-scale operation*[1] by one firm or plant or, to use Marshall's phrase, this *particular* standardization, is only a species of the genus large-scale production where large quantities of one or a few standard articles are dealt with by any number of firms, large or small.

Size can be measured as a sociological distribution between men, i.e. number of men in the group; and scale as a quantitative distribution between men (or groups of men) and work, i.e. number of men at work on each process or product. Location is ultimately a socio-geographical distribution between men and land; and integration a socio-technical distribution between groups of men and the various types of work performed—qualitative in emphasis as distinct from the quantitative 'scale'. If location and integration be dubbed, for short, questions of 'site' and of 'scope' of plant or firm, the present chapter may be said to deal altogether with the four alliterative 'S's of structure: size, scale, site and scope.

To sum up. Structural analysis in the human and social sciences, whether quantitative, qualitative, or both, breaks the whole organization down into sub-structures distinguished as groups of men under one government, men or groups in particular places, or men or groups pursuing particular acts. Wherever the whole structure is analysed by member groups, scientific enquiry is made particularly hard if it is uncertain of what particular group the scope or site, not less than the size or scale, is at issue. How often are we told of the mobility or integration or scale of an industry without knowing precisely what it is that is supposed to be moving, integrating or large-scale: the whole industry, plants, firms or just a group of men?

The easiest introduction to industrial structure in a comparison of Britain and America is to present a short table (IA) of the proportion of persons who are employed in each country in the main orders or 'sectors' of economic activity. In compiling such a table it is important to add in all persons whether employed, employer or self-employed; and

---

[1] The word operation is chosen since its first two letters are the initials of *organi*-zation and *p*roduction. Large-scale OPeration is large-scale Production within one Organization. See Florence, 'The Problem of Management and the Size of Firms', *Economic Journal*, 1934, pp. 723–9.

this usually implies using the census of population data, not labour statistics. Care is also needed, when comparing countries, that industrial classifications cover the same groups. The U.S., for instance, classes garages and restaurants under retailing. For the sake of comparison the English classification is adopted, though it is not necessarily any more logical. Thus the first two columns exactly reproduce the percentages given in the industry tables of the population censuses of 1931 and 1961 for England and Wales.[1] The third column reproduces the percentages given by the U.S. National Resources Board.[2]

The fourth column involved greater difficulties, since the percentage distribution given in the annual U.S. statistical abstracts now omits those employed in agriculture.[3] The figures I present are percentages of all the occupied population including agriculturists (both farmers and farm labourers).[4] Adjustments made, however, between distribution and 'other services' allow for transference of garages and restaurants etc. from one category to the other for comparability with the English classification.

The most striking features of Table Iᴀ are the similarity of the American and British sector structure at present and the similarity of the changes that have brought it about. The two developed countries with high standards of living are seen to have a certain similar mixture of primary and secondary production and of 'tertiary' distribution and services, and to be moving from primary toward tertiary activities.[5] England has moved further away from employment in primary agriculture and into manufacture because of its need to import food and raw materials in exchange for manufactures; America has moved further into the (tertiary) services mainly because of its higher mechanization in the other employments.

The main difference in the industrial structure of the two countries was seen in my first edition to be (in 1931–40) 'the greater proportion of persons in agriculture in America and in manufacture and mining in England and Wales'. These differences still held in 1965 but the changes between 1939 and 1964 in the two structures were remarkably similar. In both countries the proportion of persons engaged in agriculture and mining fell spectacularly and rose slightly in manufacture and in building. Only in the service sectors do the types of change differ. England is

---

[1] Scotland has a separate census. If its occupied population (numbering 11 per cent of the English) is added to build a British structure little difference is made to the table. Agriculture, distribution and public utilities would be slightly reduced; transport increased.

[2] *Industrial Location and National Resources*, 1942, p. 66.

[3] U.S. Statistical Abstract, 1966, p. 229.

[4] Ibid., p. 226.

[5] See Florence, *Economics and Sociology of Industry*, Chapter I § 2, for the general prevalence of this trend.

often thought of (by Englishmen as well as foreigners) as decadent because, compared to America, fewer persons are producing goods and more 'merely' rendering services. But in fact the opposite is true. The proportions in distribution and in other services fell in England between 1939 and 1961 (largely because of the virtual elimination of the domestic servant) but rose considerably in America between 1940 and 1964. One service is an exception, however. The proportion occupied in transport did rise in England and Wales but seems to have fallen in America, probably because the private car, not involving employment for a wage, is taking the place of public transport to a greater degree.

TABLE IA

ECONOMIC STRUCTURE: PERCENTAGE OF ALL PERSONS
ENGAGED IN MAIN SECTORS OF ACTIVITY IN U.K. AND U.S.A.

Sector[1]	England and Wales		United States	
	1931[2] (1)	1961[2] (2)	1940[3] (3)	1965[3] (4)
A Agriculture and fishing	6·0	3·6	18·8	7·0
A Mining and wells	5·9	3·0	2·0	1·0
B Manufacture	32·1	36·8	23·4	27·7
C Construction (building)	5·1	6·7	4·6	4·9
C Public utilities	1·2	1·6	1·2⎫	6·3
C Transport	6·8	7·1	5·6⎭	
C Distribution	14·4	13·6	14·3[4]	15·1
C Other services	28·5	27·6	30·1[5]	38·0
	100·0	100·0	100·0	100·0

[1] A, Primary; B, Secondary; C, Tertiary.
[2] Population census England and Wales 1931; 1961 Industry tables, Table A.
[3] See text, p. 5.
[4] Exclusive of garages and restaurants.
[5] Includes 1·5, 'industry not specified'.

The economic structure presented in Table IA is measured in terms of the occupied population, not of output. The fall in the proportion of the two primary extractive sectors and the slow increase in the proportion manufacturing (changing the total of the three from 44·0 per cent to 43·4 per cent in England and Wales and 44·2 per cent to 35·7 per cent in America) does not imply a relative set-back in their contribution to the economy. Productivity per worker has recently increased greatly in mining due to mechanization, and in agriculture due to fertilizers and selected seeds as well as to mechanization; and in manufacture horse-power per worker has greatly increased, particularly in America—from six and a half in 1940 to twelve in 1965.

Mechanization is indeed the main cause of the relative stability of the proportion of the working force engaged in primary plus secondary production in England and Wales and its decline in America compared to services and not, as some would have it, national maturity or even decadence. The use of machines allows more output to be made with the same number of human producers and results in more man-power for selling and distribution services which cannot so easily be mechanized. Another cause for the relative advance of services is higher standards of living; as communities get richer more of their income tends to be spent on such services as restaurants, travel and hotels education, medical attention; and government services, too, tend to increase.

The table of national sector structures also presents an easy way of laying down an exact definition of the field of industry. This book will concentrate in both countries on manufactures, with mining, building and public utilities on the fringe of interest, and will refer to the other sectors of the total economic structure mainly to present contrasting situations. Manufacturing industry covers a variety of occupations employed within a manufacturing business; clerks, administrators, transport and maintenance employees and labourers as well as more specialized or skilled operatives.

The distinction between industry and occupation is carried out comprehensively in both the American and the British censuses. Two relevant questions are asked by the census: a person's occupation, what he does, and a person's employer. Industry is a classification by employment. The industry, for instance, of a gardener employed on the Cathedral close by the Dean and Chapter is religion, classified under professions. The industry of a charwoman sweeping a newspaper office is the publication of newspapers. Among workers in British manufacturing generally for 1931, when the distinction was clearly drawn, only 75·5 per cent were actually occupied directly in production, repair or maintenance; 6·7 per cent were draughtsmen or on the clerical staff; 3·9 per cent were in commercial, financial or professional occupations; 2·6 per cent were in transport (e.g. delivery) or communication; and 0·7 per cent were, like the charwoman, domestic help. The occupations of the remaining 10·6 per cent were recorded as 'other labourers'.

Cutting across the industrial structure or profile, it is thus possible to speak of an occupational structure within each industry, and in this structure also, trends are noticeable in both countries. The administrative, professional and clerical occupations paid on a salary are, for instance, increasing relatively to the direct producers, normally paid by wage. This trend toward an increase in the staff-ratio is of great significance and is accorded a separate section in Chapter IV when discussing the management of a firm.

§ 2. THE WORK AND TECHNICAL BACKGROUND

The work of different industries and sectors of industry differ in certain physical, technological and distributive characteristics, which will be shown to influence deeply the different ways these industries are organized. *Physical* characteristics of greatest influence are the durability through time, and transportability through space, of materials and products; uniformity, gradability and divisibility are also important. But more basic still is the distinction between sectors producing physical goods, to which durability and transportability can apply, and industries providing services which now employ half the manpower of Britain and America. It is the answer to the question, Service or Production?, and if production, How much transportability of material or product?, that form and distinguish the main sectors of activity shown in Table IA. Thus:

(A) Service:
    (1) No materials involved: professions, public administration, communications, personal service.
    (2) Materials involved: trade, transport, property service: repairs, laundry etc.

(B) Production:
    (1) Intransportable material (extractive industries): agriculture, mining, fishing.
    (2) Intransportable product: building and civil engineering.
    (3) Transportable material and product: manufacture, public utilities.

As between different manufactures (and public utilities) there are different degrees of transportability and durability in their materials and products and these differences strongly affect the form of organization, including location. The contrast perhaps most often drawn is between heavy and light manufactures, though popular discussion seldom brings out whether it is the product or material that is heavy or light or the machines in use. For it does not follow that if materials are heavy the products or the machines are heavy. Ranking by weight of material or product all the fifty-five British manufactures for which the census of 1935 gave enough data, lightest first,[1] aluminium rolling, glass-making and butter and margarine were 40th, 46th and 49th in lightness of materials, including fuel, i.e. relatively heavy in materials; but 14th, 20th and 28th in tons per given price of product, i.e. relatively light in product. The ranking of industries in heaviness of machines measured by their horse-power per man was different yet. Cotton spinning had light material (7th in rank) and product (9th in rank), but

---

[1] Florence, 1948, pp. 160–7.

the horse-power per man ranked 49th—heaviest but six of all the industries tabulated.

Weight of materials, weight of product, and power of machines, all vary widely between industries. The tobacco industry, to quote calculations I based on the British census of production, used only 2·6 tons of materials per worker per year; on the other hand, the coke and by-products industry used 1,680 tons. The tobacco industry produced four-fifths of a ton for a thousand pounds sterling; the coke and by-products industry 628 tons. Horse-power per worker varied among these 55 manufactures from 0·2 for fish-curing and 0·4 for tobacco to 14·0 for iron and steel. More will be said of horse-power differentials to date, later.

This wide range of the physical characters of various industries may be expected to cause, and does, in fact, cause, a wide range of differences in their location, organization and methods of government.

In the first sentence of this section technological and distributive were added to physical as characteristics of industries deeply influencing their forms of organization. *Technological* is used to denote characteristics of the production technique as distinct from the inherent physical qualities of the material processed, or the product itself. *Distributive* is used to denote characteristics of the markets and marketing of the product or of the service, either to the ultimate consumer or to another producer.

Before materials become usable products, they normally pass through several technical processes, like cotton through carding, spinning, weaving, dyeing, dressmaking before it becomes clothes. Some of these consecutive processes may rank as separate industries so that one industry may be grouped as an early stage (e.g. textile) and another as a late-stage (e.g. a clothing) industry. A further important grouping often, though not always, identical with 'early' and 'late' is *process* industry and *assembly* industry. Spinning 'processes' the raw cotton, dressmaking assembles cloth into various shapes. Table IB places the more important[1] (and some other) manufacturing industries according to their position in the whole course of production. For presentation on paper it is customary to put the earlier stages of production at the top of the page, the final stages of distribution at the bottom. Though not more (or less) logical[2] than making north the top of a map, it is useful to stick to conventions understood by all, and throughout the present book this form of presentation will be used

[1] Including nearly all the larger industries of Britain and America given in Table I𝐹.

[2] As most materials are extracted from the earth it might have been more logical to put extractive industries at the bottom. The conventional arrangement is probably based on the fact that we read down a page from top to bottom.

TABLE 1b

TECHNICAL FRAMEWORK OF PRODUCTIVE AND DISTRIBUTIVE RELATIONS

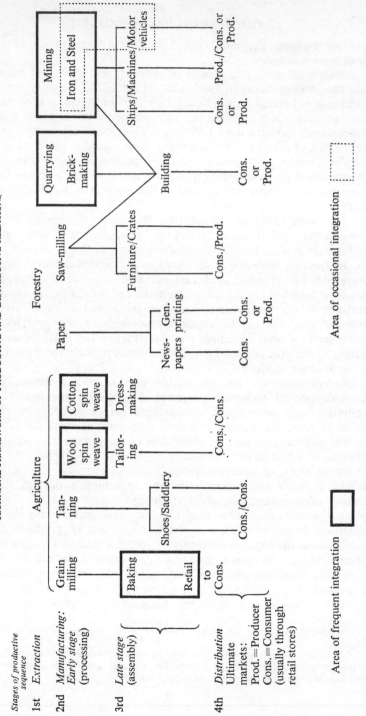

Stages of productive sequence

1st *Extraction*

2nd *Manufacturing: Early stage (processing)*

3rd *Late stage (assembly)*

4th *Distribution* Ultimate markets: Prod. = Producer Cons. = Consumer (usually through retail stores)

Agriculture

Grain milling — Baking — Retail to Cons.

Tanning — Shoes/Saddlery — Cons./Cons.

Wool spin weave — Tailoring — Cons./Cons.

Cotton spin weave — Dressmaking — Cons./Cons.

Forestry

Paper — Newspapers — Cons. / Gen. printing — Cons. or Prod.

Saw-milling — Furniture/Crates — Cons./Prod.

Quarrying Brickmaking — Building — Cons. or Prod.

Mining Iron and Steel — Ships/Machines/Motor vehicles — Cons. or Prod. / Prod./Cons. or Prod.

Area of occasional integration

Area of frequent integration

as the technical framework of reference, permitting such spatial adjectives as vertical or horizontal and lateral to be used to refer to what is in fact consecutive or contemporary in time.

Manufacturing industries employing the bulk of workers can thus be divided into early stage, usually 'process', industries as against late stage, usually 'assembly'. And late-stage assembly may assemble parts drawn from several quite different early stage industries. Lines drawn in Table IB, for instance, indicate that buildings are assembled from the products of sawmilling, brickmaking and the iron and steel industry. And though the lines are, to save confusion, not indicated in the table, the saddlery industry assembles together iron and steel (and brass) as well as leather products. Not all manufactures fall, however, into these early and late divisions. Outstanding exceptions are the pottery and glass industries, where both early processing and later finishing are usually performed in one plant, starting with the clay and sand, and ending up with ware for the consumer's house.[1] The rubber, and the hosiery industries, though they start somewhat further from the raw material, also process *and* assemble into tyres, tennis balls and stockings ready for the consumer.

Most manufactures, as Table IB sets forth, split into early- and late-stage industries. The early-stage manufactures proceed from raw materials which they process or 'refine' into more homogeneous materials that the late-stage manufactures may assemble. It is indeed the very fact that this refinement so often occurs in the technological course of production which permits the early and late stages to be performed by different plants in different industries. The refined, homogeneous and usually compact product (steel billets, cloth, flour, leather, paper) can be transported cheaply over long distances from the refining plant to the next stage, usually assembly.

Early-stage manufactures do not usually engage in assembly work and they usually change heavy material into light transportable products; but the converse is less true. Some late-stage manufactures, especially in food and chemicals, go on processing. But even in these industries the modern trend toward packaging or canning of foods, soaps and drugs for the delectation of the consumer is making the last stages an assembly technique.

Distribution (including storing and transport) to the customers can be taken as part of the technical process of supplying wants. To the early-stage manufacturer, the customer is by definition another manufacturer, but to the late-stage manufacturer the customer may be another manufacturer or the final consumer. Table IB gives examples

---

[1] But the Japanese pottery industry obeys the general rule of division between earlier and later processes. See T. Nakamura, *Journal of Industrial Economics*, 1969.

of late-stage industries making for either. The question for which of these two markets a product is destined will be found to exercise a strong influence on the manufacturer's organization. As the discussion of integration and localization will show (pp. 91–2) different methods of organizing distribution to the consumer affects the organization of production. The outstanding type of late-stage manufacturing for another manufacturer is machine-making or, in the terms of the British census, engineering. It is this industry which is the chief manufacturing contributor to capital formation, so important to the economist, and it will be referred to frequently.

To complete a technical framework of reference that claims to be realistic and comprehensive, certain industries must be added that do not fit into the *vertical* stages. The public utilities supplying electrical power, gas and water serve 'diagonally' all stages of manufacture as well as the consumer;[1] and there is a further market situation outlined on page 16 where things are taken for collection (e.g. scrap merchants, insurance agents, banks) or repair. This 'property service' tends to follow the organization pattern of personal service, rather than of manufacturing.

Apart from machine-making the bulk of manufactures fall into two technical types each with a complex or 'syndrome'[2] of at least four characters in common: the late-stage, assembly, for-consumer, from light-material type, and the early-stage, processing, for-producer, from heavy-material type. Most writers of the popular sort have seized on the light or heavy characteristic as symptomatic of the whole complex, though for the issue under discussion at the time, it may not, as we shall see, be the weight of material that really matters.

The degree to which an industry makes use of machines—its mechanization or investment generally—will be found another technological determinant of forms of industrial structure and organization. The degree of mechanization is itself determined by the physical nature of materials (e.g. greater where materials are uniform and gradable) and by the nature of the work (i.e. processing, assembly or distribution). Mechanical, piped or wired distribution or collection is achieved in the so-called octopoid industries, like gas, water, electrical supply or sewage disposal, where tentacles stretch into each home or factory. But historically, machines were first applied to the processing manufactures, cotton and wool textiles, rather than clothing; iron and steel,

---

[1] In a slightly more sophisticated version of the framework given in Table IB, Fig. 45 of Florence, *Atlas of Economic Structure and Policies*, 1970, brings power supply into the picture. In the text accompanying this figure confirmation of much of the framework is based on the national input-output tables.

[2] American evidence for this syndrome is given in the Appendix to Florence, *Economics and Sociology of Industry*, 1969 ed., and abridged below, Table IIH, p. 120.

rather than engineering; and the horse-power per man is generally at a different level in the early heavy-material, processing manufactures than in the later stage, and usually lighter material, assembly manufactures.

A high degree of mechanization, which is indicated fairly directly by a high horse-power per man, is reflected indirectly by the high financial ratios of capital to wages per year (given in the U.S. censuses of manufactures until 1921) and by high fixed assets in company balance sheets relative to total assets or total capitalization and, more broadly, by high capitalization compared to output of workers employed.

Whether the mechanization index be direct, or an accounting reflection, wide differences are found between industries. Some extremes in horse-power per worker have already been given for the census year 1935 (p. 9) and the whole range of manufactures displays great variability. In Britain tailoring and dressmaking had in 1951 a machine horse-power per worker of 0·2, cement of 25·4—127 times as much. American manufacturing industries in 1962 showed a similar wide range of variation even when joined into the 20 major (two-digit) groups. The apparel group had 0·22 horse-power per worker, the petroleum products group 89·5.[1] Financial ratios have also been shown to exhibit the same wide variation.

Fixed assets in any one period may for different manufacturers vary all the way, according to one American authority[2] from 80 per cent of tangible net worth (for example, paper-making) to 2 per cent (for silk piece goods), according to another[3] from 72·4 per cent of total capital for iron and steel to 20·6 per cent for electrical machines and 13·1 per cent for boots and shoes (where machines are largely rented). Sales per dollar of fixed property investment varied in another list from $0·70 in iron and steel, and $0·75 in petroleum all the way to $9·62 in slaughtering and meat-packing and $13·05 in tobacco products.[4] Total capitalization per wage-earner varied in a British series[5] from £3,300, £1,600 and £535 (electrical supply, gas and iron and steel firms) to £152 (clothing firms). All these industries with the extremes in high and low fixed asset ratios also had extremely high, and extremely low, horse-power-per-man ratios.

With this wide range in the technological and accounting characters

---

[1] Florence, *Economics and Sociology of Industry*, 1969 ed., Table XIX.
[2] See, for example, R. A. Foulke, *Behind the Scenes of Business*, 1937, pp. 49–53.
[3] Bliss, *Financial and Operating Ratios*, 1923, p. 165.
[4] Ibid., pp. 152 and 293.
[5] Feavearyear, 'Capital Accumulation and Unemployment', *Economic Journal*, June 1936. See also Florence, 1933, p. 94, for grouping of large American industries in 1909 according to the same test.

of manufacturing industries it will clearly not be possible to generalize much about manufactures taken as a whole. Manufactures with a horse-power or capitalization per worker ten times that of many others (or with the proportion of fixed assets twenty times that of others) will not organize or behave the same way as those others in the matter of size of plants or price policy (e.g. trade agreements) to cover fixed overheads.

Agriculture was found more prominent in the American, manufacturing more prominent in the British economy. We now reach the other striking difference in the technical background of the two countries—one that has persisted—horse-power per worker in American manufactures as a whole is at least double if not treble that in British. In 1951, the last year horse-power was measured by the census of production, the British horse-power per worker in manufacturing as a whole was 3·1. In America it was 6·5 in 1939, 9·6 in 1954 and had risen in 1962 to 12·7. Horse-power per worker is important as one of the main ingredients in labour productivity. Comparing eighteen countries, the United Nations' Economic Commission for Europe has shown[1] that there is a close positive correlation between horse-power and value of output per head in manufacturing. Italy and Czechoslovakia had, for instance, 1½ to 2 horse-power with about $500 of product per head, Britain 2½ to 3 and Sweden 3½ horse-power with $900 product per head, the U.S.A. the highest horse-power with about $1,700 of product per head. Of the 16 countries Ireland, with medium product but very low horse-power per head, is (characteristically, perhaps) the only wayward deviation from this ruling trend. The causes of the general correlation are probably a vicious (or virtuous) circle. Viciously, the less a country machines up, the less it makes per head and the less it can afford, in turn, to machine up; virtuously, the more a country mechanizes, the more it makes per head and the more it can invest and so on *ad infinitum*. Once circles start, due perhaps to labour shortage or glut, countries keep diverging unless something drastic is done, e.g. by way of planning of investment and the real enforcement of the plan. The evidence is certainly that America is increasing her already large lead in horse-power per man.

Industries within one country vary greatly, then, from one another in their intensity of investment and their consequent organization and policy; but it is significant that the same industry tends to appear in the same relative rank or grade of investment in one industrialized country as another. It was found possible to accept eighty-five industries and groupings of industries in the British census of production of 1930

---

[1] 'Motive Power in European Industry', U.N. Economic Bulletin for Europe, Geneva, 1st quarter, 1951. Table A(4) shows the trend most graphically.

and the U.S. census of manufactures for 1929 as corresponding roughly in scope. These industries were ranked each in their own country by horse-power per worker.[1]

Grouping ranks 1–17, 18–34, 35–51, 52–68, 69–85 into five relative grades, the distances between the grades of the corresponding industry in each country were distributed actually (and compared to a chance distribution) as in the first and second column of Table Ic. A later investigation, comparing the results of the British census of production of 1951 and the American census of manufactures of 1947, repeated the analysis as in the third and fourth columns.

TABLE Ic

AGREEMENT OF CORRESPONDING BRITISH AND AMERICAN INDUSTRIES
ON RANK OF HORSE-POWER PER WORKER

	1929–30		1947–51	
Distance between corresponding industries	*Actual number of industries* (1)	*Chance Random Distribution to be expected* (2)	*Actual number of industries* (3)	*Chance Random Distribution to be expected* (4)
In same relative grade	47	17	39	16
In neighbouring grade	36	27	39	26
Two grades apart	2	20	3	19
Three grades apart	0	14	0	13
Four grades apart	0	7	0	7
Total of industries	85	85	81	81

A clear bias is shown toward agreement in the horse-power grade of industries of similar scope in Britain and in America. The bias suggests that industries of corresponding scope require horse-power of relatively corresponding degree in various countries however different these countries may be in their social organization and tradition.

This in turn suggests that in the given state of knowledge in an industrialized country the investment of fixed capital is a function of the type of materials used and product made; and that whatever the government and policy developed by or imposed upon the industry, the physical and technological factors are likely to remain constant in determining structure and organization. These factors are therefore worth tabulating for future reference.

[1] Florence, 1948, p. 185.

B   15

Technical or ergological determinants:
(1) *Physical characters* of material $\left\{\begin{array}{l}\text{heaviness} \\ \text{durability} \\ \text{uniformity, divisibility}\end{array}\right.$ of products $\left.\begin{array}{l}\text{heaviness} \\ \text{durability}\end{array}\right\}$ transportability

(2) *Technological*
    (*a*) Mechanization
    (*b*) Position in productive sequence $\left\{\begin{array}{l}\text{extractive} \\ \text{early} \\ \text{later} \\ \text{distribution} \\ \text{service}\end{array}\right.$ $\left.\begin{array}{l}\text{early} \\ \text{later}\end{array}\right\}$ manufacture

    (*c*) Processing or assembly
(3) *Distributive*
    Direct to consumer market
    Retailer, wholesaler or producer market
    Mass, batch or individual distribution
    Repair work (property service)
    Collection; scrap, money (banks, insurance)
    State government market
    Export market

Recent trends in distributive are almost as important as in technological determinants.[1] The (subsidized) government market has greatly increased in the aircraft and allied industries; repair work and direct-to-consumer sales have increased with the use, respectively, of motor vehicles and public utilities and for a long time Britain and America have differed radically in the importance to them of their export market.[2]

§ 3. THE SOCIAL STRUCTURE OF INDUSTRY

At the outset of this chapter our approach was heralded as structural, and in particular as an approach through *social* structure. Technical processes and their relations, though important as determining factors, are not of primary interest, but the behaviour of human beings, logical or illogical, in the conduct of industry, and particularly the behaviour of groups and societies of human beings. In manufacturing the more permanent and regular groups are plants, firms and industries.

The *plant*, regarded sociologically, is a congregation or body of persons assembling together at a certain time and place,[3] and in this respect it is similar to the congregation of a church, or a school. It is a grouping of people in and around certain places where they work. It

---

[1] For a visual presentation of the different mixture of varieties of distributive channels for different manufactures see Florence, *Atlas of Economic Structure and Policies*, Fig. 23.

[2] Op. cit., Fig. 21 shows the much greater percentage of imports and exports to total national product in the U.K. than in the U.S. economy.

[3] For the distinction between a 'body of persons' and other organizations, see Florence, 1929, Chapter XIX.

includes farms, mines, offices, shops and stores where selling is going on, warehouses, and, most important of all, workshops and factories manufacturing goods. These factories and offices and shops are not merely themselves *congregations* of workers but tend to become part of a localization of congregations; they form industrial centres—towns that are extremely important factors in the development of industrial technique.

The industrial unit of government equivalent to the political state is not however the plant; the plant is merely a congregation of people, a 'body of persons' who happen to work together fairly persistently at certain places during certain hours. The unit of government is *the firm* or, as it is variously called, the undertaking, the enterprise, or the concern. In a multiple factory or store business—such as, in Britain, Imperial Chemicals, Boots or the Maypole Dairy, or in America, the U.S. Steel Corporation or the Atlantic and Pacific Tea Co.—it is not the factory or store that is the ultimate unit of government but the whole firm. If the plant is *the congregation*, the firm is *the Church*—the body that controls and is superior to the more visible congregation. Some plants may be identical with the firm—there are many firms, of course, with only one plant; but there are many other plants that are subsidiary plants, merely branch businesses of a main concern. And one firm is often the result of amalgamation of several firms in the past. But whatever its history the new 'combination' or 'trust' if it is under one control or government may count simply as one firm.

From the standpoint of human organization an *industry* is often defined as simply a sum of firms or plants. One economist has, in a much-used textbook, gone so far as to maintain that 'industries as such have no identity. They are simply a classification of firms which may for the moment be convenient.'[1] According to this view, an industry is a number of people, and that number is obtained by an addition sum of all the people in certain plants or firms. Just as the population of the country consists in the population of the counties within that country, so the population of an industry consists of the population of the firms or plants scheduled as within the industry. The practice of the national census of population certainly lends colour to this view. As the official British explanation has it:

The Industry to which each individual is classed has been determined (whatever may have been his occupation) by reference to the business in, or for the purposes of which his occupation was followed. Where the individual was himself an employer or was 'working on his own account' his business or profession has been regarded as the industry; but in the most usual case of individuals working for an employer, it is the nature of the employer's

[1] Robinson, *The Structure of Competitive Industry*, 1931, p. 13.

business which has determined the industry under which such cases have been classified.

This purely additive conception of industry must be modified in two respects. First and simplest the fact accepted by the census of production that one firm may operate plants in quite different industries implies that the *organizations which add up to an industry are plants not firms*. Secondly the purely additive conception of industry runs counter to the common notion of industries as easily distinguishable by the technical type of work, activity or transaction in which they are engaged. A particular industry is supposed—without reference to any organization such as plants or firms—to be performing specific transactions. Industry is thus first divided up, as in Tables IA and ID, into sectors, according to the general process performed, such as mining, agriculture, transport, manufacture, building, distribution or personal service; then further subdivided either according to the material worked upon or worked up such as manufacture of textiles, metals, etc., or according to the need supplied, such as manufacture of clothing, foodstuffs, etc., or, again according to process.

A compromise between the popular technical or 'transactional' notion of an industry and the sum-of-firms (or plants) notion, may be based on a definition I put forward some years ago[1] and states that an industry is *any kind of transactions (e.g. processes) usually specialized in by a number of plants who do not usually perform much of any other kind of transactions*.[2]

The perfectly 'clear-cut' industry is one where, as in the British match (or grain-milling) industry, all match-making (or grain-milling) is done in match-making (or grain-milling) plants, and these plants do nothing else. But most industries are not thus 100 per cent perfect. In the British motor and cycle industry, 126 plants making commercial vehicles were included in the census of 1930 since, though many of them made other products, these vehicles were one of their principal products; but 11 other plants making commercial vehicles were excluded since they mostly made other products. In short, not all motor-cars are made in the motor-car industry and the motor-car industry does not only make motor-cars. Precisely the same lack of definition is found in American manufactures;[3] in both countries

---

[1] Florence, 1929, p. 366.

[2] A fuller discussion with diagram will be found in Florence, 1948, p. 3.

[3] In its 'coverage' and 'specialization' ratios (as I say in *Economics and Sociology of Industry*, 1969 ed., p. 25).

The U.S. census of manufactures gives the proportion in which the plants of any one industry (a) cover the whole production of their principal or 'primary' products, e.g. how far grain is only milled in grain mills, and (b) are exclusive and specialize, not making other products, e.g. how far grain mills only mill grain. It is surprising

the census must determine what are a plant's principal products, and accordingly marries the plant, for good or evil, to one particular industry.

This definition maintains the popular idea of similarity of transaction throughout an industry, but avoids the conception of a certain classification of industries being something inevitable where each industry is a logical technical category, immutable and preordained. The facts are that as firms or plants give up old transactions and take on new, industries are continually changing in content and continually branching off into separate industries. There are, for instance, new industries separating off from general engineering, such as the machine-tool making and the tube-making industry; and branching off from the textile industry recently are the rayon and the waterproof industry. Allyn Young indeed considered that 'the progressive division and specialization of industries is an essential part of the process by which increasing returns are realized', and that 'industrial differentiation has been and remains the type of change characteristically associated with the growth of production'.[1] At the same time industries are also to be found coalescing. A plant will take over various sidelines: a brass-bed plant will make wooden beds and iron beds. By this 'broadening the basis' of their operation plants will be broadening industries. Another example can be taken from leather works turning out fancy goods because the market for saddles is decaying with the gradual obsolescence of horses for transport.

The reader may well think this conclusion about the definition of an industry no conclusion at all, or at least just an academic notion. If so, his attention must be drawn to the practice of the official and the business world in Britain and America, when it comes down to a practical classification.

How many *manufacturing* industries are officially recognized? The American census of manufactures for 1963 (the latest published) distinguishes 426. In the ingenious official U.S. standard industrial classification (S.I.C.) these are 'four-digit' industries. For instance, the lighting fixtures industry is coded 3642, but is a branch of the lighting

[1] *Economic Journal*, December 1928, pp. 537 and 539.

---

how little most industries' plants engage in products or processes not primary to the industry. Of the 426 four-digit individual industries, only 17 were recorded in the 1958 census with a specialization ratio under 76 per cent. High coverage is more difficult to attain; but even so only 34 of the 426 four-digit industries are recorded as 'failing' to cover in their plants two-thirds of all the products primary to the industry, i.e. had a coverage ratio less than 67 per cent. Firms, however, integrate production primary to other industries more often and cross the census boundaries more frequently than plants. They diversify more and thus become the 'conglomerate firms' we shall speak of later.

and wiring three-digit group 364 and that is part of a two-digit 'major group', 36, 'electrical machinery'. There are 20 such major groups, or 21 if the more recently formed 'ordnance and accessories' is added. Except for the food group they distinguish types of work from one another fairly logically. In particular, they distinguish (as the fourteen official British 'orders' do not do so thoroughly) the early stage, primary, industries of metal manufacture, paper, lumber and textiles from the later stage metal fabrication and machinery, printing, furniture and clothing industries. It is, however, possible to some extent to split up the British orders of industry to obtain this distinction, as I do below, p. 160, Table IIIc.

Rejecting the official as an arbiter, the reader may maintain that it is the industrialist who should decide what his industry is. This is what President Roosevelt thought when initiating the New Deal by his programme of 'good conduct' codes for each industry. He left it for industries to decide how many of them there were. The answer, excluding public utilities but including services, was 550 (or, if sub-codes were included, about 1,000) ranging in size from 283 industries with less than five thousand employees (such as the mop stick, the shoulder pad, the dog food, and the raw peanut milling industry), and one (the retail trade) with over three million employees.

Apart from the historical incident of the New Deal, industries have to be defined, in America and in Britain too, for the practical purposes of collective bargaining, trade-union organization, state inspection and control; and over and over again there is uncertainty and confusion as to the boundaries of separate industries.

With this warning of the complexities, fluctuations and uncertainties in the content of an industry, Table ID may be presented as an attempt to show, in bare outline, the structure of the whole of industry in one country at a particular period. Britain in 1969 is taken as an example. In the top line or tier are shown the British census orders of industry, which I refer to as sectors, agriculture and fishing, mining and quarrying, building, transport, distribution, finance and other orders of industry, e.g. services, public utilities. These orders together with the several manufacturing orders include the whole of the occupied population. The manufacturing orders constitute *groups* of industries: the textiles working in particular kinds of material, the metals working in another kind of material, clothing industries producing a definite product; and there are other groups of industries—too many to be put into this tier of the diagram. Finally, under the metal group there are included what are generally considered to be instances of industries or smaller groups of industries, such as the iron and steel industry, vehicles, electrical machinery, together with many other 'industries' all coming under the metals group.

TABLE ID

DETAILED ECONOMIC STRUCTURE BY SECTORS, GROUPS, INDUSTRIES, FIRMS AND PLANTS WITH EXAMPLES OF BRITISH FIRMS AND PLANTS OF ONE FIRM IN ONE INDUSTRY

	Agriculture and fishing	Mining and quarries	Construction	Manufacturing	Transport	Distribution	Other sectors or orders of industry
Sectors[1]	Agriculture and fishing	Mining and quarries	Construction	Manufacturing	Transport	Distribution	Other sectors or orders of industry
Groups[2]		Textiles[1,2]	Metals		Clothing[1,2]		Other groups of manufactures
Industries		Metal manufacture[2] (Iron and steel etc.)	Electrical machinery[2]	Vehicles[1,2]		Scientific instruments[2]	Other metal industries
Firms		Philips Electronics	Associated Electrical Industries	General Electric and English Electric Companies	Thorn Electric		Other electrical firms
Plants		Witton Works, Birmingham	Wembley Works	Trafford Park Works, Manchester	British Domestic Appliances, Peterborough	Marconi Works, Chelmsford	Peel Connor Telephone Works, Coventry	Other plants

[1] 'Orders' in the British census of production. For relative importance in both countries see Table Ia.

[2] Two digit 'major groups' in the U.S. census of manufactures.

21

The difficulty is to know where to stop in the splitting up of industries. If carried far enough one would come down ultimately to the production of a single sort of commodity. In fact, some industries which are officially recognized, such as lapidary work which figures as code number 3913 in the U.S. census of manufactures and in 1963 employed a total only of 1,535 all told, may enjoy almost this simple nature. More usually 'an' industry, however specifically analysed out, includes the production of many different articles and must remain, in the economist's theoretical 'model' (where industry is identified with one product), a group of industries.

There is therefore no purpose in introducing any more tiers into the diagram and we may proceed by choosing electrical machinery as a typical instance of 'an' industry, and coming down definitely to the firm. Several well-known firms in the British electrical industry are cited in the table, such as Philips Electronics, Associated Electrical Industries, General Electric and English Electric, Thorn Electric. Let us take only one firm, just as previously we took one sector, one group and one specific industry. In 1970 the General Electric and English Electric Company controlled works at Witton in Birmingham, the Wembley works in London, the Trafford Park works in Manchester, works in Peterborough, Chelmsford and Coventry and many other locations.

Under systems of private enterprise the government of industry, in the strict sense of government, that is, the issuing, receiving and obeying of commands only occurs within the firms. The General Electric and English Electric Company as a whole does not take commands from anybody. There is no one controlling the whole of the electrical apparatus industry from which the company would take orders. Much less is the metal group organized as a whole. Thus in capitalist industry the unit of government comes fairly low in the whole structural scheme. The study of this unit and its behaviour is the subject-matter of micro-economics, that of the whole structure macro-economics. The structure is decentralized and oscillates around the market. The top of the structure is politically an anarchy; under normal circumstances there is no one organizing the whole of industry, telling each industry how much output there should be or what prices to charge. There is no one organizing a group of industries or any specific industry, and it is not until almost the bottom of the diagram is reached that we can detect the process of full government.

Within the governing or 'rule' unit of a firm such as the G.E.C.-E.E.C. a number of plants may be organized, and these plants of a 'multiplant' firm may be in different industries. A number of complications are thus likely to mar the neatness of a diagram like Table ID —particularly overlapping. The company, which is primarily making electrical apparatus, owns glass and some general engineering works and thus impinges on the glass and mechanical engineering industries. Under one firm several different industries may be represented, and such a 'conglomerate' firm may branch out in all sorts of ways.

Under private enterprise there is indeed no limit to what a firm may provide. British railways, before being nationalized, did not confine themselves to the railway industry. They ran hotels; they ran ships; they also ran engineering and woodworking plants for making their engines and carriages. The ordinary iron and steel firm did not confine itself to making iron and steel. It owned 'captive' mines and thus 'poached' on the mining industry. And finally, take that large organization, the English Co-operative Wholesale Society. It is not merely a selling organization, with banking attached, but it also manufactures boots, clothing and food products and many other consumer's goods, and also goods required for its own production and trading, e.g. office furniture and shop fronts. No firm or plant is limited to certain definite sorts of transaction, so that a complicated jigsaw puzzle results in which each firm is trying to form and re-form the area of transactions under its regime—to change, as we shall call it, the scope of its integration. It reminds one of nothing so much as the shuffling and re-shuffling of independent principalities of central Europe during the Middle Ages; and those who have tackled the history of the Holy Roman Empire (which, as Lord Bryce said, was neither holy nor Roman nor an empire) between 1200 and 1500 will have a clearer understanding of the way in which different firms are trying to carve bits out of the industrial field as 'empires', and of the complications that arise.

The definition of any one industry is thus very blurred. We talk of such-and-such an industry and such-and-such another industry, but in actual fact logical boundaries between the two will be extremely uncertain, as census takers, who must comprehensively assign all plants to some industry or other, know to their cost, and we can only trace, with difficulty, the logic of events. Our main footholds in tracing size, scope, scale and site of industries are the structural entities known as the plant and the firm,—clearly definable. To sum up:

A *plant, factory* or *establishment* is a body of persons engaged in production (or distribution) at a given time and place, housed in contiguous buildings, and controlled by a single firm.

A *firm* is the governing organization exercising control over production and distribution and may own more than one plant. Like a state or nation a firm may be unitary or federal in government. Federal firms include all-purpose combines formed through holding companies or interlocking directors.

Where the constitution is federal the word 'firm' may refer to the whole federation or, as in Table ID, may denote the often subsidiary entities trading under a particular name.

§ 4. THE SIZE DISTRIBUTION OF PLANTS AND FIRMS

The structural approach is nowhere more clearly set off from any other approach than in the question of size or scale. The first question of structure is 'size or scale of what?' Until this question is answered, discussion can have little meaning. Here the structural is identical with the statistical and institutional approach. No statistics can be collected of sizes till the collector is told the particular body, institution or structure he is to measure for size.

The previous section has in fact analysed out what the industrial institutions or bodies are which are to be measured: the plant, and the firm including the combine. The size of these two institutions in British and American industries will be examined first as they appear in different manufacturing industries, and then any recent changes or trends in their size will be described separately for plants and firms.

(A) *The size distribution of plants and firms in different manufactures*

I stress the word distribution because a basic characteristic of the sizes of organization in a free economy is their variation, ranging widely from the single employee workshop to the mammoth plant of over 2,500 employees. Moreover there is little or no variation round a normal size, but a great preponderance of the smallest sizes. This 'skew' distribution we shall find typical of many economic and sociological measurements such as incomes, share-holdings and sizes of cities[1] and makes averages misleading. It differs greatly from the distribution of biological phenomena such as the heights of men where many are of medium height, a few short and a few tall. The latest British census (for 1963) shows 60 per cent of all plants employing 24 or less and the latest American (also for 1963) 67 per cent employing 19 or less. The distribution, as we shall see, in section (4C) has become still more widespread and 'skew' among firms.

An economist, however, is interested chiefly in the size of plant or firm from which the *bulk of output* comes. This can be indirectly indicated by the size-ranges employing the greatest proportion of workers— the most populous size, or as I shall hereafter call it, the 'prevailing'

---

[1] See pp. 217–19. Various laws have been formulated about the precise form of these distributions such as Zipf's or Gilbrat's but require further verification.

size. Different manufacturing industries have, however, very different distributions of manpower among different sizes.

In the first edition of *Logic of British and American Industry* I gave two large tables detailing the size distribution of employees among different sizes of plants in the 21 largest manufacturing industries shown by the census in Great Britain 1935, and America in 1939. In the present edition a summary description of the most populous or prevailing grade of size of plant and firm in Table IF (p. 28) replaces the statistical distribution among sizes in each industry. Any change in the size grade and the degree of the industry's localization are noted, for both countries, in adjoining columns for joint consideration.

The method of grading industries by size of plant is one I have adopted since 1935. It is explained and illustrated in Table IE by up-to-date examples from the very detailed American classification of industries and a quotation from my *Economics and Sociology of Industry*.[1]

For purposes of comparing sizes of plant at different dates a simple average is adequate; but such an average is often unrepresentative and we must now introduce the notion of a size of plant grading of industries which allows for some industries having no particular prevalent size. . . .

Using the test of 50 per cent of employees in at least two consecutive size-ranges out of the seven in Table IE (or 60 per cent of the three smaller ranges), industries that have a representative size of plant can be divided into several grades. Large-plant industries are those that have 50 per cent of all their workers in plants employing a thousand or over. Largish-plant industries are industries other than large-plant that have 50 per cent in plants employing 500 or over. Medium-plant industries have 50 per cent in plants of 100–499 workers. Smallish-plant industries have 50 or 60 per cent respectively in plants employing 50–249 or 25–249. Small-plant industries have 50 or 60 per cent respectively in plants employing less than 50 or less than 100.[2]

In other industries the concentration of workers in plants of certain sizes was not so sharp, and supplementary grades can be added for industries showing 'bias toward smaller plants' with 60 per cent of workers of under 250, and (a rare case) 'bias toward larger plants' with 75 per cent of workers in plants of over 250. All remaining industries were graded as showing no representative size of plant. An example of each of the seven more frequent grades is given in Table IE.

Many industries now have 75 per cent of their personnel employed in plants employing over 1,000. These industries may be assigned to a

[1] Ed. 1969, pp. 90–1.
[2] Unfortunately the British and the American censuses differ here in the limits to the ranges of size. Instead of 249 or 250 read in the British statistics 199 or 200; for 19 or 20, 24 or 25. The same failure in international standardization occurs in the size ranges above 1,000 employees. See below, p. 41.

THE STRUCTURAL APPROACH

TABLE IE

ILLUSTRATION OF SIZE-OF-PLANT GRADING (DISTRIBUTION IN CERTAIN U.S. INDUSTRIES OF EMPLOYEES AMONG SIZE-RANGES OF PLANT, 1963 CENSUS OF MANUFACTURES)

Industry and code number	Percentage of employees in plants employing stated number Total of employees in each industry = 100. Some size-ranges are combined: (a) 250–999; (b) 500–2,499; (c) 250–2,999							
	1–19 (1)	20–49 (2)	50–99 (3)	100–249 (4)	250–499 (5)	500–999 (6)	1,000 plus (7)	Grade * of size of plant assigned (8)
Sawmills and planing mills (2421)	24·7	19·3	17·6	16·6	9·6	7·0	5·2	Small(S)
Brick and structural tile (3251)	3·0	21·7	39·0	26·0		10·2a		Smallish(s)
Wool weaving and finishing (2231)	1·7	4·0	7·1	26·6	33·0	27·5b		Medium(M)
Mechanical measuring devices (3821)	3·7	5·1	6·0	14·2	13·4	12·7	45·0	Largish(l)
Shipbuilding (3731)	4·8	4·7	5·2	8·7	20·4		56·2	Large(L)†
Brooms and brushes (3981)	14·1	17·0	19·4	20·8		28·7c		Bias to small(ms)
Sanitary paper products (2647)	1·8	2·8	4·6	18·1	24·6	28·9	19·2	No type(X)

* Bias to 'larger' grade has been omitted as very rare.

† When grading *firms*, very large (LL) and mammoth (LLL) grades are added with 75 per cent and 85 per cent of employees in firms employing 1,000 and over.

further 'very large' grade in the series of size-grades. The same measures of size-grade may be applied to firms as to plants. Moreover the development of firms owning many plants is now on so large a scale that a third large grade should be distinguished from the merely very large—the mammoth-size structure. This super-large structure may be segregated from the very large, whenever employees in plants or firms employing 1,000 or over form over 85 per cent of the industry's total employed. Only a very few industries, however, none of them large, have any such *large-plant* structure.

Table IE serves to illustrate the surprisingly wide range of sizes of plant that occurs in an industry. Each of the twenty American major industrial groups covering all manufacturing industries had plants ranging from the minute plant employing 1–4 persons, to the mammoth plant employing over 2,500. And Table IE shows instances of *individual* industries in each grade of prevalent size yet with workers distributed in all sizes of plant up to 1,000 strong. Moreover, even in a large-plant industry such as shipbuilding, with only 4·8 per cent of employees in the smallest plants, the number of plants of that size was 1,492 out of a total of 1,964, i.e. 76 per cent of all its plants. But the very smallness of these plants means that, numerous as they are, their aggregate employment is small and of little importance to the output of the whole industry. I use employees rather than value of output as a measure of size because of the difficulty of comparing money value which varies from time to time (with inflation and deflation) and between country and country (with changing exchange rates).

The pure economist might (and occasionally does) argue as though an industry had normally an optimum (minimum-cost, maximum-gain) size to which its plants (and firms) must conform on pain of eventual bankruptcy. The statistics of the situation in Table IE do not show this clear-cut profile for two levels of reasons. The deep-seated, psychological and historical reasons will be discussed in the next chapter· Here we may anticipate at least that psychologically the wide distribution of managing ability must be allowed for, resulting in a certain scatter of size; and historically that one must expect 'lags' and 'leads': a lag or survival into a later age of plants suited in size to the exigencies of an earlier age, and also a gestation period in the course of which the efficient firm is leading up to a larger size. But the superficial reasons have perhaps more effect on the distribution of sizes of plant as tabulated, particularly the difficulty of defining an industry in practice. Few of the industries listed in Table IE are more than aggregations of plants which the census, as already explained, must assign to one industry or another but which are only roughly speaking engaged in the same sort of production.

It is almost impossible, then, to observe any one definite representative size of plant in any of the industries in Table IE. There are all sorts of sizes. But this negative statement may be qualified. Some size-classes are very much more populous or frequented in one industry than another; they include a higher proportion of workers than other size-classes. Thus we can ask, within what classes of sizes are the majority of all workers employed, and find significant differences between industries.

Since I devised this method of grading Bain has, in his *International Differences in Industrial Structure*, adopted a further summary indication of size of plant structure. In his Appendix tables he has given the size distribution of plants, measured in numbers employed, in 1951 for the United States, the United Kingdom, Canada, Sweden, France, Italy,

TABLE If

COMPARISON AND CHANGE IN TWENTY-FIVE LARGEST BRITISH INDUSTRIES AND CORRESPONDING AMERICAN INDUSTRIES: SIZE OF PLANT AND FIRM AND DEGREE OF LOCALIZATION, 1963

Name of industry (U.K. census heading, U.S. code numbers)	Total employed (thousands)*		Comparative grade of unit				Change* in size of plant grade		% Coefficient of localization			
	U.K.	U.S.A.	U.K. Plant	Firm	U.S.A. Plant	Firm	U.K. From 1935-9 to 1963	U.S.A. From 1939 to 1963	1958	U.K. Rank	U.S.A. 1947	Rank
	(1)	(2)	(3)	(4)	(5)	(6)	(7)	(8)	(9)	(10)	(11)	(12)
Motor vehicles (3717)	433·0	649·9	LL	LLL	LL	LLL	Rise 1 grade	Rise 1 grade	·388	19th	·62	21st
Iron and steel (3312)	268·9	500·6	L	LLL	LL	LLL	Same	Same	·305	14th	·51	17th
Aircraft (and engines) (3721, 2)	252·7	679·4	LL	LLL	LL	LLL	Rise 1 grade	Same	·265	10th	·68	23rd
Radio and electronics (3662, 3671, 2, 3, 4, 9)	242·1	677·8	L	LL	L	LL	Same	Rise 1 grade	·355	16th	·42/·48	15th
Printing (general) (2751, 2, 2771, 89, 91, 3)	228·2	377·9	N	N	SM	SM	Same	Rise 1 grade	·182	3rd	·22/·27/·28	2nd
Electrical machinery (3611, 2, 3, 3621, 2, 3, 6, 9, 3694)	205·8	309·5	L	LL	L	L	Same	Rise 1 grade	·298	13th	·32/·35/·25	6th
Shipbuilding (3731)	202·6	139·6	L	LL	L	L	Same	Same	·375	18th	·46	16th
Wool (2231, 83, 91)	177·0	69·8	M	1	M	1	Same	From no type	·665	25th	·60/·54	20th
Bread and flour confectionery (2051)	160·2	237·0	M	L	M	1	Rise 2 grades	Rise 2 grades	·125	2nd	·28/·14/·35	1st
Chemicals (general) (2812, 5, 2818, 9)	138·4	225·0	L	LL	1	LL	Rise 1 grade	From no type	·400	20th	·34/·36/·46/·49	12th
Printing (newspapers etc.) (2711, 21)	130·1	374·1	1	L	N	1	Same	Same	·279	12th	·20/·46	8th
Industrial plant and steelwork (3441, 3443, 3567, 3559)	124·7	222·7	1	L	N	N	N.A.	N.A.	·234	6th	·27/·28/·30/·37	7th
Hosiery (knitgoods) (2251, 2, 3, 4, 5, 9)	124·5	220·5	M	1	N	N	From no type	Same	·585	22nd	·52/·61	19th
Instruments (3811, 31, 41, 2, 3, 51, 61)	122·8	181·7	N	L	1	L	From medium	Same	·364	17th	·35/·54/·58/·61	18th

Industry (code)	Col 1	Col 2		LL	L	LL					Col 11	Col 12
Rubber (3011, 3031, 3069)	120·8	219·6		LL	N	1	Fall 1 grade	From no type	·259	8th	·41/·45	13th
Men's outerwear (2311, 2327)	113·9	196·5	N	1	N	1	Same	Same	·268	11th	·37/·33	11th
Iron castings (foundries) (3321, 3322, 3323)	112·6	199·6	N	1	N	1	Same	From medium	·350	15th	·26/·39/·42	9th
Cotton spinning (2281, 2)	104·3	75·2	M	L	M	1	Same	Same	·655	24th	·73/·65	25th
Footwear (3141, 3021)	102·3	244·4	M	N	M	1	From no type	Same	·506	21st	·44	14th
Cotton weaving (2211, 2221)	98·4	297·1	M	N	1	LL	Same	Same	·615	23rd	·70	24th
Furniture (2511, 2, 2521)	98·1	215·3	N	N	N	N	From small	From medium	·196	4th	·24/·36	4·5
Dresses, women's and children's underwear (2335, 41)	95·8	276·7	SM	SM	S	SM	Same	Same	·264	9th	·24/·49	10th
Cocoa and sugar confectionery (2071, 2)	91·8	72·4	L	LL	N	LL	Rise 1 grade	Same	·227	5th	·28	3rd
Paper (2611, 2621, 2631)	88·2	208·3	1	L	1	LL	Rise 1 grade	Rise 1 grade	·238	7th	·24/·36	4·5
Timber (2411 to 2442)	81·0	472·9	SM	SM	S	SM	Rise 1 grade	Same	·100	1st	·65	22nd

* Total of 25 listed industries U.K. 3,918·2 (U.S.A. 7,343·5).
All other industries U.K. 4,041·8 (U.S.A. 8,891·0).
Total all manufacturing U.K. 7,960·0 (U.S.A. 16,234·5).

Notes:

Column 1—Source: U.K. census of production, part 13, Table 1.

Column 2—Source: U.S. census of manufactures.

Columns 3–6—the grading is as follows

LLL = Mammoth, 85 per cent of employed in units of 1,000 or over.

LL = Very large, 75 per cent of employed in units of 1,000 or over.

L = Large, 50 per cent of employed in units of 1,000 or over.

1 = Largish, 50 per cent in units of 500 or over.

M = Medium, 50 per cent in units of 100–499.

SM = Bias to small, 60 per cent in units of under 200 (250 in U.S.).

S = Small, 50 per cent in units of under 50.

N = No prevailing type.

Column 11—Source: Stanford Research Institute. The 1947 and 1963 code numbers do not always correspond, and coefficients are not available for every industry involved. Where more than one coefficient is given, the ranking in Column 12 is by unweighted average.

Japan and India[1] in the same way as I did for the United Kingdom (1935) and the United States (1939) in my first edition (1953). But as a summary measure for each industry Bain adopts the (estimated) average size of the twenty largest plants.

In the absence of more direct statistics in many European countries, this measure is a useful indirect approach to quantifying the degree of concentration of firms that is relevant to monopoly problems. These problems will be discussed in Chapter III. Here we are concerned with the absolute size of plants which is relevant to problems of management and the efficiency of production. In view of the present near-explosion in multiplant firms soon to be pointed out (pp. 41–3), plants and firms must be kept distinct. Though the plant structure strongly affects the firm structure of any industry, there are exceptions. It is perfectly possible for an industry to have large or largish plants and yet for business not to be concentrated in a few firms—as for instance, in the U.S.A., radio which has a concentration ratio in the first four firms of only 29 per cent but an average of employees per plant of 342, over six times the overall average for all industries; or paper mills which have a concentration ratio of only 23 per cent but an average of employees per plant as high as 399.[2] In the U.K. the tinplate, explosive, cement and sugar industries all had in 1951 only a 'bias' toward large plants, yet large firms.

Devoting attention for the present to the absolute sizes of British and American plants we must question Bain's use, as an index measure, of the average number employed in the 20 largest plants. According to this measure it appears (*op. cit.*, p. 49) that the 1951 average size of the British plant is only 78 per cent of the American. A smaller country is almost bound to have a lower number of employees in the twenty largest companies of any of its industries than a large country since, with fewer plants generally, several of the smaller of the 20 largest are likely to be quite small. Bain's own comparison of the United Kingdom and the United States confirms this likelihood. The 20 largest British plants have (according to his Table 3·2) a larger average size than the 20 largest American in only 6 out of the 34 industries. But if we look

---

[1] This is an exceedingly useful table and bears out the similarity industry by industry of the size of plant distribution in the eight countries. In most of them, industries with the highest proportion of their employees in the *largest* plants are iron and steel, petroleum refining, motor vehicles, aircraft, shipbuilding, rubber; and industries with the highest proportion in the *smallest* plants, sawmills, wood containers, grain products distillers (all of them oriented to scattered materials) and the labour intensive apparel industry. In spite of all the variations inherent in different countries, factors distinctive of different types of work appear (in accord with my ergological thesis) to prevail in determining size of plant.

[2] Report of the U.S. Bureau of the Census for the Senate Sub-committee on Antitrust and Monopoly, Part II, pp. 418ff.

at his detailed appendix, we find the total percentage of employees in all plants employing 500 or more is larger in Britain in half the industries, i.e. 16 industries out of the 32. This equal vote industry by industry in size of plants (measured in employees) between America and Britain is borne out by my own surveys. Not only do the large industries seen in Table IF show the same size of plant grade in both countries but a wider comparison I made of the facts for 1929–30 and 1947–51 showed a high degree of similarity in the plant-size structure of the 47 or 48 industries which corresponded in scope for both countries and which also had some specific prevailing grade of size. Table IG shows that in 1929–30 the actual frequency with which corresponding industries were in exactly the same grade of plant size in both countries had been 2·9 times (27:9·4) as much as to be expected in a random distribution. In 1947–51 it was 2·5 times as much—26:9·6.

TABLE IG

AGREEMENT OF CORRESPONDING BRITISH AND AMERICAN INDUSTRIES
ON SIZE-OF-PLANT GRADING: 1929–30, 1947–51

| Distance between corresponding industries | Number of industries | | | |
| | 1929–30* | | 1947–51 | |
	Actual (1)	Expected random (2)	Actual (3)	Expected random (4)
Same relative grade	27	9·4	26	9·6
Neighbouring grade	17	15·0	19	15·3
Two grades apart	3	11·3	3	11·5
Three grades apart	0	7·5	0	7·7
Four grades apart	0	· 3·8	0	3·9
Total	47	47·0	48	48·0

* Reproduced from Appendix III, Table c in Florence, 1948.

In the preface of my second edition (1960) I pointed out that the British size of plant aggregating all industries was approaching the American and now that both countries have published a census for the same year, 1963, it is possible, as in Table IF (p. 28), to show the remarkable similarity of the two countries' size-of-plant structures.[1] The practical importance of this similarity is that it is not now possible to point to a smaller size of plant as a cause of the lower British productivity. Causes must be sought elsewhere.

[1] Below, in tracing the recent trend in size of plant in manufacturing generally by means of an average size, I show that, to be precise, the average British factory was in 1963 larger in point of numbers employed than the American.

In 1958 and 1963 the United Kingdom undertook a census of production and luckily the United States undertook its census of manufactures in the same years. The final results were published with considerable delay—the British census of 1963 not till 1969. It is now possible to present and compare fairly recent information.

Table IF lists, in the first column, the 25 largest British manufacturing industries that are not composite[1] as distinguished by the census of production of 1963 in order of their size in numbers employed, given in column 1. No industry that is listed employed less than 81,000. Column 2 gives the numbers employed in the corresponding American industries as far as the two enumerations can be matched; their official code-numbers are recorded under the names of the industries.

The censuses of the two countries allow a fairly accurate correspondence except for cotton weaving and cotton spinning. The two processes are far more integrated in the United States plants and probably much spinning done in weaving plants is counted under weaving.

The industries grouped to correspond with the 25 largest British industries include all American (four-digit) industries employing over 150,000 in 1963 except three: fluid milk, meat slaughtering and plastics, employing respectively 185, 180 and 166 thousand. However, even omitting these industries, in 1963 the 25 that are listed contained 7,343,500 employees in America and 3,918,200 in Britain: about a 1:2 sample of the total employed in manufacture.

From this table, with its four main sets of columns, several general conclusions can be drawn. The last two sets, dealing with changes in the sizes of plant and with localization, will come up for discussion later in part B of this section and in the next section (§ 5). Four conclusions arise from the first two sets of columns. They concern (1) the activity structure within the manufacturing sector and the prevailing size of (2) plant and (3) firms in these 25 important manufacturing industries. Finally (4) we shall be concerned with certain corollaries of the multi-plant firm.[2]

1. Like the structure of their main sectors (Table IA) the make-up within the manufacturing sectors of the British and American economic systems is surprisingly similar. The totals already quoted as employed in the 25 listed manufactures; (3,918,200 in the United Kingdom,

---

[1] Classes labelled by the census as 'miscellaneous' are omitted. General mechanical engineering and Light metal, Copper, Brass and other base metals are also too composite.

[2] Further points that arise from Table IF besides the four here mentioned are (5) the stability of industries brought out in columns 7 and 8 which is dealt with on pages 37–9; and (6) the similarity in location pattern of corresponding industries in the two countries brought out in columns 10 and 12, dealt with on pages 49–50.

7,343,500 in the United States) have a ratio of 53:100. Between the totals in all manufactures the ratio is 45:100.[1] A similar structure of economic activities for the two developed countries would thus involve each British industry employing about half the number in the corresponding American industry. In fact comparison of columns 1 and 2 in Table IF (adding together cotton-spinning and weaving for reasons already explained) shows a fairly close scatter round a 50 per cent ratio between the size of the British and the corresponding American industries. Though the ratios might be anything from 0 to infinity (if the corresponding American industry employed no-one) yet in 20 out of the 24 industries (cotton-spinning and weaving counting as one) the ratios fall within the range 35 to 67 per cent. In three industries—shipbuilding, wool and cocoa and sugar confectionery—the British employees outnumber the American, i.e. the ratio is over 100 per cent; in timber the British employees number only 15 per cent of the American.

These exceptional ratios are associated with particular resources or needs of each country, timber in America, shipping and perhaps warm clothing and food in a mostly non-centrally heated Britain. They involve an export trade from the country where the ratio is exceptionally high, an import trade to where it is low. The general similarity, however, indicates a certain balance in the economic activity structure of Britain and America. This balance can be logically expected in all developed countries when there is a fairly similar distribution of wealth and industries catering for family budgets (see III § 2) at a variety of income levels and where technology is at much the same stage.

2. The prevailing size of plants (or absence of prevalence) is the same in 13 of the 24 corresponding British and American industries. Of the remaining industries, nine have neighbouring plant sizes prevailing and for the four others there is no prevailing size. The position is summed up in Table IH, the neighbouring-size situation being shown by brackets. This international similarity of plant-size structure in the same industry is remarkable in view of the dissimilarity of Britain and America in point of size of market area, variety of climate, density of population, standards of living and national resources. It points to the importance of the type of work, i.e. the particular ergological traits of any industry.

The agreement in size of firms, also shown in Table IH is much the same as the agreement in size of plant. Again, 14 industries are in the same grade in Britain as in America and 8 in neighbouring grades. The footnotes give the three industries not in agreement or near agreement on *plant* sizes, and the four not on *firm* sizes.

3. In both countries the size of firm structure follows fairly closely the size of plant in the several industries. Naturally, because many firms

---

[1] The difference in the ratios is to be expected since the 25 British industries were listed because they were the largest.

THE STRUCTURAL APPROACH

TABLE IH

AGREEMENT ON PREVAILING SIZE-GRADE OF UNITS (PLANTS OR FIRMS)
BETWEEN TWENTY-FIVE LARGEST (NAMED) BRITISH AND CORRESPONDING
AMERICAN INDUSTRIES IN 1963

	Same prevalent size in both countries	*Neighbouring sizes**
	PLANTS†	
Very large (LL)	Motor vehicles; aircraft ⎫	Iron and steel
Large (L)	Shipbuilding	
	Radio, electrical ⎬	
		Chemicals; Rubber
Largish (l)	Paper ⎫	Industrial plant; Print news; Instruments
No type (N)	Furniture; men's outerwear ⎬	
	Iron castings	Hosiery
Medium (M)	Cotton-spinning; wool ⎭	
	Footwear, bread	
Bias to small (MS)		Timber; Dresses
Small (s)		
	FIRMS‡	
Mammoth (LLL)	Motor vehicles; aircraft	
	Iron and steel;	
Very large (LL)	Radio; chemicals	
	Rubber ⎬	Shipbuilding; Electrical; Paper
Large (L)	Instruments	Cotton-spinning; Printing news; Bread
Largish (l)	Wool; iron castings;	
	Men's outerwear ⎭	
		Hosiery; Footwear
No type (N)	Furniture	
Bias to small (MS)	Dresses; timber ⎭	

* Neighbouring grades of size in the two countries.

† Three of the 25 largest industries differed by more than one grade of prevailing size of plant: cotton weaving with largish size prevailing in America, medium size in Britain; cocoa and sugar confectionery with large size prevailing in Britain, no size in America; general printing with bias to smaller size in America, no size in Britain.

‡ Four of the 25 largest industries differed by more than one grade of prevailing size of firm: general printing has bias to small prevailing size of firm in America, no prevailing size in Britain; industrial plant has no prevailing size in America, a large prevailing size in Britain; cotton weaving has very large firms prevailing in America, no size prevailing in Britain; cocoa and sugar confectionery has very large firms prevailing in Britain, only largish prevailing in America.

34

contain plants, a greater proportion of employees in each industry is always found in the larger firms than in plants of the same size range. In many industries over 70 per cent are employed in firms employing 1,000 or over. They may be graded 'very large' and where 85 per cent are so employed, 'mammoth'. In few industries do such very large *plants* prevail. To judge from Table IF the most frequent pattern is for the prevailing size of firm to be one grade larger than the prevailing size of plant. Mammoth firms (LLL) prevail in industries where very large plants (LL) prevail; very large firms prevail where merely large plants (L) prevail: and merely large or largish firms prevail (L or l) where largish or medium sized plants (l or m) respectively prevail.

Next most frequent is the industry where the firm is two grades larger than the plant. This double deviation occurs among the large industries shown by Table IF in American cotton weaving, chemicals and paper industries and in British iron and steel, cotton-spinning, bread and rubber.

Further examples of the double deviation in the prevailing size-grade of firm compared to plant occur in industries other than the 25 given in Table IF. They will be cited in Chapter II § 5 when discussing, in general, the *logic* of this deviation between the scale of the firms of an industry and its plants located in different places. It is indeed largely a question of locational economics.

Least frequent in Table IF are industries where size of firm and size of plant are of the same grade and multiplant firms are less frequent. Five are shown in the United States: electrical machinery, shipbuilding, industrial plant, hosiery and furniture; three in the United Kingdom: dresses, furniture and timber. On the whole it is industries with smaller or no prevailing size structures where firm and plant sizes tend to be identical. Indeed, the small firms are nearly all 'uniplant'. For instance the 45,276 British manufacturing firms in 1963 employing 1–24 persons own between them 45,845 plants, an average of only 1·01 plants per firm.[1]

4. The existence in certain large industries of large multiplant firms in Britain and America carries two corollaries that make these firms more important than first appears. Their administrative headquarters are often not physically connected with any of the plants; and plants of the same firm may be located in different countries.

When separate from any of the firm's manufacturing plants, headquarters are usually sited in the centre of the largest cities and conurbations, thus increasing their congestion. The headquarters of many of the largest U.S. manufacturing corporations in 1965 listed in *Fortune* magazine were in the firm's largest plant. But 82, or 32·8 per cent, of the 250 largest firms had separate headquarters in New York; of the next

[1] U.K. census of production, 1963, Part 132, Table 13.

largest 250, 48 or 15·2 per cent. The runner-up, Chicago, was a long way behind New York with 19 headquarters among the 250 largest firms, 21 among the next 250 largest. Apparently the larger the firm the more likely are headquarters to be in the largest metropolis.[1]

The employees in these administrative headquarters are 'white-collar' staff and increase the staff ratios for manufacturing generally. If the firm is conglomerate, however, it may not be possible to assign this additional staff to any particular industry.

All plants located in a country are counted in that country's census, but when the firm is dispersed internationally only that part of the firm which is physically located in that country is counted. In short, firms will internationally be still larger and contain more plants than appears from the national census.

In the latest British census of production (1963; Part 132) a convenient table (20) gives an analysis of manufacturing industry by nationality of enterprise (i.e. firm). From this table we can calculate that the proportion of British plants controlled in 1963 by foreign firms of all nationalities were 2·05 per cent, but the proportion of employment was as much as 11·1 per cent. The proportion of U.S.-owned plants and employment was 1·45 per cent of plants and 7·7 per cent of employees. Foreign and especially American company-owned plants were thus larger than the average British-owned plant and the table tells us that the American-owned firms' capital expenditure and net output per head was also larger; £224 and £1,937 as against £114 and £1,430.

This investment of American manufacturing firms in Britain and in all foreign countries generally has been increasing rapidly in recent years. The amount of direct investment in manufacture rose for all foreign areas from $6,322m. in 1955 to $24,124m. in 1967 and only for the United Kingdom from $941m. to $3,877m.[2]

The main logic underlying international investment is one of location. If it is important to be scattered in location within a country, it is likely to be still more important to be scattered in location within a wider area of greater distances. In fact, few of the products of American-owned plants in the United Kingdom are marketed in America. They are made abroad to sell abroad, though not necessarily in the country where they are made. Great Britain is nearer to the wealthier foreign countries. In 1954 the average American subsidiary sold overseas up to twice as much as the average U.S. parent concern.[3]

---

[1] Similarly in the U.K. in 1955, 55·9 per cent of companies with assets over £25 million had head offices in London, but only 34·9 per cent, 31·6 per cent and 19·3 per cent of the smaller companies with assets of £10·1m to £25·0m, £5·1m to £10·0m and £2·6m to £5·0m. *Town and Country Planning*, March 1962, p. 123.

[2] U.S. Statistical Abstract, 1957, p. 878; 1970, p. 785.

[3] Dunning, *American Investment in British Manufacturing Industry*, p. 311.

U.S. investment in manufacture in the United Kingdom is associated with certain particular types of work. Applying my technique of the concentration quotient, Dunning[1] gives U.S. firms in Britain a quotient of 4·13 in precision instruments, 2·23 in chemicals, 1·77 in vehicles, 1·70 in engineering and shipbuilding and 1·45 in electrical goods. This means that employment, for instance, in American precision instrument firms was 4·13 times as high, and in American chemical firms 2·23 as high, as was to be expected if American firms had employed workers among the different industries in the same proportions as all firms did in the country generally.

Bringing the analysis up-to-date Dunning[2] estimates that in 1967 85 per cent of the expenditure on plant and equipment of the overseas subsidiaries of U.S. manufacturing enterprises occurred in vehicles, chemicals, mechanical and electrical engineering. As regards textiles and clothing, on the other hand, the quotient was as low as 0·06 in 1953, and in 1967 multi-national firms were 'largely absent'.

This association of the newer science-based industries with international firms points to the importance of the spread of technical know-how in explaining large firms. Indeed, Dunning quotes an estimate that one-third of the increase in Europe's exports of technologically advanced products between 1955 and 1964 was accounted for by American-financed firms. Other factors were overcoming tariff barriers and lower costs of production—particularly wages.

(B) Changes in the size-of-plant in manufacturing generally

So far, comparisons have been drawn between Britain and America, industry by industry, for the most recent census year, 1963. This is, so to speak, a static picture or 'still'. If forecasts of the future are to be made, however, we must look at a 'movie' of the trend of events up to the present. In this, manufacture will mainly be considered as a whole, not fragmented into separate industries.

What has been the trend of change, if any, in the size-of-plant structure? In America, size-of-plant statistics go a long way back, but the equivalent British statistics only date from 1935. The change in the distribution of employees among broad ranges of sizes of plant is conveniently summed up in Table IJ.

America always appears to have had a greater proportion of employees in the smaller plants, but the significant point is that since 1954 the proportion of employees in the larger American manufacturing plants, employing over 500, has fallen, whereas the larger plants have continued to increase their proportion in British manufactures. The

---

[1] Ibid., pp. 57, 58.
[2] *The Multinational Enterprise*, Lloyds Bank Review, July 1970, pp. 19ff.

THE STRUCTURAL APPROACH

TABLE IJ

SHIFT IN DISTRIBUTION OF EMPLOYEES AMONG BROAD
SIZE-RANGES OF PLANT (PERCENTAGES)*

| | Total of manufactures | | | | | | | |
| | U.K. | | | | U.S.A.[3] | | | |
	1935 (1)	1951 (2)	1959[1] (3)	1963 (4)	1909[2] (5)	1939[2] (6)	1954 (7)	1963 (8)
Plants employing								
0–99 persons	32·5	25·2	24·0	19·0	37·8	30·0	25·7	26·2
100–499 persons	35·3	32·4	30·0	31·1	34·2	34·8	29·1	30·9
500 or more persons	32·2	42·4	46·0	49·9	28·0	35·2	45·2	42·9

* Reproduced from Florence, *Economics and Sociology of Industry*, 1969, p. 90, with the British percentages for 1963 added.

[1] *Labour Gazette*, September 1959, allowing for plants employing less than eleven
[2] Wage-earners only
[3] U.S. census of manufactures

average British plant, as we shall see in a moment, now has, in fact, a greater number of employees than the American. But it must be remembered that mechanical horse-power has been substituted for man particularly fast in America and with it, productivity per worker. Thus horse-power per plant can be shown to have risen considerably between 1954 and 1963 and consequently the physical volume of production per plant, in spite of the relatively small reduction in employees.[1] While production workers per plant fell on average from 43·2 to 40·6, horse-power per production worker rose from 9·6 to 12·5. Average horse-power *per plant* thus rose from 414·72 to 507·50, or 122 per cent. It has, in fact, been estimated that American production per plant was, in 1937, 216 per cent that of 1914;[2] and after the war, the volume of output is recorded as rising continuously per (non-farm) man-hour, e.g. from 1947 to 1965 by 66 per cent.

Changes in the size of plants of particular industries varied considerably from the general trend. In America between 1914 and 1937 when plants were, for manufacturing as a whole, getting larger, 63 out of the 204 individual manufactures studied by the T.N.E.C. (or 31 per cent) fell in average number of wage-earners per plant. These falls were less in degree than the rises and were largely due either to large displacements of men by machines, if not a total decline of employment in the industry. In Britain, similarly, when between 1935 and 1948 the size of plants was rising in manufactures as a whole, it was falling in

[1] U.S. Statistical Abstract, 1970, p. 226.
[2] Florence, 1948, p. 124.

38

many particular industries—49 out of the 133 analysed, or 37 per cent. Again the falls in size were less in degree than the rises, and 27 or 58 per cent of them were in industries declining in total employment.

The stability in British industries' plant-size structure from 1930 to 1951 is shown graphically in my *Post-War Investment, Location and Size of Plant*, 1962, and reproduced in my *Atlas of Economic Structure and Policies* as Fig. 47. Of the 94 industries into which all manufactures were divided, 10 are shown to have fallen in size-of-plant grade, 19 to have risen, 65 to have remained stable.[1] The falls in size of plant-grade were associated with a fall in the total employed in the industry and vice versa. Four industries out of the ten *falling* in plant-grade, but only one of the industries out of the 19 *rising* in plant-grade fell in *total* employed. Not to miss the wood for the trees, the main lesson is, however, the stability of the representative plant-size in each industry. With one exception (carts, perambulators etc. which jumped from small to medium plant-grade) each of the 29 industries changing size of plant-grade changed only between neighbouring size-grades.

If we take each of the larger industries listed in Table IF and trace events from 1935 to 1963, the general picture of changes in the size of plants is, again, one of stability. This is the fifth of the six significant points which Table IF discloses. Of the 25 large industries 24 remained comparable[2] in scope of activity in both countries over the whole period of 24–29 years. Twelve of the 24 large British industries kept the same grade in size of prevailing plant and only one industry (bread and flour confectionery) changed more than one grade, by rising two grades. Six industries rose, and two fell, by one grade, and four changed from or to no prevailing grade. Thirteen of the 24 American industries kept the same grade in size of prevailing plant and only one rose two grades (bread and flour confectionery again). Five industries rose one grade and five changed from or to no prevailing type. There were in America no falls in grade over this period. It is clear that even over long periods changes of an industry's grade of plant-size are the exception rather than the rule. This stability during nearly thirty years in size of plant structure in given industries in spite of the changing management and ownership of plants—not to mention a world war—is further evidence of the persisting 'ergological' effect of the type-of-work characteristic of an industry.

The reader may by now be impatient to be told in a forthright manner the trend to the present day in the *average* size of plant for manufacturing as a whole and how it differs in Britain and America.

Since 1947,[3] the average size of plant in Britain measured by persons employed has, unlike in America, continued to grow until the average

---

[1] 64 if 'bias to small' and 'smallish' are considered separate grades.

[2] Industrial plant was recognized as a new category during the period.

[3] When the censuses of *both* countries included all plants employing one or more.

size for all manufactures measured this way is now considerably greater than in the U.S. In the 1963 censuses the total employed in American manufactures was given as 16,234,506, the number of plants as 306,617. The (arithmetic mean) average employees per plant was thus 53. In Britain the total employed was 7,960,000, number of plants 89,949; average per plant 88 or 166 per cent of the American size. But this arithmetic mean average is misleading when the distribution of sizes of plant is so extremely skew particularly in America where the proportion of all plants in 1963 that employed 1–4 people was as much as 36·5 per cent, though employing only 1·3 per cent of all employees.[1] In Britain the proportion employing the wider official range of 1–5 people was in that year only 21·0 per cent. As calculated from Table IK in 1963 the median average (less influenced by skew) of the plants was in America 375, in Britain 500 or 133 per cent of the American.[2]

(C) *Change in the size of firms: their inequality*

The stability in these recent years of the sizes of *plants* in manufacturing especially in America, and, in contrast, the growth of the size of *firms*, is brought out clearly in Table IK. In the United Kingdom the employment in the *plants* of 1,000 employees or more rose between 1958 and 1963 only from 34·5 to 35·6 per cent of all employment; in *firms* of that large size it rose from 55·0 to 63·2 per cent. What is now the average size of firm, is a question as popularly asked as the average size of plant (if the questioner realizes the difference). Given the skew, lopsided, distribution of firms' sizes the most representative form of average, as already said of plants, is the 'median' and the change over a mere five years is told strikingly by contrasting the 1958 and the 1963 medians— the 'half-way' point below which size as many employees were employed as above.

If in Table IK the five top and the four bottom percentages of the 1958 column for British firms are added, they show 45·0 and 45·9 per cent of all employees to be in plants employing respectively less than 1,000 and 2,000 or more. The median size is thus nearly in the middle of the 1,000–2,000 range—to be more exact, at 1,550. If the six top percentages of the 1963 column for firms are added they show 50 per cent of employees in firms employing less than 1,999; 42·8 per cent in firms employing more than 5,000. The median thus falls within the 2,000–4,999 range but nearer the lower limit—to be more exact, at

---

[1] The high proportion of small plants in America is particularly evident in the umber and wood products and the printing and publishing groups and in some industries in the food products group, e.g. cheese making, manufactured ice.

[2] The method of calculation is spelled out in greater detail for the *firms*, below (pp. 41-2).

3,240. The (median) average size of British firms (about 500 in 1935) rose, in short, between 1958 and 1963 from 1,550 to 3,240.

TABLE IK

DISTRIBUTION OF EMPLOYEES AMONG DETAILED SIZE-RANGES OF FIRMS AND OF PLANTS
TOTAL OF MANUFACTURES

Ranges of size of plant or firm, in number of employees	Percentage of total employees U.S.A.*			
	Firms		Plants	
	1958 (1)	1963 (2)	1958 (3)	1963 (4)
1–49	15·3 ⎱ 23·0%	14·7 ⎱ 22·1%	17·2 ⎱ 27·0%	16·4 ⎱ 26·2%
50–99	7·7 ⎰	7·4 ⎰	9·8 ⎰	9·8 ⎰
100–249	10·6 ⎱	10·2 ⎱	16·2 ⎱	16·8 ⎱
250–499	7·9 ⎬ 25·7%	7·3 ⎬ 23·9%	14·0 ⎬ 42·5%	14·1 ⎬ 43·3%
500–999	7·2 ⎰	6·4 ⎰	12·3 ⎰	12·4 ⎰
1,000–2,499	9·0 ⎱ 51·0%	8·3 ⎱ 54·0%	13·3 ⎱ 30·5%	12·6 ⎱ 30·5%
2,500 plus	42·0 ⎰	45·7 ⎰	17·2 ⎰	17·9 ⎰
Total employees (thousands)	15,394 = 100%	16,235 = 100%	15,394 = 100%	16,235 = 100%
Median size§ (approximate)	1,170	1,700	370	375

	Percentage of total employees U.K.†			
1–24	5·8 ⎱ 15·6%	5·7 ⎱ 13·6%	6·6 ⎱ 20·1%	6·6 ⎱ 19·0%
25–99	9·8 ⎰	7·9 ⎰	13·5 ⎰	12·4 ⎰
100–199	8·0 ⎱	6·1 ⎱	11·8 ⎱	11·6 ⎱
200–499	12·2 ⎬ 29·4%	9·4 ⎬ 23·2%	19·8 ⎬ 45·5%	19·5 ⎬ 45·4%
500–999	9·2 ⎰	7·7 ⎰	13·8 ⎰	14·3 ⎰
1,000–1,999	9·1 ⎱	8·2 ⎱	13·3 ⎱	13·3 ⎱
2,000–4,999	11·5 ⎮	12·2 ⎮	12·1 ⎮	12·9 ⎮
5,000–9,999	9·5 ⎬ 55·0%	10·4 ⎬ 63·2%	5·7 ⎬ 34·5%	5·3 ⎬ 35·6%
10,000–49,999	17·6 ⎮	23·0 ⎮	3·4 ⎮	4·1 ⎮
50,000 plus	7·3 ⎰	9·4 ⎰	¶ ⎰	¶ ⎰
Total employees (thousands)‡	7,500 = 100%	7,610 = 100%	7,680 = 100%	7,839 = 100%
Median size§ (approximate)	1,550	3,240	490	500

* Source U.S. census of manufactures.
† Source U.K. census of production.
‡ Satisfactory returns.
§ 50 per cent of employees of 'satisfactory returns' below and above.
¶ Included in previous size range.

The same contrast between the change in the size of manufacturing plants and of firms is seen in America as in Britain. Table IK shows that 30·5 per cent of all employees were in plants employing 1,000 or over in 1958 and 30·5 per cent again in 1963; but 51·0 per cent in *firms* of that size in 1958 and 54·0 per cent in 1963. The (median) average size of American *firms* changed from 1,170 in 1958 to 1,700 in 1963.

The most striking change in the size structure of manufacturing organizations between the census of 1958 and that of 1963 is thus the growth of the larger *firms*. This growth is in keeping with the increase in 'conglomerate mergers' to be noted later, but it is specially intriguing in view of the stability if not fall, in the size of plants. In fact a particular *trend* today is toward the multiplant firm which we noticed in the 25 largest industries selected in Table I F. For manufacturing industries *as a whole*, this trend has been noticeable since 1939, when the percentage of all wage earners who were in multiplant firms had risen to 56·0 from 48·4 in 1929. In 1954 the proportion of all employees who were in multiplant firms was 60·6 per cent. The proportion rose to 65·5 per cent in 1958, to 67·8 per cent in 1963.[1]

The logic of this general trend is that though increasing returns may continue to be obtained by larger and larger plants the materials they use and the markets they supply have to be found further afield. Transport and communication costs rise with size and eventually outpace the falling production cost. Locating plants near the sources of supply or markets cuts down transport costs without increasing the marketing and financial costs of the multiplant firm. Moreover, when a large firm takes on more plants it will often 'rationalize' their production. Each plant, though no larger, may be organized to specialize in particular lines of product and produce each of them economically on a larger scale. A conglomerate firm often consists in a group of specializing plants, according to the pattern D on page 68.

The growth in the size of firms raises, however, a particular problem. Growth in the average size of firms as well as of plants does not imply that all firms or plants grow. There always remains a considerable proportion of small firms or plants. In 1963, as Table I K shows, 14·7 per cent of American employees were in firms employing less than 50; these were mostly one-plant firms. This continuance of the small firm with its small plant[2] in spite of firms' increasing average size implies greater inequality of sizes. Now inequality is more of a problem in the case of firms than of plants, because firms are the units of industrial government and inequality may spell dominance within the industry by a few firms—a state of oligopoly; or by one firm—a state of monopoly. Inequality can be viewed as a concentration of anything in the hands of relatively few. When we are dealing with the firm, the

---

[1] Florence, *Economics and Sociology of Industry*, 1969 ed., p. 94.

[2] In 1937 the plants of multiplant firms employed on average 170, the plants of single-plant firms 30. By 1958 the difference had widened to 241 and 21 (U.S. census of manufactures, summary).

unit of control over production concentration becomes particularly important *vis-à-vis* the market and the consumers of the products. Chapter III, devoted to relations with the consumer, considers further the problems that arise.

To enable the reader to grasp the degree of inequality in the distribution of *firms* by size, comparisons may be made with the often quoted and well authenticated distribution of income in Britain and America. Income distribution is usually considered fairly unequal and 'skew' in dispersion, with many poor and a few very rich. To be precise, 10 per cent of all British income recipients had, in 1952, 26 per cent of total national income; and 10 per cent of American recipients had 27 per cent of national income in 1947–50[1] and in subsequent years (1960, 1965, 1967) 27 per cent, 28 per cent and 28 per cent.

This fairly stable proportion may be taken as a standard practical yardstick. But compared to the disproportion in plant and firm sizes, this standard degree of inequality in sizes of income appears mild. Employees in the largest 9·5 per cent of U.S. plants formed in 1963 73·8 per cent of employees in all plants.[2] The inequality among *firms* was still greater.

To compare statistics within the two countries, size of *firms* can be measured in net output value—termed 'value added' in America. In Britain in 1963, the 210 largest enterprises (all those employing over 5,000) had a net output of £4,983 million. The total number of enterprises was 64,367 and the total net output of manufacture £10,470 million. So 0·3 per cent of all enterprises produced 47·5 per cent of all the net output.[3] In America in 1963 the 200 largest enterprises, forming rather less than 0·1 per cent of all manufacturing enterprises,[4] produced 41 per cent of total value added.

The American statistics allow us to trace the recent changes in the

---

[1] The British contrast between the three inequalities in the sizes of income, of plants and of firms can be neatly summed up in terms of the top 5 per cent. The richest 5 per cent of British income recipients in 1959–60 received (before tax) 18·6 per cent of total national income. But 5 per cent of the largest British manufacturing *plants* employed 53·4 per cent of the total employed persons and 3 per cent of manufacturing *firms* employed 59·5 per cent of that total.

[2] Owing to the method of official tabulation, an exact ranking of plant-size into tenths cannot be obtained. Also, the precise degree of inequality is harder to supply for the U.K. because official statistics record that in 1963 5,723 plants out of a total of 89,949 gave unsatisfactory returns. Almost all of these would presumably be in the small plant category (in fact their average employment was only 21). Adding these the nearest contrast with the income inequality of the *richest 10 per cent having 26 per cent*, is that in Britain *employees in the largest 8·7 per cent of plants formed 70·8 per cent of employees in all plants*.

[3] U.K. census of production, 1963, Part 132, Table 13.

[4] Evidence of Blair at Hearings on Economic Concentration, U.S. Senate Subcommittee on Anti-Trust and Monopoly, 1964, Part I, pp. 80–1.

200 enterprises' share of value added. For 1947 it was 30 per cent. There was a sharp increase between 1947 and 1954 when the share was 37 per cent, then relative stability between 1954 and 1958 and then moderate increase, bringing the share up to 41 per cent in 1962.

But the most telling statement of all to bring out the inequality and the *growing inequality* of the sizes of American firms is the percentage of total manufacturing corporate assets held by the few largest corporations. In America in 1947 the 100 largest corporations held 39·3 per cent of the assets and the 200 largest, 47·2 per cent. In 1968 the 100 largest corporation held 49·3 per cent of all corporate assets and the 200 largest, 60·9 per cent. Between 1947 and 1968 the 200 largest had thus increased their share by 29 per cent.[1]

§ 5. PATTERNS OF INDUSTRIAL LOCATION

The plants of different industries were said (p. 4) to differ in their location or site as well as in their size. Plants being physical entities must obviously be situated somewhere and the pattern of plants of any particular industry may concentrate in some particular place or region to various degrees or may not concentrate at all. The fact that manufactures vary widely in their location pattern can be seen most simply from the tables of the U.S. census[2] showing for all cities the number of plants in all broad subdivisions of manufacture. In each of the 224 metropolitan areas with a population of over 50,000 some of these industrial sub-divisions, printing and food and drink for instance, have plants employing at least 20 workers in *every* area; other subdivisions have no such plants at all in certain areas. There are none, for instance, in 28 areas for the textile, clothing and leather group and none in 34 areas for the transport equipment group. In Britain the same differences of pattern appear. In 1958 there were no iron and steel workers at all in the whole of the eastern, southern or south-western regions and no cotton spinning in any of these or in the London region either. On the other hand workers in baking and brewing appeared in every region in fairly close proportion to the total industrially employed there.

Two questions arise. If the plants of an industry concentrate or 'localize', where do they do so, or not do so? This question is answered for various places quantitatively in terms of the degree of concentration by the location quotient which I first suggested in 1929.[3] The further

---

[1] *Economic Report on Corporate Mergers*, U.S. Federal Trade Commission, 1969, pp. 172–3. The main reason for the great inequality in assets is the inclusion here of the integrated oil companies among the manufacturing industries.

[2] *County and City Data Book*, 6197, pp. 432–63.

[3] *The Statistical Method in Economics and Political Science*, pp. 327–8, Kegan Paul.

question is, taking the country as a whole, what are the degrees of concentration and the pattern of localization exhibited by different industries? This question is answered quantitatively by the *coefficient of localization* which A. J. Wensley and I first put forward in 1933,[1] and which I developed for the United States in 1942.[2] The coefficient is based, like the location quotients, on the deviation of the distribution of workers in various industries or in various areas from the distribution over the whole of industry or the whole country. In America the 48 continental states are convenient areas; in the United Kingdom nine standard English regions are now recognized by the census, together with Wales, Scotland and Northern Ireland. The average population of the 12 areas is not dissimilar to that of the U.S. states. Percentages, then, are obtained for each industry giving the proportion it employed in each of the states or regions. If these regional percentages do not deviate from those for industry as a whole there is no localization; if they deviate much, localization is high. The degree of localization of any industry can thus be measured in one figure by the sum of plus or of minus deviations of its regional percentages from the corresponding regional percentages of industry as a whole or of the total occupied population. The totals of plus and of minus deviations will be the same and neither total can be more than 100, since each is the sum of deviations of one set of percentages from another. The extreme range of coefficients is thus 0 to 100 per cent (or 1), 0 denoting no regional deviation of the particular industry from the regional pattern of industry in general and thus no localization.

Full examples of the calculation of the coefficient of localization and the location quotients can be found elsewhere,[3] but as a simple case the derivation may be cited of the coefficient of 0·50 in 1963 for the manufacture of motor vehicles and bodies in America. The census of manufactures records the percentages of total manufacturing employees in the nation as a whole that are found in each of the 48 continental states. A similar set of 48 state percentages can be found for the employees within the particular industry making motor vehicles and bodies. Only five states had, for the motor vehicle industry, location quotients above unity, calculating on the basis of employees in all manufactures, as in the first column of the following table. If preferred, workers in all occupations may be used as a broader base than those in manufacturing. Coefficient of localization for the industry is the total of plus

[1] See *Economic Journal*, 1937, pp. 662–4. Originally extreme localization was rated 2·0 not 1·0.

[2] *Industrial Location and National Resources* (N.R.P.B.), U.S. Government Printing Office, Washington. The quotient and the coefficient are now in fairly general use by geographers.

[3] Florence, 1948, pp. 34–7; N.R.P.B., 1943, Industrial Location and National Resources, pp. 105ff; *Atlas of Economic Structure and Policies*, 1970, Fig. 35.

THE STRUCTURAL APPROACH

CALCULATION OF LOCATION QUOTIENTS AND COEFFICIENT OF LOCALIZATION

States in order of location quotient	(A) Total employees in all manufactures as percentage of all in U.S.	(B) Employees in manufactures of motor vehicles and bodies as percentage of all in U.S.	Location quotients $(B) \div (A)$	Item in calculation of coefficient of localization $(B)-(A)$ $\div 100$
	(1)	(2)	(3)	(4)
Michigan	5·67	37·97	6·69	+0·3230
Indiana	3·60	8·68	2·41	+0·0508
Ohio	7·31	16·19	2·23	+0·0888
Wisconsin	2·73	5·44	2·00	+0·0271
Missouri	2·31	3·38	1·46	+0·0107

deviations in column 4 = 0·5004. The minus deviations of the remaining 43 states will add up to the same amount. The coefficient for any industry is likely to be more precise the finer the subdivision of areas. Where the subdivisions are whole states or regions it would be more accurate to speak of a coefficient of regionalization. For rough comparison (a grading of the pattern of industries into say five degrees of localization), the data here used, which are easily accessible, are probably sufficient.

The wide variety in location pattern between different manufacturing industries has always been evident. Between different American manufactures the coefficient of localization was found to vary in 1947 from 0·14 for bread and 0·15 for ice-cream to 0·76 for fur goods, 0·83 for canned fish and 0·88 for tobacco stemming. In Britain in 1951 the coefficient varied from 0·11 for bread and also for brewing, to 0·84 for linen and 0·89 for jute, and also for tinplate.[1] For both countries the 25 manufacturing industries, large or small, with the highest localization coefficient are given in Table IID. The coefficients of localization for the 25 largest manufactures in each country are given among the last columns of Table IF. The relations between the prevailing size of plant and degree of localization of each of these industries will be taken up in Chapter II.

Services and also building have low coefficients of localization when compared with most manufactures. Taking all the sectors appearing in Table IA one by one, both countries can be shown to have a dispersed location for construction, transport, distribution (trade)[2] and also public utilities and services, except tourist services, and *high* finance; but a fairly high localization for mining and wells, and a moderate localization for agriculture and fishing.[3] The most intriguing

[1] Florence, *Post-War Investment, Location and Size of Plant*, Appendix C.
[2] See p. 116 below.
[3] For U.S.A. see also N.R.P.B. 1943, *Industrial Location and National Resources*, p. 66; for U.K., P.E.P. report on *Industrial Location*, 1938, Appendix Table I.

contrast in location patterns is undoubtedly that between the different branches of manufacture. The causes, logical and illogical, for this contrast in structure, will be taken up in the next chapter.

Meanwhile the broad results of our analysis are set out in Table Iʟ. Agriculture, mining and quarrying and the service orders of industry each have a characteristic pattern of location, but the manufacturing order has not. Some manufactures are as highly, if not more highly, localized than mining; some as dispersed as services. The reasons for the different location patterns of some manufactures are not far to seek. Several of the localized processing industries like iron and steel are material oriented or 'rooted' to localized extraction by heavy cost of transporting raw material and resemble the extractive industries in pattern of location. Several of the dispersed manufactures with low coefficients like baking are 'tied' to the dispersed consumers by the

TABLE Iʟ

GROUPING OF SECTORS BY THEIR LOCATION PATTERN

Sectors of economic activity	Pattern of 'location' (measurable by coefficients of localisation)* (1)	Subdivision of pattern (2)	(Examples)* (3)
Agriculture	Moderate localization		
Mining	Fairly high localization		
Quarrying	Dispersed		
	High localization	'Swarming' without reference to extraction or consumers	(Cotton)
	Moderate localization	'Rooted' to localized extraction	(Iron and steel)
Manufacturing	Variable	'Footloose'	(Electric machinery)
		'Linked' to other industries	(Textile machinery)
	Dispersed (low) coefficients)	Tied to consumer 'Residentiary'	(Baking)
		'Rooted' to scattered extraction	(Bricks)
Building	Dispersed		
Public utilities	Dispersed		
Services	Dispersed, except tourist trade, high finance etc.		

*See Tables Iꜰ and IIᴇ.

heavy cost of transporting products. They must reside like certain Residentiary Cathedral Canons where the consumers, the congregation they serve, reside, and thus they resemble services, utilities and building in their pattern of location. But there still remains location patterns of manufacturing not so easily accounted for, here nick-named 'swarming', 'footloose', 'linked'.

Linkage and swarming will be explained when discussing, in Chapter II, the efficiency of different location patterns. Swarming results in marked centres or localizations of specific industries with very high coefficients. Both 'linked' and 'footloose' industries show variability in the degree of localization; but only the footloose have freedom of choice in location. It is these footloose industries that the planner can use as his *masse de manœuvre*, i.e. as his manœuvrable reserves to be placed at will where required.

All these location patterns can be observed in British and in American industries. Moreover the same industry tends to have the same pattern in each country in spite of the great geographical and climatic differences. Comparison is more restricted than in the study of the relative horse-power per man compared in § 2 because coefficients had to be calculated on a different basis and on different numbers and sorts of region. In 1929–30, however, 29 industries corresponded fairly in scope in both countries and also had coefficients of localization calculable for each country. If the 29 corresponding industries are, separately for each country, placed in order of their coefficient and then grouped into five grades (the third or middle grade to contain 5 industries, all the other grades 6) a clear tendency is shown toward agreement

TABLE IM

AGREEMENT OF CORRESPONDING BRITISH AND AMERICAN INDUSTRIES
ON FIVE GRADES OF LOCALIZATION COEFFICIENT

Distance between corresponding industries	1929–30		1947–51	
	Actual[1] (1)	Chance random distribution to be expected (2)	Actual[1] (3)	Chance random distribution to be expected (4)
Same relative grade	13 ⎫ 23	5¾ ⎫ 15	17 ⎫ 36	9·6 ⎫ 24·9
Neighbouring grade	10 ⎭	9¼ ⎭	19 ⎭	15·3 ⎭
Two grades apart	6	7	9	11·5
Three grades apart	0 ⎫ 0	4¾ ⎫ 7	3 ⎫ 3	7·7 ⎫ 11·8
Four grades apart	0 ⎭	2¼ ⎭	0 ⎭	3·9 ⎭
Total of Industries	29	29	48	48

[1] For the identity of each industry, see Florence, 1948, and *Post-War Investment, Location and Size of Plant*, 1965.

between the corresponding industries in the two countries; although, as might be expected for reasons detailed below, the agreement is less clear than for horse-power per man or for prevailing size of plant. A similar study for 1947–51 showed a similar agreement.

The industries actually in the same grade of localization in both countries in 1929–30 were more than double the number to be expected on random chance distribution and there were no industries more than two grades apart, though by random chance seven out of the 29 could have been expected to be that degree different in their pattern of localization. In 1947–57 several more British and American industries were comparable making a total of 48; three-quarters of the 48 appeared in the same or neighbouring grades of location pattern.

This degree of agreement, as just noted, is not as high as the agreement for corresponding industries of the two countries in horse-power per worker or in grade of plant-size. Considerable disagreement in localization is logically to be expected on account of the different methods of calculation in the two countries[1] and the more fundamental geographical differences.

Further evidence on localization for corresponding large industries in the two countries is provided in Table IF which names the industries concerned and illustrates the differences both in calculation and geography. Geographical differences include the particular location of material resources, the variety of climate and the far longer distances involved in the United States.

Timber is an extreme case. It is grown in certain parts of America but mostly imported through several ports into Britain. There are wide differences, too, in the British and American location pattern of the aircraft industry which is more localized in America due to special climates, and of the newspaper industry which is more localized in Britain due to the sheer distances in America making any one centre for newspaper publishing impossible.

In Table IF coefficients of localization are given for the 25 largest British industries at a date as late as 1958 based on the U.K. census of production, Table 8. Though no such recent calculation has been made for the U.S. it is useful, in order to bring out a sixth point arising from Table IF, to compare these latest British coefficients with the Stanford Research Institute's coefficients calculated for America in 1947 and quoted in that table.

If the 25 largest industries are divided up according to their ranking into five grades of localization, each grade containing five industries

---

[1] Often more than one industry shown in the U.S. census corresponds to the large British industries, so more than one American coefficient of localization has often to be given in Table IF. In those industries the ranking is according to their unweighted average.

49

(first grade 1st to 5th, second grade 6th to 10th and so on), comparison of corresponding British and American grading in the manner of Tables IG and IH would show ten industries in the same grade, thirteen industries one grade apart, and two industries—aircraft and timber three and four grades apart. Clearly, and this is the point arising, Anglo-American agreement in coefficients of localization for these 25 largest industries, though not so close as for the size of firms or plants, is considerably closer than a random pairing.[1]

What has been the historical trend in the degree of localization of American and British industries? Research has only been spasmodic and the measures used not standardized. It is, however, possible to show from Wilfred Smith's data[2] that between 1851 and 1931 the British shoe industry raised its coefficient of localization from 0·05 to 0·37 and tailoring from 0·06 to 0·20. There is little doubt too that, since its industrialization earlier than any other country, Britain has kept the localizations of certain industries *in certain places* remarkably stable, though not the location of its manufactures as a whole.

In 1841 one division of a single county (Yorkshire West Riding) contained 93 per cent of England's worsted and 63 per cent of her woollen workers; Lancashire contained 70 per cent of England's cotton workers; Staffordshire 79 per cent of England's locksmiths and 65 per cent of her pottery workers; and Warwickshire 57 per cent of England's brassfounders.[3]

Though local administrative boundaries have changed somewhat, these localized industries have been shown[4] as still, in 1931, localized in the same geographical areas. The region containing Yorkshire had still, ninety years later, 80·5 per cent of Britain's wool and worsted workers; the region containing Lancashire 80 to 90 per cent of British cotton workers; and the region containing Staffordshire and Warwickshire 85 per cent of locksmiths,[5] 79 per cent of pottery and 73 per cent of brass goods workers.

The change in the location of manufactures as a whole, the movement, for instance, after 1920 from the north and from south Wales to the midlands and the south of England has, in fact, been mainly due to this very tendency of particular industries to stick to their locality. The south and midlands increased their industrial employment because their particular local industries including locksmithing, brassware and

---

[1] If, instead of being grouped into five grades, each of the 25 industries is considered separately, the Spearman coefficient of correlation between the British and American ranks in localization is 0·643, and without the timber industry, 0·788.

[2] *An Economic Geography of Great Britain*, 1949, pp. 503, 528.

[3] Day, 'The Distribution of Industrial Occupations in England, 1841–1861', *Transactions of the Connecticut Academy of Art and Science*, March 1927.

[4] P.E.P., 'The Location of Industry, 1938', based on 1931 census of population.

[5] Census of production, 1935, Part II, p. 105.

other metal working and pottery were prospering, and the industries staying in the north, iron and steel, shipbuilding, cotton, wool and worsted, were not.[1]

Some localized industries have, however, not remained where they first localized, particularly industries rooted to their materials or linked with specialized markets, when their material, or their markets, changed in location. The rooted early-stage iron and steel processes moved some years ago from the English west midlands (leaving the Black Country behind with exhausted ore and coal mines) and is now moving into the iron-fields of the east midlands. The same industry has also changed its 'seat' in America, mainly from coal toward iron ore areas (the relative importance of these two materials having changed), or toward those areas where are localized the iron or steel using industries (e.g. motor-cars) which form its market.[2]

A localized industry, neither rooted to its material nor tied to a special market, is often termed mobile. But if this indicates that the industry moves readily the adjective gives the reverse of a true impression. It is not used in Table IL. Within a single country of fairly uniform labour conditions,[3] most unrooted, unlinked localized industries show remarkable persistence in their locality—from the social standpoint (see p. 325) possibly too much persistence.

Instead of harping on movements of localized industries between regions and countries, writers should appreciate the constantly changing structure of a country's manufacturing industries. One particular manufacture will decline, like the British cotton industry (mainly localized in Lancashire) which almost halved in man-power between 1923 and 1938 and has more than halved between 1938 and 1966. Another industry will grow, like electrical engineering (largely in the London area) which more than doubled in man-power between 1923 and 1938 and has since then branched out into the radio and electronic industries. The significant movement is that the population not needed in an industry localized in one region migrates to help take up or develop another industry that has always been located in some other region.

Even so, Makower, Marschak and Robinson have shown that mobility is subject to certain limitations. During the economic recovery of the early 1930s when the motor industry was growing in Oxford, the rate of movement from other areas was roughly proportionate to the excess of their unemployment rate over that of Oxford; and mobility

[1] See West Midland Group, *Conurbation*, Table XXIV, p. 119.
[2] Isard, *Journal of Political Economy*, June 1948.
[3] A localized industry like cotton has 'moved' between regions of very different wage levels within one country (e.g. New England and the Old South); and between countries (e.g. England and Japan, 1922–39).

diminished fairly regularly the further the area was from Oxford.[1]

Movement of the particular industries themselves (i.e. a change in location), has occurred not so generally between regions as in the same region from the centre of cities to suburbs. Urbanization quotients can be calculated to measure which industries showed preferences for various degrees of centralization or decentralization. For instance, in the American book and job printing industry, the proportion of jobs in *principal cities* of industrial areas was in 1933 1·9 times the proportion for manufactures as a whole—65·5 per cent as against 35·1 per cent; while pottery, steel and chemicals with quotients of 2·3, 2·8 and 2·5 showed a still stronger bias to the *periphery* of industrial areas. Between 1929 and 1933 a fall in the percentage of jobs in principal cities was accompanied by a rise at the peripheries in knit goods, worsted goods, men's clothing, women's clothing, boots and shoes, pottery, furniture, steel works and rolling mills, steam fittings, stoves and ranges, rubber, motor vehicles, motor vehicle parts. In the whole list of industries presented by Goodrich, movement from periphery to principal city was only found for furnishing, textiles and electrical machinery.[2]

§ 6. FORMS AND EXTENT OF INTEGRATION

While size of organization is a question of man-to-man relations and location is ultimately a question of man-to-place relations, integration is a question of the relation of man, or groups of men, to type of work—man-to-work relations. It is thus more intimately connected with the technical background sketched out already. The very basis of the structure of industrial activity discussed in §§ 1–3 consists ultimately in the degrees of specialization or integration. In primitive societies there is no complete division of persons into agriculturists, manufacturers, servicers; nearly everyone is a bit of all, and organizations are not specialized; all their work activities, not to mention religious and social pursuits, are integrated. When it came, in § 4, to a definition of a manufacturing industry the degree of integration was also most relevant. Iron and steel, boots and shoes, are each counted one industry because most firms and plants now happen to integrate iron with steelmaking; boot with shoe-making.[3]

Integration is not just of philosophical interest as the basis of

[1] Oxford University Papers, October 1938, May 1939, September 1940. Quoted by A. J. Brown *Economic Journal*, December 1969, p. 773.

[2] Goodrich and others, *Migration and Economic Opportunity*, 1936, pp. 317–92, 708–34, and N.R.P.B. 1942, p. 106. This type of enquiry does not seem to have been repeated, except in particular localities.

[3] A tendency opposite to the division of industries noted by Allyn Young, see above, page 19.

definitions; it is one of the main questions of policy for the top government of any organization. Whoever has the decision what goods to make or services to provide, what not, is in fact in top control. The optimum degree of integration is the qualitative question corresponding to the quantitative question of the optimum scale of production, of how much to make.

Economists who disregard the structural approach have not sufficiently appreciated the importance of the degree of integration. Instead, till recently, they have in their theoretical models assumed, for the sake of abstract simplicity, that each entrepreneur produced only one sort of product.

In fact integration has certainly been increasing recently. Using the subdivision of all American manufactures into about 426 industries (the so-called four-digit code) the following table shows the great increase during the mere five year period between 1960 and 1965 in the number of products made by the 494 largest American corporations in 1960, some of which became merged.

TABLE In

INCREASE IN NUMBER OF U.S. FIRMS MAKING A WIDE VARIETY OF PRODUCTS*

Number of types of products	Number of firms		Change per cent (3)
	1960 (1)	1965 (2)	
1–5	180	134	− 25
6–10	147	114	− 22
11–15	85	81	− 5
16–30	71	105	+ 48
31–45	8	19	+137
46+	3	8	+166
	494	461	

* G. H. Berry, *Ohio State Law Journal*, vol. 28, no. 3, 1967.

It is noticeable by what high percentages the number of these corporations decreased which integrated only 1–5 or 6–10 products and especially by what high percentages, considering the short period of five years, the number became larger of the corporations integrating over 16 products. The trend in percentages is continuous; the greater the number of products, the more 1965 exceeds 1960 in companies making that number.[1]

[1] Thanks to the U.K. Census of Production for 1963 (Part 132, Table 16 published in 1970) the increase in integration of British firms can now also be traced. Manufactures were divided into 51 groups. In 1958 out of a total of 9,190 large or

A further temptation to over-simplification is that integration, being mainly a qualitative question cannot be handled mathematically; and indeed though the extent of integration can be pictured by the super-imposition of the area of a firm's or a plant's work over the technical structure illustrated in Table I$_B$,[1] no convenient measure has been thought out like the coefficient of localization, or the measure for prevailing size of plant.

For comparing different industries the nearest approach lies in M. Gort's 'alternative diversification measures'.[2] They all depend on a detailed standard classification of a country's industries and products such as the four-digit code and a clear decision of which among a plant's products or processes are primary to the plant—what the British census calls its 'principal products'. Elsewhere[3] I have used one of these measures of integration (the percentage of total employees that are found in the primary industries) to rank the U.S. standard 'major industry groups'. Least integrated were the tobacco industry (with 99·9 per cent employees in the primary industry) and food; most integrated, electrical machinery (with 66·7 per cent of its employees in the primary industry); next most integrated was fabricated metals. Just because it is not simple or not easily measurable, integration must not, however, be omitted as a leading and ever present factor in industrial structure and control, and some survey must be made of its extent.

Though often used, like the word combination, merely to mean the act of coming together of hitherto independent firms, integration will here be used more widely to connote a given state of affairs. Integration, to be precise, will refer to the scope of activities or transactions found under any sort of single control. The notion indicates the scope of a firm or plant and even (as in Chapter II, § 5) the scope of the activities of a locality. Integration is not used of the activities of a single person but otherwise it is the opposite of specialization and we can contrast firm, plant and local integration with firm, plant or local specialization. The activities integrated have been grouped into several types according to their technical relations.

---

[1] See Florence, *Atlas of Economic Structure and Policies*, Figs. 43 and 44.

[2] *Diversification and Integration in American Industry*, Princeton University Press, 1962, pp. 23ff.

[3] *Economics and Sociology of Industry*, 1969 ed., p. 247.

---

medium firms, i.e. 'enterprises' that employed 100 or more persons with an average of 690 employees per firm, 1,356 or 14·8 per cent employed 500 or more in manufacturing groups other than their main group. Only five years later, in 1963, the total of large or medium firms had fallen to 7,540 with an average employment of 882. Of these, 1,716 employed 500 or more in manufacturing groups other than their main group. The percentage of integration thus rose from 14·8 per cent to 22·5 per cent.

The production of many different sorts of articles at the same stage of production is sometimes referred to as horizontal integration; but to avoid confusion with the mere addition to the scale of production of the same article (to which horizontal integration may also refer) we shall follow D. H. Robertson in his use of the expression lateral integration.[1] The lateral relation may subsist between products diverging from the same process or source, or between materials converging upon the same process or market. Boots and shoes diverge from leather tanning; meat, hides, horns and bones from slaughtering; fish-hooks and needles from steel wire. Fish-hooks and artificial flies, furniture and metal springs converge on the same market. Organizations that produce meat and glue and work up the other by-products from cattle may be said to have divergent integration; organizations making both furniture and metal bed-springs to have convergent integration; and organizations that make fish-hooks, needles and flies to have both divergent and convergent integration.

Vertical integration occurs where one organization (or locality) performs consecutive processes (possibly including distribution), for instance iron and steel making, or textile carding, spinning and weaving, or making and selling shoes or pottery 'from clay to cup'. *Diagonal* integration consists in the provision within one organization of auxiliary goods or services required for the several main processes or lines of production of that organization. An organization may, for instance, provide its own designs or power, make its own tools and machines, or use its own carpenters' services for repairs.[2]

A certain degree of vertical or diagonal integration is almost invariably present in modern industrial organizations. But the precise degree of integration is not invariable. Some textile firms spin *and* weave, others merely spin, *or* merely weave. Again some firms provide all or some of their own electrical power, others buy it from power companies; some provide all or some of their own designs, others buy them from outside; some make all or some of their own machines and tools, others buy them ready made; some employ their own force of carpenters, others call them in from outside contractors, others do a bit of both. In short, processes and services may be integrated, dis-integrated or partially integrated.

Considerable research has been undertaken in America into the extent of these various types of integration under the control of specific

---

[1] *Control of Industry*, Chapter III, § 2.

[2] This integration is diagonal since the auxiliary goods or services help a number of lines or successive processes and can only be pictured as slanting into the main structure at various angles. It might perhaps be more intelligible, if instead of convergent, divergent, vertical and diagonal integration the terms 'materials', 'products', 'processes' and 'services' integration were used.

types of structure. This research has concentrated particularly on firms having several plants, the so-called central-office companies. The U.S. Temporary National Economic Committee (T.N.E.C., Monograph 27) found in 1937 5,625 firms with a central office controlling a total of 25,699 establishments or plants. Among these firms 3,574 had 11,321 plants, all pursuing the same industry. Among the remaining 2,051 firms with 14,378 plants many (1,219) had plants (10,696 aggregate) pursuing the same industry (i.e. in horizontal integration) mixed with plants pursuing different industries. The importance of these multiplant firms is that though heavily out-numbered (141,095 to 5,625) by firms identical with one plant, they employed 51·1 per cent of all wage-earners.

Here is the simplest breakdown of the structure of these central office (multiplant) firms, found in the 1937 survey:

	Total of firms	*Total of plants*
A. All the plants of the firms in the same industry:	3,574	11,321
B. Plants of firms in same and different industries:	1,219	{ 10,696 same 1,831 different
C. All plants of the firms in different industries:	832	1,851
A, B, C. Total multiplant firms	5,625	25,699
B, C. Complex multiplant firms	2,051	—

Concentrating on the 'complex' firms (B and C) with plants in different industries, what was the relative frequency in fact of the various types of integration in America? The answer is not easy, even when all complex firms have been duly analysed, since many a single complex may include integrations of various types. In all, 2,499 examples of integration were found among the 2,051 complex firms.[1] The convergent lateral relation type was the most frequent with 1,058 examples of plants so related to other plants within the same firm; next came the divergent lateral relation type with 781 examples (joint products 564, by-products 113, like processes 104); next the vertical, successive, relation type with 565 examples. As many as 95 firms had plants with a main activity that seemed technically unrelated to that of the firm's other plants. Divergent and convergent types of integration appear surprisingly frequent compared to the more usually cited vertical integration. The logic underlying these forms of integration is discussed in Chapter II.

Since the publication of this classic analysis by the T.N.E.C., integration has again come to the fore largely because of the growth in importance of the multiplant firm making a great variety of types of product. Though concentration of production under control of a few firms has not increased much *in the separate industries*, it has increased

[1] T.N.E.C., Monograph 27, Part II, Chapter VI, Tables 22–5.

rapidly for the manufacturing sector *as a whole*. Between 1947 and 1963 the percentage of total value added in manufacture as a whole produced by the fifty largest companies (to sum up the detailed record given above, p. 44) rose from 17 per cent to 25 per cent, and by the largest two hundred from 30 per cent to 41 per cent. The solution of this apparent paradox is that the larger firms are enlarging by diversifying into several industries (as shown clearly in Table IN) controlling, however, perhaps only a relatively small proportion of each separate industry. They often integrate products and processes *in no particular work relation* to one another. The term 'conglomerate firm' is now applied to this illogical-looking integrated structure. As far as it goes, the logic to which we revert later is managerial or financial. Mergers may make use of one company's able management. More often they use the spare cash reserve of one of the companies or its prestige to raise capital cheaply. We shall also point to cross-subsidization of one line of production by the profits from another line, perhaps an 'unfair' form of competition aimed at eventual monopoly.

To sum up. Some degree of integration is the rule both within a firm and a plant, and the practical question is not whether to integrate, but how far to integrate—and in what direction—a question taken up in the next chapter in connection with scale of operation. Other things, such as the number of men or amount of equipment employed, being equal, the more the integration the less is the scale of production within the organization.

CHAPTER II

LOGIC AND FACT OF INDUSTRIAL STRUCTURE

§ 1. THE MEANING, MECHANISM AND MEASURES OF EFFICIENCY

Now that the structure of industry with its firms and plants has been analysed and various possible references of size or scale of production made more definite, we may advance to enunciate, as a working hypothesis, a bold proposition. There are logical reasons for supposing that, granting the advantages of mechanical and human specialization, *large-scale production, especially when conducted in large-size firms and plants, tends to result in maximum efficiency.*[1] We shall use the expression 'large-scale operation' to refer to the large-scale production of any article or service *when conducted within one organization.*[2]

Belief in large-scale production, whether or not conducted within one plant or firm, is equivalent to a belief in the economists' law of increasing returns (or, as it is alternately called, decreasing costs), which states that the more the amount of any commodity (goods or service) provided, the greater the return or the less the cost.[3] The two alternative phrasings may indeed be combined in this way: 'the more the amount

---

[1] The proposition was bold in 1933 when I first advanced it and is still bold for an economist in Britain; but in America it is now perhaps getting rather bald. The logical application of this proposition to the actual structure of industry, however, still remains bold everywhere.

[2] Chapter I, § 1. Though not identical, large-scale operation implies *some* degree of large-scale organization, but no more than is necessary for the one article operated upon to be made in quantity. Readers who feel confused by the distinction between operation and organization may substitute in their minds mass-production within one plant for large-scale operation. The phrase mass-production is not generally used in the text because it has lately aroused too much enthusiasm and too much prejudice to be free from emotional bias.

[3] Some economists are content with this simple statement of the law, e.g. Mill (*Principles of Political Economy*, 1849, Book IV, II, § 2): 'The larger the scale on which manufacturing operations are carried on, the more cheaply they can in general be performed', or Taussig (*Principles*, 1911, 14, § 1): 'As additional supplies of a commodity are produced, the cost of each unit becomes not greater but less'. Other economists (e.g. Marshall, *Principles of Economics*, 6th ed., 1910, Book IV, XIII, § 2: 'An increase of capital and labour leads generally to an improved organization, which increases the efficiency of the work of capital and labour') include in their definition the law's *modus operandi* through changing organization. But in either case increasing returns is taken in the first instance as a relation of costs, or cost factors, to the scale of an industry as a whole or the production of one commodity, not to the size of any particular organization.

of any commodity that is provided the greater the efficiency'. For by *efficiency* I refer to a relation between return (or output) and cost (or input). Efficiency is indicated by the amount of return obtained at any given cost, the precise relation being either a ratio (where efficiency is greater or less according as return divided by cost is greater or less) or a difference (where efficiency is greater or less according as return *minus* cost is greater or less). Engineers seem to prefer the ratio, business men the differential (sales—costs = profits) standpoint. To be efficient thus means that either the average return, or the differential return is high.

The conception of economy or 'elimination of waste' is simply the obverse of that of efficiency.[1] Efficiency takes cost as given and focuses attention upon return or product; economy or elimination of waste takes return or product as given and focuses attention upon the cost incurred. To be economical (or to eliminate waste) implies that either average cost or marginal cost is lowered. The standpoint of both efficiency and economy may be combined by defining a *logical organization of industry* as one that as far as possible *yields maximum return or product at minimum cost.*

Both the return and the cost elements in efficiency or economy can appear on any one of the three levels: the monetary, the physical and the psychological. In monetary terms efficiency is the provision of maximum exchange value of goods and services at minimum expense in materials and the factors of production. It is on this level that efficiency measured as return *minus* cost is indicated by business profits. In physical terms, efficiency is the provision of a maximum volume of goods and services of given quality at a minimum use of materials, equipment and workers' time. The law of increasing return or decreasing cost is usually first enunciated by economists in these physical terms.[2] In psychological or human terms, also recognized by economists, especially Marshall, efficiency is the provision of maximum utility and satisfaction (now fashionable as 'welfare'[3]) at minimum 'real' cost or input in effort and sacrifice.

The logical reasons will first be presented for supposing economy and efficiency to result from large-scale production, carried on in one or (perhaps less forcibly) several organizations—for belief, to wit, in the economists' law of increasing returns. Three definite principles of efficiency appear in the mechanism of this law; that of bulk transactions, massed reserves and multiples. All assume an economic advantage in specialization of men and equipment and look to long-run conditions in the course of which adjustment and reorganization of factors of production, e.g. additional investment, are feasible. These principles

[1] See Florence, *Economics of Fatigue and Unrest*, p. 24.
[2] Marshall, *Principles of Economics*, Book IV, XIII, § 2.
[3] I plead in Chapter VI (p. 265) for a return to the traditional sense of welfare.

transcend the more obvious short-run increasing return due to a greater output from fixed equipment and staff and a constant overhead charge. They can be applied equally in technical production, as in management, marketing and finance activities.

The principle of bulk transactions is the simplest to understand. It is illustrated by the fact that the total monetary, physical or psychological costs of dealings in large quantities are sometimes no greater (and in any case less than proportionately greater) than the costs of dealing in small quantities; and hence the cost *per unit* becomes smaller with large quantities. A salesman, or purchasing agent, may spend no more effort in negotiating a 1,000 (£ or $) order for a given article, or a clerk in booking and filing it, than for a 10½p or 10½ cent order. Similarly a large order for a single article going through the factory causes no more cost in the tooling up and resetting of machines than a small order, and a long railway train costs no more in signalling and driving skill than a short one. Short-run increasing return mainly operates on this principle but it applies to long-run conditions too, since only bulk production for a larger market may justify innovations in division of labour and more specialized equipment. The principle applies particularly to physical properties. A large container will hold more goods per given cost than a smaller container, owing to the fact that cubic contents or volume increases more than proportionately to area of containing walls. Hence bulk transactions (whether on behalf of a whole country or 'localization' or firm or plant) permitting the use of larger railway trucks, ships or boilers tend to be more economical and efficient than transactions on a smaller scale.[1]

The principle of massed (or pooled) reserves This principle has come to the fore in many apparently unrelated branches of economic life. It appears in schemes for the decasualization of labour at the docks and underlies all forms of insurance and banking; the reserves that are economized may in fact be labour, liquid monetary resources, stocks of goods and materials[2] or any other factors in production, when the demands upon these factors are somewhat uncertain in their incidence.

To take a generalized case. Suppose that there are ten varieties of an article for each of which the normal demand is 100 units, subject however to a deviation either way of 20 per cent. Each variety must then be stocked to supply a possible demand of 120 units, leaving normally an unused reserve of 20 units. The total of these normal demands will be 1,000 units and the total of the separate reserves for each variety will be 200 units. But it is improbable that all the varieties will be

---

[1] Kimball, *Economics of Industry*, p. 165; Robinson, *Structure of Competitive Industry*, pp. 29–30.

[2] See McClelland, 'Stocks in Distribution', *Journal of Industrial Economics*, June 1960.

demanded to the maximum or minimum extent at one and the same time. In times of brisk trade five of the varieties may be enjoying the maximum demand of 120 units while the other five, if not suffering the minimum demand of 80 units, may only be demanded to a 'normal plus' extent of 110 units. Unused reserves will then be 5×10 units.

Now suppose that, fluctuations in trade remaining the same, *one* variety is manufactured on a large scale for the *normal* demand of 1,000 units rather than ten varieties each on a small scale for a 100 units normal demand. In times of *brisk* trade the same total demand as above, namely $(5 \times 120) + (5 \times 110) = 1,150$ units, no longer involves 20 per cent above normal production but only 15 per cent. Thus under similar conditions larger-scale production involves keeping a 15 per cent reserve as against the 20 per cent reserves of the several smaller-scale productions. In short, the aggregate of the necessary reserve stocks of ten varieties of product is greater than that for a similar amount of one variety, or of any variety less than ten.

This imaginary case is merely a rough illustration of the statistical theory of large numbers, based on probable error, that the greater the number of similar items involved the more likely are deviations to cancel out and to leave the actual average results nearer to the expected results. The probable deviation in orders for similar items that a reserve guards against is thus proportionally less when orders are many, and the cost of reserves per unit of output falls correspondingly.

The principle of multiples This principle was probably first enunciated by Babbage in 1832. 'When (from the peculiar nature of the produce of each manufactory) the number of processes into which it is most advantageous to divide it is ascertained, as well as the number of individuals to be employed, then all other manufactories which do not employ a direct multiple of this number, will produce the article at a greater cost.'[1] Or, in my own words, 'the smaller the scale of operation (or production) and the fewer the total number of persons dividing and diffusing their labour, the less chance there is of all of them being fully made use of as specialists'.[2] We need not enter into the superior efficiency and economy of specialization; that has been dealt with by a long line of economists from Adam Smith to the present day. But this efficiency, it must be noted, is only potential and depends for its actuality upon the *full use* of the specialists. An expert or a one-purpose machine idle most of the time is not efficient, nor would it be efficient to transfer that specialized machine or person to varieties of work for which it or he were not specialized. Specialized men and machines must, therefore, be used in their speciality up to

[1] *Economy of Manufactures*, Chapter XXI. Babbage is quoted at greater length in Mill's *Principles of Political Economy*, Book I, IX.
[2] Florence, 1929, p. 450.

capacity. But the capacity of different specialists and special machines is very different and they are indivisible; thus arises a difficult problem in 'balancing' production. Suppose that an article is being manufactured by subjection to three consecutive processes, the first a hand-process where a specialist can make 30 units a week, the second an automatic machine process where 1,000 units can be made in a week, the third a semi-automatic machine process where 400 units can be made per week. Then to employ all the specialists and special machines fully a number of units must be made per week that is a multiple of 30, 400 and 1,000; otherwise some man or machine will be partly idle. In this case the lowest common multiple 'throughput' of units that will employ specialists in all processes to full capacity is 6,000—permitting six automatic machines, fifteen semi-automatic and two hundred specialists to be fully employed. Clearly this assumes fairly large-scale production; probably, but not necessarily, by one firm or plant or within one 'localization'. The greater the productive capacity of any one indivisible[1] factor (e.g. the large container) the greater will be the necessary multiple. Hence the principle of bulk transactions enhances the importance of the principle of multiples.

Any given specialization of equipment or men involves for balanced production a large scale of operation or production; but conversely it is only a large scale of operation or production that admits of specialization with all its well-known economic advantages. It is only large-scale production that will justify a special research organization, intensive costing, or the working up of by-products able to occupy researchers, cost accountants or by-product plant profitably for their full time. Thus a *virtuous circle* is established. Specialization leads to higher common multiples, higher common multiples to greater specialization.

An important economy involving mutual reaction of specialization and large-scale production through the principle of multiples combined with the principle of bulk transactions, occurs in the employment of 'big brains'. Like the larger container one double capacity brain is more efficient than two single capacity brains since the two separate brains have probably to be co-ordinated by yet a third brain. But a double capacity brain, to yield its full efficiency, should specialize and concentrate on thinking out and solving the more difficult problems of production; production will have to be bulked very considerably to reduce the payment for the big brains to a reasonable cost per unit; and this bulking to secure economies in what is only one factor will involve a huge organization or scale of production when a multiple of the work of that factor and all other factors has to be obtained.

---

[1] The principle is sometimes known as that of indivisibility.

Are there any means by which the mechanism that has been out-lined can be verified and the strength of the three supposed principles measured? Are there any objective tests of efficiency available?

Two types of test have, in fact, already been used, the test by survival and the test of growth and decline. A grading of the prevailing sizes of plants existing at any one time in the largest industries, as given in Table IF is a review of the survivors and of growth. This process of growth in sizes of plant is directly traced in the later columns: in the U.S.A. between 1939 and 1963, and in the U.K. between 1935-9 and 1963. For manufacturing as a whole, rise or decline of the proportion employed in different sizes of plant and the survival of those sizes up to the latest census, is presented in Tables IJ and IK. That continuing life cannot be taken for granted and that a number of factors including mere newness militate against survival of all but the fittest, can be substantiated from studies of the birth and death rate of businesses. High death rates have been recorded among small firms, particularly retailers. American studies show that even in years of prosperity 'infant' death rates (death in the first year of life) of 100 to 200 per thousand are quite normal. Among manufacturers the T.N.E.C. reported that in Poughkeepsie from 1844 to 1917 only 53 per cent of firms lasted more than three years and that in three Minnesota cities the manufacturers closing during 1926 to 1930 amounted to 62 per cent of the total existing in 1930.[1] British evidence drawn from the jewellery industry and quoted below (II, § 2) in connection with the effect of size on firms' death rates, also confirms the keen struggle for survival in many trades.

Efficiency can be measured more directly, in consonance with the definitions already given, by three further tests; that of productivity, of returns (profits or earnings) and of costs per unit.

Productivity or output per man (or man-hour) whether measured in values or in physical units is, at first sight, and in popular esteem, the most obvious measure of efficiency. Net output value (i.e. value added by manufacture) is readily available from the census. Colin Clark, quoting Fabricant, has made us familiar[2] with the tendency of industries to increase their output per head as their total output grows and to increase it faster year by year than industries that are not growing. This is a partial statistical vertification of the law of increasing return which refers to return from a whole industry, regardless of the size of its plants and firms or the scale on which its various lines are pro-duced. Rostas has shown, too, that in the majority of his sample of compact and homogeneous British manufactures the net and gross value of output per worker and (where it is possible to obtain it) the

[1] T.N.E.C., Monograph 17, pp. 45, 52.
[2] *Conditions of Economic Progress*, 1951, p. 246.

physical output per worker, increases with the size of plant.[1] But this productivity is no complete test of comparative efficiency, since output per man refers to the return from one factor of production only. One operator with the help of a large overhead organization and staff and a machine of, say, ten horse-power might produce fifty per cent more output than one man without any machine, organization and staff. But if the machine were expensive in depreciation and had cost the labour of several men over a long period and the overhead costs were heavy in salaries and centralizing methods, the machineless, staffless operator with only two-thirds the output might well be the more 'efficient' proposition, taking all factors into account.

Even if net output is divided by all persons employed including staff, it varies in fact enormously from industry to industry. The British census of production for 1963 showed £4,271 net output per employee in spirit distilling, £3,204 in lubricating oils, £3,114 in mineral oil refining, £2,963 in man-made fibres, £2,872 in cement, down to £679 in household textiles, and also in dress, £669 in men and boys' tailored outerwear and £648 in men's shirts and overalls. But this does not mean that these textile and clothing industries were less than a quarter as efficient as the first mentioned quasi-chemical group of industries.[2]

To get round this difficulty net output per worker is often compared only within the same industry. But such 'industries', formed for statistical purposes, are often composite and include quite diverse types of work. Among vehicles, for instance, are motor vehicles with net output of £1,692 per person and locomotives and railway track equipment with £843; in the food industry are grain milling with £2,557 and bread and flour confectionery with £998; among chemicals are lubricating oils and greases with £3,204 (as already cited) and coke ovens with £1,534. These variations are largely due to variations in the degree of mechanization of the different industries. And, of course, plants within the same industry may have various degrees of mechanization and show variations in net output per worker. But the less mechanized plants with lower net output per worker are not necessarily the less efficient. They may have a lower cost of depreciation and interest charges to counterbalance the lower output per worker.

Owing to these various considerations I have not used labour productivity as a test of general efficiency, except where the industry is very narrowly circumscribed. But productivity is a misleading measure in

---

[1] Rostas, *Productivity, Prices and Distribution in Selected British Industries*, 1948, p. 45.

[2] This caution is not merely academic. The argument has recently been put forward that because output per worker is highest of all regions in London (with the odd exception of Wales) industry is more efficiently located there and should move in or at least not move out. See *The London Development Plan, 1969 Studies*.

less clear-cut cases. If it were possible to 'evaluate' all the other factors, capital equipment, buildings, and staff in terms of labour or some other common measure, no doubt productivity per man or man-equivalent would be an excellent test of efficiency. Some such evaluation is now being attempted at least for *changes* in production associated with *changes* in a common measure of input.[1] If money costs be used as a common measure of inputs, such a test by output per total cost of input factors is a test exactly reciprocal to that of total costs per unit of product.

Total costs will be frequently used as a measure of efficiency in the following sections but the reader (and authors, too) must beware of comparing costs calculated on different bases or arising under different circumstances. Cost-accountants are still far from unanimous on how to treat overhead allocations, stock-piling and purchases of stock at irregular intervals. Again, output produced as a sideline of one factory (undertaken perhaps just to balance up), but a main product of another, may well be more costly in the former case without reflecting on efficiency.

Profit is the business test of efficiency, as against the popular (and the engineers') tests of productivity and costs. Unlike productivity, profits *must* be measured in money terms and can only be obtained for the financial unit of organization, that is the firm, and not the plant or line of production. Put as simply as possible, profit $P = O\,(p-c)$, where O is units of output, p average price and c average cost per unit of output. P, profit, will thus be increased by an increase in price, by an increase of sales, supposing prices above costs, or by a fall in cost. The chief snag in testing efficiency, as defined earlier, in the form of profits, is the chance that profits may rise by exploitation of the customer—a risk that will be discussed later under monopoly. But assuming for the moment no greater possibility of price-exploitation by one plant, firm or industry than by another, profits can be used as a test of comparative efficiency if care is taken that all items of capital, in-put[2] or cost (e.g. depreciation, purchase of stocks) are included in the final ratios.

Since profit is not a ratio but the result of a subtraction sum, it will naturally be proportionate to the scale of operations; a large firm, other things equal, can expect a larger profit than a small firm. So a denominator must be hit upon that will indicate the scale of the resources put in—the scale of the 'in-put'. Possible indices that have

[1] E.g. Reddaway and Smith, 'Progress in British Manufacturing Industries 1948–59', *Economic Journal*, March 1960. See also Denison in *Britain's Economic Prospects* (ed. Caves), pp. 231–78.
[2] Later (pp. 150–1) I discuss items other than capital.

been used are total sales or turnover; the market value[1] of the equity share capital (usually plus general reserves); and total capital including debentures and loans and net assets. A rate of profit that is dangerously easy to quote is the rate of dividend on nominal equity capital, publicly declared; but the profit thus distributed and the shares on which it is distributed are neither the full profit nor a measure of the full resources, and can only be used as the roughest of guides. One important characteristic that these crude rates of dividend do disclose, however, is their wide variation. In the same industry, for the same year, different firms will show rates varying from 0 to over 100 per cent. Dividend rates eventually bear some relation to true profit rates, and there is no question that in comparable circumstances profit rates are a highly sensitive thermometer of efficiency. Mehta has used rates of dividend to compare the relative efficiency of Indian cotton companies of various sizes measured in spindles. Dividend rates appear to agree in the results obtained with the other measures he uses such as rate of profit on capital and funds, on 'effective capital' and on 'gross block' (i.e. fixed assets).[2]

§ 2. EFFICIENCY OF THE LARGE FIRM OR PLANT OF VARYING PATTERN. THE SURVIVAL OF THE SMALL FIRM

The bold proposition resting logically on our three principles must now be subjected, as a working hypothesis, to the test of the facts. Do the industrial structures and trends in structure disclosed in Chapter I, and the relations between those structures, validate the proposition that large-scale operation, other things equal, gives the greater efficiency? The prevailing size of plants and firms in various industries, and the prevailing degree of their localization and integration are survivals from tests of efficiency in the past; and the trends that were traced, mainly toward larger-scale organization, are probably some indication of continuing superior efficiency. The arguments that have to be added are of a different sort: qualitative appraisals from common sense or experience, or results of quantitative tests of efficiency like that of costs, profits, or productivity.

Qualitative appraisal though less exact than quantitative is useful, at least as a hypothesis for subsequent testing, if it is relevant to the particular situation at issue. Unfortunately, the lists of large-scale advantages and disadvantages so generously provided in textbooks

---

[1] But see Florence, 'New Measures of the Size of Firms', *Economic Journal*, June 1957.

[2] Mehta, *Structure of Cotton-Mill Industry of India*, 1949, pp. 161–7. The larger companies appear by all these measures more efficient, on the whole, than the smaller, and the typical size has been increasing.

often failed to visualize the structural situation. The account of economies resulting from large units often omitted to define the precise structure of the unit and cited the results, higgledy-piggledy, of different sorts of unit. In consequence the appraisals are often contradictory. Saving cross-freights and specialization of plants appear[1] side by side as results of larger firms but an approach distinguishing sorts of structure discloses that the former economy is only applicable where the distant plants of a multiplant firm produce the same article; the latter only where plants, distant or not, produce different goods. The two economies cannot be true of the same structure. In the same list again there often appears saving in handling and reheating by vertical integration, and the possibility of comparative accounting. Here again the former economy applies where there is one plant performing different processes, the latter where several plants perform the same transactions. Both economies cannot exist in the same situation.

Before quoting any further qualitative appraisals, it must be recalled that the structure of a large firm may be of several patterns, varying in precision. To visualize these patterns a plant or factory may be featured as a square, a line of production as a letter, say, x or y or z and a firm as a circle. At least seven patterns (lettered A to G) can then be distinguished varying with the features' sizes and the rigour of their definition.

(A) Three large features given in the pattern. A large firm with a single large plant making a single line product (X) on a large-scale.

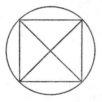

(B) Two large features and one smaller given in the pattern. A large firm making a single line of product (x) on a large scale, but in several not so large plants.

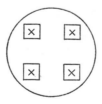

---

[1] E.g. Jenks and Clark, *The Trust Problem*, 1919, Chapter III.

(C) Two large features given in the pattern, size of the other indefinite. A large firm making a large line of product; size of plants not given.

(D) One large feature and two smaller given in the pattern. A large firm but with several (not so large) plants each making a different (not so large) line of product.

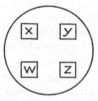

(E) One large feature and one small given in the pattern, size of the other indefinite. A large firm making several (not so large) lines of product; size of plants not given.

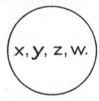

One large feature given in the pattern. Size of the others not definitely given.

(F) A large firm.

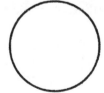

(G) A large plant, possibly with many products.

More patterns would be possible by combination of large or small scales in the three features of firm, plant and line of product, if these features were independent. But in practice they are not. A very large plant implies, for instance, a large firm. The seven patterns of greater or less definition exhaust the practical possibilities.

This analysis of structures is not just logical academic hair-splitting. A practical man of business, looking eagerly at large-scale advantages set forth in textbooks, will want to know precisely what he is to do to save cross freights or unnecessary handling and heating. Building his plant larger is certainly a different matter to him from opening a new branch, and making one article on a large scale different from a large integration of several articles. Without putting forward any new appraisals we must redesign, according to structural pattern implied, the usual classification of economies, if it is to be a classification at all, and not just a laundry list. As already illustrated these lists usually add to logical and practical confusion by mixing together economies peculiar to various forms of integration. These will be considered in § 4, their proper place.

Qualitative appraisal of economies peculiar to each pattern may be cited from the lists given by two classic American textbooks: Jenks and Clark, *The Trust Problem*, and Taussig's *Principles of Economics*. The quotations will be from the 1919 and the 1911 editions respectively, and Jenks and Clark's 13 items in their Chapter III will, in the footnote references, be numbered as in the original.

Pattern A   *Economies of the large firm with a single plant and single line of product*. This structural pattern probably gives the greatest chance for large-scale operation and high physical efficiency as already expounded under the three principles of bulk transactions, massed reserves and multiples. Specific advantages, mentioned in Jenks and Clark or Taussig's lists, which can be attributed to this particular structure, include:[1]

A1. Increased specialization and division of labour.

A2. Increased use of specialized machinery.

A3. Decreased expenses for administration per unit of output.

Pattern B   *Economies of the large firm with several (not so large) plants making the same lines of product on a large scale*.

It is often impossible to obtain a large-scale production of one and the same article without making it in one large-scale organization. Unless accurate grading is resorted to throughout an industry, different firms will in practice be making different varieties. Just as there is no localization so complete as localization within one plant, so there is

---

[1] Taussig, *Principles of Economics*, 1911, Chapter IV, § 2.

no *standardization* and mass-production so complete as the *particular* standardization (to use Marshall's phrase) within one firm.

B1. Production at least costly locations for dispersed markets or from dispersed resources. Saving cross freights.[1]

B2. Comparative accounting. Exchange of cost information between plants.[2]

B3. During business depressions selection of the more efficient plants to run full and closing down less efficient.[3]

Pattern C.   *Economies of the large firm making a large line of product.*

C1. Saving in selling expense.[4]

C2. Filling all orders promptly whatever the quantity.[5]

C3. Supplies bought to greater advantage.[6]

Pattern D   *Economies of the large firm with several (not so large) plants making different lines of product.* This multiplant pattern has few economies beyond that of large-scale finance or procurement and distribution possible to dispersed plants, and of integration.

D1. 'A large order for different classes of goods could be distributed among the different mills each one adapted for the manufacture of a particular class'[7] (and, presumably, adapted for its procurement and distribution too).

D2. 'Requirements of demand and supply readily met' by vertical integration.[8]

Pattern E   *Economies of the large firm making a number of products (on not so large a scale)* (Lateral integration).

E1. Can supply all leading qualities of goods.[9]

E2. Insurance against risks. 'In a very great enterprise, the successes may be expected in the long run to outweigh the failures.'[10]

Pattern F   *Economies of the large firm, whatever its sub-structure of plants and products.*

The superior efficiency with which production can be performed if included under the rule of one firm even though physically scattered in several plants largely centres on the acquisition and dissemination of knowledge. Knowledge is available throughout the organization of any patents, secret devices, results of technical or market research (e.g. customer's financial position). This knowledge can be communi-

[1] Jenks and Clark, *The Trust Problem*, 4th Ed., Chapter III (5).
[2] Loc. cit. (11).
[3] Loc. cit. (6).
[4] Loc. cit. (1).
[5] Loc. cit. (4).
[6] Taussig, loc. cit.
[7] Jenks and Clark, loc. cit. (7).
[8] Loc. cit. (13).
[9] Loc. cit. (3).
[10] Taussig, loc. cit.

cated effectively even though the subsidiary plants must for technical reasons be in different places, as for instance a chain of shops selling the same sort of articles, or factories distributing a heavy and unwieldy product (e.g. beer and agricultural machinery).

The possibility of wide dissemination of knowledge makes it economically worth while for a firm to specialize in research to gain new knowledge in production and distribution and to buy big brains whose 'know-how' can be widely communicated. Economies mentioned in the textbook lists which can be attributed to a large-scale of this particular pattern include:

F1. Reduction of bad debts.[1]

F2. Common use of patents, trade marks, brands and similar business devices.[2]

F3. Can command big brains. 'The first-class man is cheap at almost any price'[3] but only a large firm can pay the price and use his capacity to the full.

F4. Can distribute subordinate management and skill among a variety of jobs according to capacity.[4]

Pattern G   *Economies of the large plant whatever the firm super-structure, or product substructure.*

G1. Co-ordination on the spot. Specialization of men and machinery often compels their congregation or coincidence at one time and place. Though *localization* of separate organizations in one district may effect an approach to such co-incidence,[5] three logical reasons for the large plant seem *prima facie* obvious.

(i) Transport and routing costs in moving goods from one process to another or from process to stores or stores to process will be generally less if processes or stores are in the same plant rather than in neighbouring plants. As Babbage put it, writing in 1832,[6] 'the material out of which the manufactured article is produced, must, in the several stages of its progress, be conveyed from one operator to the next in succession: this can be done at least expense when they are all working in the same establishment. If the material is heavy, this reason acts with additional force.'

(ii) Auxiliary services such as repairs and maintenance, or tool-making, are more readily communicated with and brought to the spot if the services are part of the productive organization instead of being called in from outside.

[1] Jenks and Clark, loc. cit. (2).
[2] Loc. cit. (8).
[3] Loc. cit. (9).
[4] Loc. cit. (10).
[5] See Ch. II § 5.
[6] *Economy of Manufactures*, Chapter XXI.

(iii) Communication of plants and orders is more readily effected and their execution supervised within one plant than among several plants.

In short, the modern specialization of factors of production has increased the need for co-ordination, co-ordination is furthered by local coincidence and congregation, and a single plant is more localized than any localization of separate plants can possibly be.[1]

G2. 'A very large establishment finds it profitable to manufacture some by-products from its waste material, which, owing ... to an insufficient quantity of waste material, its smaller rival must either lose entirely or part with at a disadvantage.'[2]

These qualitative appraisals of the large-scale features, where not just a matter of time and space (as C2 and G1), all involve one or other of the principles of efficiency. The most obvious is saving in selling and buying expense and in use of brain capacity (C1, C3, F3) involving the principle of bulking; increased use of specialized labour and machinery (A1 and 2) involving the principle of multiples; and insurance against risk of experiment (E2) involving massed or pooled reserves.

It is little use advising a manufacturer that he should organize on a larger or smaller scale if he is not told what is to be larger or smaller (his factories, his lines of production or his whole firm). A fully realistic practical study of large-scale economies and dis-economies would have to consider the precise effect of each of these patterns of structure separately. Unfortunately, such studies have hitherto, with a few exceptions, not been quantitative. It is only possible to review quantitative studies of the comparative efficiency of one or two patterns, in particular the more general (or less definite) patterns (F) of the large or small firm whatever the substructure, and (G) of the large and small plant whatever the super and substructure.

Tests of efficiency of large and small firms besides that of survival and comparative growth or decline, already reviewed, are mainly those of profits. At first sight the evidence put forward by the many authorities appears to conflict; but this is largely because some authorities, like Epstein in his *Industrial Profits in the United States*, take profits on capital as the test ratio and mix all industries together. This is not a scientific procedure because it fails to isolate the fact that industries, owing to their technology, necessarily differ in the intensity of their capital investment. On the whole, small-firm industries are small capital industries and as I have pointed out[3] 'industries requiring little

[1] Florence, 1933, p. 14.
[2] Jenks and Clark, loc. cit. (12).
[3] *Economic Journal*, December 1937, pp. 633–4.

fixed capital or involving risk and uncertainty might be expected to have a higher rate of profit *per capital*. The small firm's profit is to a greater extent than the large firm's profit a payment for organization and risk-taking, and it is not logical to compare their efficiency by the rate of profit on their capital. The rate of profit of, say, a small publisher, with no capital except a desk and chair, might on this basis be almost infinite though he were not particularly efficient. This is no mere oddity; wide differences in rate of profit on capital appear as between twenty-two standard groups of American industries. In 1968, for instance[1] the range of dispersion was as wide as from 8·3 per cent to 17·9 per cent. Metal manufacturing, chemicals, paper, wood products, textiles and glass, etc., all capital intensive industries, had a 'return on invested' capital of 10 per cent or less. Publishing and printing, tobacco, soaps and cosmetics all had more than a 14 per cent return. All of them were industries of low capital intensity, but with high expenditure on marketing and advertising. Similar differentiation of these industries appeared in other years;[2] the differences were not mainly due to varying prosperity from year to year.

In short, profit rates on capital suffer as a test of efficiency, like productivity of labour from their single factor base. To measure efficiency, profit should ideally be reckoned on the input of all factors: organization, risk-taking, labour, management, land *and* capital. But short of this ideal, impracticable because of lack of data, profit per unit of capital should be compared only for firms *in the same industry*, mixing input factors in more or less the same proportions. We must keep in mind that the mix even within the same census industries is far from identical and that the smaller firms tend to have a lower proportion of capital (as shown later, II § 3, in horse-power per worker) and thus a higher rate of profits *per capital*.

Comparison of profit rates within the same industry or group of industries was carried out notably by Crum. His index was the ratio of profit (excluding taxes) to the book value of the equity and his data officially filed corporation tax returns. He found that over the six-year period 1931–6 'in all or nearly all broad lines of industry' taken separately 'large enterprise ... is more profitable than small enterprise, especially very small enterprise'.[3] The smaller enterprises were particularly unprofitable in the years of depression and show more risk in

---

[1] U.S. Statistical Abstracts, e.g. for 1970, p. 480. Bureau of the Budget grouping.
[2] Ibid., p. 484.
[3] *Corporate Size and Earning Power*, p. 7. The sizes of enterprise range from corporations with equity above 50,000,000 to equity below 50,000 dollars. Here again the result may be partly affected by using capital and not other inputs as the denominator of the ratio. The smaller the capital the higher the ratio a given profit or loss will form.

results. This may be because they deliberately took more risks or merely bore the risk during a depression, of faulty enterprise. Crum's findings on the wider variability of profits of the smaller firms are confirmed and supplemented by the 20th Century Fund[1] and more recent enquiries, though these enquiries revert to the unscientific mixing together of diverse industries.[2] The average for mixed industries showed in the boom year of 1919, and in the prosperous years of the Second World War and after, that the small or medium-sized firms often had the highest rate of profit per capital; but in the slump year of 1933 their *losses* were at the highest rate per unit of capital. In short the profits of large firms fluctuate less, due possibly to a 'cushion' of massed reserves and to some integration.[3]

For years of moderate prosperity it is worth illustrating how the rate of profit per unit of capital in different sizes of firm within the same industry depends on the precise industry concerned. Kaplan, analysing official American returns for 1939 and 1941, showed that the peak of profits in apparel and clothing was in smaller firms of the assets class, $50,000 to 100,000. 'Printing and publishing likewise reached a peak ratio near the $100,000 assets level and tapered off as greater size is attained. Leather, paper and rubber products show a similar tendency. But at the other extreme (with peak profit rates at the larger sizes) are examples in petroleum, mining and quarrying, electrical machinery and tobacco.'[4] These industries differing in the size where peak profit rates occur show a suggestive degree of identity with the industries differing similarly in the prevailing size of firm.

A recent British investigation shows considerable agreement with the American conclusion.[5] It analysed for the years 1954 to 1963 the profits of 86 companies in distribution and various manufactures (not, however, separately) according to size classes measured by their assets. Sizes varied from assets under £0·25m. to over £65m. The years concerned were fairly prosperous and the smaller firms were found on average to have higher profit rates on assets than the larger; but the variability over time of their profit rates was greater than for the larger companies.

Small firms preclude very long runs on which increasing returns

[1] *How Profitable is Big Business?*, p. 37.

[2] Osborn, *Effects of Corporate Size on Efficiency and Profitability*, 1950. In the single table (p. 50) where recent results are quoted separately for different industries profit on capital (net worth) appears, even in the prosperous years 1947 and 1948, higher for the four largest companies than for the others in thirteen and seventeen manufactures, respectively, out of twenty-three.

[3] See § 4 below for hypothesis of optimum integration.

[4] Kaplan, *Small Business, its Place and Problems*, 1948, p. 99.

[5] Samuels and Smyth, *Profits, Profits' Variability and Firm Size*, Discussion Paper, Universities of Birmingham and Aston, 1966.

depend. Why then do the smaller firms show, on the whole, higher rates of profit than the larger? Apart from the question raised above whether capital assets are a sufficiently complete measure of input, three answers may be put forward:

(1) The main answer lies in the close connection between size of firm and size of plant. Small plants are necessary, as we shall see, where materials or markets are dispersed and transport of materials or products costly. They are implicit where the markets and whole industries are small.[1] Small plants do not of course necessitate small firms and attention has constantly been drawn to multiplant firms. Nevertheless, we found in fact that these multiplant firms had large plants on the average and that the small plant tended to be owned singly by a small firm. Probably the cost of remote supervision or of distant factories is too much for the small man unable to employ others efficient enough to have powers delegated to them.

(2) The difficulties of supervision and management go beyond that of coping with a number of plants. Economists have given management as the main and an inevitable limiting factor on size of firm. In their opinion[2] the management gets positively less efficient (not just no more efficient) after a certain size is passed, and they dogmatically (and often automatically) draw a 'U' curve of costs for the firm rising from left to right as the quantity of output increases. How many blackboards have been filled lecture hour by lecture hour in British and American universities with such 'exercises in draftsmanship'.[3] For it remains an exercise. There is little factory evidence of the occurrence of any such increasing costs in the short run. Still less evidence appears in the long run when manufacturers have time to get new equipment (whether a new invention or not[4]) in order to meet enlarged orders or anticipated orders and have time to reorganize and delegate responsibilities. The art and science of delegation is so important to large-scale organization that a whole chapter (IV, below) will attend to this problem in political science—attention all the more necessary because of suspicion, voiced by Andrews,[5] of a wish-fulfilment.

Economists have found that the application to the real world of the abstract theory of pure competition requires that long-run costs should rise with increased scale. This has made it easy for the supposition to be accepted in economics that long-run costs do, in fact, rise, and, in the absence of any other plausible explanation as to why they should rise, economists have

---

[1] Florence, 1948, pp. 48–9.
[2] See also below, Chapter IV, § 1.
[3] To use Lancelot Hogben's phrase.
[4] Further hairs are split here, and the distinction between normal long period and secular period may for present purposes be ignored.
[5] *Manufacturing Business*, 1949, pp. 128–9.

tended to call in increasing managerial inefficiency as a fairly plausible hypothesis which could not easily be refuted and which could be justified by assimilating the position of the business man to that of a natural factor of production with a given 'capacity' . . .

Where economic theory appears to go wrong is that it regards the capacity of the business man as being 'given' in the same way as the fertility of a 'given' field, when that is producing a single product with given methods of production.

Land and business ability certainly have points in common. Both vary greatly in productivity and exceptional natural ability can obtain, as Marshall remarked, an income 'akin to' rent. But business enterprise today (as we must not cease to observe) is a corporate manifestation and its capacity to cope with larger outputs is not fixed but expands with its structure—and depends on the relation, to be discussed soon (Chapter IV), between the governing members of the corporation.

The contention here is not that large organizations will inevitably be more efficient than small; but simply that it is *not* inevitable that larger organizations will eventually fail because of management. Corporate management may become *more* efficient with size owing to specialization of member managers, or if it becomes less efficient, its deficiency may in effect be counter-balanced by other factors. Sometimes admittedly there will be no counter-balance. Some firms fail with size because of management, if the immediate growth in size which they attempt is too great; or if the management is incapable of adapting its structure, or (and this is important for whole industries) if each unit transaction which management tries to undertake requires close attention to detail and quick adjustment to uncertain circumstances. Farming, with its weather hazards and unpredictable animal (including pest) behaviour, is the leading case and is in all western countries carried out by small 'firms'.[1] But coping with the human animal in the shape of exacting customers is also a case in point. Many small firms survive because they give the precise and reliable service required by customers, particularly in 'jobbing' for producer-customers, with whom they keep in personal contact. They promise firm delivery dates, however unreasonable, and keep their promise; they produce the exact unstandard quality and

---

[1] 'Agriculture differs fundamentally from commerce and industries. It deals very largely with living things—animals and plants that can never be left alone for long; farmers and the leading workers must therefore reside on the spot and be ready at any hour and every day to give such attention as is necessary. . . . Both animals and plants are largely dependent on the weather, and as this cannot be forecasted with any certainty it is impossible to keep to any rigid programme of operations. The work of the day must be settled on the day itself and on the spot; everything later can be provisional only and subject to the condition: weather permitting. . . . These special characteristics of farming make it unsuitable for the operation of the great joint stock enterprises.'—Sir John Russell, *English Farming*, p. 13.

design (usually unreasonably) required and attend to the customers' complaints, however wrong-headed. For this minute attention and adjustment to detail and circumstance, patiently building up goodwill with no place for mass production, a strong and direct incentive is required; the small entrepreneur, paid for his enterprise with profit, meets the demand.

(3) The remaining causes for the survival and profitability of the small firm are negative. They are the absence of the conditions for a large firm. Small firms may flourish when no (or little) capital equipment, particularly no specialized machinery of varying capacity, is required, and little or no knowledge and research; where the market and the industry itself is not large enough; and where risks are not so high that they have to be pooled by large integration with other processes and lines of production or with marketing. At first sight this list of 'nots' seems to veto small firms in the modern mechanized, uncertain world. But it must be recalled that in the extraction-to-consumer sequence of production, the Western economy allows the widest variety of division of labour and function. A small firm may be relieved of its marketing by large wholesale houses,[1] and of its finance and capital-raising by banks, by landlords (e.g. rented shops and farms), or in other ways such as free roads for road transport, or the shoe industry's rental of machines; may be relieved of earlier or later processes by neighbouring factories in a localized production centre, of research by trade associations, universities or the state. In short, a group of specialists may grow up around the small firm either locally or (like publishers of trade journals) nationally, yielding external economies, which allow that firm to operate a single process or product on a large scale. The building industry, where small firms tackle large units of production, is perhaps the clearest object lesson in the effect of functional specialization of independent firms and persons, co-operating on single jobs. The sociologists Demerath and Baker[2] list twelve occupational roles on construction at the site:

1. Initiator	7. Subcontractor
2. Architect	8. Foreman
3. Land Developer	9. Union Business Agent
4. Financier	10. Craftsman
5. Government Official	11. Materials Manufacturer
6. Contractor	12. Materials Distributor

The small contracting and sub-contracting firm survives in building

[1] Thus large organization at one (vertical) stage or in one (diagonal) service (e.g. power stations) may often help small firms.

[2] 'The Social Organization of Housebuilding', *Journal of Social Issues*, Vol. VII (1951), p. 89.

largely because of the outside finance it gets from financier, land-developer and materials distributor, the outside research by government planner and materials manufacturer, and the outside expert guidance on quality and design from architect and initiator.

(4) Conditions explaining the survival of the small firm have so far assumed a logical structure of industry. Though the consumer with his capricious taste and predilections may be illogical in his demands, we have assumed the organization for supplying his tastes to be efficient. But this in fact is not so. Efficient large-scale structure takes time, 'lags' in overcoming inefficient small-scale structure, and, sometimes, the effort and incidental consequences of overcoming it may, by the leisurely,[1] not be considered worth while. A large-sized near-monopolist may for instance get all the profit he wants without the odium of monopoly (and, possibly, legal prosecution) by allowing a screen of small competitors to operate as a camouflage.

(5) Finally, though the opposite of lag, laziness and low-pressure, the factor of enterprise and hopefulness in the human breast continually keeps up the supply of small firms. Many of the small firms that exist at any one moment are just on their way in or out. Objective evidence of this comes from the high rates of loss already mentioned as suffered by smaller American corporations during trade depressions, and from the high mortality of small firms—almost like the rate of infant mortality of oriental countries. In the three Minnesota towns already quoted (p. 63) while only 16·5 per cent of the larger manufacturing firms of net worth over $500,000 died during 1926–30, the death rate for the smallest sizes of net worth $2,000 to $10,000 and less than $2,000 were 66·3 per cent and 87·4 per cent.[2] The working party reporting on the British Jewellery and Silver Ware industry analysed the firms localized in St Paul's Ward, Birmingham.[3] They took the ratio of deaths during the six years 1934–9 to the number of firms of the same size existing in 1939 of which the total was 1,443. Among the smallest, employing one or two persons, the death rate was as high as 62 per cent, and the rate fell continuously as the larger firms were considered: 53 per cent for firms employing 3–10 persons, 38 per cent for firms employing 11–20, 28 per cent for firms employing 21–50, 9 per cent for firms employing 51–100, only 2 per cent (only one firm died during 1934–9 though 61 existed in 1939) for firms employing over 100 workers.

§ 3. CONDITIONS OF EFFICIENCY OF LARGE AND SMALL
PLANTS AND FIRMS

Plants of different size cannot be compared in respect of profit because,

---

[1] See below, Chapter VII, §§ 3–5, especially p. 363.
[2] Kaplan, *Small Business: its Place and Problems*, 1948, p. 71.
[3] H.M.S.O., 1946, p. 104.

where a firm owns more than one plant, the plant is not the final accounting unit. But plants of different size can be compared and have been compared in respect of factory costs, particularly where they are owned by the same firm with similar accounting methods; this indeed was one of the economic advantages of a large firm of the appropriate structure already mentioned.

Little has been published recently but we know that if there is a lower cost of the larger plant, it is not achieved at the expense of labour's earnings. On the contrary, an American review of wages statistics shows the larger plant (and the plants of larger firms) to yield the higher rate of earnings per man-hour. This earnings-per-man-hour test, applicable to factories of various size as well as firms, is similar to the profits per unit of capital test applicable only to firms of various size. Both are a measure of economic return to one factor, not the output from total input efficiency.

The correlation of higher earnings of labour with larger plants has been observable for some time, though perhaps less observed than it deserves in both Britain and the United States. In 1951, annual wages and salaries per worker in British manufacturing plants rose (as shown in Table IIA) fairly continuously from £339 in plants employing 11–49 to £344, £350, £373, £390, £421, in plants employing 50–99, 100–499, 500–1,000, 1,000–2,500 and over 2,500.[1] In the United States, dividing payroll by number of employees, size-grades showed in 1963 the same consistent pattern of higher pay per employee with larger sizes of plant. The pay per employee in the plants employing 1,000 to 2,499 and 2,500 upwards was 108 and 123 per cent of that in the medium-sized plants with 500–999 employees; and in the ranges of lower sizes of plant earnings per employee fell consistently with size of plants as Table IIA shows. The positive correlation of earnings with size of *plant* is indeed more marked in America than Britain. In 1958 American *firms* showed the same progressive trend size by size. The average pay per employee in manufacturing companies employing 1,000 or more was $5,825; in companies employing fewer than 20, $3,834—a difference as of 152 to 100. The decrease was continuous throughout the nine size-ranges of companies.

The lower earnings in smaller plants could have been influenced by the smaller plants being located in regions of low pay generally. It does not appear, however, that plants employing under 100 are unusually frequent in the U.S. southern states, rather the opposite. The proportions to all plants of these small plants were, in 1963, 90·3 per cent for the United States as a whole, 88·7 per cent for the south region.

---

[1] For the sake of comparisons census size-ranges were aggregated to match the United States ranges. Unfortunately the U.K. 1958 and 1963 censuses did not include this type of analysis.

LOGIC AND FACT

TABLE IIA

SIZE OF PLANT AND PAY PER EMPLOYEE, U.S.A. AND U.K.

Size of plant In number employed	Yearly payroll		Yearly wages and salaries	
	U.S.A. 1963 $* (1)	(Relative to medium size) 500–999) (2)	U.K. 1951† £ (3)	(Relative to medium size) (4)
1–4	4,360	74 ⎱	—	
5–9	4,570	78 ⎰		
10–19	4,890	83 ⎱	339	90
20–49	4,920	84 ⎰		
50–99	4,970	85	344	92
100–249	5,110	87 ⎱	350	93
250–499	5,300	91 ⎰		
500–999	5,850	100	373	100
1,000–2,499	6,510	105	390	104
2,500 and over	7,400	126	421	113

* 1963 census of manufactures. Size of Establishments volume, Table 1.

† 1951. The 1963 census of production does not show wages and salaries separately for plants in different size-ranges; the 1951 census was thus the last to set out a table comparable with the U.S.

Quantitative enquiries into *the conditions underlying* the efficiency of large organizations have gone furthest when applied to the plant or factory rather than the firm. My own conclusion, based on bringing together American and British census data, is briefly that in both countries industries with large plants prevailing are on the whole industries with a high degree of mechanization and intense investment, and vice-versa industries with small plants prevailing are industries with a low degree of mechanization. An inkling of this tendency is provided in the footnote, p. 83, by the consistent rise in power per worker with size of plant.

The quantitative calculations on which this conclusion is based are complicated by the lack of any direct index of mechanization applicable alike to all industries. Horse-power per worker, which seems the obvious test, measures the weight of materials being processed or converted as well as the degree of mechanization;[1] and in correlating

[1] There is a clear correlation between weight of materials used for work and horse-power per worker; taking fifty-five industries where the weight data were given in the British census as well as the horse-power per worker (Florence, 1948, Appendix II) the (Spearman) rank correlation was + 0·56. In Britain the (median) horse-power per worker in 1930 was, for all assembly industries, 0·8, for all non-assembly industries 2·0. In America the horse-power per worker required in assembly in 1939 was exactly half that in other industries; 2·1 was the median for assembly industries, 4·2 the median for non-assembly. Assuming a similar degree of mechanization of assembly and non-assembly industries, a point not yet established, this would

the horse-power per worker with the prevailing size of plant in industries I found it necessary in my *Investment, Location and Size of Plant* to separate processing industries from assembly industries where weight of material is a less important factor. Among both assembly and non-assembly industries both in Britain and America, industries with large plants prevailing tended to have high horse-power per worker and these relationships (with the possible exception of British non-assembly industries) appeared statistically significant.[1]

A further step may be taken by way of consolidating the two types of industry in one table. The assembly industries often have expensive, delicate and complicated machinery, not, however, of high horse-power. It will not be too arbitrary if we reckon a horse-power in an assembly

TABLE IIB

RELATIONSHIP OF DEGREE OF MECHANIZATION AND SIZE-OF-PLANT IN
MANUFACTURING INDUSTRIES (BRITISH, 1930, AND AMERICAN, 1939)

		Prevailing size of plant*		
	Degree of mechanization	Small or smallish (1)	Medium (2)	Large or larigsh (3)

Distribution of all measurable (86) British manufactures (Modes underlined)

A	0 to ½ H.P. per man for assembly 0 to 1 for non-assembly	17	6	3
B	Over ½ to 1 H.P. per man for assembly Over 1 to 2 for non-assembly	12	6	14
C	Over 1 H.P. per man for assembly Over 2 for non-assembly	4	8	16

Distribution of all measurable (155) American mobile† manufactures (Modes underlined)

AB	0 to 1 H.P. per man for assembly 0 to 2 for non-assembly	30	5	4
BC¹	Over 1 to 2 H.P. per man for assembly Over 2 to 4 for non-assembly	19	11	4
C²	Over 2 to 3 H.P. per man for assembly Over 4 to 6 for non-assembly	15	16	11
C³	Over 3 H.P. per man for assembly Over 6 for non-assembly	11	12	17

* For precise definition of sizes see above, text p. 25. Mining industries excluded.
† Excluding material oriented industries.

[1] For details of coefficients of contingency, see Florence, 1948, pp. 103–6, 118.

justify weighting horse-power per worker by two as in Table IIB to represent the degree of mechanization of assembly industries.

industry to be the equivalent in capital investment and mechanization to two horse-power in a non-assembly (mostly heavy processing) industry. Based on this reckoning, Table IIB can be presented as a contingency table relating three grades of prevailing size of plant with three degrees of mechanization in British, four in American manufactures. In *both countries* the tendency is clear for the cells with larger relative frequency to run from top left to bottom right, that is for industries with large or largish plants (like iron and steel rolling or the assembly of electrical machines in Table IF) to be industries with a high consolidated index of mechanization. Statistical computation from all the figures shows this relationship to be fairly close and significant for both countries.[1] This statistical correlation can be interpreted indirectly at least as a factual support for the principle of multiples. The more a factory is mechanized the greater the difficulty in balancing up production (and the greater the idle overhead expense otherwise), unless the throughput of the factory is large enough to allow each stage of production the exact number of machines of efficient capacity that will give full use to all.

Similar contingency tables between horse-power per worker and prevailing size of plant were constructed separately for British assembly and for non-assembly industries in 1951 as they had been in my *Investment, Location and Size of Plant* for 1935–9. In both types of industry the coefficient of contingency became higher in the later period but was significant only for the more homogeneous assembly industries, where the coefficient 0·496 in 1935–9 was ·57 in 1951.[2]

[1] The summary measures of the degree of correlation between the index of mechanization and the prevailing size of plants are as follows when cells, in Table IIB, with expected frequencies of less than 5 are lumped together.

	Britain	America
Coefficient of contingency (C)	0·36 (upper limit approx. 0·82)	0·39 (upper limit approx. 0·87)
Measure of significance χ^2	12·72	28·20
Probability of a greater χ^2 from random sample	less than 1/500	less than 1/1000

[2] Florence, *Post-War Investment, Location and Size of Plant*, 1962, p. 9. Support for this relation of size of plant and mechanization comes from the U.S. census of manufactures for 1954, Mc 203, Table 1. Beyond a certain very small size the larger plants (larger in terms of employees) have for manufactures generally the higher ratio of horse-power per production worker.

The high horse-power ratios in the plants employing less than five is probably due to large unused capacity.

It is of interest to observe that value added, i.e. productivity, though increasing

All industries today have some degree of mechanization in their plants. Why then do some industries have small plants prevailing? The main answer, anticipated when discussing size of firms, is the economy, where transport costs are high, of proximity to dispersed materials or markets. The costs, in short, of procurement and distribution, or both, outweigh the economies of mechanized large-plant production. This balancing of opposing tendencies is nowhere more clearly evident than in the slaughtering industry, or more clearly or forcefully stated than by a British government committee on the Slaughtering of Livestock:[1]

the net operating costs per head, after allowing for the receipts on account of by-products, decrease as the scale of operation increases. At the same time, as the size of the area served increases, the cost of transport per head, alive and dead, increases. It is the interaction of these two tendencies which defines the area which may best be served by any slaughtering centre. A point comes at which the decrease in the average costs of operation consequent upon an increase in area, is more than balanced by the associated increase in the average costs of transport.

Quantitative 'macroscopic' analysis again comes to the aid of the common sense microscopic argument. The survey of localization and size of plant which has covered much the largest number of industries is that published in 1957 by the Stanford Research Institute in its *Role of Small Scale Manufacturing in Economic Development*, in which

[1] Economic Advisory Council Report, 1933, p. 52. Since 1933 the U.S. slaughtering (or meat-packing) industry has moved slightly nearer to the British pattern of dispersed and smaller plants.

with size of plant does not do so as steeply as the horse-power ratio. The effect of size of plant upon productivity appears to be mainly indirect, by permitting the use of

Range of size of plant (employees)	Ratio of horse-power per production worker	Value added ($1,000) per production worker
1–4	12·1	7·6
5–9	3·9	7·5
10–19	4·5	7·6
20–49	5·0	7·6
50–99	5·2	8·1
100–249	6·9	8·8
250–499	8·1	9·3
500–2,499	11·4	10·4
2,500 upward	11·8	11·1
All sizes	9·6	9·5

more powerful and specialized machines. Without reference to machine power, value added per worker certainly cannot be taken as a measure of the efficiency of labour as such.

coefficients as in Table IF were quoted for 322 American manufacturing industries. It applied both my measures of size of plant structure and of localization. Table IIc gives in its six columns the number of industries with no representative size of plant and those with small, smallish, medium, largish and large size of plant prevailing. The figures that appear are percentages of the total of industries within each of the five ranges of the localization coefficient. Thus the figure at the top left corner refers to 18 industries out of a total of 47 with coefficients between 0 and 0·29, i.e. 38·3 per cent of them. Reading across the table, all the rows of percentages add up to $100 \pm 0 \cdot 1$.

Running down the columns, the eye will notice a continuous fall in the first column and a continuous rise in the last column. The fall indicates that the less an industry is localized (i.e. the more it is scattered) the more it tends to have no prevailing size of plant. This 'all-sites-all-sizes law' is logical enough, since e.g. residentiary industries found in *both* small and large towns might well have plants of all sizes to fit various sizes of their markets. On the other hand, the rise in the last column indicates that the more industries are localized, the greater tends to be the proportion with a larger size of plant. There are, in fact, only very small percentages in the right hand top corner where industries are placed that have a large, largish or even medium prevailing size of plant and also little localization.

This tendency, that the more an industry is localized the more likely it is to be an industry with a large prevailing size of plant might of course be a 'spurious' correlation if the local areas or industries used as a basis were small and one large plant alone might account for the high location. But industries below a certain number of employees were omitted; and large areas were used: whole states were the local units in the U.S., whole regions in the U.K.

Two definite relations thus emerge between the location pattern and size-of-plant pattern of industries but the second relation between the patterns of high localization and large plant does not extend to low localization and small plant. We might expect the industries with small or smallish plants prevailing in the second and third columns to decrease relatively as localization increases, as a counterpart to the clear opposite tendency among large plant industries in the last column. But there is no desert of almost empty boxes in the left bottom corner similar to that in the right top and no continuous diagonal linear trend of high frequencies appears. There is thus no universal law of the larger the plants the higher the localization. Instead, there are high frequencies 17·0, 18·7, 20·9, 22·9 per cent of industries combining small, smallish or medium sized plants with localization coefficients above 0·40, 0·50 and 0·60. A third relation thus emerges that some prevailing small-plant industries are localized; examples listed in Table IF will be cited shortly.

British data on the relation between localization and size-of-plant have not been based on such a detailed classification of industries as in Table IIc but show the same associations of (a) all-size with all-sites, (b) larger prevailing plants with high localization and (c) smaller prevailing plant pattern with high localization. The logic of this last association, which is marked in Britain, is that external economies (see p. 77) within an industry of small plants are particularly strong if these plants are localized close together. Table IF shows clear traces of all three associations in its survey of all the 25 largest British industries and their American equivalents based on the most recent survey data. These associations constitute the sixth point which Table IF was said (see page 32) to bring out.

(a) The association of no prevalent size type of plant with industries of low localization. Table VF, column 3 has five no prevalent plant size (N) British industries. Two of them, general printing and furniture have the 3rd and 4th lowest localization coefficients out of 25, and none of them have any of the highest eight coefficients. In column 4 there are eight American no prevalent plant size (N) industries. Three of them, cocoa and sugar confectionery, industrial plant and furniture are 2nd, 3rd and equal 4th lowest in localization and only two are in the top half of the whole list of 25. The logic of this association, as said earlier, is that where industries are scattered they are probably scattered in a number of towns of different size and being market-oriented, have plants of different size.

(b) The association of large plant prevalence with high localization. In column 3 there are eight British industries with large plants prevailing, marked LL or L. Six of them rank among the upper half of industries with highest localization. In column 5 there are seven American industries with large plants prevailing, six of which rank among the upper half of industries with highest localization.

(c) The association of small-plant prevalence with high localization. In the British columns of Table IF, all the large industries with the smaller plants prevailing (smallish or medium) are the highest in localization: footwear, hosiery, cotton-weaving, cotton-spinning and wool, respectively 21st, 22nd, 23rd, 24th and 25th out of the 25 largest industries. There are only three other smaller plant industries (bread, timber and dresses) listed. Bread making, owing to the perishability of product, and saw-milling of timber, owing to intransportability of product, have to be spread among consumers since most of the raw material is imported. The dressmaking location pattern is a compromise between proximity to consumer and, as in London, a fashion centre localization. The third ('C') association is less marked among the larger industries of America, but it is illustrated in cotton-spinning and wool and also in lumbering.

LOGIC AND FACT

TABLE IIc

RELATIONSHIP OF DEGREE OF LOCALIZATION AND
SIZE-OF-PLANT AMONG 322 AMERICAN MANUFACTURES, 1947
Source: Stanford Research Institute

Range of localization coefficient	Percentage of 322 manufactures within each of the five ranges of localization coefficient						
	No prevailing size of of plant (1)	Prevailing representative size of plant					Total of Industries (7)
		Small (2)	Smallish (3)	Medium (4)	Largish (5)	Large (6)	
0–·29	38·3	19·2	27·7	6·4	2·1	6·4	47
·30–·39	37·8	9·8	12·2	15·8	13·4	11·0	82
·40–·49	25·6	9·3	20·9	7·0	18·6	18·6	86
·50–·59	22·0	17·0	17·0	5·1	17·0	22·0	59
·60 or above	2·1	12·5	22·9	18·7	12·5	31·3	48
Total number	85	41	62	34	44	56	322

Table IIE, below, provides further evidence of this association of very close localization with smaller or medium rather than larger plant industries. Among the 24 most localized British industries, those with prevalent medium-sized plants (marked M) outnumber industries with large plants (marked L) by nine to three. For all manufacturing industries in Britain in 1951, whatever the degree of localization, the relation was as seven to six. Among the American localized industries medium, smallish and small plant grades outnumber large (and very large) grade industries by 15 to 5.

The hypothetical argument backed by statistical correlation of the relationship between investment in machines, size of plant and a degree of localization may be set forth in the genealogy of Table IID.[1] Scientific invention is applied in the form of innovations such as new mechanical devices usually secured to the innovator by a patent on which he obtains royalties.

The links in the argument that are forged by some form of statistical correlation are marked by arrows with three-lined shafts. The remainder of the tree might be regarded as corresponding to a pure economist's 'model', but more solidly based on the facts. The statistical correlations established by Tables IIB and IIc suggest: (a) that the more mechanized the industry the larger its prevalent size of plant, which accords with the

---

[1] The ancestry is carried further back in Florence, *Atlas of Economic Structure and Policies*, 1970, Fig. 12 by indicating that invention and factory mechanization are more easily applied where materials are uniform, and transport mechanization more important where they are heavy.

law of increasing return and the principle of multiples; (b) that localized have larger plants prevalent than dispersed industries; but (c) that industries highly localized in production centres may have small or medium sized plants prevailing. Localization has been the child of cheaper transport since it has made procurements of materials and distribution

TABLE IID

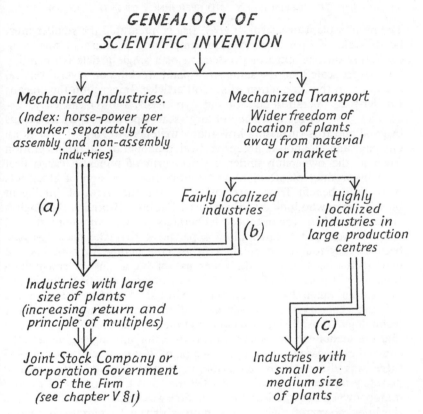

GENEALOGY OF
SCIENTIFIC INVENTION

Mechanized Industries.
(Index: horse-power per worker separately for assembly and non-assembly industries)

Mechanized Transport
Wider freedom of location of plants away from material or market

(a)

Fairly localized industries

(b)

Highly localized industries in large production centres

Industries with large size of plants (increasing return and principle of multiples)

(c)

Joint Stock Company or Corporation Government of the Firm (see chapter V §1)

Industries with small or medium size of plants

of products from and to a wide area less costly, and given the economies of large-scale production in one or a few localities a greater chance to prevail over the transport costs. It will be remembered[1] that, since the inception of railways, those British industries where the comparison was possible (such as shoemaking and tailoring) were found to have become measurably more localized. Thus mechanization of transport takes its place beside mechanization of industry as the underlying cause of larger plants or localized centres of production. Now both

[1] See Chapter I § 5.

forms of mechanization are the result of the application of scientific invention, and this genealogy is of importance in forecasting the future.[1] Since progress in scientific invention seems very like persisting, growth in localization and in large-scale organization and production looks very like persisting too.

§ 4. THE INEFFICIENCY AND EFFICIENCY OF INTEGRATION

The more a plant or a firm *of given size* is integrated the smaller must be its scale of operation. A plant employing a thousand men concentrating on one stage of production of a single article is operating on a larger scale than the same sized plant working on several vertical stages or on the production of several articles. Integration thus means smaller-scale operation and, on our hypothesis, a lower efficiency.

This thesis of the efficiency of large-scale operation is by no means original and it is surprising how many writers[2] will sing its praises on one page and on another accept vertical, diagonal or lateral integration (such as the ownership under a single firm of mines, a cargo fleet or a by-product plant) as almost automatically a sign of efficiency. Automatic benefit from integration is not the view of intelligent business men who look into their costs. Cadbury Brothers, the English chocolate makers, for instance, deliberately gave up running a fleet of canal barges, and a saw-milling department to make packing-cases, because they found independent firms, contracting for a number of manufacturers, able to make fuller use of barge and of saw-milling capacity and thus costing less.[3] The most obvious practical step in disintegration taken by manufacturers (British and American) in the twentieth century is in power generation. Under nineteenth-century technology, transmission costs of direct mechanical propulsion required that the manufacturer integrate his own prime moving engine, and the engine-house was an integral part of a plant. But between 1899 and 1963 there was diagonal disintegration in favour of public (as against privately integrated) utilities. In 1899 the total horse-power of electric motors owned by American manufactures was one and two thirds times the horse-power of their electric motors driven by purchased energy. By 1962 it was a mere fifth.[4]

Integration within a plant or a firm must be suspected therefore of small-scale inefficient production till it is proved innocent. How can its efficiency be established? The pleading follows three lines of argument,

---

[1] For the impact of science on the social relations of industry, see Florence in *Sociological Review*, January 1939, pp. 1–24.

[2] Despite Marshall's warnings in his *Industry and Trade*, 1919, pp. 197–249.

[3] *Industrial Record, 1919–39*, Bournville, 1945.

[4] U.S. Statistical Abstract, 1966, p. 782.

based on the facts and analysed by structure as established in Chapter I: (A) arguments from common costs applicable to firms or plants; (B) arguments from technical factors including distribution applicable to plants; and arguments (C) from risk and uncertainty applicable mainly to integration within a firm.

(A) The common production cost argument is the simplest. It was shown in Chapter I that integration was sometimes unrelated, but usually in terms of our technical framework was spread in vertical, lateral or diagonal directions. Now, with lateral integration, production often diverges from a common previous vertical stage also performed by the plant or firm, or converges on a common later stage so performed. If convergent integration be pictured as two lines joining one another downward like a V, this combination of lateral and vertical integration yields technical relations of a Y rather than a simple V type. Whether converging (in Y-like) relations or diverging (like a Y upside-down) the later or earlier *common* process (the stem of the Y) can often be performed on a larger scale and to fuller capacity if there is integration of the several materials used in the earlier, or of the several products in the later stages. The clue to the economy of producing together articles laterally related is that they have common costs.

Articles *diverging* from the same process have materials in common (and possibly the earlier processes) and the economy of bulking applies therefore when one organization buys common materials. Articles *converging* upon the same market have marketing costs in common (and possibly the later manufacturing processes) and the bulking of orders from customers is economical in the time of clerks and sales force, even though the order is composite and consists of a demand for several different products.

Thus where common costs arise the principle of bulking may often be invoked in favour of extension of the production of a single article to that of laterally related articles—all provided by one organization.

The same corollary holds true of the principle of multiples. If a given special machine or process in a plant cannot be used to capacity in one line of production it may be worth adopting a second or third line that would also diverge from this common process to use the idle capacity and 'balance up'. And in the case of convergent articles, it may be economical to use a selling staff of a firm to capacity by adopting subsidiary articles that they are competent to sell, so to speak, in their spare time.

Can this theoretical common cost argument for integration be supported by a widespread basis in fact? The comprehensive survey of all American manufacturing firms with several branch-plants distinguishes a special class of 'by-product' and of 'like process' manufacturing among the *divergent* integrations and a special class of 'complementary' product makers among the *convergent* integrations.[1] In the case of by-product divergence the early stages are common, though 'at some point in the manufacturing process the original raw material diverges into two parts'—the inverted Y procedure, to wit. Like-process integration, where at least one process is common, occurs particularly in textiles where a firm 'may operate establishments which spin cotton yarn and silk yarn. The same process, spinning, is applied to different raw materials, the result being the manufacture of cotton and silk yarn.'[2] Here the plants integrated with a common central process can be pictured as an X relation. The instance of complementary convergence cited is that of a firm 'whose major product is machinery', but which 'operates different establishments producing such complementary parts as nuts, bolts, foundry products, wire, steel, brass, etc'.[3] Here the convergent lines have, like a Y, a common tail.

Now integrations within multiplant firms along these common cost lines account for a considerable proportion of their type. Among the 781 divergent type integrations (see Chapter I, p. 56) by-product (λ) integrations number 113 and like-process (X) integrations 104. Among the 1,058 examples of convergent integrations 183 made auxiliary products, and 489 produced for like markets; the remaining complementary (Y) integrations, with the common vertical stage of assembly, numbered 386.

Integration, however, is not confined to the form where several plants of different industry are owned by one firm, and as already said (p. 89) an analysis has been made of the product structures of the fifty largest American manufacturing corporations, who integrated from 6 to 302 products each. The common cost looms repeatedly behind the answers of the corporations to the question why they diversified their production. But it is not the cost of a common earlier or later stage of production that appears so often in the answers, as 'research conducted as a general business policy'. Research was (in § 2) added to finance as an explanation of large firm efficiency, and to a firm that was large enough to use research organs at all, there would arise economies in using that research (like finance) to the full. As the American survey sums it up:[4] 'research may discover new uses or remove known obstacles' to new applications of existing technology and materials; and 'may bring about the production of new products because some advance is made in technology'.

The economy of integration due to common costs boils down to

---

[1] See Chapter I§6 for italicized terms.
[2] T.N.E.C., Monograph 27, p. 147.
[3] Ibid., p. 149.
[4] Ibid., p. 658.

this, that if a manufacturer has a certain unused capacity in equipment or in research or in finance (or brains of himself and staff), it may pay to 'balance up' by taking on as a side line new processes or products using that idle capacity. As a summary to the American survey puts it under the heading of utilization of resources, 'diversification may result from an attempt to make full use of managerial or manufacturing capacity'.

Sometimes the unbalance and incomplete use of common resources arises from contraction of certain lines or changes in demand. Partial substitution may then take place; a new product is integrated with reduced quantities of the old.

(B) The technical factors involved in justifying integration are chiefly portability and durability affecting integration within the plant, and quality control and supply to distributors affecting integration within the firm. The classical argument for vertical integration arises in iron and steel production where loss would be incurred if the molten iron has to cool and then be reheated in some other distant plant. The processing of by-products is usually integrated within a plant because their portability is low in relation to their value. Less often quoted are the cases, frequent in wool textile and also in motor manufacture,[1] where a firm performs an earlier stage to ensure the quality of semi-manufactured materials for the later stages of manufacture. The economies of diagonal (service) integration are based mostly on these technical grounds. The specialized auxiliary services, such as maintenance and toolmaking, available on the spot has already been given as a reason for the efficiency of the large plant.

The framework of technical or ergological reference in Chapter I included the transport, storage and distribution of goods to the final consumer. Supply to distributors may make for considerable lateral convergent integration because the retail stores, where goods are displayed and the consumer makes his choice of purchases, are in general more integrated than the factories which supply them. With a few exceptions, like furniture and shoe stores, a shop will retail the products of more than one manufacturing industry. Grocers stock biscuits, hams, jams, canned fish and the products of several other manufactures distinguished in the British and American census. Ironmongers in Britain, corresponding to hardware stores in America, may sell sacks, domestic hollow-ware, locks and keys, wire, tools, cutlery, batteries and accumulators, electric lamps, electric lighting fittings, electric heaters, paints, oil, polishes, matches, linoleum, brushes, abrasives, incandescent mantles, wallpaper, pottery and glassware, cement and some building materials—the products, in short,

---

[1] See Lavington, 'Technical Influences on Vertical Integration', *Economica*, March 1927.

of twenty-three industries recognized by the British census of production.[1] And grocers and hardware stores are by no means so integrated laterally as the American drug store or the village (or slum) 'general store', or the city department stores which sometimes claim to be universal providers. Taking a comprehensive view, though avoiding duplication, the total kinds of retail store recognized by the U.S. census of distribution in 1929 were 85, but among the total of industries recognized by the census of manufactures of the same date, I calculated that those making for retail were at least double. The original British distribution census recognized, free of duplication, 38 kinds of retailers of manufactures; the production census about a 100 divisions making for retail. In both countries, the lateral integration in shops averages wider than integration within the plants of any industry and the trend toward selling a range to satisfy the retailer would therefore make for wider integration in production. This trend is undoubtedly strong. Questioning the fifty largest American manufacturing corporations (who integrated between 6 and 311 products each) why they diversified their production, a most frequent answer given was, in order to carry a 'full line' especially for distributors or salesmen.

Distributors of radios . . . began to carry other electric household appliances when the radio business became seasonal. These distributors preferred to deal with the manufacturers who could provide a number of household appliances. Some manufacturers diversified their output to meet this need by adding air conditioning equipment, washing machines, oil burners, etc. Others found it necessary to follow suit.

In another case, a company that produced and processed oil got into the drug business through developing a mineral oil. They later added other drug-store products, including cosmetics and nasal sprays. One company interviewed was formed by a combination of retail druggists with the purpose of manufacturing their own patent medicines. This organization now produces surgical dressings, rubber sundries, grape juice, crushed fruits and sirups, envelopes, drinking cups, chocolate, cocoa, candy coatings, surgical gauze, drugs, and other articles commonly sold in drug stores.[2]

Other integrations were adopted by producers to supply a full line of office equipment. This pull from the distribution end may come from the customer not merely the retailer. An American manufacturer added furniture polish to his line of radio sets. In England I found a jewellery manufacturer who made metal badges and regalia for the Freemasons,

---

[1] The 23 products or industries are cited in the text in the order in which they appeared in the census. Only five of them (of electrical and hardware type) are subdivisions of the main 109 manufacturing industries. The remainder are main industries.

[2] T.N.E.C., Monograph 27, p. 651.

branching out also into aprons, banners and other cloth and plush goods needed by the Order.

(C) In production which anticipates demand, risk and uncertainty inevitably arise from technical progress and the sovereignty allowed an often fitful consumer, superimposed on the continued waywardness of nature and the desire of rival human producers for monopoly. The distinction between risk and uncertainty drawn by economists is that risks arise from fluctuations that can be foreseen, uncertainty from fluctuations or other events that cannot. Risks arise naturally from variations in weather and temperature; and whether it will be hot, temperate or cold, can usually be foretold. In America (though not necessarily in Britain) it will be hot in summer, cold in winter with resulting contrast in supplies and demand. Hence to keep capacity in full use, a food manufacturer will often integrate operations using summer and winter (or at least all-season) supplies, and meeting winter and summer demands. Jam and ice-cream making (mainly a summer trade in Britain) is thus integrated with the all-season, or winter, potting of meat and fish.

Seasonal fluctuations can be foreseen and are a risk that lateral integration can insure against by 'dovetailing', rather than an uncertainty. But cyclical fluctuation and secular trends are uncertain in their incidence and, moreover, do not cancel out. In the course of a trade cycle industries rise and fall together and a manufacturer can hedge, not by integrating industries fluctuating in opposite directions, but only by integrating the less with the more fluctuating industries. The likely degree of cyclical fluctuation of specific industries can to some extent be estimated from past experience. Hedging against secular trend is still more speculative. Growth and technical progress may advance fast or slow along particular lines and the more industrialized a country, the more the consumer appears prone to fashion and unpredictable changes instead of a traditional way of life upon which a producer can count. The efficient manufacturer thus often plays safe by integrating 'bread-and-butter' lines he knows to be old-fashioned in technique and demand with laterally related lines he thinks (but uncertainly) may become technically efficient and fashionable.

Human nature interferes with simple large-scale operation from another direction, however—the brain (or the breast) of the fellow producer, not the consumer. Any one manufacturer in the sequence of production may be uncertain whether the source of his materials, or his market, may not be monopolized and he himself exploited by having to pay too much for his materials or being offered too little for his product. In the first case manufacturers think it efficient strategy in the long run to integrate vertically backwards, in the latter case forwards. British newspaper publishers, largely in consequence of threatened monopolies, are integrated to paper manufacturing and American cotton and wool spinners to weaving.

In short, it is not necessarily logical and efficient for any one firm or plant to be organized for the largest possible scale of production, making one or just a very few standard products by one or a very few standard processes. There is logic in certain 'optimum' degrees of integration according to the common cost, technical risk and uncertainty factors involved.

Yet probably only a part of the integrations actually in existence can put in any such claims to superior efficiency. To start with, some of these factors mentioned in justification of integration are not inevitable and might well be diminished in strength. If fear of monopoly were abated by government action or technical progress smoothed out by amendment of the patent law, two sources of uncertainty would be cut down. Uncertainty might often be turned into a predictable risk, needing less random integration, if manufacturers, as suggested in Chapter III, used more market and even general sociological research. In 1937 I found an English baby carriage maker quite ignorant of the fact that the number of births had been diminishing in his country for thirty years previously. This manufacturer had integrated to some extent, but the obvious and perhaps sufficiently safe integration (in view of the ageing structure of the population) of baby carriages with invalid chairs had not occurred to him. Even if uncertainty and technical factors making for integration are taken as inevitable, the evidence is strong that there is much over-integration. The American survey quoted earlier (p. 56) found that many firms had plants integrated in no sort of logical technical (supply or demand) relation, or where no common costs existed. Conglomerate firms appear to integrate more unrelated products or processes than can be justified as hedges against risks and uncertainty, or as resulting in incidental common cost economies particularly from large scale marketing and finance. In my *Logic of Industrial Organization*, published in 1933 (p. 211), I cited as a warning the losses of Herr Stinnes in his empire building after the First World War, and many American conglomerates seem to be following his path in 1968–70. Conglomerate mergers are often, indeed, formed for reasons extraneous to larger-scale efficiency. Empirical studies show mergers conglomerate or homogeneous (e.g. operating geographically more widely) aim to profit from the undervaluing on the Stock Exchange of the shares of the 'mergeree', the company that is taken over; or, more generally, aim for more power.[1]

Instead of large-scale production of a few commodities, there is a wide prevalence of small-scale production of a multitude of sizes, shapes

---

[1] Developed in greater detail in the next section (pp. 109–10).

and qualities of the same sort of article. Some numerical idea of the extent to which this orgy of specifications may go can be obtained by a glance at the work of the simplication movement in the United States. Even in this country of supposed standardization it took all the energy of ex-President Hoover, when Secretary of the Department of Commerce, to get the following results for industries as a whole between 1921 and 1925. Among producer's goods the number of sizes or varieties of shovels, spades and scoops were reduced from 4,460 to 384, of grocer's paper bags from 6,280 to 4,700, of grinding wheels from 715,200 to 255,800, of warehouse documentary forms from 'thousands' to fifteen. Among consumer's goods the number of sizes and varieties of hotel chinaware was reduced from 700 to 160, of brass lavatory and sink traps from 1,114 to 72, and of milk bottles alone from 49 to 9.

Even though 'an industry' produced a great variety of patterns, and in Marshall's phrase[1] there was no 'general' standardization, it might yet be true that the firms or plants within the industry each produced one or a few of the varieties, obtaining by such specialization large-scale *operation*, and that there was 'particular standardization'. But this usually is not true. Each firm or plant tries to supply the whole gamut of varieties, and thus by competing all along the line with all the other firms or plants in the industry only succeeds in conducting small-scale operations.

The varieties of product made by firms employing no more than a few hundred workers may run into thousands or tens of thousands, as the perusal of any of their catalogues may show. It can be demonstrated mathematically that even if only one small article is produced—say an electrical switch for domestic lighting—but produced in half a dozen materials, a dozen colours, a dozen sizes and two dozen shapes, over 20,000 varieties of the product will be made.[2] What possibilities of further multiplication in the products of one firm are offered when numerous kinds of article—pots, pans, kettles, pails, skillets, griddles, mugs, dishes, tins, buckets, scuttles, cans, dutch-ovens, percolators, roasters, steamers, urns, bins—of all firms, sizes, shapes and colours are produced at one and the same time.

The English metal industries have been full of instances such as this. One firm 'makes locomotives of 24 different gauges between 18 in. and 5 ft. 6 in., and sizes may vary from 6 to 60 tons throughout the range ... consulting engineers acting for buyers may insist on variations in details to suit their own views'.[3] Not much has changed since the Board of Trade Engineering Trades Committee of 1916–17 was

[1] *Industry and Trade*, 1919, p. 201.
[2] $6 \times 12 \times 12 \times 24 = 20,736$.
[3] Balfour Committee on Industry and Trade, *Survey of Metal Industries*, 1928, p. 172.

much impressed . . . by the very large number of relatively small firms that exist—each with a separate organization, separate establishment charges, separate buying and selling arrangements, and each producing a multiplicity of articles. Some of them seemed to take a special pride in the number of things they turned out. . . . The result of many firms being employed upon producing a large number of articles in common use is the causing of confusion in the types of articles produced, so that no two manufacturers seem intentionally to produce the same article. Each one claims some special merit of his own.[1]

If the actual practice in integration goes beyond the 'optimum degree of integration' that can be logically justified by common costs, technical factors or uncertainty, why do such examples survive and why are they undertaken or deliberately maintained?

The answers, for there are several, are often clear enough.

(1) A firm or plant existing at any one time, which is over-integrated beyond the optimum may, in fact, as expected be inefficient and may be passing out of existence—failing to survive, or at least may merely be kept in existence by some sort of association or agreement to 'stabilize' prices and avoid losses in the industry as a whole.

(2) A firm may have become integrated due to a combine of previously integrated firms, some of the previously integrated products, processes or services being unrelated to the main products of the combine as a whole. In this case over- or rather mis-integration is a corollary of combination, and the combine may either be in process of shedding some of its products or processes, or some departments may be living on the fat of the others. This explanation leads to a third.

(3) The inefficiency of the particular integration of one firm or combine may be masked by the efficiency of that firm in other respects.

Though all too few in number some results have been published by individual firms of the costs and profits actually experienced on unintegrated, standard large-scale operations. Even then, most of the few published records refer to the more obvious short-period results when a given capital equipment is used to greater capacity. Printing 500 copies of a magazine, each copy was, for instance, found to cost $1·75, printing 10,000 copies, each copy to cost $0·167. This increasing return was due to the fixed constant overhead of editing, setting up type, proof-reading and corrections costing no more for the 'bulk' 10,000 than the small-scale 500.

Two classical examples, one American one British, can be given of large-scale economies of standardization or 'disintegration' in the long period when time is allowed for investment in new capital equipment. The British case history is that of the amalgamation of Hans Renold's and the Coventry Chain Company, when the amalgamated

[1] Op. cit., p. 146.

firm reduced the production of varieties of cycle and other chains from 123 and 1,249 to 6 and 221, of pedals from 69 to 16, of hubs from 47 to 21 and of other cycle fittings from 1,276 to 358. One manifest economy, according to Sir Charles Renold, was in the holdings of stock or 'inventory'. 'Centralization of stock and of their control and the reduction of varieties by standardization have enabled a permanent reduction of stock investment to be made of some £60,000 on a stock of £438,000.'[1] The principle of massed reserves seems to have operated fairly strongly.

The American example tested efficiency by profits not costs, and refers to a number of firms in an industry. Between 1922 and 1926, though production by itself made least profit, oil industry corporations that refined only, or refined and marketed only, had a considerably higher profit than corporations which integrated production and refining, or production, refining and marketing.[2]

Many other instances of standardization by firms are reported but usually without accurately measured results or with no results at all;[3] frank disclosures of costs or profits are far to seek that will test the principles of bulk transaction and massed reserve.

§ 5. THE LOGIC OF LOCALIZATION AND DISPERSION

Before arguing the particular efficiency of localizing an industry the sort of facts under discussion must be recalled. The localization of industry may describe any one of four structural situations: the unequal density on the land of the total industrial population *anywhere*; high density of the total population *somewhere*; the localization of a particular industry *anywhere*, measured by the coefficient of localization; and the localization of particular industries *somewhere*, measured by the location quotient of that industry in that place. Chapter I purposely did not stress the relative density of the general industrial population either anywhere or somewhere. General *urban* concentration occurs in most countries and has probably occurred at all times. Populations are and have been concentrated in capital cities and at favourable conjunctions of land and water, like ports, or river crossings; or in areas where nature is bountiful in mineral deposits or land fertility. What is characteristic of industrialized countries and was measured by the location quotient and the coefficient of localization (ratios of persons to persons, not directly of persons to land) is

[1] Sixth International Scientific Management Congress, Development Section, p. 41.

[2] *Recent Economic Changes*, Vol. I, p. 194.

[3] Three American instances of deliberate reduction of varieties of products are given in Florence, 1933, pp. 27–9.

that certain particular industries have persisted over many years in setting themselves off from the distribution of the population in general, and thus from final markets, and often regardless of natural bounty in material or in fertility.

Table IIE lists for each country the 24 sizable industries (employing at least 10,000 in 100 plants) which were most highly localized according to the last American calculations of the coefficient (1947) and the nearest date for Britain (1951). Almost all are localizations that have existed for some time and are known to have persisted in the British calculations for 1958.[1] As can be expected from the agreement (shown in Table IM on page 48) between the location patterns of British and American industries, several industries appear 'matched up' in both lists such as lace, cotton-weaving and spinning (i.e. yarn in the U.S. census), textile machinery, plate and pottery industries. Whether in both or only in one list, a not unexpected point is the number of industries that are (in the terminology of Table IL, p. 47) linked to other industries or else rooted.

In the American list, tobacco stem, canned fish, cotton seed mills and poultry dressing, plywood, sawmills, cooperage, stocks and refractories can be said to be 'rooted', i.e. raw-material oriented, and, in the British list, blast furnaces and coke ovens. The larger number of 'rooted' industries in America points to the wider variety of climates and natural resources, particularly timber; a variety that British industries cannot match. Linked to other industries (which are themselves more or less localized) are oilfield and textile machinery, machine tools, marine engineering and tinplate and steel sheets using products of the iron and steel industry.

The rooted and linked localizations occur in industries that use localized materials or supply products for localized industries, when materials or products are costly to transport compared to their value; here Weber's law[2] applies that the location of industry will be such as to make the total ton–miles of transport to and from the industry a minimum. Lack of durability of materials and products and the need for communication and contacts between supplier, producer and consumer also have a localizing effect.

Where transport, durability and contacts are less important the industry may be considered footloose. For the jute industry in Dundee, for instance, seen at the top of the localization table, the raw materials come from thousands of miles away and the market is the whole country, if not the world. The advantages of localization in that case lie mainly in the external economies of plants 'swarming' together.

Few manufactures seem to localize at the precise mathematical point

[1] U.K. census of production.
[2] Weber *Über den Standort der Industrien*, 1909. Translated by C. J. Friedrich, Chicago, 1929.

between market and material where transport costs are least—that is, further from the market when products are relatively portable, further from source of material when materials are more portable. Such compromise between market and material orientation is infrequent because manufactures might then fall between two stools. There would be a costly break in carriage between materials and market and the plants would neither be able to integrate locally with their material and the necessary services, nor yet would the management be in contact with the market.[1]

TABLE IIE

AMERICAN AND BRITISH MANUFACTURES MOST LOCALIZED

(All employing over 10,000 in over 100 plants ranked by their coefficients of localization)

Prevalent size of plant in brackets: (S) = small; (sh) = smallish; (M) = Medium; l = largish; L = large; (LL) = very large; (N) = No prevalence).

Rank	American census of manufactures 1947	Coefficient based on states	British census of Production 1951	Coefficient based on regions
1st	Tobacco stem (M)*	·88	Jute (M)	·89
2nd	Canned fish (M)	·83	Tinplate (l)	·89
3rd	Cotton Seed oil (sh)	·81	Linen (M)	·84
4th	Fur goods (S)†	·76	Pottery (M)	·77
5th	Oilfield machinery (l)	·74	Cotton-spinning (M)	·74
6th	Cotton yarn (M)	·73	Lace (S)	·72
7th	Cooperage stock mills (sh)	·72	Cotton-weaving (M)	·71
8th	Cotton broad weaving (L)	·70	Wool and worsted (M)	·69
9th	Poultry dressing (sh)	·68	Steel sheets (l)	·65
10th	Textile machinery (L)	·66	Coke ovens (M)	·62
11th	Plywood (M)	·66	Linoleum (L)	·62
12th	Sawmills (S)	·65	Needles (N)	·60
13th	Earthenware (utensils) (l)	·65	Hosiery (N)	·58
14th	Rayon yarn throwing (M)	·65	Blast furnaces (l)	·57
15th	Silver-ware and plate (l)	·64	Carpets (L)	·55
16th	Veneers (sh)	·63	Marine engineering (L)	·54
17th	Lace (M)	·62	Plate and jewellery (sh)	·54
18th	Watches and clocks (L)	·62	Textile finish (M)	·53
19th	Motor vehicles (LL)	·62	Textile machinery (l)	·53
20th	Photo equipment (L)	·61	Machine tools (N)	·53
21st	Children's dresses (S)	·60	Boots and shoes (M)	·53
22nd	Distilled liquor (l)	·60	Fur (S)	·53
23rd	Clay refractories (sh)	·60	Chains etc. (N)	·51
24th	Wool yarn (M)	·60	Tools and implements (N)	·51

*Refers to 1958; size not available for 1947.
† Fur total employees 8,000; plants 196.

Where high localizations of industry exist and survive it is not, in many cases, because of low transport cost in procurement of materials

[1] See Hoover, *The Location of Economic Activity*, 1948, Chapter III.

or distribution of products, but to some other economy or set of economies.

The economy to which the facts seem to point has been stated before, but not sufficiently stressed in comparison with the cost of transport theories. Weber referred to it in explaining the factors in 'agglomeration' and 'labour orientation'. The pool of expert labour to be found where an industry was localized has always been held an asset just as a pool of semi-skilled labour in any big city or region is an asset to industry generally. Besides expert labour a 'localization' will, it is agreed, bring and retain specialized expert services and will make for efficient distribution by enabling purchasers to 'shop around' on the spot. Most of the economist's 'external' economies (arising where an industry grows apart from growth in its constituent firms or plants) are economies of localization.[1]

But what has not been valued at its true importance in a large localization of an industry is the possibilities of division of labour between plants in 'linked' processes, products and service industries. The advantage of full use of specialist plants can be combined with proximity. Several specialized plants, if close enough together, may have much the same economies as the separate departments of a large plant; distance between them need not be much further and—unless the single large plant has a particularly efficient internal transport system—transport need not be more costly.[2] A given scale of production by several small firms will undoubtedly offer more points where the powerful profit incentive, discussed later (pp. 337–8), is applied than a large plant with a salaried servant of a joint stock company in charge. The close localizations shown in Table IIE are in many cases associated with smaller and medium-sized plants, as indicated by the letters within brackets.

The facts leave no doubt that for certain general services like power generation and distribution and telephone communication, large local concentration with high density of consumers is more efficient and cheaper than scattered consumption. These services are increasingly being used, and help to explain continuing urbanization. The thesis of the efficiency of the localization of particular industries hinges essentially on the existence in a close localization of a fairly logical specialization and linkage between the neighbouring plants. Just as a single large plant may be more efficient if integrated to some degree, particularly in its services, so a large locality may derive economies by a local integration. Are such large local integrations to be found in fact?

[1] Marshall, *Principles of Economics*, Book IV, IX, § 7. Robinson, *Structure of Competitive Industry*, IX, § 3.
[2] Using roads built and maintained at public expense may, in fact, be less costly for the firm.

The industry tables of the British census of population permit an answer drawn from facts and not fancy, wherever a true conurbation exists. The word conurbation was brought into respectable usage by the 1940 report of the Royal Commission on the Distribution of the Industrial Population. As its etymology implies[1] it should refer to several cities situated close together, and where these cities have a separate official existence the census collects the occupations and industries of their inhabitants separately. The large conurbation in the west midlands of England consisted in 1931 of twenty-eight separate authorities, among which Birmingham and five Black Country towns ranking as county boroughs were granted a very detailed classification of people into industries. Analysis of the data, accessible in the west midland group's *Conurbation* and elsewhere[2] established three conclusions.

(1) Seventeen of the main census industries were by the test of location quotients localized in the midland conurbation area, of which twelve were related metal industries with a measurably high degree of linkage.[3]

(2) The main metal industries were found repeatedly as a pattern in very close proximity to one another. Within this pattern common single-process industries (like founding, forging, galvanizing, tinning, japanning, enamelling, stamping and piercing), and also industries making common components and requirements (like iron and steel tubes, or nuts and bolts, or engineers' tools) could be distinguished as fairly highly localized in all areas. Upon this firm floor, industries making specific metal goods like motor-cars, jewellery, plate, stoves, pins, could here and there build up very close localizations: in the jewellery quarter of Birmingham one short street, surveyed twenty years ago by my pupil Mr A. J. Bennett, contained forty businesses, twenty-five in the jewellery trade, and ten working for it as bullion dealers, stone-merchants and scrap and sweepings merchants. Work was 'put out' or 'subcontracted' if orders were too many, thus adjusting output

[1] Prefix *con*—Latin *cum*—meaning with, together, altogether, completely.— *Concise Oxford Dictionary*.

[2] *Conurbation*, The Architectural Press, 1948, Chapter VIII. Florence, 1948, Chapter IV.

[3] Just as the coefficient of localization measures how some particular industry deviates in its location from the general working population, so a coefficient of linkage can be worked out to show how one particular industry deviates in location from another particular industry. As the coefficient approaches unity and there is little deviation the two industries are to that extent geographically linked. Fairly high coefficients of linkage have been measured between metal industries; for instance, 0·54 between the American stamped and pressed metal industry and the hardware industry (N.R.P.B., Industrial Location and National Resources, p. 119) and 0·832 between the British Motor Cycle Accessories Industry and the Non-Ferrous Tube and Pipe Industry (Florence, *Statistical Journal*, 1944, Part II, p. 106).

to capacity. Porters and errand boys and girls 'toting' goods from plant to plant linked processes, like the internal transport system of a large factory, and formed a substantial part of each firm's staff.[1] In other areas these microscopic intensive 'insights' were still lacking and we could only work out the 'macroscopic' quotients that indicate the close localization in county boroughs of whole industries making specific goods. In West Bromwich the hollow-ware industry had in 1931 a location quotient of 40·8, in Wolverhampton the lock industry 50·9, and in Dudley the chain and anchor industry 83·8. This means that Dudley, a town of fifty thousand inhabitants, within a radius of just over a mile, had over eighty times as many anchor and chain workers as would be expected if the industry were evenly distributed throughout Britain. As an incidental comment on the need to analyse minimum transport cost in procurement and distribution, Dudley had little coal or iron left with which to make anchors and is almost as far from the sea, where anchors are used, as it is possible for Britons to live!

(3) Industries and sub-industries were technically linked (i) vertically, like non-ferrous refining and non-ferrous wares, especially plate and jewellery; (ii) convergently, like bolts, rivets, tyres, accessories and tubes 'feeding' the assembly lines of other local industries like railway carriages, cycles and especially motor vehicles; or like leather and brass wares for assembly into saddlery; (iii) diagonally, like construction engineering, engineering tools, foundries and other metal processes as a service to a number of local industries. Besides direct technical links there were (iv) more indirect, social, relations. Though chiefly a localization of metal industries, the midland conurbation includes also a localization of the cocoa, chocolate and sugar confectionery industry, employing women to men in the proportion of two to one. The logic here is that metal industries tended to employ a greater proportion of men to women than the proportion available in the community; hence 'balancing' industries found a plentiful supply of woman-power. The census of 1963 shows metal industries still highly localized in the west midland conurbation. But probably because these industries now employ their share of women, the cocoa and chocolate industry has developed on Merseyside where unoccupied women were more available.

All this complex 'concatenation' of linked industries was localized in an area with virtually no natural resources left and no water transport except a few small canals! The Birmingham and Black Country conurbation is an object lesson in the economic advantage of localization in and for itself, without reference to nature. Its one natural

[1] For a map of the extreme localization of jewellery and gunsmiths' trades in central Birmingham, see Florence, *Atlas of Economic Structure and Policies*, 1970. Fig. 48.

'facility' is a position more or less in the centre of England. The whole of the Birmingham and Black Country complex of linked industries could probably flourish anywhere else, so long as the place was not too far from the centre of the country. But the emphasis of this statement is *whole complex* as well as *centre of country*. All the industries must move together like a swarm of bees, hence the appellation 'swarming'. Their site would probably have to be somewhere within the elongated pentagon containing only one-seventh of the area but two-thirds of the population of England and Wales, with London as its base and south Lancashire and west Yorkshire as its apex. The shape, as opponents of this economic centralization of industry have not been slow to indicate, is that of certain ancient coffins.

With the coming of the motorized age and the ability of more and more people and goods to travel longer distances from place to place, conveniently and without trans-shipment on the way, the built-up conurbations or metropolitan areas so clearly defined in census reports have become less significant. For some areas and industries the 'city region' is rather the significant unit of localization. This expression is much used today among geographers and planners, for instance both in the main Maud Report on Local Government and in Mr Senior's Memorandum of Dissent, 'city region' is often used rather vaguely and almost invariably without industrial content. However it has been defined[1] as 'a conurbation or one or more cities or big towns surrounded by a number of lesser towns and villages set in rural areas, the whole tied together by an intricate and closely meshed system of relationships and communications, and providing a wide range of employment and services.'

What this definition does not state is that many such city regions specialize in certain particular closely-meshed industries and provide the linked special services, supplies and markets these industries need. In *Conurbation* a series of bar-charts showed this specialization clearly for the six county boroughs within the west midland conurbation. In each of them the bar representing the proportions employed in metals stuck out at least two and a half times the length of the bar representing the proportion so employed in England and Wales, i.e. the location quotient of each county borough was at least 2·5. The proportions have changed little since, but the further point to be made here is that in certain boroughs just outside the conurbation the same specialization in metals (excluding the heavy metal manufacture and ship-building orders V and VII) is to be found as in the boroughs *inside* the conurbation. To quote the county census reports of economic activity for 1966, the location quotients of the total of the three light metal orders (VI,

---

[1] Redcliffe-Maud Report, Vol. I, Chapter I, par. 10, note.

engineering and electrical goods, VIII, vehicles and IX metal goods not elsewhere specified) were for the six county boroughs inside the conurbation:

Birmingham	2·5
West Bromwich	2·4
Warley (previously Smethwick)	3·1
Walsall	2·6
Wolverhampton	2·4
Dudley	1·7

But outside the conurbation many surrounding boroughs had much the same if not higher location quotients for the three light metal orders:[1]

Coventry	4·0
Rugby	3·5
Redditch new town	2·0
Stafford	2·4

Another large city region extending beyond a conurbation is that centring on Manchester. The south-east Lancashire conurbation specializes intensively in the cotton industry. Within this conurbation Bolton and Rochdale had in 1966 a location quotient for cotton-spinning as high as 21·0 and Oldham, 17·8. But outside this conurbation surrounding towns also had quotients for cotton equally high—to cite only county boroughs, Blackburn 18·4 for cotton-weaving and Burnley, 16·8. It is a notable example of extreme localization that the weaving and spinning towns are separated respectively into northerly and southerly groups. But clearly the two processes are linked and the whole area can be brought into the definition of a city region wider than a conurbation.

Examples of smaller city regions extending beyond a hub city are the Leicester hosiery region and the Northampton shoe region. The city of Leicester had in 1966 a location quotient for hosiery as high as 24·4, the county of Leicestershire outside the city a quotient as high as 18·6. The city of Northampton had in 1966 a location quotient for footwear of 24·3; the county of Northamptonshire outside the city a footwear quotient, even higher, of 33·3.

[1] Since I wrote this account of the economic aspects of a city region Lomas and Wood have published their *Employment Location in Regional Economic Planning* (Frank Cass, for the West Midlands Social and Political Research Unit, University of Birmingham, 1970). Here maps and diagrams are shown of the 'functional relationships' within the west midland metal and engineering industries, a distinction being made between the linked 'assembly', 'process and requirements' and 'component' industries. The towns studied round the conurbation are more numerous than the four which I cite but the importance is again shown of the conurbation industries, foundry work and general engineering.

So long as streets are not congested there are great economic advantages in an urban city region with all services and linked industries near at hand as well as special markets. The thesis of economic advantages in concentrated, linked, industries built up on British factual evidence has been put forward even in the country of wide-open spaces. In America E. M. Hoover[1] considers that these economies 'rest on the same basic principles' as those I advanced to explain the economy of large-scale operation, namely multiples, massing of reserves, and bulk transactions.

The principle of multiples means here that in a large industrial concentration the specialization of functions as between firms can be carried further. Certain operations and services that a firm in a smaller place would have to do for itself can, in the city, be farmed out to separate enterprises specializing in those functions and operating on a large enough scale to do them more cheaply.[2] The principles of massing of reserves means that in a large city the individual firm can operate on a hand-to-mouth basis of materials and supplies, secure in the knowledge that more can be obtained at short notice if necessary. The principle of bulk transactions refers here essentially to the economies of large-scale transfer and terminal handling.

If localization is economically so logical, why are any industries left dispersed? The answer lies mainly in the dispersion of the population over the land for past reasons (not necessarily economic today) and for present reasons mainly related to the extractive industries. Agriculture has to be extensive and mining and fishing are scattered or at least sporadic since minerals and fish are dispersed by nature. Where its materials or products are heavy or not durable, manufactures will be rooted or tied near the scattered materials and markets, and will have to be carried out in small plants where the available supplies and markets are small. Both for Britain and America Table Iꜰ shows examples in furniture and bread. Smaller industries, too, with a low coefficient of localization, (i.e. dispersed and in contrast to the localized industries of Table IIᴇ) have in both countries small plants prevailing or have no particular prevailing size of plant. Examples are soft drinks, milk products, concrete or cement, bricks and miscellaneous building materials. A further logical reason, besides the needs of heavy or perishable materials or products for manufacturing industries with scattered and therefore small plants, is the need for personal contacts with the population generally, and not with any particular industry. Examples seen for both countries among the 25 largest industries in

[1] *The Location of Economic Activity*, 1948, p. 120.
[2] This specialization is illustrated in the printing business. City printers often have their machine typesetting done by special composing shops. Similarly, garment manufacturers rely on contract shops and specialized producers who may concentrate on such single steps as buttonhole making (Hoover's note).

Table I*F* are dresses and general printing. Among smaller industries requiring contact with the market of the general population are all repairing and 'property-servicing' as in garages, laundries and shoe-repair shops.[1]

The localization of some industries that is actually found in practice, (e.g. swarming) and the dispersion of others (i.e. rooted, tied, foot-loose) can, thus, both be defended as logical up to a point; but this does not mean that all existing locations are logical, from the purely economic standpoint. It is often maintained that the manufacturer himself knew best and knows best where to put his factory and that things should be let alone without any state or local planning. But factories are durable, and we must realize that decisions to locate factories some-where, taken in the past by the profit motive, would not always be the decisions taken under the present circumstances; and even at the time were not always in each individual case, taken on a strict calculation of profit. The following situations, at the time the decision was taken and at the present time, must be envisaged as possible, and have frequently occurred:

(1) Firm makes decision irrationally, no calculation of profits. Factories have been built without thought in the habitual location of the industry, or, 'to please the wife', near the metropolis.

(2) Firm calculates profit, but incorrectly for the time itself. Many firms, because the initial costs and trouble are smaller, take over existing premises that happen to be for sale. They fail to weigh in the balance the long-term costs of a possibly unsuitable location. It must be realized that decisions on new locations do not often occur in the course of a single-plant firm's history and that its staff is not experienced or trained to evaluate the factors involved. A large multiplant firm will be more prepared for location choosing.

(3) Firm calculated profit correctly for the time itself, but:
(*a*) Incorrectly for present-day circumstances.
(*b*) Correctly for present-day circumstances.
    (i) Profit no measure of the balance of social benefit over cost.
    (ii) Profit a fair measure of the balance of social benefit over cost.

In this analysis only in case 3*b* is policy logical, for present economic reasons, and only in case 3*b*(ii) logical on national grounds.

---

[1] Labour may now be listed beside transport costs and convenience of personal contact as a logical reason for dispersion. With fuller employment and housing shortages the search for available unskilled labour has moved firms in many industries to scatter branch plants. For America, see the National Industrial Conference Board's *Decentralization in Industry*; in Britain, government policy has prevented many firms extending their existing plants, and induced them to open branches in the 'development areas' where a large supply of labour was available.

In growing industrial communities cases 3a of obsolescent logic are likely to be frequent. A site near a city centre economic fifty years ago is now likely to be congested, preventing expansion and causing transport 'jams' and engrossing land required for shops, offices, assembly halls, where centrality is more important than for manufacturing. These prior claims eventually assert themselves, offering high rents or high purchase prices for the central sites and the migration (Chapter I, § 5) of plants to the suburbs may be largely accounted for in this way. But adjustment is slow and erratic and town planning, particularly the development of new towns, is taking the place of the slower, though often correctly groping, economic forces.

The case for town planning and the planning of industrial location generally rests on stronger ground when we consider the case (3b, (i)) where private economic profit may involve social losses. Outstanding examples were the British depressed areas of south Wales and the north east coast. These areas are two of the most richly endowed by nature in the whole world, with coal, iron-ore and the sea, found in juxtaposition. In consequence shipbuilding and iron and steel making were exceedingly profitable and other industries neglected; there was little chance of industrial work in the area for a woman. When the cyclical depression, to which they are peculiarly liable, hit these capital investment industries, there was 50 per cent unemployment among men coupled with the continued 'unoccupation' of the women. Ever since the Distribution of Industries Act of 1945, the British government has been charged with developing these areas and has attempted to 'balance' the coal and capital goods industries employing men only with more stable industries employing women (if footloose industries of this description are available for manœuvre).

A 'balanced' industrial structure is, however, in danger of becoming a fetish and of throwing away the economies of local specialization. The pursuit of private profit does not violate the logic of social stability when it so localizes an industry that an area specializes in producing for common, stable, consumer wants. Burton-on-Trent specializes in beer, but need not fear a slump. Such a lack of balance is not of social consequence, particularly if the industry happens to employ all sections of the population. It is specialization in unstable industries with restricted employment that leads to widespread unemployment and unoccupation in a region.

If a balance of industries is desired in addition to localization of those industries, the mathematically inevitable result is, to use Cobbett's phrase, a 'great Wen' of a metropolis, or a conurbation like Birmingham with a dozen or so highly localized industries. Unemployment may then be diluted at the cost of congestion with its slums, ill-health, liability to pollution, long journeys to work and vulnerability to air attack.[1] Large urban areas have certainly been increasing under the system of private profit. Between 1910 and 1946, cities of over 500,000 in America rose from 7 to 21 in number. But big cities have increased under other systems of industrialization such as Russia's, and seem economically logical and likely to become increasingly so until traffic congestion seizes them up, perhaps. The telephone systems and electrical power transmission and other public utilities become cheaper with high density of population. Canal and railway transport first made possible industrial localization away from material or markets, and the cheaper transport now offered by road services enables production to be centred still further from supplier and consumer for all but very heavy goods.

To sum up in relation to the size of plants discussed already. It is customary to interpret the location pattern of manufacturing industries mainly as a balancing of cost of procurement (transport of material and fuel from their natural sources) or costs of distribution (transport of product to market) as against the costs of smaller scale manufacturing nearer to materials or markets.[2]

This interpretation is supported by one of the outstanding facts disclosed in the more recent reports of the British and American census, the fact, namely, of the rapid growth of the multiplant firm to which Chapter I drew attention, and which runs parallel to the growth of the 'chain-store' multiples in retailing. The multiplant firm pattern is illustrated above (II § 2, p. 68) by structural pattern (B), if the several plants each make the same product, by pattern (D) if they make different products.

Many large industries were shown in Table IF to have a size structure of firms that was one grade larger in scale than the size-structure of plants, and several industries were cited that had a size-structure of firms two grades larger, notably bread, rubber and iron and steel. Among smaller British industries the census of production shows a similar two-grade divergence in the cement, sugar, fertilizer, metal box and building material industries. Table IF also shows a two-grade deviation of size of firms from size of plants in corresponding large American industries: paper, chemical, cotton-weaving. Among other industries the U.S. census of manufactures shows a similar double, or even wider divergence in oil-refining and the metal can, cement, fertilizer and beet-sugar industries.[3] Within such industries the structural pattern is

[1] Royal Commission on the Distribution of the Industrial Population, 1940. For full *pros* and *cons* see Florence, 'Economic Efficiency in the Metropolis,' in Fisher, *The Metropolis in Modern Life*, Doubleday, 1955.

[2] See Hoover, *The Location of Economic Activity*, 1948, especially Chapters 2 to 5. Dechesne, *La Localisation des Diverses Productions*, Brussels, 1945.

[3] The percentages of total employed that in 1963 were in plants and firms of stated size are detailed in the text, p. 109.

mainly of B type and the economy involved mainly of B1 type.[1]

Apart from the cotton industry, these industries where firm-size diverges so considerably from plant-size have unusually high transport costs in relation to the value of material or product, either for supplying raw materials or marketing the product. A similar cost is incurred if supplies or products are perishable, as in the baking industry, or where metal boxes or other containers have to travel empty and are then packed with perishable fruit or vegetables. The logic underlying this

Industry	Plants	Firms
Metal can	59% in sizes 250–999 (medium grade)	88% in sizes 1,000 and over (mammoth grade)
Cement	83% in sizes 100–499 (medium grade)	77% in sizes 1,000 and over (very large grade)
Fertilizer	54% in sizes 50–249 (smallish grade)	80% in sizes 1,000 and over (very large grade)
Beet sugar	70% in sizes 100–249 (medium grade)	91% in sizes 1,000 and over (mammoth grade)
Petroleum refining	50% in sizes 1–999 (no prevailing size)	87% in sizes 1,000 and over 82% in sizes 2,500 and over (mammoth grade)

Further evidence of divergence of plant and firm sizes is given in Blair's evidence before the U.S. Senate Subcommittee on Anti-trust and Monopoly, 1965, Part 4, pp. 1536–71, 1719–31.

big-firms-with-smaller-plant structure is that the industry concerned is (1) capital intensive, (2) either requires raw material or supplies a product that is heavy, perishable or (like metal boxes) bulky *in relation to its value* and (3) has scattered demand for its product or scattered supply of its materials. To avoid costly transport its plants must be scattered (and therefore smaller than if output was concentrated), so as to be near the market or the area of supply.[2] But to raise the necessary capital cheaply the industry may need a large scale financial organization.

This need has been disputed in the controversy arising from recent large conglomerate mergers. A staff report of the U.S. Federal Trade

---

[1] See above pp. 67–8.

[2] In calculating transport costs a paradox must be taken into account. It is not sufficient merely to measure the transport costs actually incurred by an industry. Over a distance some costs are sometimes so high that evasive action is taken and they are not incurred. Brick-building or a cement works are located next to the clay or limestone quarry, laundries and repair work next to the consumer being serviced and the freezing plant next to the food producing plant. Thus the paradox is that industries showing practically no transport costs are potentially industries with the highest costs, and whose location is closely determined by transport costs.

Commission[1] sums up a series of empirical studies over the years 1951 to 1961 which compare firms that merged and that did not merge. The merged, active firms' profit performance was inferior whether measured in terms of return on stock-holders' equity or in terms of stock market price gains. These findings were held to support the conclusion that mergers were undertaken to serve the interests of management who are more concerned with size, growth and power than 'profitability'. A somewhat similar conclusion has been reached in Britain by Newbould.[2]

The British Monopolies Commission has shown that two-fifths of the growth between 1958 and 1968 of the largest companies was attributable to acquisitions by merger rather than self-generated.[3] But the profitability of the merger is likely to depend on the compatibility of the types of work being merged. The commission (*Survey of Mergers, 1958–1968*, H.M.S.O., 1970) found 55 per cent of mergers and 66 per cent of the assets involved occurred 'within the same classification of industries', that is, were not conglomerate but were usually dispersed in location. This type of 'horizontal' merger is the more likely to profit from economies of scale in production and marketing.

Thus location, integration and motives of rulers are interrelated. As shown later (Chapter V), some companies appear to be management controlled. Plausibly, growth with consequent prestige mainly actuates the management-ruled; but profit maximization, possibly based on monopoly power mainly actuates the shareholder-ruled companies.

Comprehensive tabulation of the actual pattern of the location of all British and American manufacturing industries, as in Table IIc, shows many of them to be dispersed with small plants prevailing. The logic here is that the transport of product to the scattered consumer outweighs in cost the economies of large-plant production. But the converse is not shown from the tables; the industries most highly localized, and usually localized at some distance from raw materials, are not particularly the industries with the largest plants but often are industries with medium or even small plants. To outweigh the cost of transport from materials as well as to consumers it is not apparently necessary to obtain the internal economies of a large plant; localization of many small or medium plants, carrying external economies, can act as a substitute. The medium and small plants in these localizations often specialize in linked industries, thus showing plant disintegration but local integration. Most of these localized integrations are economically logical but may involve narrow specialization locally in industries

---

[1] Hearings before the U.S. Senate Subcommittee on Anti-trust and Monopoly, 1969, Part 8A, pp. 100–1.

[2] *Management and Merger Activity*, Guthstead, Liverpool, 1970.

[3] The 40 largest in terms of assets showed nearly a 200 per cent growth.

subject to unemployment risk and not occupying women. If specializations in several types of industry are added, risk declines but the area is liable to become a conurbation or megalopolis.

§ 6. AGREEMENT AND DIVERGENCE OF LOGIC AND FACT. MANUFACTURING AND OTHER SECTORS

Enough has been said to show the discrepancies between the logical theory of efficiency and the actual facts of industry. If we adopted the attitude of the engineer the facts might undoubtedly be brought closer to logic on the physical plane. The president of the engineering section of the British Association in 1932 considered that the engineering mind 'involves a certain faith in the obtaining of good by logical procedure to that end. This quality of logicality is partly inherited, but only brought to full efficiency by being trained and spurred to overcome difficulties successfully.'[1] Suppose a man with such an engineering mind to be given the powers of full dictatorship to re-organize American and British industry, or for that matter the industry of any country. Undoubtedly he would insist upon larger-scale production, and he would be supported by the theories we have advanced, though before sweeping away all the small-scale transactions and organizations of his country he would be wise to enquire how the existence of these apparently illogical scales can be explained. In this chapter the theory or working hypothesis was advanced that seemed justified by the economist's law (and certain observed data) of increasing return. Other things equal it was supposed that the larger the scale of production, the lower the costs per unit and the greater the return. Structure organized toward this end of larger-scale production was therefore provisionally labelled logical.

The scale of production refers primarily, as in most classical statements of the economist's law, to the quantity made of a given commodity however many producers make it, in however many factories, in however many places. But to reach minimum costs and maximum returns and efficiency, there is a logical basis for planning large-scale lines of production by large firms in large factories or at least by large localized production centres. The economy of firms, factories or centres making any commodity on a large scale implies specialization and standardization. But we found the existence of certain distributive and 'risk' factors in nature and human nature to condition, by a practical economic logic, some local dispersion, and some integration, the opposite of specialization. A survey of the existing facts showed a wide variation even within single industries, for instance, in size of plant. Nearly all industries had some, and many industries

[1] See Florence, 1933, p. 42.

E   111

had a prevailing proportion of, small scales of production, small plant and firms, scattered location and wide integration. The question then comes, does a practical economic logic admit of these departures from the original working hypotheses based on physical efficiency. The answers given have been partly yes, partly no. Yes, if however logical the producer, whether a manufacturer or not, he must deviate from large-scale industry in order to cope with the illogic of consumers or other producers. No, if the producer himself appears to be the source of illogic.

A manufacturer is not working in a vacuum and must often depart from logical large-scale principles by reason of physical nature, including human physique and physiology and of human nature, particularly when collecting his material and distributing his products.

Physical nature was shown directly to affect the location of industry; and lies behind many of the uncertainties and fluctuations against which small-scale production and integration was undertaken. The size of markets or of sources of supply of manufacturers may be physically restricted for reasons of dispersion and cost of transport and for reasons of variation and discontinuity.

Low transportability of *product* applies to baking, or printing, where transport of product is difficult either because of the sheer bulk and weight, or because physical deterioration sets in early, or, as in the case of 'job' printing, because of the number of times the job has to pass backwards and forwards between producer and consumer before both are satisfied. Hence where the population that requires these products is physically scattered, production must also be scattered in many small plants. *Materials* that are difficult to transport and are scattered geographically in small quantities are important in the brickmaking industry, using heavy clay deposits, and in the repairing (and laundering) of scattered property. Hence bricks and repairs cannot for physical reasons be produced in a few places on the scale that would be most efficient.

People vary in their physical needs, they vary in the sizes and shapes of their feet, heads and bodies. Hence shoes, hats and clothing cannot be produced in enormous quantities to meet *one* uniform type of demand. Soil and mines vary physically in the quality of their supplies. Hence to that extent the working up of these raw materials into products cannot be achieved on a large scale. And not only is there variation in materials and need at any one time, there is also variation from time to time. Physical needs are different in summer and winter, in hot and cold climates. Different materials are harvested at different times or are accessible at different times. This instability makes continuous mass-production logically impossible.

Departures from theory on account of *human nature* (especially the producers') and human institutions (especially those in which the producer himself partakes) are not so lightly to be considered logical. When all physical reasons for small-scale production and organization have been taken into account, there still remains a wide area where large-scale production and organization is technically possible in manufacture but is not in fact adopted. Physical restrictions apply indeed to plants rather than to firms. For a wider explanation we must turn to historical, psychological and sociological factors in the behaviour of the human consumers and producers. In this sense the facts are illogical. The engineer in his logic, based purely on physical and technical considerations, would not take account of them in trying to obtain maximum efficiency. He would assume complete adaptability in human nature to the conditions of production he imposes. Or, short of that, he would force human beings into accepting the more efficient production. He might be prepared not only to plan production, but to plan consumption. This is apparently the policy of the engineer already quoted.

There is a waste of heat in domestic fires, waste of by-products in the consumption of coal, thereby producing dirt; waste of fresh air by pollution; waste of sunshine. . . .
    If engineers were in control, they would so order matters as to neutralize this waste at the source. . . . People should be prohibited by law from burning soft coal, as they are in Paris. They would then be compelled to burn carbon in a bright cheerful fire making no smoke, or to use gas.[1]

If, however, the consumer is to be left free to demand the products he wants, however wasteful and inefficient their use and production, then the historical, psychological, sociological conditions supervene which only the social sciences can try to comprehend.

    The present structure of production has its roots in history. Many of the small plants that exist at any one time have survived from days when small plants were necessitated by the restrictions of markets and sources of supply due to less efficient conditions of transport, communication, and technique generally. Logically under modern conditions the larger organization should immediately outdo the presumably less efficient smaller organization; but in fact there is a lag, owing to the stickiness or 'friction' of the market, i.e. the slow adaptation of the consumer, and owing, on the production side, to the difficulties in the rapid growth of organizations.[2]

    The dead hand of past technical conditions is not the only source of illogical industrial organization. Industrial organization consists of

[1] Florence, 1933, p. 46. A Clean Air Act was passed in Britain, 1956, prohibiting smoky fuels in certain areas. Householders' conversion of open fireplaces is subsidized.
[2] See Edith Penrose, *Theory of the Growth of the Firm*, passim.

human producers and its purpose is to provide human consumers with goods and services on a large scale at the minimum cost. The human beings who are the producers and consumers may not permit this. As producers they may resist the necessary specialization, adjustment and re-organization, especially redundancy; as consumers they may resist standardization and scientific fuel or apparatus and, by the variability of their demands, introduce uncertainty and small-scale buying, even though economic inefficiency and loss or waste of income result. This behaviour may be due to sheer stupidity or inertia or else to a preference for other values above the economic. We know statistically from intelligence quotients (as well as by personal experience) how widely human beings vary in their intelligence or at least their mental alertness. Though bearing this in mind, we shall concentrate rather on difference in the value preferences and attitudes of consumers and (in Chapter VII) producers.

The manufacturing industries hitherto kept in the centre of the picture are probably more free from nature and human nature than either the extractive industry rooted to the land or the distributive and service industries tied to the consumers' whims and habitat. In spite of that, the British and American extractor or distributor or servicer makes

TABLE IIF

MANUFACTURING AND OTHER SECTORS OF INDUSTRY RANKED BY A ROUGH
MEASURE OF SIZE-OF-FIRM

| Order of industry | U.S.A., 1940 census* | | | U.K., 1951 census* |
	Rank (1)	Ratio of employees to manager or proprietor (2)	(3)	Rank (4)
Mining (coal)	1st	65·0	98	3rd
Railways	2nd	34·0	100	1st
Manufacturing	3rd	21·8	19	4th
Public utilities	4th	16·2	99(a)	2nd
Road haulage	5th	13·2	5	7th
Services(b)	6th	5·9	3	8th
Finance	7th	5·0	16	5th
Construction	8th	4·7(c)	15	6th
Trade	9th	2·3	2½	9th
Agriculture	10th	0·6	2	10th

* U.S. statistical abstract: e.g. 1950, p. 184 (not repeated in later abstracts); U.K. census of population.

(a) Gas works form a much higher proportion of utilities than in America.

(b) Excluding public administration and education; and private domestic and professional where there are no proprietors or managers.

(c) Census of construction, 1939: Ratio to active proprietor and firm members including self employed.

a valiant effort toward the logic of large-scale operation and organization. Because of nature he fails to achieve large-scale organization in
agriculture, and because of human nature, disposed to living in small
scattered family homes, he fails to achieve it in much house-building and
retailing trade and servicing. But he has achieved large plants in mining
(partly because of nature's concentrated, localized mineral deposits) and
in the wholesaling, supermarket and department stores section of
distribution, and large firms in some sections of building and road
service and in chain-store retailing (where bulk-buying looms large),
banking (especially in Britain), and insurance. Though to collect
savings from scattered homes bank branches must be scattered and
small, the principle of massed reserves is powerful in building up large
firms. Table IIF presents the evidence on size of firms both for Britain
and America. The ratio of employees to proprietor or manager is the
measure common to all industries (manufacturing or not) nearest to
indicating the size of firm. The two countries have, however, different
definitions of proprietors and managers and too much weight must not
be placed on the precise differences in ratios for the same order of industry. What is significant is the rough similarity in size-of-firm ranking
among the orders of industries within each country. What differences
there are in ranking are mainly due to a difference in laws. Britain allows
large-scale banking and even before their nationalization (e.g. in 1921)
encouraged large-scale amalgamation of railways. In both countries the
ratio is larger than that for manufactures in mines and railways,
indicating a larger unit of government. Nature makes for large size
in mines (especially coal mines), by concentration of deposits, but
large organization in railways is associated with intensive investment
of man-made capital. In both countries nature keeps agriculture
organized to a small-scale by the scatter and extension of cultivation
entailed. The small firms in the service industries—in trade and in
road haulage—are associated with a scatter of the population served
and the consequent scatter of the workers occupied in these orders of
industry. The small firms in building are associated not only with
specialization by independent outsiders (see § 3) but with the industry's
intransportability of product for a scattered demand, and the large
proportion of repair service on existing scattered building. The British
government's working party on building found that in 1949, 86·5 per
cent of the operatives in small firms employing under six workers were
on repairs, maintenance and conversion of houses, but only 11·9 per
cent of the operatives of the largest firms employing over 5,000. This
percentage fell continuously between these two extremes of size of firm[1]
showing a high negative correlation between size of firm and proportion

[1] H.M.S.O., Report 1950, p. 5.

Size of building firm: number of employees	1–5 (1)	6–19 (2)	20–99 (3)	100– 499 (4)	500– 99 (5)	1,000– 4,999 (6)	5,000 and over (7)
Percentage of operatives on repairs, maintenance and conversion	86·5	71·5	53·8	37·6	27·2	21·8	11·9

of its operatives on repair, rather than new construction. The relative dispersion of operations in these small-firm personal and property-service industries was measured in the following low coefficients of localization —extremely low when compared with the coefficients of manufacturing industries listed in Table IF.

Coefficients of localization	Britain[1]	America[2]
Building	·12	·065
Road haulage	·07	·09[3]
Trade	·06 ⎱	·086[4]
Banks, finance, insurance	·19 ⎰	

[1] Based on Appendix Table I, P.E.P. report on Industrial Location, 1939.
[2] N.R.P.B., 1943, Industrial Location and National Resources, p. 66.
[3] All transport and communication.
[4] Combined under trade.

In both countries, in short, large-scale organization is strongly determined in all sectors of industries, as in manufacturing, by the pattern of location and the 'hard' physical and distributive factors indicated at the very outset of our enquiry.

§ 7. SUMMARY: THE ERGOLOGICAL SEQUENCE

At this point it will be useful to review the facts assembled so far, and to sum up as a probable hypothesis the sort of logic to which the facts seem to conform generally and not merely in the manufacturing sector.

In the first edition of this book I made several references to the characteristics distinguishing each sector of a country's economic activity. These have all been retained in the present edition with explanatory text.

(1) On page 8 the existence or not of materials used in work and their degree of transportability is cited as a main distinction between the different sectors of economic activity.

(2) The Table IB (page 10) the linkage is analysed between sectors (and industries) and in particular the different stages in the web of links in production and distribution occupied by the different sectors and industries. The earlier stages are usually extractive, the later an assembly and servicing type of work.

(3) On page 44 transportability and other physical characters such as durability, homogeneity and divisibility are set out, together with

technological and distributive factors as ultimately 'determining structure and organization'.

(4) In Table Iн and IIе (pages 34 and 99) the different sectors are distinguished by location pattern and by size of firm in America and Britain—part of their structure and organization.

Thus the ergological thesis (derived from the Greek *ergon*, work) is developed that the characteristic of the work distinguished in (1), (2) and (3) determined the forms of social structure such as are measured in (4). Type of work includes the supply of materials and resources that are used whether transportable, uniform, durable, etc., and the demands of the market that are met. The word technical used in my first edition, though it might cover materials as well as technological methods of production, fails to indicate that conditions of the market are included. Yet the nature of the materials and of the market is often fundamental. The development of technology such as the extent to which mechanization can proceed depends, for instance, on whether materials are uniform or whether the demand is of mass market type and stable; and if it is a consumer's, not a producer's, demand, whether it is a 'speciality' or convenience goods.[1]

In a recent representation of the family tree of descendants of scientific invention as on page 87 I have in fact added high in the diagram further ancestors—weight and uniformity of materials and products—for the application of scientific invention is conditional on this uniformity,[2] and the overcoming of weight by mechanized transport.

Realistic analysis of economic structure and government, to quote the subtitle of this book, thus looks for logic ultimately to the hinterland of supply and demand, materials and markets.[3] This hinterland conditions the 'background' degree and direction of technology such as mechanization and automation, the technology conditions social structure such as the size, location and integration of plants and firms, the structure in turn conditions the extent of various forms of government, such as incorporation measured in Table Vа (p. 207) for the various sectors. Different types of government may well behave differently and have different characteristic policies so that a final level may be added. These policies may affect any of the earlier levels. The policy might aim to broaden the type of work by, say, diversification, to change technical methods by more ploughing back of profits, to

[1] See Heflebower, 'Toward a Theory of Industrial Markets and Prices', in *American Economic Review*, Vol. XLIV, pp. 121–39.

[2] See Florence, *Economics and Sociology of Industry*, 1969.

[3] In Fig. 10 of Florence, *Atlas of Economic Structure and Policies*, 1970, I picture a perspective of this systematic study.

relocate or to increase the number, or size of plants or firms by merger. The sequence has indeed a feedback element.[1]

The sequence from type of work to form of government and policy may be illustrated from professional services, as of lawyers, consultants or private medical practice in the service sector, and from vehicle making in the manufacturing sector. Policy and behaviour is not determined only by the single preceding level, i.e. the form of government, but by all the levels. This indeed is the point of 'ergo-' in 'ergological'. The type of work placed in the top level, its markets and materials, demand and supply is always influential.

TABLE IIG

ILLUSTRATION OF THE ERGOLOGICAL SEQUENCE

Type of work	Vehicle manufacture (Assembly stage)*	Medical practitioners (in U.S.A.), consultants and other professions (e.g. lawyers)
Market demand	Mass consumer and producer	Producer and consumer
Materials supplied	Uniform semi-manufactures	None
Technology (Scientific invention)	Capital intensive (Mechanized)	Little fixed capital
Location pattern	Concentrated	Dispersed over regions but localized in towns and cities
Prevailing size of plant organization firm	Large Very large, mammoth	Small Small
Prevailing form of government	(U.K.) joint stock company (U.S.) corporation	Entrepreneur or partnership (Owner-manager)
Policies of the organization's government	?Prices enough to deter competition ?Merger into larger firm New designs and advertising	Charge what traffic will bear In U.K., no advertising

* See below, Table IIH.

The route whereby scientific invention has led technologically to mechanized industries and transport, structurally to a localized pattern and large size of plants, was charted in Table IID and represents the sequence found in vehicle making. Professional services with a 'personal

[1] See Table III in Florence, *Economics and Sociology of Industry*, 1969.

contact' market and little mechanization, represents a different case with different structural consequences.

The association of events at the different levels is much the same in Britain and America, and the agreement which appears in Tables Ic, IG and IH between the horse-power per worker and the size of plants and firms, and the location pattern of the corresponding industries in Britain and America, is strong evidence of the ergological influence of the type of work upon industrial organization in spite of national differences.

This book deals primarily with the industries within the manufacturing sector and though the difference in the nature of the work of the different sectors is greater, the same sort of analysis can, has been and will be applied. Table IB, as already said, places several manufacturing industries as well as whole sectors in their stage of production: Table IL (p. 47) illustrates the varying location patterns of manufactures by examples from different manufacturing industries. Indeed, many manufactures resemble certain non-manufacturing sectors in their characteristics. Baking and printing resemble retailing and services in their dispersed location alongside their consumer markets, brickmaking and iron and steel resemble mining in their dispersion (or concentration) near the extraction of the raw material. We may thus speak of extractive-type manufactures and service-type manufacture such as repair of buildings and other 'property services'. Unless large enough to develop their own external and internal economies, early stage manufactures tend to be of extractive type located near source of supply, 'material oriented'; later stage manufactures to be of service type, market oriented, near the source of demand.

Though differing less than between whole sectors, many of the work and structural characters of the manufacturing industries within the manufacturing sector show statistically measured differences that are considerable.

In the appendix to the first edition (1964) of *Economics and Sociology of Industry* I listed the half dozen to a dozen separate British industries that were at the extremes of such measurable characters as linkage with extractive industries, capital intensity, degree of localization, growth and fluctuation in employment, ratio of staff to operatives, size of plants and firms and their diversification, extent of incorporation, mergers and monopolistic concentration, often known as market structure. In the appendix to my second edition (1969) I was able to be more comprehensive, thanks to the bracketing of all American manufactures into a score of fairly distinctive major groups. These groups I ranked in respect of much the same measured characteristics as the British individual industries and, to give the complete range of variation, the lowest and highest measures (ranked 1st and 20th respectively) were stated. Even within the nine assembly-type industry groups Table IIH shows how wide is the range of variation.

TABLE IIH

A SYNDROME RANKING (SMALLEST FIRST) AMONG ALL NINE ASSEMBLY-TYPE U.S.
MAJOR INDUSTRY GROUPS IN RESPECT OF FIVE MEASURABLE CHARACTERISTICS

Code	Name of group	Horse-power per worker (1)	Size of plant (a) (2)	Size of firm (b) (3)	Concen-tration ratio (c) (4)	Extent of merger (d) (5)
23	Apparel	1	1	1	1	1
25	Furniture	5	4	3	2	4
27	Printing	3	5	4	3	5
31	Leather (mainly shoes)	2	2	5	5	2
35	Machinery	8	6	6	6	6
36	Electrical machinery	7	8	8	8	8
37	Transport equipment vehicles	9	9	9	9	9
38	Instruments	4	7	7	7	7
39	Miscellaneous (e)	6	3	2	4	3
Range of character from 1st		0·22	9%	8%	13·4%	6·3%
1st to 9th rank 9th		9·60	84%	81%	61·3%	34·0%

(a) % in plants employing 500 or over.
(b) % in firms employing 2,500 or more.
(c) Percentage of total shipments by the four largest firms.
(d) Percentage of employees in mergering firms 1959–62.
(e) The largest are jewellery, costume jewellery, musical instruments, games and toys, signs and advertising displays.

Associations were found between the measured characteristics at the different levels. Thus nine American major industry groups classified as engaged in assembly work were, at the level of technology, ranked according to the measure of intensity of capital provided by the U.S. census of manufactures' horse-power capacity per production worker. Comparing their work and technology ranking in column 1 with the nine industry groups' size-of-plant ranking in column 2, the Spearman 'foot-rule' coefficient of correlation[1] is as high as 0·769.

This enquiry into the statistical association of an industry's particular type of work and technology with its prevailing size-of-plant can be carried further and associated with its prevalent size-of-firm, with the concentration of output in its largest firms, who might thus govern an industry *oligopolistically* (to be discussed in Chapter III) and even with its policies of *merger*, of particular interest to economists today. Among industry groups with assembly type of work Table IIH can

[1] $r = 1 - \dfrac{6\Sigma d^2}{N(N^2-1)}$ where d^2 is the sum of the squares of the deviations of one set of ranks from the other. N is, in this case 9.

indeed provide rank correlation coefficients with the horse-power per worker (in column 1) as high as 0·65 for size of firm (in column 3); 0·70 for concentration (in column 4); 0·77 for a policy of mergers (in column 5).

A *prima facie* case is suggested for the association of these characters at the different levels illustrated in Table IIG; and even for a policy of merger. The form of government of institutions influences, in turn, business behaviour and policies, and it is policies rather than forms of government in which economists are mainly interested, when studying the provision and exchange of goods and services. Thus our analysis proceeds from the economic facts of demand and supply, markets and materials, needs and resources to the economic policies involving the *amount* of goods and services to be provided and exchanged at a price. But the mere existence of needs and resources does not determine economic policy directly and automatically. Their influence can only make itself felt through technology, social structures of varying size, scope and site, and forms of government. Thus human instincts, sentiments, complexes, habits and customs must be taken into account if our study is to be something more than mere algebraic formula with the human factor as X. The following chapters will attempt to evaluate the human forces that make for illogical relations with the consumer and inefficient organization of producers; but they will also attempt to show how such forces can be harnessed and stimulated to increase industrial efficiency and to bring actual organization somewhat nearer to a logical plan.

CHAPTER III

THE RELATIONS OF INDUSTRY
AND CONSUMER

§ 1. PLANNED AND FREE CONSUMPTION. THE COSTS OF DISTRIBUTION.

EFFICIENCY, as defined in Chapter I, may be measured on any one of three levels—the physical, the pecuniary or economic, and the psycho-physiological. Hitherto we have considered mainly the physical level. The physical volume of output per man-hour or machine-hour worked was held to be increased by large-scale production and operation. But as soon as relations with the consumer are considered, there comes the question whether the physical output turned out is needed or wanted and demanded. Engineers have told us that, if left alone as technocrats to run the economic machine, they could produce things in much greater quantities per man or machine, and that they are baulked in doing so by the middleman distributor. This may well be true; but suppose the consumer does not demand, or want, or need, those 'things', what then? The physical things will merely pile up in warehouses to rust and rot, and in the end it will be worse from the standpoint of efficiency than if they had never been made. Room will be taken up and when rot has gone far enough decay will spread throughout the land. It is ultimately not the middleman or the economist who prevents the engineer's dream from fulfilment, but the demand, wants and needs of the consumer.

In recent years the importance of the distinction between producers' (or capital) goods and consumers' goods has been stressed by economists. Among consumers' goods and services the distinction between those meeting demands, wants and needs respectively is equally vital to an understanding of the whole (and not just the economic) situation, and I shall repeatedly make the distinction as I have in the past.[1] Briefly, a *demand* is a want for which the consumer is prepared to pay a price, a *want* is any thing or service the consumer desires or seeks, and a *need* is any thing or service the consumer *ought* to have to keep alive and healthy or to keep efficient or simply because somebody (not necessarily himself) thinks he ought to have it. Thus while demand is an economic conception, want is psychological, and need, partly at least, ethical. And before the engineer and technocrat sets about putting the world right, he must be clear whether he is going (1) merely

---

[1] E.g. Florence, *Uplift in Economics*, § 6. American edition, *Sociology and Sin*.

to supply things and services the consumer wants and is prepared to pay for, i.e. demands; or (2) to supply things and services the consumer wants but can't always pay for; or (3) to supply things and services he (the engineer, or some other authority) thinks the consumer ought to have.

All of these three ultimate policies are feasible and have already to some extent been tried by different communities. The policy of supplying demands is the general tendency in capitalist countries but exceptions occur when houses are subsidized out of taxation, or education and the use of roads allowed gratis entirely from taxation.[1]

A pattern of consumption planned by the producers would enormously simplify the organization of production. There would be fewer problems in distribution; so much of a series of articles is planned to be consumed and just so much is produced, and put on the consumer's doorstep. Precisely those articles which can be produced economically in large quantities can be planned to be consumed. This producers' dream was, broadly speaking, adopted by Soviet communism; but whether the whole quantity produced was wanted by the consumer and sold was another question.

Convenient as this planning of consumption is to the engineer and producer, the fact must be faced that Western European and American communities will not permit their consumption to be planned by some supreme economic authority—they would call it a dictatorship. They do not 'want' the goods or services that any all-highest authority would consider they 'needed'. Though moving toward equal distribution of income by progressive taxation and other devices, they do not even seem to contemplate such complete equality of incomes as would ensure every consumer equal preference in satisfying his 'wants'. We must therefore abandon the immediate possibility of production for needs or wants only, and must concentrate on the problems of a continued production for the 'demand' of private consumers with different incomes.

The consumer thus left free to obtain whatever goods and services his income permits, immediately creates difficulties. He or she persists in demanding things in small lots, thus preventing the economies of bulk-transactions. This habit of petty purchasing is chiefly due to the institution of the family household and the space wanted for living requirements. Goods are purchased by the housewife for the consumption of small scattered groups usually of two to five persons and seldom more than seven or eight. Hence sales are retail, on a small scale, and have to be distributed on a small scale. And since the housewife has usually little reserve cash and is not selected primarily for her buying

---

[1] See below, Chapter VI, § 1.

efficiency, there is a hand-to-mouth buying and much 'human' feckless-ness, caprice and lack of efficient calculation. This, and the pleasure many housewives find in gossiping with the shopkeepers, may, and does, keep going many an inefficient hole-and-corner shop, perhaps a 'Ma and Pa joint', willing to extend credit—and chit-chat[1]—but charging a necessarily high price to cover unnecessarily slow turnover and high retailing costs per unit of sales. If purchases were made in bulk as for the army, for restaurants and for factory canteens the retailer, and possibly the wholesaler as well, might be eliminated.

Given the institutions that are part of the way of life of Western civilization, we must therefore add to the costs of actual production heavy costs for the distribution of products among individuals in small scattered families. If delivery-wagons are expected to take a loaf of fresh bread or a pound of coffee or some small toy miles away to a single house, the wages of the driver and the errand boy, not to mention the fuel and wear and tear of the vehicle, must be included in the cost of distribution. Long journeys may be (and are) avoided by distributing the shops themselves widely over the area of population; but in that case the scale of organization and operation will be small and probably expensive. The most logical solution would be so to group orders in time and place that *large-scale deliveries* from a large central store could be made systematically door by door for every door, road by road, in a whole neighbourhood like a postman's round. Possibly, if the community were keen enough to reduce the costs of distribution which they so loudly criticize, some compulsory regulation of buying habits to ensure such concentration of delivery might be agreed upon. But for the present we must assume free purchasing habits side by side with free consumption, and shall try to disentangle the logic and the illogic of distribution to consumers under such circumstances.

As things are, the gross margin exacted by the distributor certainly appears high. A 'classical investigation' in America[2] showed that in standard lines such as groceries, where the distribution margins are lowest, 20 per cent of the final price may go to the retailer and 9 per cent to the wholesaler, in addition to 12 per cent for the producer's own marketing cost. Thus total distributive charges were 41 per cent, cost of actual production charges 59 per cent of the price to the final consumer. And grocers appear comparatively moderate in their charges. In the shoe trade the retail margin alone was about 30 per cent, in stationery 35 per cent, and in jewellery 40 per cent; in dry goods and also drugs the

[1] 'The independent shopkeeper . . . adds to the pleasure of life for people who do not regard shopping as a disagreeable necessity, but who, when they have time for it, regard it as a pleasant way of spending time'—Dr. Dalton in the House of Commons, as President of the Board of Trade, Hansard, 23 July 1942.

[2] See McNair, *Economic Journal*, December 1930.

wholesale margin alone was about 17 per cent. When transport is added to wholesale and retail trading, the cost of distribution was estimated as almost 59 per cent of the retail price of all goods sold in 1929 to the American final buyer.[1]

A yet more detailed classic of distribution cost was an analysis of British experience in 1938 by Jefferys. For groceries 20 per cent of the final price was found to go to the retailer, 3 per cent to the wholesaler, 8 per cent for the producer's own marketing cost. Though the British wholesaler and producer apparently each took less, the retailer took the same percentage as the American. As in America, other less standard lines showed higher distributive cost than groceries. The shoe retailer took 29·5 per cent, the stationer 40 per cent, the jeweller 41 per cent.[2] For all consumer's commodities the producer's, wholesaler's and retailer's distribution costs, or gross margins, were respectively 5–6 per cent, 4–5 per cent and 26–8 per cent of consumer's expenditure. The varying costs for the different stages in distribution, indeed the very existence or non-existence of these stages, are not arbitrary. Retailers, for instance, are usually non-existent for producers' goods, there are none in iron and steel, ship-building or cotton-spinning; but they are thick on the ground in consumers' goods such as clothing, food products and tobacco. The precise structure of distribution of the various manu-factured goods is now measurable in the British census of production for certain years. The census for 1951, for instance, gives in its Table 6 an analysis of the 1948 sales of each of the 135 manufacturing industries then distinguished and in my *Atlas of Economic Structure and Policies*, 1970, Fig. 23, I have presented some of the contrasting patterns graphic-ally. The contrasts are certainly striking and in explaining them I pointed to certain distinctive features of the work entailed.

Patterns of distribution channels will be set by answers to such questions as how far the goods of varying design require lengthy inspection by the pros-pective consumer; how far they are fairly homogeneous and uniform; whether the market is the final household consumer, or another stage in manufacturing. Beer does not require the lengthy inspection by consumers required in choosing between the great variety of motor-car models. It is, accordingly, transported straight from brewery to the retailing (and serving) public houses. On the other hand, motor-car manufacturers make use of *wholesalers* and retailers to display their goods. They had no retail outlets of their own and sold 44·8 per cent of their product to independent wholesalers (much of it exported) and 28·0 per cent to the industrial consumer.

Tailoring and dress-making is at the other extreme to brewing in requiring display of a variety of designs for the consumer's inspection. . . . This industry relies for distribution to the extent of 32·6 per cent on independent whole-

[1] 'Does Distribution Cost Too Much', 20th Century Fund, 1939, pp. 117ff.
[2] *The Distribution of Consumer Goods*, 1950, p. 69.

salers, 39·3 per cent on independent retailers, 9·5 per cent on their own wholesale department and 10·6 per cent on their own retail branches. The rubber industry illustrates a structure of distribution channels catering both for the final consumer through wholesalers, and also for a further stage in manufacturing providing tyres for assembling the completed car or cycle. While 34·1 per cent of their products go to rubber manufacturers' own wholesale branches and 34·2 per cent to independent wholesalers, and 24·4 per cent go to other productive underakings.

In cotton spinning by far the highest percentage goes direct for consumption in other industries particularly, of course, by transference to cotton weavers.

Much the same contrasts are found in the distribution patterns of the American industries, and this correspondence is further evidence for an ergological interpretation in the nature of the work. The 1929 U.S. census of distribution, indeed, published an illuminating set of charts for fifty-six manufacturing industries, and a summary for all manufacturers, in a report on the distribution of sales of manufacturing plants.[1] As in Britain the clothing industries had a high percentage of their sales distributed directly from factory to retailer (for men's clothing 63·0 per cent, for women's 83·1 per cent of all sales), motor-cars had high sales to wholesalers and retailers (33·2 per cent and 38·2 per cent), cotton goods had high sales to other industries, and 'converters' and the rubber industry had high sales both to wholesalers and other industries (i.e. for consumers' replacement and for the original motor vehicle assembly).

The two most surprising findings perhaps were the similarity of the British and American distribution cost-structure for the same types of product (illustrating again the pre-eminence of technical or ergological over national factors); and, for some types, the high cost of distribution defrayed by the producer himself. British makers of electrical goods spent 13 per cent of the final retail price in distribution; American baking corporations spent 24·07 per cent and 3·03 per cent of the value of their sales for selling and advertising, and a sample of corporations making perfume and cosmetics 10·01 per cent and 20·65 per cent.[2]

These margins were by no means, however, all middlemen's profit. When analysed it was found that about half the retail margins and two-fifths of the wholesale margins went in wages and salaries to employees, and much of the remainder in rent, interest, heat and light, maintenance, insurance, and advertisement. Where salaried managers control

---

[1] An 'Analysis of the Distribution of Manufacturing Sales' was also given in the 1958 census of manufactures, but omitted the clothing group of industries and all charts.

[2] Federal Trade Commission Industrial Corporation Reports, quoted by Duddy and Revzan, *Marketing*, 1947, p. 620.

the business the actual dividend to the shareholder owners often appeared indeed as a mere one or two per cent on sales. The popular clamour against distributive charges is thus often misdirected. It is not the net margin that accrues after costs are subtracted from gross margin that is excessive and capable of reduction, but the costs themselves. Are there too many people engaged in distribution?

From Table IA it appears that in the last 25 to 30 years the proportion of total occupied persons who are engaged in distribution has fallen slightly in Britain and risen slightly in the U.S. The difference between the two countries is due partly to the aftermath of the Second World War when Britain rationed and cut down drastically in consumer goods and has had to make more goods for export. The significant ratio of *distributors* to farm, mine and factory *producers* changed in England and Wales between 1931 and 1961 from $\dfrac{14\cdot4}{6\cdot0+5\cdot9+32\cdot1}$ to $\dfrac{13\cdot6}{3\cdot6+3\cdot0+36\cdot8}$ i.e. from 32·0 per cent to 31·1 per cent, in the U.S.A. from $\dfrac{14\cdot3}{18\cdot8+2\cdot0+23\cdot4}$ to $\dfrac{15\cdot1}{7\cdot0+1\cdot0+27\cdot7}$ i.e. from 32·3 per cent to 42·0 per cent.

The particularly high proportion of the U.S. occupied population devoted to commerce, as well as services is noted by Bain[1] and attributed to the 'substantially higher per capita income of the United States and the much greater productivity of labour in agriculture'. Higher productivity of American labour in mining and manufacture thanks to greater mechanization may well be added. Selling the larger product requires more distributors, since mechanization is only slightly applicable. Social structure and deployment thus depend upon technology, and technology in turn upon the type of work involved. It is the U.S.A. rather than England that is now the 'nation of shop-keepers'.

The criticisms popularly levelled against the middleman have permeated technological circles and the president of the engineering section of the British Association for 1932 is found referring to the middleman (together with the economist!) as 'that curse of civilization'. This criticism mainly attacks the number of retailers at the final stage in direct contact with the public. Another point of attack is the number of stages that goods must pass through before they reach the public. Indeed the word middleman is often confined to the jobber, agent or wholesaler who is seen to stand between—in the middle of—producer and retailer. Now the number of such stages is a direct consequence of the small scale on which either production or retailing, or both, is organized. Somewhere in the process of production and distribution, efficiency seems to demand large-scale organization. If in any one line

[1] *International Differences in Industrial Structure*, 1966.

of goods and any marketing area there are a hundred small producers and a thousand small retailers there may, of mathematical necessity, be a hundred multiplied by a thousand contacts between them. Salesmen, orders, deliveries, invoices, bills, receipts will be thus multiplied a hundred thousandfold. But let three large wholesale firms intervene in the middle and the possible contacts will be reduced to three hundred between producers and wholesalers plus three thousand between wholesalers and retailers, a total of three thousand three hundred, instead of a hundred thousand. This difference can be well understood by reference to the telephone network. If a thousand individual subscribers were directly connected with every other in a district with a thousand subscribers, the necessary lines to bring them all in contact would be $999+998+997+\ldots$; but introduce one large telephone exchange or centre and the necessary lines are reduced to one thousand connecting that exchange with each subscriber. Thus in a world of small-scale individual firms *indirect* sale through wholesalers is necessitated by the comparative economy of a large-scale 'wholesale' junction or exchange, interposed in the process of piecemeal distribution.

High distributive costs remain, even under co-operative trading and direct sale by integration of distribution with production; they are largely due to the great number of assistants employed only slightly cut down by supermarket methods, the large stocks held, the roomy and central sites required for display, and the real costs involved if the consumer expects to be served attentively at frequent intervals in small lots of wide variety neatly packed and delivered over great distances. This extravagant expectation may have been raised by competition in service rather than price. It is one of the drawbacks of the high-pressure salesmanship and the competing designs described later (§ 5) among rival producers and distributors.

§ 2. THE LOGIC AND ILLOGIC OF FREE CONSUMPTION

The private consumer, free to purchase according to his individual demand, however costly his methods of purchasing, might be assumed to demand goods and services with a certain substratum of logic that would help the more logical producer in his struggle for standardization and efficient large-scale production.

In the first place, every consumer's demand will be based, partly at least, on the bare needs for keeping alive and must include essential foods, clothes, fuel and housing accommodation. These physical necessities will therefore be demanded on a large scale by the population as a whole.

Secondly, human nature is notoriously conventional. Plain gold wedding rings could be turned out by the hundred thousand with fair certainty of sale,[1] and in the recent past aspidistra, plaster figurines and lace curtains for front window display safely grown and manufactured for stock. Men's clothes are likewise preferred of uniform pattern. True, the vagaries of fashion dictate the clothes of women and alter styles from season to season. Nevertheless at any *one* moment fashion implies a great degree of uniformity and conformity. Fashion, as Nystrom[2] speculates, probably depends on a quite natural hunger for companionship and a human instinct to accept a common uniform leadership.

One of the most characteristic results of the desire for companionship, that is, to be with other people, is a tendency to be like the people we want to be with, in appearance, in ways of thinking, in methods of expression, in manners, in dress and in fashions. The desire for companionship leads to conformity, and the group once formed of people with common basic interests and similarities in turn demands conformities not only from its present members, but also from those who would join the group. . . .

Groups are tyrannical. To conform is the easiest way of getting along; to be different in thinking, in manners, in dress or other forms of expression is to invite the belief in others that one is queer.

A third characteristic of a market, however free, that might be expected to help in large-scale production is the great proportion of industry engaged in making 'producer's goods', machines and machine parts, equipment, tools, supplies, materials for further production. In America four-fifths of all manufactured products in terms of values go direct to industrial users (mostly for further processing or assembly) and nearly a third end up as finished producer's goods. Two consequences should logically follow.

(i) The final consumer's vagaries need not affect the intermediate product, for highly differentiated articles may be made for the final consumer from the same material by the same type of machine and of almost exactly similar parts differently arranged or finished.

(ii) Buying and selling methods and habits between men of business might be expected to be more logical than those practised where small individual families are represented, not by a professional, but merely by a typical specimen of humanity—the housewife.

These expectations of logical behaviour are not always fulfilled. Mr. Hoover, in his campaign to reduce variety,[3] found a lack of standardization and simplification among producer's as well as consumer's goods, and the producer is offered almost as many varieties of goods and services to choose from as the final consumer.

While the designs of producers' goods appear as various as those

[1] There are over four hundred thousand marriages per year in Britain, and over two million in the United States.
[2] *Economics of Fashion*, pp. 59, 60.
[3] See page 95 above.

of consumers' goods, the methods of handling and passing on these goods from producer to producer are often as petty and niggling as the methods of distribution to the final consumer. Goods are wanted by producers in a hurry, usually owing to lack of planning, and the producers making for these producers must spend a large part of their energy and time in 'chasing' goods through their works for early delivery. Odd, irregular lots are ordered at odd, irregular times, and congest the orderly flow of work through the plant. Finally, different producers even within one trade have entirely different methods of accounting and checking quality and vary in the reasonableness of their complaints. All these idiosyncrasies must be attended to and a 'complaint book' kept to sort the unreasonable from the reasonable. It was a maker of *producer's* goods who once complained to me that the 'consumer is always *un*reasonable'.

To sum up. A certain standardization of free consumption is logically indicated on the ground that certain forms of consumption must necessarily be preferred before others. The poorest class of final consumers have to restrict expenditure to physically necessary wants. The next poorest class of final consumers restricts expenditure in some degree to physical plus conventional necessaries. The producer-consumer is a buyer of standard parts, materials, and machines, though not to the extent that might be expected. This leaves the well-to-do final consumer as the main source of variability in consumption.

Generalizing from a great number of family budgets in the 1880's Engel formulated his law that families with the larger incomes spend a less proportion on food and other standard necessaries of life such as fuel and lighting. Since his time, repeated comparison of the budgets of families of different incomes in various countries have confirmed this law.

In my *Atlas of Economic Structure and Policies*, 1970, Fig. 65, I have compared the proportion of income spent on a wide variety of uses by British middle-class households with incomes of at least £40 per week, as against the proportion spent in the same year (1962) by all households. Engel's law is seen to follow through logically. At the higher incomes the proportion falls which is spent on the physical necessities of food, housing, fuel and light and (though only slightly) clothing, and on the 'conventional necessity' of tobacco. At the other end of the spectrum the proportions rise, with the higher incomes, on household durables, such as furniture, and also drink; and they rise greatly on services and saving. If savings and taxes are excluded, the proportions, based on consumption only, rise with higher income also on clothing and transport.[1]

Looking into a future with rising incomes, the pattern of spending

[1] A more detailed analysis of household consumption given by Tipping, *Applied Statistics*, Vol. 19, 1970, pp. 1–17, confirms and accentuates these differences. Here

by the majority of families could be forecast as approaching that of the richer class. On the other hand if deviations from the average standard of consumption become smaller—if net incomes after taxation should become more equal—wants will come nearer to primary or standard needs. There will be more families with lower middle incomes mainly devoted to food, clothing, housing and possibly some conventional necessaries, and fewer families with very high incomes most of which might be spent on any sort of want. In Britain fuller employment and the welfare state are certainly forces making for greater equality and with a high and progressive income tax, there are now fewer high net incomes. But there are opposing forces; where inheritance is permitted, the differential birth-rate tends to create more poor and fewer rich. Hence we must assume that variation and diversification in type of wants and demands will remain an important factor in free consumption. This contention may be contrary to the popular view that man in industrialized society is becoming daily more standardized, but it is strongly supported by Leonard Woolf.[1]

In the aristocratic societies of the past there were enormous differences between the classes, but it is doubtful whether within each class there was any more room for free development of individuality than there is today. . . . The lower classes were standardized by poverty, overwork, and ignorance. . . . There is certainly more scope for individuality and people are more highly individualized today than they have ever been in the world's history.

This individualization of man presents increasing difficulties to the producer. The consumer's variability, his lack either of uniformity and conformity with others or of stability through a period of time, his irrationality and lack of logic, involves uncertainty in the sale of the producer's product. F. H. Knight sums it up.

The lower wants of man, those having in the greatest degree the nature of necessities, are the most stable and predictable. The higher up the scale we go, the larger the proportion of the aesthetic element and of social suggestion there is involved in motivation, the greater becomes the uncertainty connected with foreseeing wants and satisfying them.[2]

§ 3. THE VAGARIES OF FREE PRODUCTION, DESIGN AND DISTRIBUTION
FOR FREE CONSUMPTION

The difficulty of coping with variability in consumption is greatly magnified wherever production proceeds in long and round-about

[1] *After the Deluge*, 1931, pp. 269–70.
[2] *Risk, Uncertainty and Profit*, 1921, p. 265.

the highest grade level of income is compared not just with the general level but with various other grades of incomes.

anticipation of demand, and wherever output is made for stock and the equipment and machinery for that output planned and tooled up in advance. If production were entirely to order, as in the case of bespoke tailoring, there would be no risk of financial loss on account of output not saleable. But if large-scale production is to take place, part of the output at least must be made ahead of orders, and the risk incurred of investing in capital that may become idle overhead.

The consumer is presented under the system of competition with all sorts of goods and services ready-made to choose from, but which of them will be chosen and sold is wrapt in uncertainty. The main, but uncertain, limit to large-scale production, unavoidable if the consumer's demands are to be catered for, is the law of diminishing utility. As production of any article or the provision of any one service is increased, the demand for additional units of it will diminish and the price which will permit the sale of the total amount produced or provided must fall. The precise percentage by which the price must be reduced, to sell a unit percentage increase in output, is known as the elasticity of demand, demand being the more elastic the less the price-reduction needed. In a system of free consumption this diminishing demand is due to two conditions, of which economic textbooks often only mention the first: psycho-physiological satiation of the individual consumer's wants, and the economic exhaustion (or default) of the poorer consumer's income. Thus the producer is deterred from large-scale production of the same article unless prepared to reduce his price, because he fears that the rich may be satiated after consuming a certain number of those articles, and the poor may never be able to pay for more than an occasional unit.

But this natural physiological satiation, and the economic default that is unavoidable if inequalities in income persist, are increased by the producer's own tendency to multiply sorts and varieties of articles and services. The consumer, so far from being discouraged from abandoning one sort or variety of consumption, has so many varieties of the same kind of article or service to choose from, that he naturally turns from one to the other as his fancy tickles him. Here is a vicious circle that for the sake of efficiency should be avoided. For fear of satiating the consumer, the producer provides a variety of goods and services, each on a small uneconomical scale, but that very variety distracts the consumer of any one sort and stimulates him to turn from one sort to another, thus perpetuating the high-cost small scale of production.

Unquestionably the consumer, if left to himself, would want (and demand) *some* degree of variety. He may have artistic leanings, may be a snob, may want to be different from other people, to enter another class, or to indulge in conspicuous waste;[1] he may have exotic tastes

[1] See Veblen, *Theory of the Leisure Class*, 1899.

and crave novelty and titivation. Some degree of variety permitting the selection of the fittest is a condition of progress, but there is no unavoidable reason why such customers should be encouraged to multiply sub-varieties and sub-sub-varieties of consumption at any one time as they are by the bright salesman who represents the producer. Mr Henry Ford, essentially the engineer, put the case clearly in discussing his 'T' model:[1]

It is strange how, just as soon as an article becomes successful, somebody starts to think that it would be more successful if only it were different. There is a tendency to keep monkeying with styles and to spoil a good thing by changing it. The salesmen were insistent on increasing the line. They listened to the 5 per cent, the special customers who could say what they wanted, and forgot all about the 95 per cent, who just bought without making any fuss. . . .

Salesmen always want to cater to whims instead of acquiring sufficient knowledge of their product to be able to explain to the customer with the whim that what they have will satisfy his every requirement—that is, of course, provided what they have does satisfy these requirements.

Therefore in 1909 I announced one morning, without any previous warning, that in the future we were going to build only one model, that the model was going to be 'Model T', and that the chassis would be exactly the same for all cars.

In contrast to Mr Ford's policy of standardization in any given period, most producers not only provide the widest and wildest multiplicity of goods and services to suit every existing demand of every possible consumer, but attempt to create or maintain species of the same variety of article or service that no consumer ever thought of wanting. The producer often imagines certain features are wanted and insists on pressing them on reluctant customers who would be quite satisfied with a plainer and perhaps cheaper article. Pottery is turned out that, according to some technical, professional, standard in the producer's, but not necessarily in the lay customer's mind, has qualities of perfection in its glaze or texture; metal goods are ground and finished to a degree far beyond the average consumer's requirements (and purse); British villas have gothic and tudor features added; American homes, colonial styling, all highly desirable in the architect and housebuilder's eyes, but not necessarily so in those of the home-builder. Domestic utensils, too, are produced in the wierdest and most inconvenient shapes.[2]

The fact that machinery permits any one given pattern to be reproduced in thousands of copies might be expected to make the producer careful of his original design. Curiously enough, this is not so. So far

---

[1] *My Life and Work*, 1922, pp. 71–3.
[2] See *Art and Industry*, Report of Committee appointed by the Board of Trade, 1932, Memorandum by Roger Fry.

from studying the consumer's wants and taste and possibly trying to educate him to some standard model found most fit for its purpose, the producer appears almost to treat him with contempt. I once asked the foreman of a British factory department specializing in expensive cut-glass ware, who was responsible for the design which appeared to me atrocious. The answer was, 'Oh, me or the boss, when we have the time to spare.' If a special designer does exist in the factory, his education in design is often no deeper than a night-school, and his aim no higher than to compromise between existing and often incompatible 'best sellers'.[1]

The public at large is perhaps willing to accept better designs than it gets. 'After all, people are forced to buy what is before them, but they often do so of sheer necessity and without approval.'[2] The conventional dictum of Consumer Sovereignty that the community of consumers is 'the controlling employer in the productive system', and 'the business man simply one of many faithful servants',[3] is today seldom true as regards design of product. In fact, the initiative in proposing comes from the producer or the distributor—the consumer merely disposes; he buys the proposition or leaves it on the retailer's shelf.

To quote Schumpeter:

Innovations in the economic system do not as a rule take place in such a way that, first, new wants arise spontaneously in consumers and then the productive apparatus swings round through their pressure. . . . It is the producer who as a rule initiates economic change and consumers are educated by him if necessary; they are, as it were, brought to want new things. . . .[4]

Hoyt[5] applies this view forcibly to the initiation of designs and the stimulation of an artificial advertisement-led demand.

Today certainly the producer tries to direct the preferences of the consumer. 'See this,' said the producer, 'and this; and this. I made them for you. Take them, try them. Now I'll think up something else for you.' The consumer is so confused by the multitude of offerings that he rarely conceives anything new himself. . . . Whatever can be made by the use of power machinery, that the producer tries to make. Then he sets about to teach the consumers to want it.

Galbraith has in his *New Industrial State* (1967) pursued still further the possibility of a capitalist 'techno-structural planning of consumption, replacing market decisions till it corresponds almost to the

---

[1] See Pevsner, *Industrial Art in England* 1937, esp. pp. 193–4.

[2] Roger Fry, op. cit., p. 46.

[3] Plant, *Economica*, 'Trends in Business Administration', February 1932, pp. 45–62.

[4] Schumpeter, *The Theory of Economic Development*, 1934, p. 65.

[5] *The Consumption of Wealth*, p. 111.

Soviet consumption planning referred to in § 1. At present, however, western communities are some distance from being thus totally committed. Before making pronouncements as though there were a general situation, analysis must look into the very different structures of particular types of industry, and the probable causes, permanent or impermanent, underlying these differences. So far as the causes lie, ergologically, in the type of work involved, differences in the degree of competition or monopoly are more likely to be permanent.[1]

The climax to the orgy of designs and showmanship is reached at Christmas time when the shops are filled with a plethora of 'novelties' that no consumer would think of wanting for himself and which he is only 'taught' to buy (for others) in the glow of the Yuletide spirit. But it clearly pays the distributor not to let down at any season. In America Christmas is preceded by Thanksgiving in November, Thanksgiving by Hallowe'en in October, and Hallowe'en by the start of the school year in September. Here's the reaction of an American returning after a stay of twenty years in England.[2]

When September came round there was a great to-do about getting the sweet co-eds off to college. For weeks shop windows and advertisements plugged the wardrobe, the face-cream, the tooth paste, the hair-do, the perfume she simply had to have if she wanted to 'dazzle that date'. Every advertisement teemed with very young girls perched on very long legs in sports clothes, in campus togs, in evening get-up, surrounded by admiring undergraduates. From the advertisements it appeared that young men, if any, *en route* to college, needed very few supplies, but that every young woman in America was just off to higher education whose main purpose was to attract the male. The shops swarmed with fond mothers and strong-minded daughters who argued incessantly over the choice of purchases. I searched for any reference to the instruments of learning—books or papers or dictionaries. Some shops suggested that the young should be provided with typewriters, the only refinement, I believe, which schools and colleges do not themselves supply. . . . Finally I ran across a necklace made up of tiny pencils, slates and rulers. The tools had not been completely forgotten.

Free enterprise in consumption aided and abetted by free enterprise in production and distribution has resulted in such a multiplication of sub-varieties of goods in shops that a few really different well-thought-

---

[1] Certainly the increasing capital intensity of many technologically developed industries makes such planning, helped by advertising and sales promotion, acceptable to the producer technocrats. But industries that are both concentrated and highly powered are mostly confined (see my *Economics and Sociology of Industry*, 1969, Table XIX, Columns Ici and vb) to the chemical, petroleum and primary metal and, perhaps, paper and transport equipment groups. They are not the whole economy.

[2] Lella Secor Florence, *My Goodness! My Passport*, 1941, pp. 161–4.

out patterns cannot at any one time be produced economically on a large scale to satisfy any given want.

Confusion is made worse confounded, however, by the changes in demand through a period of time, consequent upon unstable incomes. This again forms a vicious circle in the relations of producers and consumers. Fear of a fall in the prices of his products induces the producer in his capacity as employer to dismiss employees, and in his capacity as investor to cease ordering machines and equipment. The dismissed employees will no longer have the means to demand even those products that they used to consume quite steadily, and the makers of machines and other producer's goods will find their market collapsing. Thus standard production is thrown still further out of gear. No class of consumption, however stable in normal times, is immune from this type of variation that is due to the productive machine itself. The poorest class must cut down their consumption of needs, the next poorest their conventional necessaries, just as consumers of producer's goods cut down *their* orders. This fluctuation of demand from time to time presents a more serious limit to large-scale production methods than the diminishing utility at any one time. Plant and organization laid down against a fairly stable maintenance or development of consumption is rendered idle and production may become more costly than if no such plant or organization had ever been introduced. It is this very risk of fluctuations in consumption that has in fact induced producers to 'hedge' by lateral integration (particularly of the divergent type) which implies a smaller and less efficient scale of operation.[1]

Are there no means of reducing the risk of large-scale production by foreseeing and thus forestalling both the variability of demand among consumers at any one time and the trend and fluctuations of demand from time to time!

§ 4. FORECASTING AND MARKET RESEARCH

In spite of these vagaries in the type of products and the proportion of given products demanded by final and producer consumers and in the methods of production and distribution, certain strands of logic run through the tangled web and make a more or less logical pattern. It is up to the producer out for efficient large-scale operation, to find the precise manifestations of this logic, and base his marketing policy upon it, if he, in his turn, is to be logical.

Engel's law has already been cited that the proportion spent on food is less at the higher income levels. It is laws of this type, grounded on the

[1] See Chapter II, § 4.

collection and statistical analysis of the facts of the situation, which must provide the logical producer with a basis for action.

Engel's law is of practical importance to the structure of industry because it points broadly to means of reducing uncertainty as to the direction of free consumption. Any one consumer is free to eat, heat, dress, and light himself as he likes, but taken *en masse* consumers behave in certain predictable ways; there is a certain regularity in the pattern of consumption. This logic underlying much of free consumption helps the logic of free production because the more certain a producer is about the behaviour of his market the less risk he feels he is taking in plumping for the production of particular articles to satisfy the market. Instead of insuring himself and hedging against uncertainty by integrating and making on a small scale a whole series of products *some* of which he hopes may sell, he will feel able to concentrate more safely on a few articles each produced on a large scale. A number of 'Engel' types of research into consumption may be set forth, all of which should help a manufacturer in concentrating upon certain products in a large way.

(A) Analysis of consumption by types of customer and the frequency of the different types:
  (1) According to income (e.g. Engel's law itself).
  (2) According to physical features.
(B) Analysis of effect upon consumption of changes:
  (3) Through time in total national income; trade cycles; varying propensity to consume as against saving.
  (4) In consumption of linked goods.

(1) A producer should contrive to analyse his customers or possible customers into fairly uniform, standard types or classes, within which large-scale standard lines of consumption are possible, and to find the relative frequency of each type. Analysis of consumers according to their income is important because the more stable demands based on physical and conventional needs are to be expected of the poorer classes.

Engel's law applies to whole categories of articles, food, household requirements, clothing. What is required by the would-be large-scale producer is similar laws or regularities applying to specific articles. Here empirical research has made considerable progress in recent decades[1] and has added to the economist's conception of elasticity of demand (or more precisely price-elasticity), already defined, that of income-elasticity. While to the producer price-elasticity is the precise

[1] See Means, *Patterns of Resource Use*, U.S. National Resources Committee, 1938. Stone, 'Analysis of Market Demand', *Statistical Journal*, 1945, pp. 286–382.

proportion by which price must fall to sell a unit percentage increase in output, income elasticity is the precise proportion by which the income of the consumer or a community must be higher to sell that percentage increase in output.

(2) Cutting across the income classification are many other useful classifications, notably that by personal features, since people vary physically in the sizes and shapes of their bodies and consequently *need* different sizes and shapes of clothes and shoes. Shoe manufacturers have made a study of what the statistician calls the 'frequency distribution' of lengths and widths of feet. It was found[1] that of every hundred men in America ninety required shoes of fairly normal width and length. Of these, three required size 6 shoes of normal range of widths, eight size $6\frac{1}{2}$, fourteen size 7, eighteen size $7\frac{1}{2}$, twenty size 8, thirteen size $8\frac{1}{2}$, eight size 9, three size $9\frac{1}{2}$, two size 10 and one 11. These 90 per cent with normal size of feet could be further sub-divided according to the precise width of shoe required within the normal range. Thus among the twenty men requiring the most frequently required length (i.e. size 8), one would require B width, three C width, seven D width, eight E width and one EE width. With this sort of simple knowledge, applicable in many directions, large-scale manufacture for stock in anticipation of demand is a less uncertain gamble. Even where still a matter of trial and error, hit and miss, there is less error and more hits.

(3) The producer can also seek to forecast changes in consumption, either through a period of time or as a consequence of changes in prices. This involves analysing the changes in wants and demands with variations in national income, and the likely changes in incomes upon which these changes in demand depend.

Changes in British and American real income have, in the past two centuries, showed a gradual but fluctuating increase per head. The forecasting of the trade cycle has now a long history. It is essentially an attempt to foretell probable aggregate sales. For, given the aggregate costs, it is not the future prices of a unit of his product that the producer wants to know but his aggregate receipts. This, when aggregate costs are subtracted, will tell him total profit.

Assuming that a satisfactory index of aggregate sales is obtained for a sufficiently long period in the past, it has been possible to trace a series of repeated cycles of prosperity and depression extending over similar spans of years, leading to the expectation of further cycles of similar span in the future. But if such exact recurrence in the index of sales can neither be found in the past nor expected of the future, it may yet be possible to find symptoms in other indices of a coming change in aggregate sales. It may be found that changes in aggregate sales are

---

[1] Nystrom, *Economics of Fashion*, p. 460.

always preceded by, say, changes in prices of industrial shares on the Stock Exchange, or in rates of short-term interest or in wholesale prices of goods or in exports. In that case the producer will be provided with a signal, red or green as the case may be, of coming depression or prosperity.

With improving statistical field-work and measurement these forecasts, if intelligently interpreted by the producer, would prevent his infection from wild hearsay rumours and seizure by herd-instinct;—an instinct which appears as panic at times of falling sales and purchases, and yields to unthinking optimism in times of prosperity. He should be enabled to act more logically on the basis of contemporary facts, former experiences, and economic reasoning.

(4) The trend of changes in consumers' wants and demands with differences in their income can be estimated by recourse to inductive statistical enquiry. Some *a priori* conceptions can also come to the aid of the logically-minded producer, for instance, that of joint or linked demands.

After the First World War, the official statistics of the numbers engaged in specific industries showed that in Britain industries linked with housing expanded more than most other industries. While the average increase in all workers nationally insured against unemployment between 1923 and 1929 was 8·4 per cent, workers engaged in making artificial stone and concrete increased 72·1 per cent, in making heating and ventilating apparatus 61·1 per cent, in electrical wiring and contracting 44·4 per cent, in making paint and varnish 44·2 per cent, in making bricks, tiles, pipes, etc. 41·4 per cent, in stone-quarrying 39·6 per cent, in slate-quarrying 38·5 per cent, in making wallpaper 35·9 per cent, and furniture 33·1 per cent. Only one industry linked with housing, carpets (1·1 per cent rise), was below the average rise.[1] Building itself rose 21·2 per cent in men insured.

Similarly in America between 1919 and 1925, among the twelve industries increasing most in the number of wage-earners employed, seven were linked with housing: plumber's supplies (increase of 145 per cent), carpets and rugs (48 per cent), steam fittings (38 per cent), brick-making (34 per cent), furniture (29 per cent), hardware (23 per cent), paints and varnishes (19 per cent).

[1] *Ministry of Labour Gazette*, November 1929, pp. 392–7. This passage was published in 1933 in my *Logic of Industrial Organization*, p. 71. If producers had then betted on a continuance of the trends I indicated, they would have prospered handsomely. All the ten industries linked to housing with one exception (slate quarrying) but including carpet making expanded more rapidly than the average for all industries. The all-industry average rise in the numbers insured between 1929 and 1938 was from 8·4 per cent to 24·6 per cent above 1923—an increase of 16·2 points. The rises in these industries linked to building were from 24·5 to 226·4 points, with an average of 84·6 points.

These figures show a general secular trend towards an increased desire for housing partly to make up for war-time deficiency and for the auxiliary products in joint demand. If producers of the type of goods required followed the figures and adopted or adapted their products accordingly they might reduce their risks of unsold merchandise. For the trend displayed by these statistics is not mere accident; the trend might indeed have been expected *a priori* from what we have called the logic of consumption. As real earnings rise (i.e. money wages in terms of retail prices) in the way they did both in America and Britain between 1923 and 1929, in Britain between 1933 and 1939, and again in both countries between 1945 and 1951, people may be expected to spend proportionately less of their total income on the necessary food and fuel, and more on comparative luxuries such as more refined house furnishings.

To sum up. The risks of the large-scale free producer in relation to the free consumer point to the necessity of a market research and forecasting on the part of the producer which will look into the facts and possibilities of the actual situation. Market research, apart from the question of channels of distribution, aims at determining the design of the product and the qualities and varieties to be provided; the amount of each quality or variety to be provided, and the price to be charged.

Instead of a multitude of designs, hit upon by chance fumbling, imitation or compromise and finding a market by a process of trial and error—most designs being errors—efficiency requires that within one line of goods only a moderate number of carefully thought-out designs be standardized which will both answer wants of most consumers and be amenable to large-scale production. This policy of simplification based on previous research has been carried out by a number of firms and has resulted in great economies and greater output.

The amounts to be produced in each design and the prices to be charged for them depend at any one time on the price and income elasticity of demand,[1] and over a period of time, on fluctuations in their saleability. To avoid undue risks, the policy of the producer on price and amount produced must be based on some estimate of such factors derived from his market research.

§ 5. COMPETITION AND COMBINATION, SALES PRESSURE AND ADVERTISING

To a policy of large-scale operation based on market research and forecasting, however, business men will raise one insuperable objection. It can be expressed in one word—competition. One or a few producers, they will say, do not operate in a vacuum. Supposing any producer does,

---

[1] See above, § 3, pp. 131–6.

by market research, gauge correctly the future of the market and the present elasticity of demand for a standard product; and suppose he foresees correctly that by lowering prices 10 per cent, a thousand more of the sort of product he makes can be sold next year. Can he proceed with confidence to manufacture a thousand more units and to re-organize his total production by such methods of large-scale operation that the average cost and the price can be reduced by 10 per cent? By no means. First of all, he does not know how far his competitors have not made the same correct estimates of the market and all of them not likewise be trying to capture the demand for the additional thousand units. And since he *and* his rivals cannot each and all of them sell the additional thousand units, it is best to be cautious and continue with the old and small-scale methods for fear of an over-production in the industry as a whole.

But suppose, in the second case, that he knows his competitors are all old-fashioned and unlikely to have undertaken any market research, or to have any inkling of the possible lucrative expansion of the market. He might then suppose that new large-scale methods of operation permitting a 10 per cent cut in his costs and prices on a given product would not only capture the new thousand units but eat into his competitors' original trade to the tune of several additional thousand. Assuming economic man, this certainly ought to happen. If a consumer can get the same article 10 per cent cheaper he should (if he is as alert and calculating as economists used to assume) immediately and eagerly transfer his custom to the cheaper producer. But again, this *in fact* is not always so. Modern economists admit that there is generally a 'stickiness', 'friction' or imperfection in any market which prevents the cheaper firm's product from having an infinite increment of demand and capturing the whole market for that product. Almost every producer has some pocket of monopoly, since there is usually a willingness on the part of the group of buyers who constitute a firm's clientèle to pay, if necessary, something extra in order to obtain the goods from a particular firm rather than from any other.[1] This pocketing of a clientèle can be achieved by a trade-mark and will outlive the changing of the actual producer, as with a doctor's practice, so that the consumer's custom can be bought and sold in the form of goodwill. Moreover, if there were any marked tendency for the consumer to desert his original but more expensive producer, that producer, whatever his costs and lack of fore-sight, would be likely to cut prices to meet the new competition. Hence the (cheap) large-scale producer would have an uphill fight to dispose of his additional product, and the increased marketing costs necessitated might soon offset his decreased producing costs.

[1] Sraffa, 'The Laws of Returns under Competitive Conditions', *Economic Journal*, December 1926.

Under actual conditions of competition the producer, then, cannot be logical and, by large-scale operation cut costs and price to capture the market, either because his fellow-producers may be equally logical and prepared to capture the market or at least determined not to lose markets; or if other producers are not logical and determined, he cannot be logical, because, in an imperfect market, the consumers are illogical and refuse to be captured even to their own economic advantage. Have we then reached a dead end?

There are several possible exits to the apparent impasse. One is combination between erstwhile competitors so that they may between them share, in some logical manner, the original and the forecasted increase in demand. Other exits are to break down the competing producer's resources, or the consumer's illogic.

Much of the general policy of industrial firms has always turned on questions of war or peace in their relation with other firms. In fact, we speak of trade wars though often under the delusion that these only occur between producers of different nationality. Thus infiltration, strategy, tactics, campaigns, resistance and other military terms can suitably form part of the producer's vocabulary as they do of his practice, and part of the political science of business lies in estimating the relative power of competing businesses.[1]

The normal method of defeating inefficient producers under the system of full-blooded competition between a number of small producers was to bankrupt them; and during early capitalism new or more efficient firms could and did replace others, as (in Marshall's famous analogy) new trees in a forest replace the old. Knock-out competition has employed all methods from fair to unfair, ranging from the legitimate policy of lower prices based on lower costs to sabotage and (e.g. in the Chicago beer trade under prohibition) mass murders. To the loser, competition is always 'unfair' and usually 'cut-throat'; but the theory of laissez-faire and individual capitalist enterprise depends for its validity, as Keynes reminds us with his parable of the giraffes,[2] on the survival only of the fittest for some purpose or object such as reaching to the topmost leaves. Those individuals who move in the right direction will destroy by competition those who move in the wrong direction.

This implies that there must be no mercy or protection for those who

---

[1] This paragraph is reproduced substantially as written in 1933 (*Logic of Industrial Organization*, p. 82). Since then a whole theory of duopoly and oligopoly has been based on the somewhat similar analogy of games (see *Theory of Games and Economic Behaviour* by Neumann and Morgenstern), and in which military terms like strategy are constantly used. The phrase 'barriers to entry' has been introduced by Bain. To continue the military analogy 'trenches' might be used to indicate barriers achieved by cutting prices.

[2] Keynes, *The End of Laissez-Faire*, 1926, p. 28.

embark their capital or their labour in the wrong direction. It is a method of bringing the most successful profit-makers to the top by a ruthless struggle for survival, which selects the most efficient by the bankruptcy of the less efficient. It does not count the cost of the struggle but looks only to the benefits of the final result which are assumed to be permanent. The object of life being to crop the leaves off the branches up to the greatest possible height, the likeliest way of achieving this end is to leave the giraffes with the longest necks to starve out those whose necks are shorter.

In the course of this struggle for existence the 'representative firm' might gradually have become larger. But technical and financial conditions, such as the difficulty of new firms immediately securing extensive and expensive plant needed for optimum efficiency, have latterly slowed down this process of replacement. Like modern wars between States there is a heavy price to pay by the ultimate victor no less than by the victim. Cut-throat price-cutting in a war between firms with high fixed costs may have to proceed to a level below that of the prime costs even of the more efficient firm, and for a considerable time after the war may involve 'spoiling the market'. Consumers who have stocked up during the time of cut prices may have no need to buy long after hostilities have ceased. Realizing this loss to both sides, the modern strategy of industrial warfare is usually to bring to terms, thus enlarging the size of firm or association, rather than to fight to a finish. Competition is not necessarily a tactic opposed to combination but may merely be its prelude.

The important question in that case is whether the more efficient firm will or will not become the predominant partner in the larger alliance. When in the past the consumer stuck to his original supplier though his products were dearer for the same quality, and thus obstructed and ultimately perhaps bankrupted new and possibly more efficient competitors, it was often from some instinct or sentiment of loyalty or camaraderie. His supplier might have been some 'pal' of his, or at least a good fellow whom he did not wish to hurt or offend. But it is doubtful whether this sweet human reasonableness in favour of friends, however inefficient, will continue under the attack of 'high pressure' salesmanship, and intensive advertising directed towards the selling of specific brands of goods each produced on a large scale. Formerly goods and services were bought because so-and-so made them or so-and-so sold them and *he* could be trusted; but except for so-called prestige advertising, specific goods and services are now brought to the attention of the consumer on their own alleged merits.

This advertising of specific goods introduces an uneconomic illogical artificiality into the demand for them. Consumers react to emotional appeals and sentimental clap-trap, are influenced by telling posters with bright colours and snappy wise-cracks, and are gulled by half-truths flashily presented. The mere repetition of the name of a brand may finally put it over. Consumers fail to inspect quality or check the prices of the goods themselves. The demand is artificial in the sense that it is built up on high pressure advertising 'copy' that has little relation to the real qualities of the product. Luscious girls or Regency bucks have little real connection with cigarettes or whisky— yet the goods are demanded because of the image or aura of beauty or the halo of snobbery thus artificially created. For self-protection against this 'hot air', societies of consumers like the Consumers' Research Inc. or Consumers' Union have organized themselves in America and in Britain the Consumers' Association. They issue bulletins exposing hyperbole and the puffing of inferior goods. The quality of advertised goods are analysed by experts and openly given good or bad marks according to their 'value for money'.

The law of libel, it was said, prevents this self-help by consumers in Britain.[1] The British consumer is perhaps more phlegmatic in temperament and traditional in outlook and thus less subject to the illogic of high-pressure sales and advertising companies than the American; nevertheless the logic even of his demands can be artificially channelled by subtle 'low pressure' understatements. I have overheard the sales department of a food factory say to a possible client in the most gentlemanly Oxford tones, 'I say, old chap, you don't *really* want our stuff, do you?'—and make the sale.

If large-scale production of a well designed standard article is to find a market there is just as much need for consumer education and breakdown of his illogic in Britain as America. Once freed from 'ballyhoo', advertising of specific goods may help rather than hinder the large-scale production of new standardizable designs as against a variety of conventional patterns, and may permit consumers conveniently to compare prices and designs of competing products and so to prefer the best value for money. Advertising may teach consumers to like the standard article which is cheap because produced by economical methods, and even to alter their habits, traditions, or craving to be 'different' if these involve unnecessary and illogical expenditure.

In short, with the modern spirit of scepticism, coupled with wider education, logical comparison may take the place of both gullibility and sentiment, and service or product may be more likely to win the consumer on its merits of quality and cheapness.[2] Advertising can be used to break away from mere tradition and to stimulate the consumer to demand the article which by large-scale methods is the most efficiently produced, and gradually to get trade into fewer hands, thus

[1] But has not stopped rapid growth since 1957 of the Consumers' Association.
[2] This hope, originally expressed in 1953, is not materializing. Advertising copy (and songs) seem more irrational than ever on television.

enabling each to produce on an ever larger scale. This does not necessarily mean monopoly. There is a long way to go between the thousands
of firms to be found in so many industries and say the dozen or so of
large firms or combinations that might each have a sufficient portion of
the trade to be able to produce efficiently on a large scale.

A monopoly undoubtedly results in certain economies, especially
in marketing, over and above those which are due to the maximum
scale of operation it makes possible, and which might be obtained
equally well under oligopoly or a few competing large-operation firms.

(1) In some cases concentration of all production and service of a
given sort in the hands of one firm is the only recourse for obtaining a
sufficiently large scale of operation to yield maximum efficiency. This
situation is particularly likely where the total industry is small and there
is room for one efficiently sized plant or firm but not two. Here the
economy of a monopoly is merely incidental to the need for large-scale
operation, monopoly is efficient only because it is a condition of
achieving the necessary scale. Other economies are, however, intrinsic
to monopoly.

(2) In 'octopoid' industries like water, gas and electricity supply,
telephone service and sewage disposal, delivery to (and collection
from) scattered homes, stores and factories has been effectively
mechanized by piping, cabling or wiring and a duplication or still
greater multiplication of these physical tentacles along parallel routes
is most wasteful of fixed overhead costs. In the heyday of capitalist
enterprise competing gas mains ran under the same London streets; and
in some American towns there were two competing telephone systems
—since few subscribers wished to be available to only half their friends,
most clients had to be on both systems, with consequent duplication of
lines, centres and exchanges. Even where delivery (or collection) is by
hand, not by physical tentacles, as for newspapers, milk, coal, mail,
garbage, a unification with one route serving each house consecutively
in order, is a great saving over competing routes each serving a house
only here and there.

(3) Consumers faced by a monopoly can be forced to be reasonable
in the designs demanded. They would have to accept any standardized
cheaply producible article or go without. The trading habits that are
often equally unreasonable and illogical could also be eliminated; a
firm or an association of firms that had a monopoly of transport or
credit facilities could force traders to send consignments in bulk and to
pay within a reasonable time. Without monopoly such logical standardization would be impossible since even one competitor could 'cut
the throat' of standards however reasonable. The counterpart of the
monopolist (or single seller) forcing the consumer to be reasonable and
logical is the monopsonist (or single buyer) forcing the supplier to be

reasonable and procuring standard materials cheaply and conveniently. Though efficient from the monopolist's, and monopsonist's, standpoint, however, both cases may easily develop into exploitation, which will be considered shortly.

(4) While competition exists, even though it is only between two organizations, high marketing and advertising costs are likely to persist, including the risk of overproduction and uncertainty of prediction mentioned earlier. It is not till monopoly is achieved that the combative competitive element in these costs is eliminated.

The conclusion is thus reached that if the marketing costs of larger-scale operation are not to offset the production costs, and in some cases if production costs are to be at a minimum, monopoly may need to be established. Monopoly achieved by a knock-out war among competitors is extremely costly under modern conditions of high fixed overhead costs and of established staff in works management and marketing. The bankruptcy owing to external circumstances of a firm whose specialists have long worked as a co-ordinated team and the substitution of a new organization in its place, may not always induce greater efficiency.

In its policy towards mergers the British Labour government of 1964–70 encountered this very dilemma of either monopoly or else high cost and competition. A firm becoming larger through merger could benefit from the economies of scale in production, marketing and finance; it has a chance of lower costs than those of smaller firms. But if its larger size gives it a monopoly (or a near monopoly) of a market it may charge a higher price or may be careless in seizing its chance of lower costs.

In a largely trading country such as Britain the merger which a government is fostering, though it may reduce competition among home producers is still subject to competition from foreign producers and in fact the merger may be fostered for the very purpose of strengthening the home competitor against giants from abroad. Of course, if fair competition is the object, the government must not in logic impose prohibitive tariffs on the imported products. A brief attempt is made in the next section to co-ordinate the economic and the structural approach to monopoly.

§ 6. MONOPOLISTIC STRUCTURE AND THEORY

Much has been written by economists about monopoly, duopoly, oligopoly and the exploitation of the consumer by one, two, or a few sellers; much about monopsony, duopsony, oligopsony and the exploitation of the supplier by one, two, or a few buyers; much also about imperfect or monopolistic competition and the trust problem. Here, the structural aspect of monopoly is of prime interest, and we shall attempt to show the relationship of a monopolistic structure in modern industrial organization to the type of problem that worries the economists—monopolistic being used to cover one, two, or a few sellers (or buyers). The economist is chiefly interested in the terms of exchange, the amounts of goods, services or factors exchanged and the prices, wages, profits, etc., at which they exchange.[1] To him the 'problem' of monopoly is the power it gives the monopolist to charge the consumer (or if he 'discriminates', *some* consumers) a higher price (or the monopsonist to extort from the supplier a lower price) than would result from perfect competition. The monopoly prices tend to restrict production and employment by limiting the demand of the consumer, and in the long run limiting the supplier. Monopolists may also slow down progress to keep up profit on existing equipment.[2] They may thus misdirect the allocation of resources. The private monopolist, it is held, is likely often to exercise his power since under certain conditions his profit can be increased by this exploitation of consumers and suppliers.

The economist's approach has often been confused with the structural or organization approach by such terms as the trust problem, the combination movement, or the take-over. It is too often assumed that whenever firms combine, it is to exploit the consumer or supplier, or conversely that all exploitation is organized by combinations and trusts. Both assumptions are untrue. Monopoly exploitation has arisen without combination by sheer knock-out competition; combination often occurs simply to increase the size of firms and reduce costs.

In setting out the relations of the economic and the structural or organization aspects a deliberately systematic presentation is thus needed. An orientation chart, Table IIIA, presents the two aspects in parallel columns. In the midst of the right-hand column *economic* aspect is monopolistic *exploitation* and the economist focuses on its precise definition, its causes placed above (arising *from* what conditions and *for* what objects) and its results placed below.[3] In the forefront of the

---

[1] This was my definition in 1929 of the scope of economics generalized from the actual contents of economic textbooks and lecture courses, as contrasted from what economists said economics was about. At that time the emphasis was put on prices rather than the amounts in exchange. But with the publication of Keynes' Theory of Employment in 1936 the emphasis has shifted and economists now also discuss amounts exchanged (e.g. total national income; trade returns; aggregate employment). My definition is more realistic now than when first put forward.

[2] See Allen, 'Economic Progress, Retrospect and Prospect', *Economic Journal*, September 1950, pp. 473–4.

[3] This pattern of an orientation table with its indentation to indicate super-, co-, and sub-ordinate relationships was suggested in my *Statistical Methods in Economics and Political Science*, Chapter XII. Here instead of the symbols N, O, P, R, to indicate and standardize the four causal relationships, cause, objective, policy and results, the words *from, for, by* (or *through*), *hence* have been used.

TABLE IIIA

ORIENTATION CHART FOR PROBLEMS OF MONOPOLY AND CONCENTRATION

Organization aspect	Economic aspect
PRIVATE MONOPOLISTIC STRUCTURE	
Def. Large units of control relatively to total sales (output − export + import). Oligopoly.	
From	
(1) Legal restriction on sales. Tariffs, patents.	
(2) Technical restriction (indivisibility of plant).	*From* (1) Inelastic supply, e.g. barriers to entry, due to
(3) Large units, financial strength.	←————monopolistic structure.
Through	(2) Inelastic demand.
(*a*) agreement between firms,	
(*b*) association of firms, with organization (easier if localized).	
(*c*) mergers into larger firms (e.g. joint stock holding cos.).	
(*d*) knock-out competition between firms, fair or unfair.	

For	Maximum or satisfactory (secure) profit	*For*	Maximum or satisfactory (secure) profit.
By	(i) Lower costs of production.		
	(ii) Lower competitive wastes.		
	(iii) Exploitation————————————→	EXPLOITATION	
	of consumer	*Def.*	Price higher than marginal cost under perfect competition. Discrimination. Restriction of output. Restrictive practices.
	of supplier		
	(monopsony).		
	(iv) Checking use of new inventions which would scrap existing inventions.		
		Hence (A)	Potential competition and substitution brought back into play (self-regulating equilibrium).
STATE COUNTER-ORGANIZATION		*Or* (B)	Lasting exploitation. Misallocation of resources. Need for state action.
Regulatory commissions. Nationalization. Planning controls. (Maximum prices). ←————————————			

left-hand *organization* aspect lies the monopolistic structure of an industry, defined as the situation where units are large relatively to the industry's total sales and which forms the focus for enquiry, concerned with the causes *from* and *for*, and the means *through and by* which monopolistic structure arises.

A continually reciprocating interaction occurs between organization (or structure) and economic activity (or policy). Large structures can often by their financial strength adopt a policy of barring competition in their own or (by cross-subsidization) in other industries and thus set up a circle proceeding from strength to strength. Many would call this is a vicious circle calling for state intervention. Tracing reciprocal action back and forth between the two 'aspect' columns, organizational and economic, of the orientation chart (Table IIIA) is not merely an academic exercise but an attempt to suggest government policy. Through mergers, for instance, into larger firms (left-hand column *c*), barriers to entry (right-hand 1) may be erected which by unfair competition (left-hand, *d*) may lead (right-hand B) to lasting exploitation. This calls (left-hand column) for various forms of state counter-organization.

The ground the two aspects have in common is indicated by phrases appearing at the same level in each column, such as maximum or satisfactory (secure) profit and exploitation. Thus, a condition *from* which exploitation may arise on the supply side is a monopolistic structure with large units of control; and one of the causes of a large unit organization may be the desire *for* maximum profits obtainable not just by the lower cost of maximum-scale production or by cutting the marketing wastes of competition, but by economic exploitation and checking innovation. Of exploitation economists have written plenty, but of checking innovation they have written too little. Large firms have the resources to promote research conducive to technological progress, but the same resources may be used to defend established positions, for instance, by 'defensive' research or by building up hedging patents round a basic invention. Recognition of problems like this, which mean that monopolistic practices have different significance for the public interest at different stages of the industry's development, has called forth the concept of workable or effective competition first associated with the name of J. M. Clark. This concept involves applying tests of competitiveness which focus on the actions and reactions of types of industrial leaders under actual conditions of organization along the lines pursued later in Chapter VII, particularly leaders' response to the stimulus toward innovation.

If we pursue down the chart the logic of events and facts in the relations of a monopolistic production structure to the consumer, the practical question is whether the existence of exploitation shows the need for intervention by the State, and if so, the precise form of organization required to counter exploitation.

It is a possibility (A on the chart) that a price higher than cost will bring into play the forces of potential competition or substitution. New firms, tempted by the high margin of profit, may enter the same market or consumers may switch to alternative types of product or counter-vailing power may be organized on the opposite side of the market.[1] In either case, because supplies are increased or demand

[1] Multiple retailers in America oppose large producers, and strong farmers' organizations oppose monopsonistic food and tobacco manufacturers. See Galbraith, *American Capitalism*, 1952, especially Chapter IX.

decreased, prices and profit margins will fall and exploitation may cease or be reduced. Stigler maintains,[1] on the basis of industry-by-industry analysis, that the popular thesis of competition declining steadily in America is 'partly fictional history'. Certainly the growing absolute size of plants and firms analysed in the preceding chapter is, as Stigler says,[2] 'irrelevant to the question of competition'. Larger and larger plants and firms may well continue to compete so long as their industry is large enough to contain two or more of them.

With self-regulating equilibrium or counter-vailing power, there will be no need for intervention. But American enquiries into the facts of prices and division of markets[3] have disclosed the probability (B in the chart) of a lasting exploitation in particular industries where a few firms control the bulk of the output, split the sales, and thereby fix the pattern. This situation calls for an intensive analysis of the structure, government and policies of such firms (not just theoretically, of 'the' firm) as in Chapters IV and V.

Empirical research on exploitation is gradually accumulating but does not always confirm the positive correlation of profits and concentration of an industry. Bain, to quote Hart,[4] found that for the period 1936–40 the average rate of return in the high concentration industries was higher than in the other industries. Stigler also found a significant correlation between concentration and profitability for this period, though the correlation was not significantly different from zero for the later period 1947–54. Hart himself found evidence of a lack of association between concentration and rate of return in British industries, 1951–4. Before concluding that concentration and monopoly exploitation are only occasionally connected, two questions must, however, be considered, one technical, the other institutional.

In the first edition of my *Economics and Sociology of Industry* (1964, p. 241) I give the ten British industries with highest and lowest ratios of fixed assets per person employed in 1954, cited from Barna.[5] Now the ten industries with highest fixed assets per employee, £2,950–£12,680, have on the whole higher concentration than average, while the ten

---

[1] Stigler, *Five Lectures on Economic Problems*, 1949, pp. 46–59. See also Adelman, *Review of Economics and Statistics*, January and May, 1952. Replying to five critics, Adelman notes that all agree 'that since 1931 there has at least been no further concentration'. In this controversy concentration refers to the *relative* share of *large* firms in *one* industry, not their *absolute* size. In 1947, indeed, Adelman estimates that as few as 139 still held 45 per cent of the assets of *all* manufacturing corporations. For the position in 1968 see above, p. 44.

[2] Op. cit., p. 52.

[3] E.g. Burns, *The Decline of Competition*, 1936.

[4] P. E. Hart, *Studies in Profit, Business Saving and Investment in the U.K.*, London, Allen & Unwin, 1968, p. 259.

[5] *Statistical Journal*, Part I, 1957.

industries with lowest, £590–£1,170, have lower concentrations. Thus the technical question is whether using the single factor capital-assets as the denominator of the rate of profit does not artificially reduce the apparent profit on the capital-intensive concentrated industries and introduce an inbuilt bias toward a high-concentration-*low*-profit correlation.

The institutional question is the possibility that the management-ruled companies (governed by salaried executives holding little of the capital) constituting probably the majority of large companies by 1947–54 may be monopolist in policy, but not for the sake of profits so much as for growth, or even ease of mind freed from the anxieties of competition. Certainly it is relevant to bear in mind the lower average of ratios of net income to net worth occurring from 1952 to 1963, according to Monsen, Chiu and Cooley,[1] by the manager-controlled firms in the same mixture of industries. These ratios measure the return on owners' investment. Is it too simple an explanation to assume that manager-ruled companies will be less keen on maximizing this return than the investors?

Given a monopolistic structure and lasting exploitation, counter-organization is called for against unnecessarily high prices to consumers, against restriction of output (with consequent unemployment) and, possibly, against the checking of technological progress and the misallocations of resources. The precise measures the state may take is a matter of organization rather than economics, and an arrow refers across to counter-organization in the left hand column of the orientation table. It will be discussed later (Chapter VI) under regulatory commissions, nationalization and planning control.

The moral of this orientation and the previous discussion it co-ordinates is that the structural, organizational, approach gives substance to the economist's more abstract approach to monopoly in several ways; notably (*a*) in keeping the economics of large-scale operation before the eyes of the theorist arguing about monopoly, (*b*) in ascertaining which (if any) of the economists' models are nearest the methods of organization actually adopted by most monopolies (e.g. agreement, association, combination) and the extent of this monopolization, (*c*) in detecting the degree of concentration and the danger of monopoly in particular industries, and pin-pointing the need for state counter-organization.

(A) By stressing the differential effect (e.g. the tendency to increasing returns) on efficiency and cost, of scale of production and the size of plant and of firm or combine, the analysis of organizations may give point to the real difficulties of measuring monopoly exploitation.

[1] The Effect of Separation of Ownership and Control on the Performance of the Large Firm', *Quarterly Journal of Economics*, 1967, pp. 435–47.

Theoretical economists like A. P. Lerner have proposed as an index of the degree of monopoly some comparison between actual price and marginal cost, since price should equal marginal cost under perfect competition. Owing to the different costs under different scales of operation, such marginal cost has, in practice, unfortunately proved impossible to measure.

The economist's difficulties arising from differences in cost of production due to changes in scale of organization, production and operation may be illustrated by a simplified comparison of costs, profits and prices in two situations. Let us suppose that by becoming larger through knock-out competition or combination, and producing an article on a larger scale with more efficient machines (old or new in invention), a firm's cost of production for that article, apart from profit, is reduced by a fifth from 10 (£ or $) to 8. But this firm is now so large, compared to the total industry, that it can exploit its consumer monopolistically in the sense that it increases (e.g. doubles) its margin of profit, obtaining 2 (£ or $) instead of 1 (£ or $).

Structure	Comparative cost	+	Comparative profits	=	Price to consumer
Competitive structure (many small-scale producers)	10 (£ or $)	+	1 (£ or $)	=	11 (£ or $)
Monopolistic structure. One or a few large-scale producers	8 (£ or $)	+	2 (£ or $)	=	10 (£ or $)

Is the consumer really 'exploited' in the new situation? He actually pays less than before, but there is a higher margin of profit which may or may not have been necessary to call forth the new structure. This contrast in situation, though simplified, is by no means an unrealistic illustration, and is probably of frequent occurrence. It may lie at the bottom of the observed fact that after a monopolistic combination is set up in an industry, its prices may fall and profits rise at the same time.[1]

(B) The structural approach may also give substance to economic theory in observing the extent of the various means by which organizations have actually widened their control (e.g. by association, combination or enlargement through competition) and thus testing which of the rival economists' 'models' are nearer reality. The colourful model of two (or a few) large-scale strategists playing a game (like red versus white chessmen) has challenged[2] the (greyly) imperfect competition model which not so long ago displaced the two alternative models

---

[1] See National Industrial Conference Board, *Mergers in Industry*, 1929.

[2] See Neumann and Morgenstern, *Theory of Games and Economic Behaviour*, 1944; the question of the level of authority at which such a strategy is decided upon is taken up below, Chapter IV.

of (black) monopoly or (white) perfect competition between numerous suppliers.

The various forms of organization for widening control have been covered in textbooks. The main subdivision usually made is between temporary trade associations (for single products or groups of them) ranging all the way from gentlemen's agreements without any documentation[1] through formal written agreements between firms without co-ordinating organization, to trade associations with a formal constitution and a secretariat (and possibly a common profit and loss pool) on the one hand, and on the other permanent combines, with the distinctive power (as against associations) of making central decisions for all purposes, especially investment.[2] Midway between the association of independent firms and the combine which organizes all functions of the constituent firms is the federal form of the syndicate in which otherwise independent firms set up an organization for a specific function such as selling. The all-function combine has several varieties of organization from the type where nominally separate companies have *interlocking directors* or one company is a *holding company* owning a controlling number of shares in other 'subsidiary' companies, to a complete merger where the separate identity of the constituent companies is swallowed up. The complete range of agreement and combination, of which combines are only a section, might be captioned 'from gentleman to cannibal'.

When their purpose is considered monopolistic, associations are usually known as *cartels*, combines as *trusts*, though before 1914 the word cartel was used more narrowly for the selling 'syndicate'. Cartel and trust have, however, become terms of abuse and, in an unbiased discussion of the forms of business alliance, are best not used; not at least until the degree of monopoly aimed at or achieved is ascertained. The object of the alliances which is beyond controversy is that of enlarging the area of application of such top policy decisions as the price to be charged, the output to be sold in any market or the financing of investment. Combination between firms may therefore be considered, in the first instance, as of the same nature as the trend, already considered, toward the large-scale organization of firms and can be justified or condemned on much the same grounds of logic and efficiency.

Associations or combines do not necessarily result in monopoly,

---

[1] G. Picton, *Commercial Agreements*, Cambridge (Bowes & Bowes), 1952.

[2] A combine differs structurally from an association as a single, federally governed, state from an alliance of states (Florence, 1929, pp. 336, 394), has more functions and usually integrates a wider set of products or processes. A longer life is only incidental and not always true. Many gentlemen's agreements have proved of long standing.

nor are they the only method of achieving monopoly. 'Knock-out' competition may do that as well. But if some of a few large firms in a small industry combine together the now still fewer and larger firms and combines may well dominate the situation. The relevant facts in British industry were originally brought out by the enquiry of Leak and Maizels[1] who amplified the data of the census of production of 1935 by considering the size of 'business units'. A business unit means to Leak and Maizels 'a single firm or aggregate of firms owned or controlled by a single company, control being defined as ownership of more than half the capital (or voting power) of each firm'. The organization of joint stock companies permitting such a method of control will be detailed in Chapter V; the definition of a unit clearly includes holding companies plus their subsidiaries, as legally recognized. In manufacturing as a whole the effect of this inclusion upon size-of-organization statistics is considerable, as already seen (Table IH) in contrasting size of plant with size of firm structure. American *plants* employing in 1963 over 2,500 included 17·9 per cent of the total employed in manufacturing; but *firms* of the same size included 45·7 per cent of the total employed. British *plants* employing in 1963 over 10,000 included only 4·1 per cent of the total in manufacturing, but British *firms* of the same size included 32·6 per cent of the total. Taking particular *large* industries one by one the same wide divergence of firm from plant structure is seen in Table IF, by lettering indicating grades of size.

In many industries the economist must clearly reckon with the very large firm or combine; but it must again be stressed that the *absolute* size of a firm or combine, though important to its efficiency, is irrelevant to monopoly, unless that size is large relative to the *whole* industry. If no competing output is imported, output from one firm equivalent to 100 per cent of the whole industry would indicate a complete monopoly, a similar percentage by two firms a duopoly, and so on. Calculations of the percentages of total output achieved by a small number of firms known familiarly as 'concentration ratios' are considered in the next section.

Studies, though less comprehensive, have also been undertaken of the approach toward a monopoly by various other forms of combination such as the interlocking directorate. In America in 1938 the National Resources Committee published in its *Structure of the American Economy* (pp. 158–62) charts of interlocking directorates among 250 large corporations showing very wide 'interest groupings'. In Britain in the inter-war years some facts of interlocking were uncovered largely by way of propaganda, for instance in Haxey's *Tory M.P.* Quite recently, and more objectively, Beesley has traced the interlocking of

---

[1] 'The Structure of British Industry', *Statistical Journal*, 1945, pp. 144–51.

directors between all companies in the British midland metal and metal-using industries and found that, in 1948, a connection could be detected between companies employing as many as one-third of all the workers in the industries. Further, the companies displayed a very marked concentration in the large plant, heavy investment industries. He considers that the significance of this 'interest group' lay not in actual co-ordination of the companies' policies—of price, for example—in particular industries, but in its usefulness as a protective device to ensure that individual investment decisions were not injurious to the other members of the group. The danger in this lay, he holds, in delaying or 'stunting' innovating activity.[1]

When the interlocking directorate and the holding-plus-subsidiary combine are added to the trade association and the complete merger, the reduction of competition *appears* formidable. One important distinction must here, however, be drawn between the combine or merger form of organization, and the association. The association usually covers in its operations specific products or processes. The firm belonging to an association which fixes the price of only one or a few of the firm's products, may well be making a range of hundreds of products in several different industries. There may thus be more associations than 'industries', as commonly defined in the census,[2] and yet only a small proportion of the hundreds of products that are made by each of hundreds of firms may be covered by associations. For estimating the extent of monopoly within any census industry, combines and mergers, since they affect all the products of the factories combined or merged, are more significant than trade associations.

Significant too, are the technical relations, the degree of integration of the firms combined or associated. A monopoly position depends on competition being eliminated in one product or process, not directly on vertical or even lateral integration. Cartels in fact occur chiefly between firms in horizontal relation, i.e. engaged in the same product or process. Combines, on the other hand, often occur between firms in vertical relation. Directors interlock, for instance, between British electrical engineering firms and (before nationalization) electrical supply companies; and between breweries and hotels dispensing the beer. A structural approach to discover the conditions from which monopoly arises, may thus usefully extend the analysis of forms of combination to the correlation of varieties of these forms with varieties of integration.

(C) A third way in which the structural approach may help the theory of monopoly is the practical possibility of detecting in what

[1] Ph.D. thesis, Birmingham.
[2] Associations, together with outsiders recognized as in the same trade, may define an industry, in the sense of a sum of firms or plants competing for the same market, more realistically than the wider census categories.

countries, industries or types of industry the tendency to monopoly, and thus the danger of exploitation, is the strongest. This work of detection is developed in the next section. Structural analysis cannot perhaps do more than establish the 'whereabouts' of monopoly and the areas within which monopoly exploitation may be lurking, but at least many unlikely regions will be eliminated and attention directed to real situations.

§ 7. DETECTING MONOPOLY

The structural approach to the degree of monopoly in particular countries and industries had realistic starting points in American and British enquiries (all based on comprehensive surveys of census statistics) in which measures were worked out for various industries of the degree to which production is concentrated in a very few firms or combines. In *Structure of the American Economy* the U.S. National Resources Committee published, under the direction of Gardiner Means, a ratio of the persons employed by the four largest producers (or companies) compared to the total persons in the industry, for industries distinguished by the census of manufacture in 1935. The T.N.E.C. in its Monograph 27 gave a similar ratio of concentration for 1,807 products made by these industries. For Britain in 1935 Leak and Maizels gave the proportions of persons in the largest three business 'units' for 302 trades or subdivisions. These units include holding companies with their subsidiaries. Twenty of the trades covered were not manufactures, and of the manufactures 108 were main industries as recognized by the census of production, the rest subdivisions.

Since the publication of these pioneer enquiries both the American and British governments have published statistics of industrial concentration at regular intervals.

The simplest way to review the past and current industrial incidence of concentration is to present for the latest year available two tables: IIIB giving for each country the distribution of all industries over the same levels or ranges of concentration; IIIc attempting to show in what different types of industry high or low concentration occurs. Since the main theoretical and practical importance of industrial concentration is its possible monopolizing effect on the market for the industry's product, its measurements, in short, of 'market structure', the more recent statistics use sales or shipments as the unit of account, not number of employees.

Table IIIB distributes all manufacturing industries according to the same four ranges of concentration-ratio, in both countries for 1935, and again at the latest available count—1958 for Britain, 1963 for America.

TABLE IIIB

PERCENTAGE DISTRIBUTION OF ALL INDUSTRIES OVER FOUR RANGES OF
CONCENTRATION RATIOS BASED ON SALES, U.S.A. AND U.K.

	(Total number) (1)	Percentages of total number			
		0–19% (2)	20–49% (3)	50–69% (4)	70% (5)
1935					
1. British industries	(118)*	37	40	14	9
2. British 'sub-divisions'	(234)*	25	46	15	14
3. American 4-digit industries	(275)*	27	46	15	12
1958-1963					
4. British 'industries' 1958	(123)†	29	43	15	13
5. American 4-digit industries 1963	(417)‡	21	50	18	11
Large (a)	(110)	28	45	17	10
Medium (b)	(87)	23	48	21	8
Small (c)	(220)	18	54	16	12

* Reproduced from Florence, *Logic of British and American Industry* (1953), Table IIIc; numbers reduced to percentages.
† U.K. census of production for 1958, Part 133, Table 5.
‡ Report by Bureau of the Census for U.S. Senate Subcommittee on Anti-trust and Monopoly, Part II, Table 6.
(a) Sales $1,000m. and over, annually.
(b) $500m. to $1,000m.
(c) Below $500m.

The sources of the data are given in the footnotes. Reporting on 1935 I noticed in my first edition the similarity of the two distributions; for instance 46 per cent of industries had in both countries concentration-ratios between 20 and 49 per cent. The similarity persisted in 1958–63. Britain had 28 per cent, American 29 per cent of its industries with concentration-ratios between 50 and 100 per cent. The similarity in levels of concentration is, however, not so great as appears because the British concentration refers to the employment or sales of the largest three firms compared to that of the total number in the industry, the American to that of the *four* largest. In short British industry (if firms or enterprises are defined similarly in both countries) is the more concentrated.[1] Moreover, the British census divides up industry into fewer classes in 1958–63, 123 as against 417, and their finer classification of markets should give American industries higher concentration-ratios; so here again British concentration is indicated as actually

[1] How much more can only be estimated. Clearly the fourth largest firm has a lower share of the market than the third, the third than the second, and the second than the first. Hence the sales of the largest four cannot be more than 1⅓ of the sales of the first three. Since sizes of the largest firms taper off rapidly they are probably considerably less than 1⅓.

higher than appears from Table IIIB. But the factor of the greater American distances now come into play. We have to consider only the competition that is accessible to the consumer. Unless its plants are scattered throughout the country or its products are very transportable, a firm making products in Californian plants does not compete with a firm in the same industry with its plants in New York. With American distances in mind it is not possible to say whether the United States or the United Kingdom has the more concentrated industries.

The lower half of the table subdivides the more detailed American classification of industries into three sizes of industry, according to its total sales. It is clear that large American industries with sales over a thousand million dollars per year are not more prone to high concentration than smaller industries. If again we group companies according to concentration ratios above or below 50 per cent each of the three size-classes of industry show an almost exactly similar proportion of industries (27 per cent, 29 per cent and 28 per cent respectively) with 50 per cent ratios or over.

Among the several points which Table IIIB brings out, the most important for its bearing on the monopoly prospects is the trend over the years in the level of concentration. For a fair comparison from year to year of the distribution of industries over time, one must be sure that the industries compared correspond in scope. Two requirements are involved, one stricter than the other. Industries must (a) be part of an equally finely subdivided classification, for, as Shepherd points out[1] 'the measured degree of concentration increases with the fineness of industry definition'. The simplest test of fineness is the total number of industries into which the whole manufacturing sector has been divided. This requirement is satisfied when we compare the 234 British subdivisions (line 2) and the 275 American industries (line 3). It can be seen that the distribution was then extraordinarily similar. Both countries had the same 46 per cent incidence of 20–49 per cent concentration-ratios and the same 15 per cent of 50–69 per cent ratios. The requirement is also satisfied when comparing for 1935 and 1958 (lines 1 and 4) the 118 and the 123 British divisions. Here we see a distinct fall from 37 per cent to 29 per cent in the lowest concentration-ratios and a rise from 9 per cent to 14 per cent in the highest ratios. In short, an increase in concentration. For the trend in American manufacture it is permissible, perhaps, to compare the distribution among the 275 industries of 1935 and the 417 of 1963 (lines 3 and 5). Here stability seems to reign. The proportion of industries falls off at both ends of the scale, though rather more severe at six percentage points among the industries of lowest concentration.

[1] 'Changes in British Industrial Concentration 1951–8', *Oxford Economic Papers*, November 1965.

The relative stability of concentration in the different industry groups is found combined nevertheless with the steadily increasing concentration for industry as a whole, pointed out already (Chapter I § 6)—a paradox explained by the emergence of the integrated, conglomerate, firm straggling over several industry groups.

The more strict (*b*) of the two requirements for fair comparisons of industrial structure is that the scope must be closely examined qualitatively, since official classification and definition often change from time to time. Here we must rely on special enquiries. Several enquiries have been made into British trends in which each industry was compared year to year and only those industries admitted where the definition has not been changed at all in the meanwhile. From 1935 to 1951 Evely and Little[1] found 41 comparable industries: 27 had increased in concentration, 14 diminished. Between 1951 and 1958 Armstrong and Silberston[2] found 63 comparable industries: 36 had increased in concentration, 16 diminished and 11 were unchanged or indeterminate. A similar period was covered also by Shepherd.[3] He found, among 73 industries he matched, that 49 had increased in concentration, 13 had diminished, and 11 showed no change.

Shepherd has also traced the course of concentration ratios in American industry. He reported that the general extent of concentration in individual industries did not change substantially during 1947–58 and that stability was not just due to 'offsetting rises and falls by individual industries, within the general distribution. . . . The actual changes seem to me to have been relatively modest. There have been changes of course; a rise by 10 points or more in 35 industries, a fall of 10 points in 39 industries out of the whole range (of 426 industries).'[4]

Now comes the question whether the similarity in the national distributions of concentration-ratios generally, is also true industry by industry?

Table IIIc uses the framework of the 20 American major industry groups so as to include all branches of manufacture. Each major group is then assessed quantitatively along a scale of concentration. For the American assessment I use in column 1 the semi-official assessment presented by Dr John Blair to the U.S. Senate Subcommittee on Antitrust and Monopoly. The assessment is based on the proportion of shipments from those industries within the group, which showed a concentration of shipments (i.e. sales) of 25 per cent or more from the four

---

[1] *Concentration in British Industry*, 1960, pp. 151–5.
[2] *Size of Plant, Size of Enterprise and Concentration in British Manufacturing Industry 1935–57, Statistical Journal*, Part III, 1965.
[3] Loc. cit.
[4] U.S. Senate Subcommittee Hearings on Economic Concentration, Part 2, 1965, p. 637.

TABLE IIIc

RANKING OF ALL MAJOR INDUSTRY GROUPS IN CONCENTRATION-RATIO

Proportion of U.S. and U.K. industries among total in group with ratio of 25% or more

	U.S.A. in 1963*		U.K. in 1958†		
Major groups	Industries with 4 firm concentration-ratios of 25% or over, weighted by their sales (1)	Rank (2)	Industries with 3 firm ratios of 25% and over plus one point each for (lettered) industries‡ (3)	Divided by total of industries in the group (4)	Rank (5)
Food	52·6	7th	9aaa	12/14 = 0·90	14th
Tobacco	100·0	20th	1b	2/1 = 2·00	20th
Textiles	76·4	13th	7c	8/10 = 0·80	12th
Clothing	15·7	2nd	1	1/8 = 0·12	4th
Timber	11·4	1st	0	0/3 = 0·00	2½
Furniture	23·1	3rd	0	0/3 = 0·00	2½
Paper	68·7	11th	2	2/3 = 0·67	9th
Printing	25·6	4th	1	1/2 = 0·50	5½
Chemicals	76·9	14th	12dddd	16/13 = 1·22	17th
Petroleum	97·1	19th	2e	3/2 = 1·50	19th
Rubber and plastics	36·8	6th	1	1/2 = 0·50	5½
Leather (shoes)	63·4	9th	0	0/4 = 0·00	1st
Stone, brick etc.	63·6	10th	3f	4/6 = 0·67	10th
Primary metal	95·1	17th	2gg	4/4 = 1·00	16th
Fabricated metal	34·3	5th	5	5/7 = 0·70	11th
Machinery	68·9	12th	7	7/11 = 0·64	8th
Electrical	66·7	16th	5	5/6 = 0·84	13th
Transport equipment	96·1	18th	6hh	8/6 = 1·33	18th
Instruments	81·3	15th	2	2/2 = 1·00	15th
Miscellaneous (and ordnance)	60·4	8th	4j	5/8 = 0·62	7th

* Source: Hearings of U.S. Senate Subcommittee on Anti-trust and Monopoly.
† Census of production for 1958, Part 133.
‡ *a–j Concentration-ratios over 70%*
    (a) Sugar 96·0%, spirit distilling 91·0%, margarine 80·2%.
    (b) Tobacco 94·1%.
    (c) Man-made fibres 89·4%.
    (d) Explosives 92·6%, dyestuffs 83·8%, vegetable oils etc. 75·4%, soap etc. 71·7%.
    (e) Mineral oil refining 87·9%.
    (f) Cement 86·3%.
    (g) Cans and metal boxes 87·0%, steel tubes 84·8%.
    (h) Railway carriages 70·5%, locomotives 90·9%.
    (j) Small arms 84·8%.

largest producers. Column 2 *ranks* the industry groups[1] according to

[1] This ranking appears in Florence, *Economics and Sociology of Industry*, Table XIX, column V B.

this assessment. For the British assessment I group industries as nearly as possible to correspond to the American grouping though, owing to overlapping in their contents, the American 'primary' metal and 'fabricated' metal groups cannot be separately identified with the British 'metal manufacture' and 'metal goods not elsewhere specified' and must be combined.

To assess the British degree of concentration of the whole group I use an unweighted procedure. The number of industries concentrated 25 per cent or more is given in column 4 and one point is added for each letter indicating industries of extreme concentration with the result shown as a percentage of total shipments (given for 1958 in column 4). Comparability within each country is provided by the columns (2 and 5) of ranks, and the additional feature of the letters to refer to particularly high concentration, i.e. 70 per cent or more of particular industries, within the group. The names of these industries appear in the footnotes. Where two or more British industry groups show (by comparing the column of their concentrated industries with their total of industries) that their concentration-ratios are of equal value, rank is ceded to the group with most letters indicating very high concentration; and when there are no letters it is ceded to the larger absolute number of concentrated industries.

The earlier table has already established the very similar level of concentration in British and American industries; here it is the comparative position, i.e. the ranking, of corresponding groups of industries that is of particular interest. Inspection of Table IIIc shows the ranking to be very similar in both countries and it can be asserted that high concentration and the hazard of monopoly arises in both countries in the area of tobacco, chemicals, petroleum refining, electrical machinery, transport equipment and, in view of the many very high ratios in the food group, certain food industries. Areas of low concentration, presumably with considerable competition, occur, again in both countries, in timber, furniture, clothing and printing. Type of work certainly has more influence on concentration than the size of the industry. The seven highest concentrated major industry groups in America, ranking 14th to 20th are among the eight highest concentrated British industry groups ranking 13th to 20th.

To sum up: when an industry is concentrated in a few firms or businesses in Britain (or America) it tends also to be so concentrated in America (or Britain). In spite of the different geographical, economic, political and social characteristics of the two countries, the degrees of concentration of control (whether monopolistic or competitive) show a similarity for corresponding industries. This similarity of structure industry by industry is a further result of physical, technological and distribution (i.e. the ergological) characteristics of each industry,

161

including inelasticity of demand and of supply. These characteristics are apparently important enough to override national peculiarities in resources, climate and customs—in nature and nurture. Without discovering and taking account of them, effective control of monopoly may well prove impossible.

Once we have measured in what industries production is particularly concentrated, two practical questions are worth asking. What were the causes of the concentration, and what positive evidence exists that the power thus concentrated results in the exploitation of the consumer or supplier?

Some clue to the causes is provided by finding that the degree of concentration is much the same for the same industries in both countries, and that the concentrated industry groups—chemicals, petroleum refining, electrical machinery, transport equipment and tobacco—have certain characteristics in common. They are capital-intensive, science-based or puff-needing (or a mixture thereof) involving difficulty in raising sufficient capital for equipment and building, and presenting in the words of Bain a high 'barrier' to competition. Other barriers to competition are the need of research staff for scientific innovation, and, particularly with consumer goods such as motor-cars and tobacco, for consultants on puffing wares by advertising. Both research staff and advertising campaigns may need capital beyond the means of most new firms. But it is always possible for a firm established in some other industry to integrate and 'cross-subsidize' into the new venture, probably financing early losses from its established interests. The recent development of conglomerate firms may well be attributed, among other factors, to this possibility of hedging against risk, or establishing monopoly.

As to some resultant exploitation the main test must be high rates of profit though, as already pointed out, if costs are lowered by large-scale production, higher profits are not necessarily due to higher prices, but maybe to greater efficiency.[1]

Empirical quantitative research is comparatively still scarce and almost confined to America.[2] But if they are to help solve the monopoly problem realistic economists should look into the determinants of profit differences. Certainly the more an industry is concentrated in control, the more important it is to determine the policy and the

[1] This is the Morton's Fork of the profit measure. Gifts were extorted from King Henry VIIth's subjects for two opposite reasons, because they obviously lived well, or because they lived ill and had presumably saved money. Similarly if profit is high the firm can be charged with monopoly; if it is low with inefficiency.

[2] See Florence, *Economics and Sociology of Industry*, Ch. VIII § 3. I quote reasons for this scarcity from Hutchison, *The Significance and Basic Postulates of Economic Theory*.

economic performance of the controllers within the individual firms in which output is concentrated. No longer are the total supply and total demand in the market the sole determinants of prices. Prices are to some extent at least 'administered' by the monopolist or oligopolist firms. It is important therefore to turn attention to the type of government within these large firms. Does concentration of power hold good within these firms as well as within the whole industry in which these firms predominate? Is there, in short, a two-fold process—concentration piled upon concentration?

The next chapter will analyse the division of work and government within large industrial organizations. The following two chapters will try to pinpoint the centre of government in a large capitalist firm and to contrast its functioning with alternative forms of industrial organization such as the nationalized public corporation, or the co-operative society.

CHAPTER IV

RELATIONS WITHIN THE MODERN FIRM. MANAGEMENT AND TOP GOVERNMENT

§ 1. THE TREND OF INVESTMENT AND EMPLOYMENT. OVERHEAD COSTS

THE structure of industry in Britain and America is marked, as already described, by large organization, organized marketing policies and monopoly or oligopoly. The attention of the economist must therefore be directed less toward the equilibrium of supply and demand and the higgling on the market of hundreds of small firms, and more toward the complex organization of policy making and of government within the few large firms who are able to exercise some influence on production, price and progress. This internal organization should logically have developed to realize the advantages of large-scale organization and to exploit the possibilities of monopoly or oligopoly. The top controllers of most large firms do, in fact, spend considerable time and thought on their price and output policy in any given line of product. Modern technical progress also forces the top control to think hard about investment in machines and technical processes generally and also in the employment of expert specialists. The economy of large-scale operation ultimately depends upon *the full use of mechanical and human specialization*. Once relations with the consumer are so organized that a large-scale of production is feasible, then the producer may invest in the special machinery, equipment and plant adapted to the particular variety of product concentrated upon, and may proceed to employ separate specialist managers.

The facts show that investment in machinery and equipment has already proceeded far. Plants and firms have increased in the number of men employed, as shown in Chapter II; but they have increased still more in their capital. While, in America, in 1879 the capital invested[1] was 2·94 times the annual cost of wages in manufacturing industries, in 1899 the ratio had risen to 4·23; and between the same years the ratio of horse-power to wage-earners rose from 1·28 to 2·05.[2] In 1899 the American census of manufactures on which these figures are based started excluding establishments with products valued at less than $500 (and in 1919 $5,000 per annum) and later dropped the calculation of capital invested; but comparing comparable figures the

---

[1] This includes working capital (e.g. stocks) as well as fixed capital.
[2] Florence, 1948, p. 126.

ratio of horse-power per production worker increased between 1899 and 1919 from 2·18 to 3·33; in 1929 it was 4·91, in 1939 6·52, in 1954 9·58, in 1962 12·49.[1] It is noticeable that there is little here of the deceleration often presumed of settled economies. In the five successive periods (of from 8 to 20 years each) the increased rate of horse-power *added* per *production* worker, per decade, was 0·57, 1·58, 1·61, 2·04 and 3·55—a progression faster at the end than the middle. In Britain, however, progress has been more erratic. Between 1907 and 1924, the official Committee on Industry and Trade quoted a rise in the horse-power *available* (including reserve or idle) per worker[2] which was from 1·63 to 2·54 for the bulk of manufactures. Between 1924 and 1930, according to the census of production the horse-power *in use* per worker rose in all factory trades from 2·02 to 2·44.

Unfortunately only in one year later than 1930 did the U.K. census record horse-power capacity—1951. For all manufactures it was, then, 3·1 per worker. The added horse-power per worker in the three periods 1907–24, 1924–30, 1930–51 thus amounted to 0·20, 0·70, 0·31 per decade—the latter including a period of depression and a long war.

Consequences of this continued technical revolution and deeper investment are first, and most physically obvious, a higher output per worker; second, more risk of failure to cover greater overhead costs —an additional type of problem requiring more planning by the top control of firms; third, a higher proportion of managers, supervisors, technical assistants and office staff per manual worker.

If the intensity of investment be measured by horse-power per worker it is not difficult to trace its effect upon output per worker when comparing different countries, different industries with varying horse-power per man, or different times within the same country for the same industries. Comparing American and British manufactures as a whole, Rostas considers that the American output per worker was, in 1938, over double that of Britain, and the horse-power per worker was then probably nearly three times as high.[3] In both countries output per worker has since increased with the increased horse-power per worker.[4]

The increased investment in fixed specialized plant, machines and mechanical and chemical processes has been reflected in a disproportionate increase in fixed overhead costs, compared with the prime cost of raw materials and of wages and labour costs that *vary with the output*. In modern organization this implies that during a trade depression

[1] U.S. Statistical Abstract, 1970, p. 715.
[2] *All* workers are included in the denominator so that the intensity of mechanization is greater compared to the U.S. than appears from the crude ratios.
[3] Part of the general trend for a country's productivity per man to be proportioned to horse-power per man, mentioned (Chapter I, § 2) in the technical background.
[4] See below, Chapter VI, § 6, for detailed estimates of this 'progress' up to 1963.

or any other crisis for the firm, more factors prevent costs being adjusted to the lower output.

Certain costs are *constant* over time regardless of output, or at least *not adjustable or variable* in proportion to output. Such are the costs of obsolescence and depreciation (though not wear and tear from actual work) of the specialized plant which once laid down for a specific purpose cannot, without additional expense, be adjusted to other uses. Lumped by accountants into overhead, are also costs *common*, but not easily allocated, to different processes. Some of these, like supplies of oil, vary proportionately with output and should not be included with the constant overhead. Others are common and more or less unadjustable to output, largely because they are indivisible. If the output of any one process has to be cut down or even cut out altogether these indivisible common costs must continue in full strength, not because they cannot, physically speaking, be cut down, but because the full or nearly the full 'quantum' is required for the remainder of the processes. The clearest examples of such common costs are the heating, lighting and ventilation of a room which must be heated and lit and ventilated *en bloc* as a unit throughout the scheduled hours of work, even though in some parts little or no output is being turned out. The administrative staff is another such cost. A complete foreman must continue to be employed even if his departmental output is halved. It is the old problem of indivisibility of economic units. You cannot have half a foreman, or half a heated room.

The special problems raised by these constant and common indivisible overhead costs and requiring preparatory planning may be illustrated from the alternative employment policies for meeting a fall in demand: either working all short-time or dismissing some workers as 'redundant'. In both cases output falls, and the costs will increase per unit of output of all items that are 'constant'.

A short-time policy may not, however, increase some of the cost per unit of output (as dismissals will) on the items that are 'common'. Heating, lighting and power generation and transmission by shafting can be restricted to the precise shorter hours or fewer days when persons are employed in the plant; and where shorter hours per day are worked and lighting and heating costs are different for different hours, the least costly can be selected. If fewer hours are worked per day in winter, the hours naturally lightest and warmest may be selected. On the other hand, the dismissal policy can reduce overhead costs by dismissing men on the less efficient machines or in complete sections of the plant, dispensing with all lighting, heating and power-transmission there—as well, possibly, as some of the supervisory staff.

When no machines were used and equipment was of the simplest, the men employed could be hired and fired as demand fluctuated, involving no cost of idle overheads. But with intense investment in machinery it is logical, for maximum efficiency or minimum loss, to plan ahead with the policy of getting the most out of the fixed equipment. It is logical, for instance, to employ machines full-time or as full-time as possible, by shifts of operators.[1]

More intense physical investment and increased productivity per

TABLE IVA

STAFF RATIOS: THE PROPORTION OF SALARIED STAFF TO PRODUCTION WORKERS ('OPERATIVES'), 1947–1967

| Census year | U.S.A.* | | U.K.† | |
	Non-production workers§	Production workers	Administrative, technical and clerical staff	Operatives
1947	—‡	—‡	1,093 (19·9)	5,487 (100)
1950	2,991 (25·4)	11,779 (100)	—	—
1954	3,755 (30·4)	12,373 (100)	1,417 (22·8)	6,234 (100)
1958	4,359 (37·4)	11,666 (100)	1,653 (27·1)	6,108 (100)
1963	4,729 (38·5)	12,232 (100)	1,856 (30·9)	6,016 (100)
1967	5,423 (38·7)	13,975 (100)		

* Statistical Abstract, 1970 pp. 713, 716–17.
† Census of production for relevant year.
‡ See text for non-availability (p. 168).
§ Workers in administrative offices, independent of plants, are included.

direct labour usually entails an increased ratio of (indirect) labour and salaried managers, foremen and office staff. Machines displace direct labour but more staff is required to cope with the greater number or complexity of machines and the greater output. Additional planning logically connected with intense investment because of the need to get the most out of fixed equipment, also entails additional staff.

The facts follow this logic of increased office staff and middle-rank management, as Table IVA shows, both in Britain and America. In 1947 the U.S. census substituted in place of the division between 'wage-earners' and 'salaried officers and employees', a category of 'production workers'. This change prevents a standard series of indicators for the staff ratio continuing up to the present. In Table IVA I take the balance of all employees who are not production workers to be indirect staff including salaried office workers, typists etc. They may not, however,

[1] Objections by labour to this logical policy are discussed in Chapter VII, § 1.

be exactly comparable with the British or with the previous American category. In 1950 a further change was made by the U.S. census; headquarter administrative offices independent of the plants and works auxiliary to manufacturing were included. These have, of course, a particularly high staff ratio, almost 100 per cent. So Table IVA can only start the American columns in 1950.[1]

The balance of employees that are not production workers has been rising fast from 1950 to 1967 and their ratio to production workers still faster, faster indeed than the contemporary rise in Britain of the staff to operative ratio. This fast increase in the white- over the blue-collar worker is a fairly universal phenomenon in industrial society. Mechanization and the increased productivity of the production workers which staff have to cope with, is not the only cause. Research staff and technologists have increased greatly in science-oriented industries. Some critics of state interference blame increased form-filling. Other critics the firm's own bureaucracy and excessive paper work. Melman's conclusion[2] quoted in my first edition that high staff ratios are not associated with large firms requires further examination in the light of the new size of enterprise data of the U.S. 1963 census. As larger and larger enterprises (i.e. firms) are considered, the ratios (which do not include workers in headquarter offices) rise from firms employing 50–99 at 26 per cent, 100–499 at 29 per cent and 500–999 at 31 per cent, to firms employing 1,000–2,499 at 32 per cent and over 2,500 at 37 per cent.

Two considerations must modify conclusions from these statistics that appear to confirm Parkinson's Law of unnecessary overhead staff costs in large organizations. Value added per employee (production, not staff) as shown in the last column of the table on p. 83 is much higher in the larger sizes. If we may judge from the 1954 census (the last to publish this type of analysis) this progression is due mainly to the greater mechanization of the larger plants (see footnote accompanying the table) and, as already said, it is the larger firms that own the larger plants. Machines replace the production worker and the increased output from their use will need increased staff more or less proportionately. When workers in headquarters offices are added, this rise with size in the staff-ratio becomes considerably steeper since headquarter workers are almost entirely staff and only the large firms have headquarters separate from operating plant. But the other consideration which will be taken up shortly is the changing economic structure; highly staffed have been taking the place of low-staffed industries.

If we compare not times, or sizes of organizations but countries, a striking similarity appears between the rank of American and British manufacturing industries in the order of their staff ratios. The American

---

[1] See Florence, *Economics and Sociology of Industry*, Chapter I.
[2] Op cit., p. 140.

major industry groups differ widely in their staff ratios (from 10·7 per cent to 38·3 per cent in 1958, to be exact). The highest ratios are given in my *Economics and Sociology of Industry*[1] as those of petroleum, printing, chemicals, food, instruments and electrical machinery. In Britain the manufacturing orders (or industries corresponding to the American major groups) have a similarly wide range in staff-ratios (from 12·1 per cent to 37·1 per cent) and those which have the highest staff ratios are much the same.[2]

The American major groups with the lowest staff-ratios are, lowest first, leather (mainly footwear), textiles, tobacco, clothing and lumber. Again these are also the British industries with the lowest staff-ratios except for tobacco (which in Britain contains a much lower proportion of cigar-making); furniture (7th lowest in America) takes its place among the five industries with the lowest staff-ratio. This international agreement in the ranking of staff-ratios, and the wide range of these ratios, testifies strongly to the influence on organization of the type of work. Each industry group is defined by its work fairly similarly in each country; but in other respects the countries disagree. The agreement on staff-ratio industry by industry prevails despite wide disagreement between the two countries in size of markets and the distribution of resources such as raw materials and food.

The further question, however, what precise characters in the work can be linked with this two-nation staff-ratio ranking, is not easy to answer. It is an important question because, apart from the social significance of the rise of the 'white-collar' bourgeoisie, a high staff-ratio points to high overhead costs and a possible Parkinson's Law source of inefficiency which some industries may suffer from more than others. If this law were a true hypothesis explaining the extent that staff grew disproportionately to the size of organizations, the staff-ratio ranking would be closely correlated, positively, with that of the size of plants or of firms. Rank-correlation of the twenty American industry groups shows, on the contrary, a low positive and a (low) negative coefficient for staff ratios when correlated respectively with plant and with firm size.

Another hypothesis is suggested by the parallel rise in the course of time (already traced for manufactures as a whole) of the staff-ratio with mechanization. But again comparing the twenty American industry groups there is little correlation in their ranking according to staff-ratios and to horse-power per worker.[3]

[1] Appendix, Table XIX.
[2] See U.K. Annual Abstract of Statistics, 1967, Table 141 and census of production, 1963.
[3] *Economics and Sociology of Industry*, 1969, (Appendix) Table XIX. Columns Iᴅ and Ici.

One difference does seem, however, to distinguish industry groups with higher from groups with lower staff-ratios. It is the comparative senescence of the industry. Of the twenty American major industry groups, five diminished in number employed between 1947 and 1964: textiles, leather (mostly footwear), tobacco, lumber and petroleum.[1] All except petroleum were among the five with lowest staff-ratios. British experience is much the same. Of the industry groups corresponding as closely as possible with the twenty American, six fell in number employed (or rose less than the all-industry average): textiles, clothing, footwear, furniture, tobacco and petroleum.[2] All except petroleum refining had staff-ratios below the average for manufacturing as a whole—the first four, considerably below. At the other end of the scale, not that of senescence but adolescence, American industry groups which proportionately increased most in numbers employed between 1947 and 1964 were electrical machinery, transport equipment, chemicals, instruments, rubber and plastics and printing. These six industries were all among the seven with highest staff-ratios. Thus the British high-staffed industries were, as already said, the same as the American and they were also in both countries the fastest growing 'adolescent' industries.

There is a difficulty, however, in measuring the growth of an industry simply by the growing total of number employed. Many industries have developed as a result of new technologies so radically applied that the number of operators or 'production workers' has been reduced absolutely. This explains the exception of the petroleum industry to the association of high staffing with adolescence when measured by growth of employment. It is in fact an exception which proves the rule! Petroleum reduced its production workers from 146 to 105 thousand between 1939 and 1964 but increased its horse-power capacity per production worker from 22·84 to 89·46, a fourfold increase which contrasts with a mere doubling for all manufacture as a whole. The real growth of an industry must be measured by other indicators beside number of personnel, such as increase in equipment capacity or assets, or by indices of the value or volume of its output.

The increase in the proportion of staff is so universal a modern trend in industrial development[3] and apparently increasing so steadily, that it should be analysed in greater detail. It must first be recognized that the increase in the ratio for manufacturing as a whole is partly due to the changing composition of the manufacturing sector. Different manufactures differ widely in their staff-ratio, and the particular industries

[1] U.S. Statistical Abstracts, 1950, pp. 760–70; 1966, pp. 768–72.
[2] For difficulty in measuring the growth in petroleum refining by numbers employed, see p. 44.
[3] *Economics and Sociology of Industry*, Chapter, I.

which have a high ratio are growing faster and are in the total composition becoming more important, those with a lower ratio becoming less important. But as well as this, each industry is increasing its own ratio, marking the greater part played by the two elements of technology and management. Technological development has already been shown in Chapter I as dating back many years, by the increase in mechanical capacity per producer. In recent years it can be measured, also, by expenditure on research and development and by the number of scientists and technicians in industry. Expenditure on research in British industry runs particularly high in aircraft—in 1964–5 it was just over £500 per worker. In other industries it ranged downward from £300 in petroleum[1] and £255 in electronic equipment to £120 in chemicals and £50 in mechanical engineering including instruments. In the remaining manufactures, research expenditure was negligible. In spite of the relatively high expenditures just mentioned the research expenditure per worker for manufactures as a whole was only £53.

American statistics of the number of scientists and technicians in 1967[2] when divided by the totals employed in each industry group yield the following percentages: ordnance and accessories 24 per cent; petroleum refining 15 per cent; chemicals, and also instruments 11 per cent; vehicles (including aircraft), and also electrical equipment 10 per cent. Again, as in Britain, the remaining industries are rank outsiders. In spite of these high ratios in these six major groups the average ratio for all manufactures is only 5·9 per cent.

When scientists are subtracted, the 'net' staff ratio may be said to represent mainly the growth of management and its attendant clerical work, and the decline of the skilled craftsman. In fact as British statistics distinguishing skilled from other operatives show,[3] a ranking of the ratio of skilled to total employment among the industry groups would run almost exactly opposite to their ranking by staff ratios. Clothing, footwear, timber and furniture, leather goods and shipbuilding, with staff ratios of 20 per cent or less have over 135 men and women classed as skilled, to every 100 semi-skilled or other operatives. The two large high staff-ratio groups with ratios of 28 per cent or more, chemicals and vehicles, have less than 25 skilled.[4]

Looking into the future one may perhaps prophesy that industries with the syndrome adolescent, science-based, capital-intensive, high staffed, few craftsmen, will gradually be displacing the others as adolescents do in the human population and that training in technology

---

[1] Annual Abstract of Statistics, 1967, p. 138.
[2] U.S. Statistical Abstract, 1970, pp. 526, 718.
[3] Annual Abstract of Statistics, 1967, p. 112.
[4] Annual Abstract of Statistics, 1967, p. 112. No skill classification is made for engineering and electrical goods.

and management will become of more practical use than long apprenticeship. This prophecy is independent of the answer to the question whether a basis in science and high staffing causes growth or growth causes science and high staffing to be applicable. Both processes may be at work in a 'virtuous circle', through economies external because of more firms or internal because of larger firms. A growing industry may be able to use relatively more specialized and research staff and scientific innovation; more staff and innovation may in turn help growth.

§ 2. EVOLUTION OF SPECIALIZED MANAGEMENT

The increase in salaried staff compared to operatives is not merely quantitative in interest but marks a qualitative structural change in the corps of managers. Management becomes more specialized and more graded into ranks from general manager to foreman and chargehand.

The relationship of employment and investment between different persons arose when the trader, originally working with his own hands and using his own capital resources, gradually hired men to work for him and borrowed capital to work with. The one-man trader may in fact be pictured as splitting up his activities and assigning some of them to specialized labourers and investors, leaving himself the work of management or general control.

In 1909, the U.S. Census of Manufactures tells us (1939, p. 67), there were 4·1 proprietors or firm 'members' to a hundred wage-earners. Since then division of labour has taken place devolving much management upon salaried officers. This division of managerial function had developed far by 1939. Proprietors and firm members decreased absolutely, and compared to salaried officers and employees were by then (for every 100 wage-earners) only 1·4 to 20 instead of 4·1 to 11·9. The qualitative subdivision of managerial function corresponding to these quantitative data may be illustrated thus:

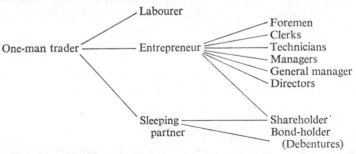

The owner-manager entrepreneur has almost disappeared in

manufacturing and his functions of taking risks with his capital and of managing are shared between shareholders, directors and managers. In addition to the increase in fixed capital, therefore, large-scale operation and organization involves separate, specialized management. And just as the internal organization of producing and distributing firms may be slow in adapting itself to the greater use of fixed capital, so the organization may also be slow in adapting itself to the more efficient use of the specialized management that is required in the economy of all large-scale operations.

Most economists used to agree that the chief obstacle to the extension of the size of firms is due to the limit of the work that a single man can do in controlling large-scale operations. Thus J. H. Jones writes:[1]

After a certain stage has been reached in the growth of the unit the economies either remain constant or, in many cases, grow less. The final limit is set by the difficulty experienced in securing ability of a sufficiently high order to direct the policy and organization of the unit. The latter becomes too unwieldy for effective control.

E. A. G. Robinson[2] also saw in the factor of management a definite limit to the scale upon which firms can be organized.

There must come a point at which the machine is too unwieldy to be managed, a point at which the gains of increasing size are so negligible that the still increasing costs of co-ordination are likely to exceed them. In this the managerial optimum differs from the technical optimum. The latter affords only a minimum scale below which the greatest efficiency cannot be achieved. Additional output may be produced under conditions of approximately constant cost. But if the managerial optimum is exceeded, costs, through declining efficiency and the need for additional co-ordination, begin to rise. The managerial optimum sets, therefore, not only a lower, but also an upper limit to the scale of operations.

This view of the economists neglects the distinction between large-scale organization and operation. The limit to single management is obviously reached much sooner when the particular size of the firm is due to a great complexity of organization with a variety of goods made, each on a small scale, than when the same size is due to one article specialized upon in a large-scale mass operation.

Most of those who have made a special study of organization, however, differ from the economists.[3] They come to the conclusion that no limit is set to the size of organization, if correct principles are adopted to enable the single leader to delegate control.

'The vastest organization that the human mind can conceive will not

---

[1] *Economics of Private Enterprise*, 1925, pp. 123–4.
[2] *Structure of Competitive Industry*, 1931, p. 48.
[3] Ord is an exception in agreeing with the economists. See note below, p. 195.

be too vast for efficient one man leadership if the (hierarchical) and functional principles are correctly applied.' These principles in the sharing of government lift the limits to the magnitude of an organization. 'Without these principles, all operations of any magnitude would be absolutely dependent for their creation and permanence on an administrative genius of corresponding magnitude, and could not hope long to survive the removal of such genius.'[1]

Undoubtedly there are men who would be competent to head industrial organizations of almost any size, but accepting the 'normal' distribution of inborn abilities, it is usually assumed that such geniuses are rare, and that the average head of a business is not competent to manage on a scale beyond a certain point. When the size of his firm is small, and all contacts with his subordinates are personal and 'face-to-face' the problems of communication and identification are simple and direct. But with growth in the size of organization, management becomes corporate and shared, and, as stressed later, labour identifies itself less with the management. There must be delegation of powers, so as to relieve the strain and responsibility of the man at the top, and some restructuring into small groups, identified with a part of the production. Delegation, indeed, must be conceived not as just unilaterally a process of decentralizing. It also covers *not centralizing*—not allowing powers to accrue to the top if autonomy and local responsibility at lower levels will serve instead. This two-way reference of delegation, though not strictly applicable to *external* price, output and investment policy, is important in the internal organization of labour for production and will be reverted to (Chapter VII, § 1) when discussing factory and group autonomy. Problems constantly arise at the front line, the 'spear-head' point of contact of direct producer with production; but they must not be allowed to rise too high before decision, particularly where only interpretation of rules already settled is concerned.[2] If it is needed to remind readers, the phrase local autonomy will be coupled with delegation.

Delegation so far from being a necessary evil of large organization may actually achieve additional economies. I question (Chapter VII, § 6) whether geniuses need be quite so rare in British industry; but however rare, a genius may through his delegates exercise a wider influence, and, by division of labour, the delegates may acquire dexterity in their management speciality, and specialities can be fitted to each manager's innate special talents.

The growth in the proportion of salaried staff to operatives, and the fall in proprietor and firm members which accompanies the growth

---

[1] Mooney and Reiley, *Onward Industry*, p. 308.
[2] Florence, *Labour*, 1949, p. 191.

in the size of plants and firms is the outward, visible and statistically measurable sign of the inward division in the work of managing plants and firms. This division raises problems which the social sciences should be prepared to tackle.

More managers, sub-managers and office staff are created to assist the head of the business. In the final section of this chapter the functions will be considered that must be reserved for the top-level government of a business. This and the following sections will take up the relations between the top and subordinate, middle-level, specialized managers which tend to further efficient large-scale operation. The economy of large-scale operation consists partly in the very fact that specialized managers can be used to their full capacity; but the difficulty then presents itself of determining relations between these managers and sub-managers, so that their interests, authority and work will not conflict.

As industry becomes conducted by fewer and larger organizations, questions of political science becomes more important relatively to questions of economics. In earlier times when a vast number of small firms were competing for the consumer's custom, and haggling and higgling one with another, the questions of price and the other terms upon which they bought and sold were determined by the aggregate supply and demand on the market where goods and services were exchanged; but in the twentieth century the area where exchanges are carried on, the area of Economics, has become more restricted. Price on the market is often a matter of a few big firms' policy, and more of the key transactions of industry are carried on *inside* the organization, without exchange for a price. Now relations of persons *within* an organization are an important part of political science. It is true that till recently political science has confined itself to questions of State, but as I have illustrated elsewhere,[1] scientific laws or generalizations applied to the State are also applicable in industrial, or indeed in any large organization.

By an organization is here meant any body or association of persons within which there is normally a government or rule relation (authority with sanctions, discipline and commands issued and replied to). This definition obviously includes industrial firms and trade unions, as well as armies, churches and states. Within the small industrial firm typical a hundred years ago, there were simply two sub-structures or parties, the governing or ruling entrepreneur-employer-capitalist and the governed, ruled, employee-workers. Within this simple firm, problems of internal government centre on the relations of hiring (and firing) and training the workers, providing sanctions or incentives to work and

[1] Florence, 1929, especially Chapters III, IV, XIX, XX.

testing consequent labour efficiency by reference to output, absence and labour turnover rates.

As soon as the ruler-party becomes several people (shareholders, directors, managers) the study of government includes the relations internal to the governing party, as well as those between the governing and the governed party. Instead of one person—an unlimited monarch or autocrat—making rules or laws, executing and adjudicating on them (steps which he may or may not distinguish psychologically), there will be (more or less formally) a separate legislature, executive and judicature, as in constitutional state governments with their 'separation of powers'. Within the legislature or rule-making body, moreover, separate people may be initiating, discussing, formulating and finally deciding the rules, laws, policy or strategy. And within the executive or administrative function, separate people may be planning, organizing, commanding, co-ordinating and checking up.[1] The structural approach, heralded in the first chapter, cautions us not to abstract and split functions with their characteristic '-ing' endings unless they are split observably between persons, bodies and social structures like the legislators, administrators and adjudicators, or planners, organizers, etc. (with their characteristic '-or' or '-er' endings). These relations between the substructures or organs internal to a complex government each with different powers may be called the 'procedure' of government. For perpetuating and developing procedure, some specific method out of various alternatives[2] will be devised of *structuring* the government, that is of creating new substructures (boards, cabinets, departments, committees or individual posts *et al.*), and of *manning* them, that is appointing persons—by nomination, election, co-option *et al.*, on principles of seniority, merit, nepotism *et al.*—to those substructures of government. In short, as well as relations, a *procedure* for deciding policy external to the whole organization (e.g. price to customers) and policy external to the ruling party but internal to the organization (i.e. relations of ruler and ruled like training policy) there will be relations, a *constitution* for organizing, structuring and manning, the ruling party itself.[3] The structure involved in these internal relations can be shown on what industrialists call their organization

---

[1] In his *Exploration in Management*, 1960, Lord Brown illustrates effectively the applicability of the notions of political science to industry.

[2] See Florence, 'The Method and Content of Political Science', *Aristotelian Society Proceedings*, 1933–4, especially pp. 127–8.

[3] The similarity in the procedure and constitutional concepts and devices of complex state and industrial organizations makes the need obvious for a common political science. Lord Salisbury, incidentally, thought (Woolf, *After the Deluge*, pp. 210–11) the most 'natural' and the highest type of organization for regulating the nineteenth century state to be that of the joint stock company. He was, however, writing before he was Prime Minister.

chart. This is a diagram that sets forth as in Table IVB the respective functions and positions of the individuals forming the corps of managers. Relations of rule and appointment are usually traced vertically, downwards; relations of work, i.e. division of labour, at the same level of rule are traced laterally, and thus the system of relations within any one firm may be depicted as a whole, including relations of the ruling corps with the ruled rank and file employees.

European pioneers in the political science of industrial organization include Fayol and Urwick. Fayol, whom Urwick introduced to the English-speaking world, distinguishes six groups of 'operations' which occur in business undertakings: technical, commercial, financial, security, accounting and administration. Apart from accounting (which in the form of budgeting and statistical recording of costs, is coming into greater prominence) these groups of operations clearly correspond to Robinson's grouping of functions on which different optimum sizes of units depend:[1] the functions of producing, marketing, financing, guarding against risks and fluctuations, and managing. All except the last of these operations, the administrative or managing functions, are peculiar to business and Fayol, like a true political scientist, is interested most in this 'administration'. He subdivides it into five specific 'elements' of planning, organizing, commanding, co-ordinating and controlling (i.e. checking up on results). His 'administration', as Fayol himself says, thus involves more than what is usually understood by managing. To include all functions or operations at topmost as well as lower levels, the word government is here proposed. No word short of this (such as management or 'administration' itself) covers external policy toward the outside world as well as internal relations and the total procedure of legislating, execution and final adjudication involved in top-level planning, organizing, commanding, co-ordinating and checking up. The word 'control', formerly usable, now suggests imposing limitations or merely exercising a general supervision, not active operation, and will only be used, and then sparingly, for active top-level government when qualified as top control.

In America the political science of business organization was carried further by the analysis of relations within that prevailing form of business organization, the corporation. Works that have contributed to this analysis include Berle and Means' *The Modern Corporation and Private Property* (1932), Barnard's *The Functions of the Executive* (1938), John C. Baker's *Directors and their Functions* (1945), Gordon's *Business Leadership in the Large Corporation* (1945) and Ruml's *Tomorrow's Business* (1945). In a chapter on 'Business as a Rule-Maker' Ruml maintained that

---

[1] *Structure of Competitive Industry*, 1931, Chapter II–VI.

TABLE IVʙ

SAMPLE ORGANIZATION CHART OF LARGE FIRM

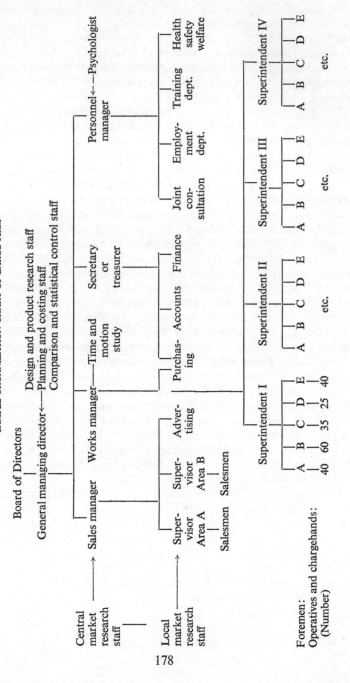

Board of Directors

Central market research staff ⟶ Sales manager   Works manager   Secretary or treasurer   Personnel ← Psychologist manager

General managing director ←— Design and product research staff
Planning and costing staff
Comparison and statistical control staff

Local market research staff ⟶

Supervisor Area A   Supervisor Area B   Advertising   Time and motion study   Purchasing   Accounts   Finance   Joint consultation   Employment dept.   Training dept.   Health safety welfare

Salesmen   Salesmen

Superintendent I   Superintendent II   Superintendent III   Superintendent IV

Foremen:
Operatives and chargehands: (Number)

	A	B	C	D	E
Superintendent I	40	60	35	25	40
Superintendent II	A	B	C	D E	etc.
Superintendent III	A B	C	D E	etc.	
Superintendent IV	A	B	C	D E	etc.

It is in no sense a figure of speech to refer to a company like the American Tobacco Co. and to each of its counterparts, large and small, as a private government. A business is a *government* because within the law it is authorized and organized to make rules for the conduct of its affairs. It is a private government because the rules it makes within the law are final and are not reviewable by any public body.

This statement justifies economists taking a more sophisticated interest in what political science might have to say on various procedures in decision making, in appointing top staff, in decentralization or in constitution building. After all, these are the very activities which political scientists and the more realistic lawyers study in organizations other than industrial.

Political science also deals with questions of power and conflict and can bring experience and analysis of other organizations (including the state) into the present pluralist situation in industry where trade unions, though independent, participate in management.[1] The best known exponents of this extension of political science into industry include Drücker, *The Practice of Management* (1954), Eels, *The Government of Corporations* (1962)[2] and contributors (lawyers and economists) to the *Corporation in Modern Society* (1959) edited by Mason.[3]

In Britain D. H. MacGregor was outstanding among economists in comparing industry with 'the other great systems of administration, political, military and ecclesiastical'.[4] And Sir George Catlin, among political scientists, has long advocated the extension of his science to organizations generally[5] and at least one industrialist, Mr Wilfred (now Lord) Brown in his *Exploration in Management* describing his own

---

[1] The trade union presence is taken into account below in discussing (VI § 7) alternatives to capitalist government (VI § 3), the government of nationalized industries (VI § 5), the test of democracy and (VII § 1) labour relations in capitalist industry.

[2] See review article by L. Tivey in *Political Studies*, June 1966.

[3] This integration of economics and law, not to mention political science, has furthered hopes I expressed in my *Statistical Method in Economics and Political Science* (1929) and *Logic of Industrial Organization* (1933) p. 118. One passage is particularly relevant (p. 220) from the contribution of Earl Latham, Professor of Political Science at Amherst: 'The corporation is a body politic which exhibits describable characteristics common to all bodies politic. In a functional view of all such political systems it can be said that there are five essential elements: (1) an authoritative allocation of principal functions; (2) a symbolic system for the ratification of collective decisions; (3) an operating system of command; (4) a system of rewards and punishments; and (5) institutions for the enforcement of the common rules. A system of organized human behavior which contains these elements is a political system, whether one calls it the state or the corporation.'

[4] 'Rationalization and Industry', *Economic Journal*, December 1927.

[5] *A Study of the Principles of Politics, 1929: Systematic Politics*, 1962.

organization, the Glacier Metal Company, uses as chapter heading the 'executive system', the 'representative system', the 'legislative system' and the 'appeals procedure'.[1]

It is, however, sociologists who are now making the running both in America and Britain. A semi-dependent 'organization science' is becoming recognized, based largely on the work of Max Weber;[2] but a wider integration in human sciences, including social psychology, is forming under the heading of behavioural sciences.

The concept of 'behaviour' is closely related if not interchangeable with economists' 'conduct' or 'policy',[3] and so far as it covers price policy, wage policy, product policy or market policy, it is more directly the concern of economists than organization science. But institutions such as control by ownership of capital with consequent 'alienation' of workers influence policy, and organization and economic behaviour should be studied together.

The exponents of the new sociological integration are many. They and their leading works, in order of publication date, include:

H. A. Simon, *Administrative Behaviour*, 1945, Collier-Macmillan.

A. W. Gouldner, *Patterns of Industrial Bureaucracy*, Routledge & Kegan Paul, 1954.

P. Bendix, *Work and Authority in Industry*, Chapman & Hall and Wiley, 1956.

R. K. Merton, *Social Theory and Social Structure*, 1957, Glencoe, Ill.

P. Selznick, *Leadership in Administration*, 1957, Evanston, Ill.

J. G. March (and H. A. Simon), *Organizations*, Chapman & Hall and Wiley, 1958.

R. M. Cyert (and J. G. March), *A Behavioural Theory of the Firm*, Prentice-Hall, 1963.

J. W. McGuire, *Theories of Business Behaviour*, 1964, Englewood Cliffs.

These writers are sometimes classed as a structuralist school. They are distinguished as critics of the human relations approach represented by Mayo rather than as reversing the classical analysis of systems of organization.

It was this classical analysis that I followed in my first edition when discussing the logic of various forms of delegation of government

---

[1] *Economics and Sociology of Industry*, 1969, Chapter VIII § 2.

[2] Etzioni, *Modern Organization*, 1964, Chapters 3 and 4.

[3] E.g. Caves, *American Industry—Structure, Conduct, Performance*, 1964, Chapter 3.

where the question arises, who it is that makes what decisions—a central point in the structuralist's analysis. As the title and contents of Chapter I of this book indicate, I stressed a structural approach. I adhere therefore to my original classical-structural treatment of relations within the firm, while noting the illuminating interpretations and some modifications to be added in consequence of the new analysis and research of both the human relations and the structuralist school.

One illuminating *interpretation* of the hierarchical structure shortly to be described is Simon's observation that as the levels get lower, decision-making forms a smaller element, actual performance a larger. A significant *modification* added by the human relations school is, precisely, to modify the rigidity of the formal rules. The chart given as Table IVB should, for instance, be read liberally. The span of control for industries need not always be limited to five; and allowance in the scope of their work must be made for the personalities and peculiar abilities of the various office holders. Moreover, people do not act simply as individuals, they have informal relations and act in groups, not as atoms in a 'rabble'. Most of the necessary modifications, particularly those of the human relations school refer to the stimulus to work treated in Chapter VII rather than to the organization of work.

In discussing organization as we are here, the main thesis to be considered is ergological, that the type of work being undertaken and its supply and demand conditions are strong determinants of the form of structure and government. The more important characteristics of different types of work were indicated in Chapter II; and contrasted illustrations were given of the effect of supply and demand conditions upon location patterns, the size of plants and firms and firms' predominant form of government (whether by entrepreneur, or professionally managed company *et al.*), drawn from vehicle manufacture and retailing. Top general authority in industrial organizations was referred to as top-level government or, not to make it appear too formal, top rule or leadership. This top-government includes the decision-making in all the elements of administration recognized by Fayol: planning ahead, organizing the structure of the governing party (creating structures and manning them), co-ordinating the structural parts, commanding the subordinate staff by incentives or coercives, controlling or checking results.

There are shades of decision making from the pale automatic act by habit or rule of thumb or general principle previously decided, to decision by vivid hunch or the most intense evaluation and ratiocination. Habit and rule of thumb and general principle are methods of relieving the top government from the strain in too much new decision making—are methods of decentralizing nervous effort—and occur frequently in business procedure. Though decisions on prices involving real thought may be made in a crisis, prices may normally be determined by a fixed rule as to the margin to be charged above average costs—a 'ritual' with 'priestly' and 'lay' codes (strict and less strict) discussed by English economists as alternative to profit maximization.[1] Again, output may be automatically reduced as stocks pile up to a certain tabooed amount; there may be some liquidity 'fetish'; or orders may be accepted, again almost ritually, to keep machines running near capacity.[2] These codes of conduct do not necessarily mean that no commands are issued, but that a subordinate can give orders in the place of top-level government. The practical question is how far the danger of irrational traditional action outweighs that of overloading top-level with decision making.

Since most economists are of the opinion that the larger a firm becomes the more 'unwieldy' it is for top government, attention, when studying internal organization, must be focused on one particular problem: *how, by organizing responsible sub-, and sub-sub-structures and co-ordinating them, to relieve the load on the men in top government of a large organization, so that they may be free to concentrate their thought on high policy and the means to plan, command and check that policy efficiently with expert management and advice.*

The nature of the high policy of a large industrial firm will be assessed at the end of this chapter. In the next three sections we shall discuss three main principles of organizing by which, singly *or jointly*, this focal problem of efficient large-scale management may be tackled. Following the definition of efficiency already given (Chapter II, § 1), efficiency of management is measured by its cost relative to output. Larger output will naturally involve increased staffs and increased expenses of management, but the critical question is whether management expenses will, with larger scale, increase less or more than output. Delegation of power will mean some increase in managers and specialists; but if, by relieving the load on top government, the increase achieves a proportionately greater increase in volume or, rather, value of output, the change makes for efficiency.

The three main principles of organizing the efficiency of which are to be discussed can be distinguished as hierarchical, functional and line and staff.

§ 3. LOGIC OF HIERARCHICAL DELEGATION

The system of organization which has grown up with the growth of most industrial firms may be called hierarchical, since its prototype may

---

[1] See *Economic Journal*, December 1950, pp. 771–80; June 1951, pp. 426–32, discussion of Andrews, 'Manufacturing Business'.

[2] Katona, *Psychological Analysis of Economic Behaviour*, 1951, p. 253.

be found in Church organization. But this system is also known as the military system, since traditionally it was the form of organization found pre-eminently in the army and navy. In all these systems the relation between ruler and ruled is more important than division of work. One or more persons are placed under a superior, that superior under a 'super-superior' and so on, and each of these superiors exercises a rule over their subordinates that extends to all types of work. There is, in fact, a regular chain of authority covering all functions and extending all the way down the line. Thus, to take one example of Church hierarchy: in 1930 the Bishop of Birmingham had two archdeacons under his rule, the Archdeacon of Birmingham and the Archdeacon of Aston respectively. The Archdeacon of Birmingham had five rural deans and each of the rural deans in the Archdeaconry of Birmingham visited from fourteen to twenty-one beneficed clergy. We may say that there are a series of ranks extending up from the beneficed clergymen, through the rural deans and the archdeacons to the bishops; and above the bishops, of course, two archbishops.[1]

This pyramid of ranks, the higher the rank the fewer the incumbents, is yet more familiar in the army, with its corporals, sergeants, lieutenants, captains, majors, colonels and generals. And the same series of ranks grow up in industry as the firm gets larger. There are, as Table IVB sets forth, foremen, superintendents, managers, and general managers. It is true that these industrial ranks have not a distinctive official uniform, such as the military general's stars or cocked hat or red tabs, or the Bishop's gaiters or the titles of Rev., Venerable, Very Rev., Right Rev., My Lord, and Your Grace, marking the upward sweep of the hierarchy. But there used to be signs of such distinction in the bowler or derby hat which the foreman was informally privileged to wear when walking about the works and the 'Mr' preceding his name when he was addressed.[2] The differences in status are great enough even in industry, and as the higher ranks withdraw themselves into their offices, important psychological results accrue.

Hierarchical structure lightens the load on top-level government by certain rules of communication which must be obeyed on pain of uncertainty and confusion in all executive rule and work relations.

(1) Commands should only be given to (and information received by) subordinates through their immediate superior. There should be no by-passing or skipping of links in the chain of command.
(2) Commands should only be received by subordinates from (and information given to) *one* immediate superior. There should,

---

[1] Birmingham Diocesan Kalendar [*sic*], 1930–1.
[2] See Barnard, *Organization and Management*, 1938, p. 218, on human need of titles and insignia (e.g. gowns, gaiters) by which status is established and maintained.

in short, be only one chain or line of authority, and a *unity* of command.

These rules are only too often broken, especially in British companies of the family business type. A scion of the family, in virtue of his lineage, is often placed upon the board of directors at the top of the hierarchy, and also employed in an executive capacity as a sub-manager, or even as a sub-sub-manager. He appears at the top of the line of command and also half-way down. Thus his immediate superior in his executive duties who is purely a manager, not on the board of directors, is placed in a distinctly awkward position. On certain subjects he may be skipped out altogether, since the young scion may take his orders direct from the board, and in other subjects he may find his orders to subordinates duplicated or even countermanded by the young scion. Subordinates of both these men may, in fact, be breaking the second principle by taking orders from two sources.

A third rule of the hierarchical system arises from the physiology and psychology of fatigue and has been named the span of control.

(3) There is a limit to the number of subordinates that can be *directly* commanded by one man.

General Sir Ian Hamilton[1] declared: 'The human brain cannot directly control more than five or six other brains'. And in fact the practice in the armies of most countries has been to arrange the commands so that (at least in the higher ranks, where other personal contacts have to be made beside relations with subordinates) four is the maximum number of direct subordinates within the span of control, and more than five rare. But the span of control varies with the type of work, and a survey by Dale of 47 large American companies reported spans for the corporation president of up to 21 subordinates. In only 13 of the 47 companies was it six or less. The most frequent span was 7 or 8, found in fifteen of the companies.[2]

At the lowest level of industrial authority a group of direct workers may be formed under a chargehand or foreman numbering much more than four or five. The average size (probably too large for efficient face-to-face autonomy) of such a primary group has been found in British manufacture to be about twenty-four.[3] This is in keeping with the strict phrasing of Hamilton's Law about the span of control which

---

[1] Urwick, *Management of Tomorrow*, 1933, p. 60.

[2] Dale, *Management Theory and Practice*, 1965, p. 289.

[3] *Occupational Psychology*, January 1952. In Table IVB, charting an organization for about a thousand souls, the rank of chargehand has, for simplicity, been omitted and the numbers appearing at the lowest level are in consequence higher than this average.

refers specifically to the number of 'brains' controlled. Brains presumably implies subordinates with problems of control of their own, not routine or direct labour.

The organization of many industrial firms has made the efficient application of the hierarchical principle difficult by overloading superiors. If a manager were commanding six sub-managers, and a seventh, or eighth, or ninth sub-manager were required, all these nine tend to be placed directly under the manager without much thought of the strain involved. Organizations have grown haphazard, one subject of command being added to another, bit by bit, and at no one point has it been realized that a thorough reorganization was necessary all through the system. One experienced industrialist told me that he found it necessary to reorganize every time the size of his business multiplied by three, but the less thoughtful business chief is inclined to add superior co-ordinate and subordinate structures as opportunity offers without seeing the wood for the trees—and to make a jungle of it. To quote Mr Churchill's experience of the First World War's Ministry of Munitions:[1]

The growth of the Ministry of Munitions had far outstripped its organization. A year had passed since its creator, Mr Lloyd George, had moved on to still more intense spheres. The two gifted Ministers who had succeeded him, Mr Montagu and Dr Addison, had dealt with the needs as they arose, shouldering one responsibility after another, adding department to department and branch to branch, without altering in essentials the central organization from the form it had assumed in the empirical and convulsive period of creation. All the main and numberless minor decisions still centred upon the Minister himself. I found a staff of 12,000 officials organized in no less than fifty principal departments each claiming direct access to the Chief, and requiring a swift flow of decisions upon most intricate and inter-related problems. I set to work at once to divide and distribute this dangerous concentration of power.

Under a new system the fifty departments of the Ministry were grouped into ten large units each in charge of a head who was directly responsible to the Minister. These ten heads of groups of departments were themselves formed into a Council like a Cabinet. . . .

The relief was instantaneous. I was no longer oppressed by heaps of bulky files. Every one of my ten Councillors was able to give important and final decisions in his own sphere. The daily Council meeting kept them in close relation with each other and with the general scheme; while the system of committees of councillors enabled special questions to be brought to speedy conclusion. Once the whole organization was in motion it never required change. Instead of struggling through the jungle on foot I rode comfortably on an elephant whose trunk could pick up a pin or uproot a tree with equal ease, and from whose back a wide scene lay open.

[1] *The World Crisis 1911–1918* (abridged), 1931, p. 708.

The number of ranks in the hierarchical system must then be increased with the total size of the organization, just as in the army, *given a definite number of men* in the platoons, companies, battalions, brigades, etc., these men must be commanded by officers of a definite number of ranks. In Table IVB a fairly typical large organization is depicted in which a hierarchical system gives command to the works manager over four superintendents each controlling five foremen. Foremen usually control a varying number of men according to technical requirements; but if we suppose forty men to be an average number under one foreman,[1] it follows that five foremen will control two hundred men, and four superintendents (under one works manager), each with five foremen, will control eight hundred men. Thus the employment of eight hundred men in the productive departments implies four ranks, and if the number of men were doubled, a further rank would have to be added to avoid the overloading of any officer in the superior ranks.

It is only by adhering strictly to these three rules—the chain, unit of command, and the span of control—that the hierarchical system can so lighten the load on the top government that it can efficiently execute large-scale industrial operations, and industrial firms have been slow in realizing this necessary logic of the hierarchical government of large-scale operations. But there are sources of *in*efficiency logically *inherent* in the pure form of the hierarchical system, and however closely hierarchical principles may be adhered to, a limit will be set to large-scale organization if reliance is placed solely upon a hierarchy of command. These inherent inefficiencies in the hierarchical system may be summed up under three headings:

(1) Failure to get correct information and to act upon it.
(2) Red tape and bureaucracy.
(3) Lack of specialized skill of experts.

(1) While commands go down the line under the hierarchical system information is supposed to be coming up the line. Thus, while the sales manager gives orders to the travelling salesmen under his command, these salesmen, in direct touch with the retailers or customers, should be giving the sales manager information as to the difficulties in selling the various lines. But the main defect of the hierarchical system is that such information tends to be neglected for the very reason that it comes from a subordinate. The history of the actual conduct of military organization during times of war is full of instances of neglect of information often vital.[2]

---

[1] See footnote 3 above, p. 184.
[2] See Liddell Hart, *The Real War*, pp. 194, 236, cited in Florence, 1933, pp. 124–5.

(2) Red tape and bureaucracy are words often flung in the teeth of hierarchical organization. When these words are used they seem to refer to such rigid adherence to formalities that rules become masters rather than servants. Max Weber in his analysis of bureaucratic structure stresses a certain imperviousness to changing circumstance and technique, a fatal flaw in industries depending for progress on investment in new inventions; and an exceedingly roundabout method of making decisions. That decisions can only be reached by long-drawn-out correspondence and negotiation, would follow strictly from the principles of hierarchical organization. Thus, in Table IVB if foreman A under superintendent I wishes to consult on business with a foreman under superintendent IV, he would have to ask permission first of superintendent I. This superintendent would have to approach the works manager, and not till then could the works manager give orders to superintendent IV to order the foreman under his command to meet foreman A. This procedure is found to occur in practice all over the world and in all walks of life where the hierarchical and military principle flourishes unmitigated. The classic tangle of red tape and etiquette was that cut by Florence Nightingale in the Crimean War. When some dilapidated rooms in the Barrack Hospital of Scutari had hurriedly to be made capable of accommodating beds for a new batch of wounded

the proper course was that a representation should be made to the Director-General of the Army Medical Department in London; then the Director-General would apply to the Horse Guards, the Horse Guards would move the Ordnance, the Ordnance would lay the matter before the Treasury and if the Treasury gave the consent, the work might be correctly carried through several months after the necessity for it had disappeared. Miss Nightingale however . . .[1]

(3) The lack of specialized skill is inherent in the leading characteristic of the hierarchical system, namely, that each executive is responsible for *all* subjects in his department. Thus, the head of a factory department would buy his own material, design his own products, engage his own labour, keep his own records, and set his own standard of output and costs; while the foreman in any one shop might set the piece rates, train new men, supervise the quality of the work, keep the plant running, and determine the speed and feed of the machines. In short, each commander is inclined to be a Jack-of-all-trades and master of none.

§ 4. LOGIC OF FUNCTIONAL DELEGATION

Because the hierarchical system failed to give top-level government

[1] Strachey, *Eminent Victorians*, Penguin edition, p. 145.

expert management or advice, a new principle in organizing industry (stressing work rather than rule relations) was advocated by such men as Frederick Taylor, the founder of scientific management. The leading characteristic in the new organization is that at each hierarchical level specific functions common to all or several departments are each placed in the hands of a man specifically qualified, and instead of giving attention to all the factors in one department, he gives attention to one factor in all departments.

Taylor began his attack at the bottom rank of the industrial hierarchy, that of the foreman. He advocated the creation of functional foremen—an inspector, a gang boss, a speed boss, a repair boss, a time clerk, a route clerk and a disciplinarian—each of whom should look after a different factor in the workshop.

But while Taylor was consciously reorganizing the lower ranks of the industrial hierarchy, the upper ranks were being functionalized by sheer force of circumstances. Practically every firm in England and America that employs more than one hundred men, will have the functions of management split into at least three divisions. There will be a works manager to control actual production; a sales manager to distribute the products; and a third official of equal rank, known in Britain usually as the secretary, who may have subordinates in organizing the accounts, controlling finance, and sometimes purchasing raw materials. In America the purchasing agent is usually co-equal with the sales and works managers or subordinate to the works managers. Three specialized managers under the general managing director are shown in Table IVB, together with a fourth specialized manager more and more frequently found in the larger British and American firms, namely, the 'labour', 'personnel' or 'industrial relations' manager. One or two other functional managers are also sometimes found in the top rank—depending on the technology—for instance, where capital investment is intense, the engineer or maintenance, designs and research managers. But the precise details need not occupy us, and there is little difference in essentials between British and American practice. All that need be noticed is that under the functional system, the work of government is divided in each rank so that there is not merely a system of superiors and subordinates, but a series of posts of co-ordinate authority and differentiated functions. These functions are different in respect of type of work performed, not merely as those of travellers under the sales manager in respect of territory covered.

The functional system has logical rules for the efficient relief of large-scale top level government, no less than the hierarchical system.

(1) The functions into which the work is split up should be collectively exhaustive; there should not be gaps, where no one is told off to function.

(2) The divisions of the work should, for the sake of economy of effort, be mutually exclusive; that is to say, there should be no over-lapping, poaching and duplication of work.

(3) Each division should contain related subjects. The work required of each division should be fairly similar so that the differences in the work within each division should be less than the differences of the work in different divisions.

Functional systems have grown up haphazard, just as hierarchical systems have done, and many an industrial firm is found with a functional system that violates these rules, and thus leads to obstacles in the efficient carrying out of large-scale operations. The best documented instance of such mal-assignment of functions has been given in great detail by Urwick. The organization concerned was a well-known British firm, above average in efficiency. Yet such glaring examples occur of the violation of the rules of organization both hierarchical and functional given above, that some of the details are worth stating.

First of all it was found that the line of command was uncertain.

Quite a number of executive officers in the concern had not the least idea to whom they were responsible. The reason was in itself plausible. In the course of many emergency appointments, personal difficulties had arisen. Mr A. was quite willing to act as Mr B.'s assistant, and, indeed, to accept all his instructions from Mr B. But he would not on any odds admit that he was officially 'under' Mr B.

In dealing with these difficulties, the Directors had tried to avoid using the big stick. In many cases, recalcitrant Mr A.'s had been allowed to continue to report to a Director in theory, though in practice they were really responsible to somebody else. On the other hand, where it had been necessary to increase the responsibility of some members of the staff—the Mr B.'s—they had never been granted officially the authority to discharge those responsibilities. They had been told to get along with the Mr A.'s.[1]

The third functional rule was in particular sadly violated. The chairman and six directors were employed full time as executive managers, but most of them exercised authority over the most diverse functions. Three directors appeared to be mainly in charge of production. But one of these in charge of 'box mills' managed men's and women's employment, wages, cost and pensions, staff office, buildings and estates and the laboratory; another in charge of the manufacture of three types of product also managed the time office and the fire brigade; and the third in charge of a fourth type of product also managed the canteen. A fourth director appeared to be mainly in charge of finance, but also purchased stationery and fancy boxes, and took charge of planning, transport, stores and packing, statistics and

[1] *Re-organizing an Existing Business*, Fourth International Scientific Management Congress, Paris, 1929.

costing, as well as the production of three further types of product. A fifth director appeared mainly in charge of purchasing but also managed the technical library. A sixth director appeared mainly in charge of equipment but also interested himself in research groups. It was in fact only the seventh director, in charge of sales, who definitely confined his attention to one function and managed travellers' sales and advertising and nothing irrelevant to these matters.

Let us suppose, however, that the functional system is efficiently and logically carried out and that there are no violations of its principles. Is it possible to say that in such a case industrial firms would be organized for successful performance of large-scale operations, and in particular for taking the load off top level government? Undoubtedly many firms, particularly in America, have moulded their organization upon this system but yet they have often found in the functional structure some logically inherent inefficiencies. In the first place, much that was efficient in the hierarchical structure for executing efficiently the commands of top level government had been swept away. The functional foreman idea clearly contravenes the law of unity of command. The operative takes orders not from one foreman, but from several, whose orders might well conflict, and Taylor's plan was soon found to be unworkable.[1] It is clear that if decisive action is to be taken at least a backbone of authority must be left. The hierarchical line of command cannot be entirely abandoned, and there must be some superior to whom every man in an executive or operative capacity can look for definite orders. In the second place, with division of functions and specialization has come a certain loss in co-ordination. Apart from the friction, jealousy and rancour that are apt to spring up between departments, there is an inevitable getting out of touch. This is particularly clear in the division between sales managers and works managers. Orders may be booked by salesmen that owing to overloading of productive equipment can only be produced at great cost and with little or no profit, while conversely, articles may be produced that can only be sold at a loss or not at all. Under a purely hierarchical system, where one top level individual attends to both selling and producing, he will produce with a definite knowledge of the possibility of the market, and he will market with a definite knowledge of the possibilities of production. But a division of function (for instance different men doing the designing and the making) may result in demarcation disputes to be adjudicated by the top authority thus further over-loading him, or entail the creation of a further job, that of co-ordination or liaison. In the former case there is additional inefficiency, in the latter additional expense.

[1] Fayol, *L'Administration industrielle et générale*, 1916; C. Myers, *Business Rationalization*, 1932, pp. 36–44.

§ 5. LOGIC OF STAFF-AND-LINE DELEGATION

There has been a gradual trend from the hierarchical system of delegation, to a functional system of division of labour in management. Both systems of organization, however, have been faultily applied, or even when logically applied have been found to possess inherent sources of inefficiency. The hierarchical structure, so well suited for the efficient communication of commands, limits the use of expert management and advice; the functional system, allowing the use of expert managers and advisers, divides up the execution of commands too much for effective large-scale operation. A system is thus sought which will relieve top government by striking an efficient balance in the division and concentration of rule and work. Such balance applied in industry is probably nearest approached, logically, by the line and staff system.

The conception of a staff first arose in the army as a result of the need of the top command for information. Information, if it comes from the lower ranks, is liable, as said already, to be neglected. To remedy this source of inefficiency, military commanders gradually delegated power to certain persons to specialize in giving information. Thus, the quarter-master found places for an army on the march in which to camp or 'quarter'. Information had to be collected and inferences drawn from it in the form of recommendations. In addition to informing the commanding officer, these specialists would draw up an assessment or appreciation of the situation and tender advice accordingly. Gradually the advisory function of the staff was developed, so that its advice was expected to be acted upon, and plans were prepared to facilitate the necessary action. Thus, Mooney and Reiley[1] point to information, advice and facilitation as the three purposes of a staff system. The staff works out plans for various contingencies upon information acquired, and devises the detailed methods of carrying out these plans. In short, though the staff forms no part of the hierarchical 'line' system of command, and is only attached to it as line-and-staff suggests, it influences the policy of executive officers within that system at various points.

This 'influence' is shown in Table IVB by means of arrows, converging from the margins. Thus the general managing director may have a staff that advises him as to the design of product, and the methods of producing it, by undertaking research, planning, costing and statistical control (i.e. comparing or checking the actual achievement as against the plan). In the second rank, the sales manager may be advised as to advertising methods, or price and output policy, by a staff specializing in market research, and the labour manager may be advised

---

[1] *Onward Industry*, 1931, Chapter 23.

as to the selection of labour by a psychologist, and as to piece-rates by a time and motion expert. In the third rank there may be a staff for market research attached to each area sales supervisor and this local staff may be advised by the central market research staff. It is to be noticed that none of these staff officers are part of the hierarchical backbone formed by the managing director and his subordinates and foremen, nor part of the functional division of powers seen in the division between sales, works, and labour managers. The staff are specialists in research, planning and checking of results, in which much statistical control and paper work may be involved; but they do not directly command on their own authority.

The practical difficulty of grafting a staff system on a purely hierarchical or military order, can be realized from a passage in which Sir Winston Churchill described his efforts to introduce a staff on the army pattern into the British Navy early in 1914.

The dead weight of professional opinion was adverse. They had got on well enough without it before. They did not want a special class of officer professing to be more brainy than the rest. Sea-time should be the main qualification, and next to that technical aptitudes. Thus when I went to the Admiralty I found that there was no moment in the career and training of a naval officer when he was obliged to read a single book about naval war, or pass even the most rudimentary examination in naval history. The Royal Navy had made no important contribution to Naval literature. The standard work on Sea Power was written by an American Admiral.[1] The best accounts of British sea fighting and naval strategy were compiled by an English civilian.[2] 'The Silent Service' was not mute because it was absorbed in thought and study, but because it was weighted down by its daily routine and by its ever-complicating and diversifying technique.[3]

In spite of difficulties the chief source of inefficiency in the military or hierarchical system has undoubtedly been corrected by the addition of staff officers. Information actually collected and sifted can no longer be spurned, staff officers will be more open to outside changes of thought on technical inventions, and above all they will be men of specialized skill, experts in the full sense of the word.

The staff system and its paper-work (if not overdone and merely idle overhead) corrects the inefficiency of a pure hierarchical line organization which excludes experts and specialists; it may also avoid in the form of a general rather than a specialized staff the lack of co-ordination and the violation of unity of command implied in the functional system. Knowledge will be divided up among several persons, but supplied by a general staff to one central authority, and this central authority will

[1] Admiral Mahan.
[2] Sir Julian Corbett.
[3] Churchill, *The World Crisis 1911–18* (abridged), 1931, pp. 74–5.

have unity of command. Additional co-ordination may, however, be obtained either by giving the staff a part in the *general* executive line work, or by a system of committees, where the staff advisers may meet all the functional managers whose activities need correlation.

A *general* staff for a large industrial firm with executive powers to relieve the co-ordinating load of top rule can be modelled on army structure. According to Urwick:[1]

The duty of the staff as defined in British military regulations is 'to assist their commander in the execution of his functions of command and to assist the fighting troops and services in the execution of their tasks'. Moreover it is further expressly stated that 'the main object of staff organization is to ensure a smooth and efficient co-ordination of effort between all portions of the force'. Staff officers have a special form of authority. They alone 'have authority to sign on behalf of commanders. Every order and instruction issued through the staff is given by the authority of the commander and on his responsibility.'

In any large formation there are staff officers of the various branches into which the staff is divided at each level of command, or if not staff officers, officers acting in a 'staff' relationship to their commander. That is to say, at each subordinate co-ordinating point there are individuals with this special form of delegated authority whose primary function it is to secure co-ordination, to ensure that whatever the task set, all the arrangements made by specialists and 'line' alike, dovetail into each other.

The staff thus constitutes, as it were, a third dimension in military organization, linking 'line' and specialists both vertically, laterally and diagonally.

Staff thus fall into two types in relation to line officers; specialist experts advising line officers (illustrated in Table IVB); and a general executive aid with a special form of delegated authority co-ordinating at each level down the line. As Urwick sums it up[2] the executive staff 'are not individuals who specialize in any kind of work, but individuals who specialize in the functions of command and especially in co-ordination'.

The difficulties, if not the impossibility, of the delegation of co-ordination was raised by economists in the nineteen-thirties and ever since has bolstered up the theory mentioned earlier (p. 75) of the limits and the increasing cost of the management factor.[3] More discipline would have been brought into the discussion if the well tried terms and distinctions of political science had been relied upon. Kaldor uses co-ordination partly for executive co-ordination, once a policy has been

---

[1] *Public Administration*, October 1935, p. 14. The theme is developed in Gulick and Urwick, *Papers on the Science of Administration*, 1937.
[2] *Management of Tomorrow*, 1933, p. 66.
[3] Described in Chapter II, § 2 and IV§2.

decided upon, where delegation is perfectly feasible;[1] and partly for legislative procedure in reaching decisions. He holds that[2]

You cannot increase the supply of co-ordinating ability available to an enterprise alongside an increase in the supply of other factors, as it is the essence of co-ordination that every single decision should be made on a comparison with all the other decisions already made or likely to be made; it must therefore pass through a single brain . . . given the state of technical knowledge and given the co-ordinating ability represented by that enterprise, the amount of 'other factors' which can be most advantageously employed by that enterprise will be limited, i.e. the supply of 'co-ordinating ability' *for the individual firm* is 'fixed'.

Robinson summed it up that 'the task of co-ordination cannot be multiplied in parallel. It is of its essence that it is single.'[3] This series of axioms somewhat reminiscent of scholasticism are not based on experience of business. They ignore the fact that co-ordination in policy decisions has been achieved for organizations such as the state or a whole army, very much larger than any firm; and that certainly for the army, decisions may have to be, and have been, reached just as quickly as for a firm. The general staff helps to make decisions by supplying information and formulating specific plans to meet various likely situations; there is, in short, the possibility of delegation to the staff of functions previous, as well as subsequent, to decisions—a delegation that can greatly amplify the scope and powers of top government.

Inefficiencies adding to top rule's load are logically inherent in the staff and line, as in other types of delegation. A staff officer may have been a successful empire-builder,[4] or the top authority may have been seized with over-enthusiasm for the principles of scientific management and organization, or else cleverly sold on the subject. In consequence over-elaborate systems certainly have been set up by some firms, in which the increased number and expense of staff and unproductive labour goes far beyond the increase, if any, of output and therefore

[1] When a top ruler takes a decision involving consequential and correlative changes in organization and subsidiary policies, those changes can be and are brought into line by delegation to an executive co-ordinator. Eisenhower, we read, for instance (Wilmot, *The Struggle for Europe*, 1951, p. 208), 'delegated to Tedder the intricate task of co-ordinating the efforts of the British and American heavy bombers and of Leigh-Mallory's A.E.A.F.' See also Florence, *Economic Journal*, December 1934, pp. 726–8.

[2] 'The Equilibrium of the Firm', *Economic Journal*, March 1934, pp. 68–9.

[3] 'The Problem of Management and the Size of Firm', *Economic Journal*, 1934, p. 248.

[4] Empire-building is particularly difficult to check where the objective effect on output of an increase in subordinates is not directly measurable. The staff has no departmental output of its own.

becomes uneconomic.[1] Part of the increase in staff-to-operative ratios in Britain and America displayed in Table IVA, though certainly not all, may have been this futile overhead.

The danger is also inherent in staff and line organization of creating back-room boys or a superior highbrow set who may further increase the 'idle' overhead. Certainly the staff have been pictured as sitting at headquarters devising paper forms and questionnaires to annoy the executive line officers and the men doing the 'donkey work' at the actual front. In both First and Second World Wars some still remember, even if they cannot print, what the infantry-man in the trenches thought of the 'red-tabs' or 'brass' *segregated* at the base.

Wherever the pure line system of command is abandoned and co-ordinate officers are created either for functional, or advisory or executive staff purposes, it is essential to mutual understanding and *aggregation* that a common meeting-ground be found for ideas and complaints. The logical meeting-ground is a committee where the functional executives on the same level of authority (e.g. sales, works and personnel managers) can co-ordinate their policies, or the advisory or executive staff and the executive functionaries may get together as a body to discuss plans and the difficulties of their execution and achievement. Under the staff and line system committees are particularly important. By this device, headquarters thought and front-line action may be harmonized, opinion and experiences pooled, predilections and complexes ironed out and what Mooney and Reiley have called a common 'indoctrination' achieved. The executive 'line' gets to understand and feels itself identified with the staff plans and the staff gets to understand and feels itself identified with the work of the 'line'.

Committees in an industrial firm, as elsewhere, raise of course new possibilities of inefficiency. Where two or more persons have to be gathered together time will be lost by the mere need of gathering them and, when gathered, by the slow progress of deliberation and arriving at a decision. And when the number of persons on the committee are more than a certain modicum, not only are a great aggregate of man-hours lost to productive work, but the actual efficiency of the deliberation may suffer through 'too many cooks spoiling the broth', and through the need for greater tact and secrecy. Though a certain number of persons are usually required on a committee to ensure all sides to a problem being heard (otherwise there is no point in the committee), a rule of optimum size of committees may be advanced (like the maximum span of control) that *there is some optimum number of members of a committee, above which efficiency is lost.*

The staff and line system coupled with co-ordinating committees is

---

[1] See especially Ord, *Industrial Facts and Fallacies*, 1950.

probably that best adapted for the efficient large-scale production of a few articles within one firm, i.e. for large-scale operation. If with lateral or vertical integration many processes are performed or many products made each on a small scale, many separate departments must be created each with an executive officer in charge and the organization logically tends to the hierarchical or functional pattern. But with con- centration upon a few processes or products, departments may logically be fewer, while staff services can be extended. It will pay, if there are only a few processes or products each on a large scale, to do more specialized but co-ordinated planning and checking on the specific problems of each, and to discuss in committee the closely related work of those thinking and acting upon a single process or product.

Industrial organization needs to be adapted to type of market and type of production: mass, batch, individual craftsmanship or servicing.[1] Industrial practice in most firms has not yet fully adapted organization to the technical requirement of large-scale operation. The full economies of large-scale operation have often not been realized owing to a lag in changing over from a hierarchical or functional system to a staff and line system. Such a lag has led to inefficiency where the technique of large-scale operation has already been introduced, and has prevented its introduction where conditions would otherwise have been favourable. The vicious circle thus reappears. The large-scale operation to be logic- ally expected from its economy is neglected for lack of a staff and line organization; the possibilities of the staff and line system neglected for lack of the large-scale operation to which it is politically suited.

§ 6. THE CORE OF TOP GOVERNMENT

The new problems in organization that arise as a result of the increase in specialized fixed capital and specialized management have now been considered. Industrial organizations have on the whole been slow in adjusting to the new technical and ergological conditions, though occasionally too rash. They have not relieved the load of their top-level government as much or as efficiently as was feasible, and have thus not made full use of the possible economies of large-scale organ- ization and operation.

Nevertheless, some progress is being made in the internal relations of large-scale organizations as well as in their outside commercial relations with consumers, so that large-scale operation is becoming manageable. Power is delegated and delegated powers co-ordinated in such a way that there is only a core of top-level government left with a few essential powers. What are these top powers?

[1] Joan Woodward in *Industrial Organization; Theory and Practice*, 1965 has reviewed the facts of over 200 factories in South-East England and put this need most clearly.

Men at the top level of authority, who need not be in continuous session, are those making the final decision on general policy. In industry this policy deals with the question of the kinds of products, and amounts of those kinds, to make (e.g. whether to expand or contract) with the related question of the prices to charge; and in modern mechanized industry with the question of the amount and kind of equipment in which to invest (e.g. how much of the profits to re-invest). With these questions of policy may go questions of general strategy; especially the attitude to competitors or potential competitors: whether to combine or associate with them, follow their lead, or engage in genuine (so-called 'cut-throat') competition.

In our terminology management, an art with a scientific basis, is the full-time execution of policy—including subsidiary strategy, tactics, supervision and discipline. The distinction is one of degree—higher levels of rule and authority as against lower levels—but wherever the line be drawn, management without adjective is taken as subordinate and corresponding in state government to work done by civil servants; top government to that of the legislature or cabinet, and occasionally the court of appeal. Like the state legislature, the top government of a large business firm breaks new ground, makes new rules, lays down general principles in the conduct of a business, initiates high policy.

In a progressive economy the distinctive feature of high policy as against mere management is 'enterprise', and modern economists often define the top deciders of policy (whoever they may be) as *par excellence* entrepreneurs. This is confusing since earlier economists defined (and modern economists assume in practice) an entrepreneur as a man who manages and owns all or much of the capital of a firm. Only a small share of business is done in America and Britain today by such entrepreneurs, but enterprise, or the need for it, remains. In essence enterprise is the carrying out of something new: a new product or an old at a new (usually lower) price, or new combination of factors (especially more investment of capital);—all new policies which involve the taking, if not the bearing, of financial risks. Schumpeter has made us familiar with the innovator who, as he says, may be a promoter, a financier or an engineer and not necessarily a manager at all. His use of the word entrepreneur for this independent man of enterprise, though historically correct, adds yet another definition to current usage. As far as humanly possible amidst the confusion now engendered, I shall confine the word entrepreneur to the owner-manager, and this will not imply that enterprise can only be found with that entrepreneur. On the contrary, a great number of types of business leader (of which the entrepreneur is only one) will be tested for enterprise among other reactions to large-scale problems.[1]

[1] The confusion in thought involved by these differences in definitions and

In the content of its policy an economic organization such as an industrial firm has objectives different from that of a state, a church or an army. But the sharing of rule between persons and bodies of persons in a hierarchy, functionally or otherwise, makes all large organizations kin in that their top rule must have further powers besides policy-making to enable its high policy to be put through efficiently. Fayol included organizing, commanding, planning, co-ordinating and checking up in his 'administrative operations'. Hierarchical structure relieves top rule from much commanding, and staff and line structure from much of the planning, co-ordinating and checking up. But organizing in the wide sense of the power of high appointment (or *manning* of upper posts) as well as the power of organization proper (*structuring*[1] or creation of the upper posts) must be 'reserved'. It must remain on the shoulders of the top rulers, together with the power of final adjudication of cases on appeal.

Perhaps the chief sanction of top rule is the activity of appointing and dismissing. He who appoints, promotes or dismisses is in control of him who is appointed, promoted or dismissed, and this function of 'manning' the organization is by no means just a paper right that has no practical influence upon the efficient government of industry. Employment, the hiring and firing of labour, consists essentially in this very activity of appointment, and dismissal. From the lowest rank of control upwards the vesting of the right of appointment is all important. As Knight puts it:[2]

The foreman who passes judgment on the abilities of operatives and takes the responsibility for their performing in accordance with his expectations finds himself in turn in a similar relation to his own ranking superior in the organization. . . . His responsibility is in turn transferred to the higher official (superintendent or what-not) who selects him, assigns him to his work, and hears appeals in those still rarer questions which he refers higher up for decision. . . . On up the scale the same relations hold good until we come to the supreme head of the business.

The activity of organizing is distinct from that of deciding high policy, as starting an association is distinct from commanding it; and, properly, it is distinct from that of appointing since it is a creation of structures or posts rather than the manning of those structures or posts.

[1] The *Concise Oxford Dictionary* gives 'furnishing with organs' as the first meaning of organizing, precisely what 'structuring' refers to; since structuring is unfamiliar, organizing will be retained whenever this primary meaning is clearly intended.

[2] *Risk, Uncertainty and Profit*, 1921, pp. 296–7.

assumptions is of practical importance when discussing incentives to the policy of various types of business leader. The differences are therefore detailed and illustrated at greater length in Chapter VII, § 4 under the heading of 'the entrepreneur'.

In state government organizing (i.e. structuring) includes the top power of making or amending the constitution. But since any large organization consists of a series of super-structures, co-structures and sub-structures, organizing must also occur at different levels of rank. There is super-organizing, co-organizing and sub-organizing. Super-organization creates the first-rank posts, probably the second-rank and possibly the third-rank posts, but it usually only mans the first-rank posts and possibly the second-rank posts, leaving manning of the third-rank posts to the first-rank men. Thus in Table IVB the general managing director might perhaps arrange the scope of the work, the department of each superintendent and foreman; but while appointing the superintendent himself, he might leave the appointment of the foreman to the works manager.

An important principle thus arises in the reservation of ultimate control for the supreme authority, a principle applying probably in all efficient forms of organization, political as well as industrial. It may be worded as follows: While commanding is a relation between *immediate* superiors and subordinates, appointment of subordinates is usually reserved to super-superiors and organization to super-super-superiors. The actual operatives are, for instance, given orders and managed by their immediate superior, the foreman, but they are usually appointed and dismissable only by a super-superior, either the immediate superior of the foreman (i.e. the superintendent), or in a functional structure the personnel manager, acting 'over the head' of the foreman. And when it is a question of organizing a foreman's department in the sense of creating so many sub-divisions, so many posts of time clerks, inspectors, tool-setters and operatives then it is the super-superior or even the super-super-superior, the works manager or the general manager, to whom that power is usually reserved.

Finally there is the power of adjudication reserved to top rule, corresponding in the state and the political scene to that of the judicature. One of the inherent inefficiencies of functional structure has been indicated as the overloading of top rule with demarcation disputes and other cases of friction between co-ordinate officers. An organization efficient in relieving top rule will reduce top adjudication to a minimum, but some cases will always remain of appeal to top level after failure to conciliate, mediate or arbitrate at lower level.

Within a large organization the functions thus centralized at the core of top government are the functions of deciding external policy and (internal) organization including appointment, structuring (the creation of tasks or posts to which powers are delegated[1]) and co-

[1] The question who does the structuring has hitherto seldom been asked, let alone answered; but Dale in *Planning and Developing the Company Organization Structure*, 1952, cites practical experiences.

ordination, and the function of final adjudication. The extent of the functions and powers of the central core as against that of the subordinate posts is not fixed either in fact or logic, but varies with size and, in organizations of similar size, varies according to the various technical and branch plant structures of the organization distinguished earlier. If each of the branch plants performs *like* transactions (see II § 2) and the large size of the organization is due simply to repetitive extension, powers and functions can be, and are, more centralized. If branches and plants perform *unlike* transactions and the whole organization integrates a variety of different industries the branch should logically, and often will in fact, have more functions and greater powers delegated to it. To quote Sir Charles Renold, 'because of the great variety both of activity and circumstances such an organization is almost bound to be decentralized. Authority must be relegated to near the scene of action.'[1] This is a simple corollary of the fact already noted, that the more variegated and integrated an organization *of given size* the less easy it is to manage centrally on a large scale and the greater need to delegate.

The technical and structural distinction drawn in Chapter I between firms having plants with like or unlike transactions and the consequent degree of centralization is independent of the system of government. Some *capitalist* firms such as banks and insurance companies have branches with like jobs and centralized authority. Others have branch plants with unlike jobs and decentralization, such as Unilever or Imperial Chemical Industries. Plants of the I.C.I. are grouped into several manufacturing divisions according to industry and the divisional boards may do anything except for a list of reserved powers reminiscent of federal government. Some *non-capitalist* organizations such as the Post Office or the nationalized Coal Board also have like-job plants, and centralized authority; others, such as the co-operative factories or nationalized transport activities have unlike jobs with authority more decentralized and delegated.

§ 7. THE QUESTION WHO GOVERNS AT THE CORE, AND WHY: THE NEXT
THREE CHAPTERS

This chapter has been devoted to problems of structure, such as over-centralization, bureaucracy, remote control, common to all forms of large-scale government, leaving the question of who does the governing in capitalist, nationalized and co-operative industrial organization to the two following chapters.

A political science which investigates the common problems of internal organization that nationalized rule shares with consumers' or capitalist rule or any other system of government—problems of policy

[1] Milward (ed.), *Large-Scale Organization*, 1950, p. 220.

decisions and their execution, of internal organization, of appointment and of adjudication—must be a science based on sociology and psychology. If the organization of government is the first consideration, the type of person obtained or obtainable for positions of ultimate control in that organization, the second; his response to various sorts of stimulus, follows naturally as the third problem. The efficiency and the aims with which large-scale operations are conducted depend ultimately upon the ability of certain persons to organize and to appoint suitable persons for managing that organization or for appointing in their turn further persons to sub-manage. It is vital to any explanation of inefficiency to enquire into the capacity and the response to incentives of these 'key' persons, and to probe the logic which has entrusted them with this position. This enquiry will be undertaken in the last chapter, and will lead us into the psychology of investor, manager and top ruler, and the sociological factors which conduce and induce to efficiency on their part. At first sight it would appear that a wide gulf was set between state government (the orthodox subject of political science) and business government, by the fact that businesses but not states have profit as their main incentive. This gulf has, however, been partly bridged by the institution of the business corporation or joint stock company. Many of the key men, the top rulers, in these business institutions are paid by salary like the top rulers of the state governments and some of their main incentives are similar to that of politicians and statesmen: prestige, power, interest in work, identification with the organization or other non-economic stimuli.

The important if passive role of labour must all the time be realized. Labour is not integrated into the organization for the positive control of nationalized or co-operative any more than capitalist concerns. But the employee may put a veto upon efficiency *or inefficiency* by his negative control (individually, or collectively—formally or informally through trade unions) in refusal to work on certain terms, say the shift-system or dilution of labour or unhealthy and dangerous physical conditions.

Elton Mayo and his associates have made us familiar with the informal organizations of groups of workers who have codes of behaviour which may or may not coincide with the rules of the formal organization. A group of bank-wirers in the Hawthorn works had the rule that you must not be efficient beyond a certain degree and as a sanction on this taboo put the word 'rate-buster' on violators of the rule.[1]

Employment implies not only appointment by, and subjection to, the employer's command but also a money payment or some other means, short of the sanction of coercion, to simulate efficient execution

[1] For social psychology applied to problems of formal and informal organization at higher levels, see Homans, *The Human Group*, 1950, especially pp. 369–414.

of the employer's commands. Any investigation of the logic or illogic of actual organization must enquire how far such pecuniary payment is effective, as against traditions, taboos and rituals, and how far it would be more efficient to give the present 'mere' employee more psychological interest and more participation and positive control. Control by consumers or by the state are not the only alternatives to control by the capitalist, and many schemes of workers' control have been committed to paper. Few, however, have actually proved efficient, and it is probable that other means must be found for 'securing labour's interest' in both senses of the phrase, i.e. for securing the employee's co-operation and ensuring that he is not exploited in his wages and other terms of employment.

As Catlin puts the modern conception of political science[1] control is not confined to the exercise of an authority which can impose its will upon others by compulsion, but consists rather in a 'parallelism of wills in terms of concurrent interests'. How far the interests of labour are, or can be made, concurrent with the efficiency of industrial organization, and its will parallel with that of the top 'core of control' must also come under discussion.

This 'two-way' view of command has been repeated specifically for industrial government by Barnard. He defines authority in action within commercial organizations as 'in the character of a communication (order) in a formal organization by virtue of which it is accepted by a contributor to or "member" of the organization as governing the action he contributes'. If economics deal with demand and supply in a market; politics may thus be said to deal with orders and their acceptance, or with 'command and reply' in an organization. In industrial organizations labour, and sometimes capital and enterprise, do not always 'reply'—and we must find the reasons why.

---

[1] *A Study of the Principles of Politics*, 1930, p. 70.

CHAPTER V

GOVERNMENT OF FREE ENTERPRISE
CAPITALISM

§ 1. GROWTH OF THE CORPORATION AND JOINT STOCK COMPANY

IN the last hundred years the capitalist system of control has been undergoing a profound change dictated by that very enlargement in the scale of organization indicated in Chapters I and II. This change and the reason for the change is evident from successive American censuses of manufactures.

As the average size of plant has increased, measured in number of wage-earners employed, capital invested or output produced, so has the proportion of all wage-earners, capital or output controlled by *corporations* as against partnerships or individual traders. In 1904, 23·7 per cent of all plants but 70·6 per cent of all wage-earners and 71·9 per cent of output added by manufacture were under the control of corporations. In 1939, 51·7 per cent of all plants but 89·4 per cent of all wage-earners and 92·6 per cent of all net output was under the control of corporations.

The British census of production till recently said little of the extent to which the British equivalent of the corporation, namely the joint stock company, controlled manufacturing industry; but judging from other sources there is no doubt of a development similar to that of the American corporation. Writing in 1776 Adam Smith thought

The only trades which it seems possible for a joint-stock company to carry on successfully, without an exclusive privilege, are those, of which all the operations are capable of being reduced to what is called a routine, or to such a uniformity of method as admits of little or no variation. Of this kind is, first, the banking trade; secondly, the trade of insurance from fire and from sea risk, and capture in time of war; thirdly, the trade of making and maintaining a navigable cut or canal; and, fourthly, the similar trade of bringing water for the supply of a great city.[1]

Even half-way through the nineteenth century the economist McCulloch thought that joint-stock organization was only applicable to undertakings which would 'admit of being carried on according to a regular systematic plan. . . . Companies were in all respects unsuited for the prosecution of ordinary industrial pursuits, whether belonging to

---

[1] *Wealth of Nations*, Book V, Chapter I, Part III, Art I.

203

agriculture, manufacture or commerce.'[1] And a witness before an official committee held that 'a washing company can never supersede washerwomen, washerwomen will always undersell them.'[2]

In fact, there was at that time little joint stock in Britain's manufacturing—or laundries. In 1875 a whole miscellaneous class of stocks and shares that included manufacturing and public utilities formed only 4·9 per cent of all securities, including government stock, listed on the London stock exchange, amounting to less than a fifth of the railway securities; and in 1885 the total paid-up capital of English and Scottish joint stock companies was only £495 million. By contrast in 1933 the stocks and shares in manufacturing and public utilities alone were 16·5 per cent of all securities amounting to *three* times the railway securities; and in 1935 the paid-up capital of all joint stock companies was £5,640 million, more than an eleven-fold increase since 1885[3] with much the same price level.[4]

More recently it was possible to measure the relative importance of joint stock company transactions in British manufacturing by quoting the taxing authorities on the proportion of the total trading profit (true gross) of an industry attributed to companies.[5] Adding the nineteen groups of manufactures that were recorded, the *gross true income* for *all* trades was, in 1948–9, £958·3 million; that for companies and local authorities £855·3 million. No local authorities traded in manufactures so joint stock companies apparently earned 89·3 per cent of the manufacturers' income. This was an advance on 1938–9 when the proportion was 84·2 per cent. The high proportion of income accountable to joint stock companies out of earnings of all firms was true of the bulk of manufacturing sub-groups.

In my *Ownership, Control and Success of Large Companies* I measured the importance in 1951 of joint stock companies, in all sectors and in the manufacturing sector divided into 27 different industries. Tests of the importance of the incidence of large companies with assets of over £2½m. were the number of such companies, and the total of these companies' assets per 100,000 employed in the whole industry. The differences between industries corresponded noticeably with the differences in their capital intensity as measured by horse-power per worker. Of the 11 manufacturing industries with the highest incidence (all those, in fact, containing large companies owning total assets of over a million

[1] Hunt, *The Development of the Business Corporation in England 1800–67*, 1936, p. 132.
[2] Loc. cit.
[3] Edwards, *Evolution of Finance Capitalism*, 1938.
[4] Mitchell and Dean, *Abstract of British Historical Statistics*, pp. 476–7.
[5] 92nd Report of the Commissioners of H.M. Inland Revenue, 1949, Cmd. 8052, pp. 57–69.

per 100,000 workers in the whole industry) 8 industries had over 6·5 horse-power per worker—more than double the 3·1 average for manufacturing. In the sectors other than manufacturing only two, shipping and other non-nationalized transport and communications, had more than £1m. of assets per 100,000 workers owned by its large companies. Building, wholesaling and retailing, catering and hotels all had £0·2m. or less.

In America the importance that the corporation has acquired in manufacturing, particularly, can be brought out by the official statistics of aggregate business receipts.[1] Whereas the receipts from all active corporations was 4·5 times the receipts from proprietorship and active partnership in the total of all economic sectors; it was 41·5 times in the manufacturing sectors.

Clearly in Britain, America and other industrialized countries the corporation or joint stock company is now, in manufacturing, the dominant form of capitalist undertaking and is gradually becoming still more dominating. The recent tendency towards combines, especially in the form of holding companies, does not alter the situation. For the holding company which controls several corporations or joint stock companies by ownership of the majority of their voting stock is itself a corporation or joint stock company.

Large-scale organization was found to be associated with intense investment (Chapter II, § 3) so that this connection of incorporation with large-scale organization connects, indirectly at one remove, incorporation with investment. And data from a census of at least one industrialized country (Germany) establishes a high direct correlation of horse-power per worker with proportion of workers in corporations. Among the 384 manufacturing industries recognized by the German census of 1925 there was a clear trend for industries with a high proportion of workers in corporations (Aktiengesellschaften) to be industries with a high horse-power per worker.[2]

Thus the logic of technical and technological factors seems to extend through industrial structure right into the heart of industrial government. The rule that those industries have the most incorporation which have a large-plant pattern and deep investment can be generalized to cover orders of industry outside manufacturing. For the same period, 1937–8, I made a comparison (Table VA) of the proportion of business done by companies or corporations in the nine main economic sectors both in America and Britain, including public utilities, mining and transport before they were nationalized in Britain. This comparison is worth setting beside Table IIF (page 114) comparing sectors in respect

---

[1] Statistical Abstract, 1970, p. 474.
[2] See Florence, 1948, pp. 99–100.

of size of firm, made about the same period. Table VA shows a remarkable agreement between America and Britain. The ranking of nine orders of industry according to the proportions of business transacted or of trading profits under corporate government is exactly similar in the two countries, and the individual entrepreneur or partner in both countries seems to prevail only in trading, construction, services and agriculture. Comparing with Table IIF these latter four sectors again appear in the bottom half of the list, as having the smallest firms.

These two correlates of incorporation, the size of firm and power per worker, suggest indeed the underlying logic for the present prevalence of the corporation and joint stock company. The large capital per worker required for an organization with a large number of workers cannot be obtained from an individual entrepreneur's own resources or that of his immediate circle, or his bank; he must borrow funds from the public and thus form a public joint stock company or corporation. Intermediate stages in the sequence of forms of government from one-man enterprise—stages determined largely by the intermediate size of the capital—are the partnership, and, among British companies, the private company with two to fifty members, and no right to invite public subscription.

In the Limited Public Company, liability is limited to a loss of profit and of the capital invested in the company, but partly owing to the fixed overhead costs of this capital discussed earlier (IV § 1) the losses at risk may be considerable.[1] Bonds or debenture stock may have been issued, interest on which will rank as a prior charge on earnings before dividends. If this interest is not paid the company is involved in bankruptcy. Debentures and bonds thus secured and entailing less risk to the owner carry no votes and illustrate, negatively, the connection between control and risk-bearing.

There is some positive correlation, industry by industry, between the proportion of debentures issued and the intensity of capital, 'high gearing' being found in industries such as electric light and power, iron and steel, and breweries and distilleries where fixed assets loom

---

[1] See, for example, *Economic Journal*, December 1931, pp. 577–83; September 1933, pp. 453–9. In Britain during the year 1928 a total of 277 new issues of ordinary, preferred and deferred shares, and of industrial debentures, were brought out on the market, the total capital subscribed amounting to £114,916,582. By 1 May 1931, the total market value was estimated to have sunk to £68,133,615, a net capital depreciation of 41 per cent in two and a half to three and a half years. By April 1933, two years later, the market value of these issues had sunk to £60,443,071—a total depreciation of 47 per cent. One hundred and six of these issues were for companies which were wound up before 1 May 1931, or whose shares had no ascertainable value. For earlier British experience of the survival and death rates of companies, see MacGregor, *Enterprise, Purpose and Profit*, 1934, pp. 99–120.

TABLE Va

MEASURE OF DEGREE OF INCORPORATION IN DIFFERENT SECTORS OF INDUSTRY

| America, 1937 | | | Britain, 1937–8 | | | | |
| Rank | Order of industry | Percentage business done by corporations 1937* | Order of industry | Trading profits (£000,000)† | | | Rank |
				Companies and local authorities	Total for order of industry	Percentage companies and local authorities out of total	
1st	Public utilities (electricity and gas)	100	Public utilities (electricity, gas, water)	55·1	55·2	100	1st
2nd	Mining	96	Coal	19·2	19·3	} 94	2nd
			Other	4·1	5·2		
3rd	Manufacturing	92	19 groups of manufactures	300·5	362·3	84·2	3rd
4th	Transport	89	Railways	28·2	28·2	} 83·7	4th
			Road transport	21·8	33·6		
			Shipping	14·4	15·1		
5th	Finance	84	Insurance, banking and finance	48·3	71·7	} 71	5th
			Finance abroad	6·2	6·2		
6th	Trade	58	Retail trades	45·4	144·4	} 44	6th
			Wholesale trades	54·6	84·1		
7th	Contracting and construction	36	Building and contracting	9·0	35·4	26	7th
8th	Services	30	Professions	1·3	76·5	} 15	8th
			Entertainment and sport	8·9	13·1		
			Other services	10·6	53·2		
9th	Agriculture	7	Agriculture and horticulture	7·8‡	108·4‡	7	9th

* Lynch, *Concentration of Economic Power*, p. 94, quoting T.N.E.C.
† 92nd Report of Commissioners of H.M. Inland Revenue, 1949, Cmd. 8052, pp. 57–74.
‡ Only a small number of farmers were assessed in 1937/8–39/40. The figures given are for 1948–9.

large.[1] Power to issue debentures thus again illustrates the point that the purpose of forming companies or corporations is to tap wider sources of capital, where much capital is technically required.

The growth in the company form of industrial government can be thought of as a further generation in the family tree drawn on page 87 and is so depicted. Corporations or company government are shown as 'issuing' from large-plant industries and as demonstrably correlated with them. This applies not only to manufacturing but to all orders of industry. Comparing the ranking given both in Table VA and Table IIF (p. 114) the industries with large percentage of incorporations (public utilities, manufactures, mining, rail transport) are on the whole also the industries with many employed per manager; the industries with small percentage of incorporations (agriculture, construction, road haulage and trade) those with few employees per manager. This development in the company form of industrial government has been going on to some extent in all industries, hand in hand with the structural trend, already noticed, toward more staff per worker, a division of labour among managers, and a sharing out of the entrepreneur's functions. But it is time the formal organization of this all-important institution of the joint stock company, or corporation, were described.

A company or corporation is 'formed' with a constitution (together with a statement of the capital and the directors' names) by a financier or 'promoter' or group of promoters or a merchant bank—a prospectus being issued to the public to obtain subscriptions to the stock or capital. It may be wound up or be merged in another company or be reconstructed. But here we are interested in the company as an established unit of government; not in its birth or death or other events in its history and only incidentally its rebirth in reconstruction.

Like the government of democratic states, corporations and joint stock companies decide upon a policy legally by majority rule, though the majority is of shares not heads. And, like the government of most states, they have a written or partly written constitution, which prescribes the various structures or organs of government and their functions and interrelations in coming to a decision, and prescribes also how to amend or reconstruct the constitution.

The formal constitution derives from three sources of authority. The most fundamental of them is the corporation or company law of the land, which in England and in Scotland is nation-wide, in America only state-wide, varying in content among the fifty states. Under these laws and their judicial interpretation the joint stock company and the corporation are each of them a legal entity endowed with

---

[1] Grant, *A Study of the Capital Market*, 1937, p. 167.

perpetual succession, capable of holding property in its own right, of incurring debts and of suing and being sued as a distinct person, and both have limited liability so that in the event of failure members cannot lose more than their original investment in the company.

The legally established constitution of these companies or corporations consists in two organs: a shareholders' meeting which votes according to the nominal value of the voting shares, and a board of directors. The board appoints its own chairman and also the top manager or executive—in America the president; in Britain the managing director, who has considerably less power than the president. British companies are divided into private and public. Private companies consist in less than fifty shareholders, the transfer of shares is restricted and there is no public invitation to subscribe, or requirement to publish accounts. The public companies are the more important and correspond to the American corporations in not restricting the number of shareholders or the transfer of shares and in requiring the publication of a balance sheet duly audited at least once a year. A company or corporation must have a regular (usually annual) meeting of the proprietors or shareholders which (i) elects a board of directors of not less than a certain number for a specific period, after which directors must be re-elected if they wish to continue, (ii) (in Britain though not usually in American states) sanctions and may reduce the rate of dividend, (iii) must be presented with, and may discuss, the results of the year's transactions, particularly a balance sheet.[1] Under company law all amendments to the constitution such as a change in the capital must be sanctioned by shareholders, usually in an extra-ordinary meeting.

In the formal structure and organization within the law of particular companies two further documents are involved, usually issued by the promoters of the company. The more fundamental instrument is in Britain named the memorandum of association, in America the certificate of incorporation or charter. It sets forth the name and location of the company, the scope of its objects and the total of its capital, and confirms that liability is limited. The actual procedure of government, especially the relations of shareholders and directors, of any one company within the terms of its memorandum or charter is stated for the English joint stock company in its articles of association, for an American corporation in its by-laws. In spite of certain standard by-laws or articles (e.g. 'Table A' for British companies), we find for different companies and corporations in fact quite a wide variety in the number and type of directors, the qualifying shares they must hold and their tenure of office before re-appointment. Wide variety will also be found in the division of shares into categories (e.g. ordinary or

---

[1] A. B. Levy, *Private Corporations and their Control*, 1950, p. 734.

'common stock', deferred, preferred, preference) and in the arrangements for shares to carry votes or multiples or fractions of votes. The significant general trends to be discovered in this variety will be discussed later.

The logical theory clearly enunciated in the law and the two instruments setting up the corporation or joint stock company is that the shareholders who bear this risk should have top control—a theory

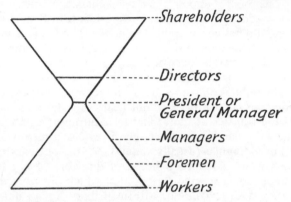

D. H. Robertson considers 'may almost be described as capitalism's "Golden Rule" '.[1]

Joint stock government is pictured[2] above as proceeding like the sand in an hour-glass from the wide top (to represent the thousands of shareholders) down through the narrows representing the dozen or so of directors, and the waist representing the managing director and president. From this point the execution of the shareholders' and directors' policy widens out again in a hierarchy of ranks and functions as detailed in Table IVb, till at the base as many workers are represented perhaps as shareholders.

The risk-bearing shareholders, in short, are considered logically also to be the risk-takers in the sense of those laying down the policies of the organization—policies that will involve various degrees of risk.[3] Otherwise, excessive risks may be taken by policy makers such as the president or general manager who are personally often safe from the direct consequences, owning few shares. For the sake of efficiency in government, the powers of appointing top managers, reorganizing the upper

[1] *Control of Industry*, 1923, p. 89.

[2] See Florence, *Atlas of Economic Structure and Policies*, Fig. 56 for detail.

[3] The nature of the risk and the probability distribution and uncertainty of various degrees of loss is measured in Florence, *Ownership, Control and Success of Large Companies*, pp. 162–8, and illustrated in Chapter VII, § 2, of the present book in discussing the stimulus for risk-bearing.

management structure and deciding policy are delegated by share-holders to the board of directors who appear at the top of the chart in Table IVᴮ and just above the waist of the hour-glass. In the capitalist company or corporation the shareholders meeting should in theory be pictured in the organization chart as on top even of the board. The members of the board (whose private interest is supposed to be identified with that of the company or corporation by holding quali-fying shares), are appointed and their appointment periodically reviewed by the annual shareholders' meeting, which also decides their scale of remuneration. Shareholders can check up on results—in theory again—from the published and duly audited annual balance sheets, and, in fact, will occasionally read newspaper comment in the financial columns of their favourite daily newspaper. Amendments of this constitution, such as an increase of the share capital, requires still further reference to the shareholders' meeting. If a certain proportion of shareholders agree, meetings may be called without reference to the directors. In short, it is the shareholders who, in law, are sovereign. But are they sovereign in reality?

§ 2. THE SHAREHOLDERS' ACTUAL PART IN GOVERNMENT. LAW AND REALITY

The dominant capitalist forms of organization, the corporation in America and the joint stock company in Britain, have, formally and legally, two main organs of government: the shareholders' meeting and the board of directors. The remainder of this chapter will deal with the question of who exercises top rule—in which, or within which, of these two substructures the bulk of top level government is to be found in Britain and America *de facto* and not *de jure*. 'Within which' is added because the possibility must not be ignored that one or some of the directors, or one or some of the shareholders and not all of them *as a body*, may actually wield top rule.

Do the shareholders as a body wield top rule in the typical corpora-tion or joint stock company in fact as they do in law? An answer can be made fairly definitely, No, except in times of extreme crisis in the company's life such as the threat of a take-over bid.

In normal conditions the shareholders elect, in law, the board of directors and the board of directors appoint the top managers, i.e. the 'officers'. Since 'the *crucial* decision is the selection of men to make decisions', Knight, in a book[1] often quoted by economists, makes this election the essential link between ownership and management. It is a link allowing the owning shareholders who take the profit in the form of

---

[1] *Risk, Uncertainty and Profit*, 1921, p. 297.

dividends, also to exercise top control and to be identified as entre-preneurs.

But in fact the shareholders neither initiate nor discuss, but merely confirm as though by rubber stamp, the election of the directors. Evi-dence has accumulated that directors to be elected or re-elected are nominated by the existing directors or a group of them; and normally there is only one list of nominees. The system of election is, in short, co-option and single-party co-option at that. As Ruml puts it,[1] 'the fact is that the shareholders elect the directors but they do not choose them. They are chosen by the board of directors itself which makes the nomination.'

The reasons for the lack of real function and power in the body of shareholders as a whole are revealed partly by companies' or corpora-tions' articles of association, but mainly by a realistic structural analysis of the actual shareholders and the distribution of shares among them. Some companies have in their articles restricted voting power to certain classes of shares. According to a random sample of British companies taken in 1935

The voting rights of shares tend to be more unequal in the larger than the smaller English companies. A line may conveniently be drawn between com-panies who have one denomination of shares only, or allow equal rights (i.e. one vote per given value of share) to all denominations; and companies, on the other hand, who granted unequal voting rights as between denominations —e.g. that preference shares may not vote unless their dividend is in arrear. Greater inequality of rights in larger companies was evident in all sections of the random sample of English companies, but full details were only obtained for the Iron, Steel and Coal, and the Brewery and Distilling sections. Dividing companies into two sizes, small where capital was £200,000 or less, large where it was more than £200,000, unequal rights were set up by seven large brewing companies out of nineteen, but only by two small brewing companies out of fourteen. Eleven large iron, steel and coal companies out of nineteen set up unequal rights, while all four of the small coal, iron and steel companies allowed equal rights.

Among the eighty largest English trading companies . . . the ratio of capital with full voting rights to total capital . . . was 100 per cent (i.e. equal rights) for only twenty-eight of the companies. For thirty-one companies, voting capital formed 61 to 99 per cent of total capital, for eighteen the ratio was 21 to 60 per cent, and for three it was 20 per cent or less. Clearly the larger companies show a wide variety but, on the average, their votes are more unequally shared, conducing to at least *partial* divorce of control from ownership.[2]

[1] *Tomorrow's Business*, 1945, p. 71.
[2] Florence, 'The Statistical Analysis of Joint Stock Company Control', *Statistical Journal*, 1947, Part I, p. 13.

In some American companies, too, according to Gordon[1] voting power is granted to only a small issue and the bulk of the stock may be left with no vote at all. 'Not only preferred but also common stock may be without voting rights.'

The main reason, however, for denying that shareholders as a whole wield top powers in the government of companies and corporations lies in their situation and behaviour. To start with, there are too many of them for effective deliberation and decision.

In 1950 the American Telephone and Telegraph Company had 985,583 stock-holders, General Motors 410,480 and the U.S. Steel Corporation 195,218. Since then the number of stock-holders in the United States generally has increased fast. In 1952 the total of individual stockholdings has been estimated at 6,490,000, in 1956 at 8,630,000, and in 1965 at 20,120,000. The number of corporations has not increased so rapidly—672,071 in 1952, 1,423,980 in 1965: a rise of 111 per cent as against the shareholdings rise in number of 212 per cent.[2] Thus more and more shareholdings per corporation appear on average.

Shareholding is not nearly so dispersed among the general population in Britain but among the 98 very large industrial and commercial companies analysed for 1951 in my *Ownership, Control and Success of Large Companies*, I estimated that twenty had over 25,000 shareholders of which three, Lever Bros, Imperial Chemical and Imperial Tobacco, had over 160,000;[3] not more than eight had under 3,000 shareholders.

It may be estimated with some confidence that the bulk of industrial transactions both in Britain and America are conducted by companies or corporations of 2,000 shareholders or more. And it is an intriguing discovery (though not particularly significant) that a large company's average number of shareholders—the nominal entrepreneurs and employers—are of much the same order of magnitude as its employees —often rather more numerous. But the certain and significant fact is that even with a mere two thousand of shareholders, so far below the number for the largest companies, an effective general meeting is obviously impossible. If all holders turned up the meeting would fill a typical assembly or town hall and resemble a political rally (given over to mass-appeal propaganda and emotion) rather than a deliberative and policy-deciding organ. In point of fact the usual shareholders' meeting is only attended by a minute fraction of the shareholders, perhaps fifty or a hundred and not representative at that, but, all too often, cranks and busybodies.

Apart from their sheer quantity, the ineffectiveness of shareholders as a whole is also due to their quality. The great majority of persons

[1] *Business Leadership in the Large Corporation*, 1945, p. 162 and footnote.
[2] U.S. Statistical Abstract, 1970, Sections 14 and 16, pp. 391 and 459.
[3] Op. cit., pp. 196–217.

holding shares are either ignorant, business-shy, or *too* busy—or any two of them or even all three. Many shareholders are children or very old people, and to judge from British evidence nearly half are women, many of them shy (with or without reason) of business. A sample enquiry into forty British companies typical of all sizes, found the proportion of women shareholders varying from 61 per cent to 20 per cent, with an average of 40 per cent of all single accounts; in addition there were 8 per cent on average of joint accounts.[1] Many investors are retired and living mainly away from business centres. Compared with the distribution of the population the shareholder in these typical companies had a propensity to live in London, the home counties (including Sussex), southern or south western England because 'he is to be found in his retirement and his wife in her widowhood, in the pleasanter climes'[2]—'climes' physical and psychological, represented by Kensington, Cheltenham and other inland spas.

American evidence is much the same as to the high proportion of women stock-holders; in fact they number over half.[3] If anything, absenteeism is likely to be still more marked with the long distances from commercial centres of the main retirement areas such as California, Arizona and Florida.

Apart from the ignorant and business-shy, likely to be passive, not to say sleeping, partners in industrial government, are there not knowledgeable and business-like investors in industrial companies? Yes, in plenty. They are, roughly speaking, of three sorts. Men and women engaged in other business or professions, transient speculators, and corporate institutions. Not all shareholders are private persons, and those that are institutions are probably neither ignorant or business-shy. In America L. H. Kimmel investigating corporations of all sizes covering 83 per cent of all shareholdings in 1951 found that 92 per cent of holders of common stock were persons, holding 57·4 per cent of the stock; 4·5 per cent were fiduciaries (trustees, etc.) holding 6·9 per cent of the stock; 1·2 per cent were brokers and dealers holding 10·2 per cent of the stock; 0·6 per cent were foundations holding 1·9 per cent of the stock; another 0·6 per cent were nominees holding 10·1 per cent of the stock; and the remaining 1·1 per cent (mostly other corporations) held 13·4 per cent of the stock.[4] In Britain a sample enquiry into forty companies typical of all sizes[5] showed 95 per cent shares owned by

---

[1] Ellinger and Carter, *Financial Times*, 2 March, 1949.

[2] Ibid.

[3] U.S. Statistical Abstract, 1966, p. 472.

[4] *Share Ownership in the United States*, 1952, p. 15. For further analysis of nominee shares see footnote, p. 227. The type of holders of the 20 largest shareholdings in large British and American companies is given below, p. 215.

[5] Ellinger and Carter, *loc. cit.*

persons and only 3 per cent by corporate and charitable holders and 2 per cent by nominee companies. But Parkinson, analysing *the large holdings* (of over 10,000 shares) only, in 30 large companies found that for the ordinary stock the distribution of holdings and capital involved was:[1]

Large holdings in large British companies	Percentage of holdings		Percentage of capital	
Persons	42·5 ⎫		36·4 ⎫	
Trustees	4·5 ⎬ 51%		2·4 ⎬ 42%	
Banks	3·9 ⎭		2·9 ⎭	
Insurance companies	10·3 ⎫		5·6 ⎫	
Investment trusts	8·0 ⎬ 22%		5·3 ⎬ 31%	
Other companies	3·7 ⎭		20·4 ⎭	
Nominees	27%		27%	

Parkinson's data cannot be directly compared with the preceding data since his data refer to large holdings in large companies only, but the evidence suggests that the institutional shareholders are more important in the larger than in the smaller companies. The importance of the insurance companies as large investors in large companies is confirmed by my own survey of the 98 largest English industrial and commercial companies in 1951. Each of seven insurance companies appeared among the 20 largest shareholders in ten companies at least. To be exact the Prudential, the Pearl and the Royal London Mutual appeared among the 20 largest shareholders of 47, 33 and 27 respectively of these 98 largest companies.

Individual persons are the largest category of investors, but each person holds, on average, a smaller number of shares than companies or corporations. We shall revert to this later as an indication of who it is that sits in control.

A further set of definitely business-like shareholders is indicated by the brokers just mentioned. They and perhaps others hold their shares transiently, either for their own or their clients' benefit, and have in the terms of personnel management a high 'labour turnover'. Buying and selling on the stock exchange so frequently, they regard their shares as a commodity rather than as a true investment in an enterprise. If such an 'investor' is dissatisfied he will not turn up at the next shareholders' meeting but may just sell out; or he may sell out just because he is satisfied—with a rise in price and a margin of profit! The shares sold on the New York stock exchange divided by the total listed securities gave in 1967 and again in 1968 a percentage of 22—not far from an average factory labour-turnover rate.[2] And like labour turnover

---

[1] *The Ownership of Industry*, 1951, p. 46. The figures here given are percentages of the large holdings, not of total capital in 1941.
[2] U.S. Statistical Abstract, 1970, p. 457.

there have always been wide variations from firm to firm. Stockder[1] quotes for 1919 the following turnover rates on the common stock of well-known American corporations: American Telephone and Telegraph 15·9 per cent, Cluett Peabody 18·3 per cent, New York Central RR 30·6 per cent, International Harvester 63·5 per cent, American Smelting and Refining Co. 332·6 per cent, U.S. Rubber Co. 641·0 per cent, U.S. Steel Corporation[2] 640·8 per cent, American Car Co. 711·8 per cent, American Locomotive Co. 1,092 per cent, International Mercantile Marine 1,549 per cent, United Cigar Stores, 2,600 per cent. It has been said that labour is only 'loosely associated' within business organizations, but I know of no turnover rates to show any labour quite so loose as the shareholders in their association with these latter corporations.[3] It is no doubt true that only some of the shareholders, particularly the brokers, are really 'loose', but the same co-existence of a hard core and a loose fringe is also true of the structure of labour turnover; and the fringe of shareholders appears often more loose and the core perhaps less thick.

Business and professional men form a certain proportion of shareholders. But possibly more important than that, professional men may advise the otherwise ignorant and business-shy. In Britain the legal profession of solicitors (unknown as such in America where the word means something quite different) perform this function of advising clients, including trustees, how to invest their estates. Business and professional men (and women) may well invest part of their own wealth outside their main line of business. But just because they *are* knowledgeable and business-like they will probably have the sense, even when dealing with events outside their special ken, to spread their risks. They will tend to fragment and scatter savings in a wide variety of companies or corporations. The extent of this spread was studied in Britain in 1949 by finding what proportion of a sample of investors in any one of forty typical companies of various sizes were also investors in the ordinary shares of two well-known large companies.[4] The answer was 24·2 per cent in one company, 19·6 per cent in the other. The authors estimate that though the total of shareholdings in Britain may have run to ten million and over, there were about that time only a million and a quarter shareholders. A similar spread of risks producing a total number of shareholdings much greater than the total number of

---

[1] *Business Ownership Organization*, p. 94.

[2] The proportion of brokers shares in this company is given by Stockder as 32 per cent in 1920, 58 per cent in 1916.

[3] MacGregor, in his *Evolution of Industry*, 1913, pp. 121–2, suggested (before such turnover rates were calculated) that in many cases through the management the labour would employ the capital rather than the capital the management.

[4] Ellinger and Carter, loc. cit.

shareholders has also been measured in America.[1] Even business-like and intelligent shareholders therefore are not likely to attend to the business of any one company in which they have shares, because they have shares in so many others.

The final consideration making for sleeping shareholders or, in Veblen's phrase, absentee-ownership of the average shareholder is connected with this fragmentation. The vast majority of shareholders usually hold a very small share in the total voting capital. The distribution of shares among the shareholders of companies is in practice most unequal, quite as unequal as the distribution of income over the population. As votes are in proportion to shares, this inequality normally debars the average shareholder from any chance of influencing decisions.

The precise degree of inequality in distribution has been put in many ways, graphical and tabular. The distribution of the sizes of shareholdings in large companies is almost universally more unequal than the distribution of incomes within a nation[2] When it comes to a 'take-over' and the shareholders do have the final decision (in that case whether to get merged), the critical point is *what number or proportion of shareholders can muster 50 per cent or thereabouts of the vote*? The smaller the number of shareholders who can in any single corporation or company wield a majority vote or a virtual majority, and the larger the number with a minority vote or virtual minority vote,[3] the more likely it is that an oligarchy can be established and that the average voter will find himself powerless. Absolute *numbers* of shareholders per corporation should therefore be tabulated, as well as the proportion they form of all shareholders.

A classical study of the distribution of shares among holders was undertaken in America for 1937 by the T.N.E.C.[4] Table VB sums up their findings on the distribution of the common stock for corporations of different size. One point to focus upon is the number and proportion of shareholders per corporation required to obtain a majority, that is 50 per cent, of the total shares. In the last three columns the 186 smallest corporations with assets under a million dollars are shown to contain an average of 13 (or 1·9 per cent) of the shareholders with 69·8 per cent of the shares; in the corporations larger than this a majority of shares appears to be held by *just over* 0·2 per cent to 0·5 per cent of the shareholders. Among the 47 corporations with greatest assets an

[1] Gordon, *Business Leadership in The Large Corporation*, 1945, p. 156.

[2] See above, p. 43 and for a simple presentation of income distribution see my *Atlas of Economic Structure and Policies*, Fig. 61.

[3] The adjective 'virtual' has been added of set purpose. Its significance will be made clear shortly.

[4] Monograph 30.

TABLE Vb

DISTRIBUTION OF SHARES AMONG SMALL, MEDIUM AND LARGE SHAREHOLDERS IN CORPORATIONS OF VARIOUS SIZES

Size of company in assets ($000,000)	No. of corporations (1)	Total common stock or ordinary shares outstanding (000) (2)	Small holdings 0–1,000 shares			Medium holdings 1,001–5,000 shares			Large holdings Over 5,000 shares		
			Shareholders		Shares	Shareholders		Shares	Shareholders		Shares
			Average no. per corporation (3)	(Percentage total holders) (4)	Percentage of total shares (5)	Average no. per corporation (6)	(Percentage total holders) (7)	Percentage of total shares (8)	Average no. per corporation (9)	(Percentage total holders) (10)	Percentage of total shares (11)
AMERICAN 1937–9*											
Under 1	186	119,990	620	(92·4)	16·1	38	(5·7)	14·1	13	(1·9)	69·8
1 and under 5	443	153,626	1,320	(97·5)	36·4	27	(2·0)	16·6	6	(0·5)	47·0
5 and under 10	217	86,421	2,190	(98·0)	41·1	36	(1·6)	19·3	8	(0·4)	39·6
10 and under 20	181	108,583	3,130	(98·0)	37·9	55	(1·6)	17·3	12	(0·4)	44·8
20 and under 50	164	159,523	6,280	(98·6)	39·3	71	(1·1)	15·6	16	(0·3)	45·1
50 and under 100	74	117,092	11,790	(98·9)	41·3	108	(0·9)	14·4	27	(0·2)	44·3
100 and under 200	66	184,268	21,260	(98·8)	32·6	208	(1·0)	15·5	50	(0·2)	41·9
200 and under 500	51	227,653	29,140	(98·9)	38·8	265	(0·9)	12·6	68	(0·2)	48·6
500 and over	47	449,129	83,755	(99·1)	43·3	609	(1·7)	12·4	135	(0·2)	44·3
All Sizes	1,429	1,606,284	7,350	(98·7)	38·9	78	(1·0)	14·4	19	(0·3)	46·7
Manufacturing only	779	766,966	6,620	(98·6)	41·5	74	(1·1)	15·5	19	(0·3)	43·0
BRITISH 1941†		(£1,000)									
30 Large companies	30	236,124	26,570	(96·4)	40·1	853	(3·1)	24·0	132	(0·5)	35·9

* T.N.E.C., Monograph No. 30, pp. 107–5.
† Parkinson, *Ownership of Industry*, pp. 61–2. Nine companies had a total (nominal) capital ordinary and preference of £10–75 million; nine £5–10 million; six £3–5 million. Shares were of slightly lower denomination than the American.

218

average of 135 out of 84,000 shareholders per corporation hold a near majority (i.e. 44·3 per cent) of the shares. How far such a comparatively small number as 13 to 135 can, with a majority or virtual majority of the shares, form an oligarchy to control the whole corporation will be discussed in the next section. All that is to be established here is that the vasty majority of shareholders have little say. Politically they are a 'ruck'. At every size of company except the smallest, 97·5 per cent or more of the shareholders have between them a clear minority of the shares, and even among the smallest companies 92·4 per cent own but 16·1 per cent of the shares. In the largest class of corporations the average of 135 shareholders per corporation (0·2 per cent of all shareholders) have each on average a holding of 14,300 shares (amounting in total to 44·3 per cent of the shares), but the 83,755 small shareholders per corporation (99·1 per cent of all shareholders) have on average a holding of only 233 shares apiece.[1] For corporations of all sizes an average of 19 shareholders have an average of 25,300 shares apiece, while 7,350 shareholders or 98·7 per cent of all shareholders have, on average, only 217 shares apiece. Roughly the same inequality is true of the *manufacturing* corporations of all sizes, and it is noteworthy that the contrast of large and small shares does not differ greatly in the large from the bulk of corporations.

The distribution of shares among shareholders in the thirty large British companies analysed by Parkinson can be tabled under the same ranges of small, medium and large holdings. Compared with the American corporations which (except for the two top rows of small corporations) cover much the same sizes of companies, the distribution of shareholding is almost equally unequal; 0·5 per cent of shareholders own 35·9 per cent of the ordinary shares and a further 3·1 per cent own another 24·0 per cent. There is again a ruck of small-holders, 96·4 per cent of all shareholders—an average per company of 26,570 shareholders (out of 27,555) own on average £118 or 0·00145 per cent of the total of ordinary shares apiece, while the average share of the 132 larger shareholders is £52,000[2] or 440 times that of the numerous small shareholders.

It is true that *if* the small shareholders got together and were unanimous they could build up a majority vote. As Mr Austen Albu put the matter during a House of Commons debate: 'There must always be a majority shareholding in any company. One has only to get

---

[1] 44·3 per cent of 449,129,000 divided by 47 corporations averaging 135 large shareholders = 14,300; 43·3 per cent of 449,129,000 divided by 47 corporations averaging 83,755 shareholders = 233.

[2] Parkinson, op. cit., p. 43. This is a larger absolute number than the large American holders partly because the British shares were of somewhat lower denomination.

enough people to combine to have a majority, then one has a majority shareholding.'[1] But against this possibility is the huge absolute number of shareholders and the exiguous fractional vote each carries in consequence of his very small holding. Except in most exceptional circumstances there is not a contest in which two or more rival parties organize all the voters. Normally only one party is in the field, namely the corporation or company's existing government, represented by the board of directors, and little 'getting together' occurs among the small-holders who are, for reasons already given, likely to be indifferent and to vote equally for or against the board recommendations, if they vote at all. It is irrelevant therefore to collect statistics of share distribution in order to search, as Parkinson does, for a pivotal shareholder who is presumed to hold the balance between contending policies. Certainly one cannot speak of 'the extremely important tactical significance of medium holdings'.[2] The statistics, so admirably collected, tend rather to prove, as will be argued later, that a few shareholders usually own a sufficiently large minority of shares to have a decisive vote, a virtual majority on policy and organization, as against a large number of indifferent shareholders with a nominal majority but virtual minority of voting power.

The meeting of all shareholders is legally the sovereign assembly of a company or corporation. But the quantity and quality of most shareholders in any one company and their quick turnover, divided interests, spreading of risks and small holdings leads to the expectation that the shareholders' meeting will be *de facto* neither well attended nor effective. Absenteeism is normally over 99 per cent and the 'rump' of the 'ruck' that attend, together with those attending by proxy (including probably large shareholders), will simply rubber-stamp the balance sheet, the decisions on policy and organization, and the nominations to vacant directorships made by the directors. Normally, shareholders' meetings (ordinary or extraordinary) only exercise real control when a take-over bid offers to buy their shares, or transactions have gone wrong and dividends cannot be paid—but usually so wrong that the company or corporation faces bankruptcy and control is in fact and in law rapidly slipping from shareholders to debenture or bond holders, or a bank or other creditors.

This passivity of shareholders at their annual meeting, when business is flourishing, normal or not too abnormal, is subject to occasional exceptions that prove the rule. Mr Lewis Gilbert, described by the *New Yorker*[3] as a 'crusader who has dedicated his life to improving the life of the moderately well-to-do' is such an exception. His crusade,

[1] Hansard, 18 May 1949, p. 518.
[2] Parkinson, op. cit., p. 96. See below, p. 232.
[3] 11 December 1948.

the rousing slogan of which is 'Divided, the Management Rules—United, Stockholders Participate', points to certain glaring deficiencies in existing procedure such as holding meetings in inaccessible places, consenting to excessively large payments to directors, or not reporting to shareholders on proceedings. Some of the reforms proposed as a more democratic regime for shareholders, such as the election of auditors by the meeting and a vote on the distribution of profits (downwards at least), has always been the practice in Britain. Indeed, as long ago as 1912 it was pointed out by a (presumably neutral) German[1] that the American corporation was 'curiously enough particularly undemocratic as compared to British companies'. But, compared to the German Aktiengesellschaft, both countries in his opinion left little power to the shareholder.

§ 3. GOVERNMENT BY BLOC-HOLDER

The shareholders as a body, whatever their legal position, do not in fact grasp the helm of government of the corporation or company. The possibility is not excluded, however, that some of the shareholders, particularly the holders of a large bloc of shares, may in fact steer the ship. This possibility is a plausible hypothesis well worth trying out. Lord Woolton, speaking in 1947 as president of the Royal Statistical Society,[2] maintained that 'the policy of no well directed company . . . was controlled by the shareholding at all', and that 'no amount of investigation as to shareholdings could ever give any guidance as to the policy of companies'. Other business men, however, like Lord Camrose in his *British Newspapers and their Controllers*, make no bones about investigating shareholdings as the obvious key to policy, and goes so far as to suggest of one newspaper, that a 20 per cent holding of its ordinary capital gives a control 'which could not be easily disturbed by a hostile combination of other holders'. But we anticipate. . . .

First, we must think of a number of persons not too large to prevent some sort of personal contact and yet large enough to control among most companies or corporations a sufficient proportion of votes to give a virtual majority. The number hit upon early (about 1937) in my own investigation into British companies was the twenty largest share-

---

[1] R. Liefmann, *Die Unternehmungsformen*, Stuttgart, 1912, Chapter II, 3.

[2] *Statistical Journal*, Part I, 1947, pp. 24–5. This school of thought stresses, as did Lord Woolton, 'that the trade of the country was in the main controlled by personalities . . . not shareholding' or finance. The same simple psychological view was put forward by Pierpont Morgan in explaining his financial colleagues' power over subsidiaries and 'affiliates', before the Pujo committee in 1912–13. See Allen, *Lords of Creation*, pp. 169–87.

holders, about a normal size for a committee or board; and significantly enough the same number was picked in America by the T.N.E.C. Though an arbitrary number (fifteen might be sufficient; or twenty-five or thirty not too large for contact), it is the twenty largest shareholders that will be adopted as a standard procedure. This number proves justified in practice by facts which will appear shortly.[1]

What proportion of the total ordinary shares (or common stock); or, better still, what proportion of the voting shares[2] do the twenty largest shareholders possess in British companies and American corporations?

Finding the twenty or any other number of the largest shareholders is laborious and both the T.N.E.C. investigation in America and my own in England[3] have been confined to the very largest corporations or companies—in America the 200 largest non-financial, as of 1939; in England the 85 industrial (i.e. manufacturing) and commercial companies not nationalized in 1950 with over £3 million of capital in 1936.[4]

Although picked out by different tests the two lists are important and fairly comparable; they refer to neighbouring years. Both lists are free of duplication and exclude subsidiaries of companies already on the list. The 200 largest American non-financial corporations (among which were 96 manufacturing with 101 common stock issues and 30 'other' corporations, not railroad or public utility, with 31 issues), had about 40 per cent of assets of all non-financial corporations;[5] and the 85 largest English manufacturing and commercial companies probably owned and controlled with their subsidiaries a fairly similar proportion of the assets of all such companies whatever their size. But it is not only the high percentage of all assets in all industries owned, or even of all transactions performed, by those largest companies that makes them important. There is also the monopolistic or at least oligopolistic powers of these firms within a single industry whether fully exercised or not. One or other of the listed 85 largest English companies, or of the 126 largest American industrial companies, operates in each of most of the industries given in Table IIIc where the index of concentration was found so high.

Qualitative comparability of the English and American list of largest companies is approached by selecting only the manufacturing and 'other' non-financial American corporations. The net American total of 96 manufacturing and 30 'other' corporations (of which 12 are

---

[1] P. 225, i.e. a sharp taper in the sizes of the largest holdings.

[2] See above, § 1.

[3] Scottish companies registered in Edinburgh were excluded. There were only two which, if English, would have qualified for the list—'British' may, perhaps be used.

[4] Appearing in the section of the *Stock Exchange Year Book*, 1936, named 'Industrial and Commercial' together with shipping and the brewery sections.

[5] T.N.E.C., Monograph 29, p. 23, refers to 1937–9. The English list refers to 1936.

'merchandizing') is matched by the English list of 58 companies manufacturing, and 24 others, the majority in commerce.[1] All the English companies had, by definition, an issued capital of £3 million or over; this is probably equivalent to from £6 to £12 million of total assets. All the American companies had *total assets* of over $60 million, equivalent, perhaps, in 1937 to rather over £12 million.

Table Vc gives a measure of the importance of the largest twenty shareholders in these large companies in both countries. In Britain the measure is the percentage of all voting shares, and in America the

TABLE Vc

PERCENTAGE OF SHARES HELD BY TWENTY LARGEST SHAREHOLDERS AS A WHOLE
IN 82 LARGEST BRITISH* AND 126 LARGEST AMERICAN INDUSTRIAL COMPANIES
1936 AND 1937–9†

Proportion of shares held by largest 20 holders (identified or not) %	American corporations' common stock issues‡ 1937–9					English companies (voting shares) 1936			
	Manufacturing (1)	Mfg. (less oil, iron and steel) (2)	'Other' not financial (3)	Total (4)	% (5)	Mfg. (no iron, steel or oil) (6)	Commercial (7)	Total (8)	% (9)
0– 9·9	3	(3)	1	4	3 ⎫ 31	6	1	7	9 ⎫ 22
10–19·9	32	(24)	5	37	28 ⎭	8	3	11	13 ⎭
20–29·9	23	(13)	6	29	22	15	2	17	21
30–49·9	22	(18)	8	30	23	10	4	14§	17
50 up	21	(15)	11	32	24	19	14	33	40
Total	101	(73)	31	132	100	58	24	82	100

* Excluding from the largest 85, three companies with special voting provisions.

† This table differs from somewhat similar summaries of the T.N.E.C. tables given by Gordon (*Leadership in the Large Corporation*, p. 32) in two respects:

(1) All the 20 largest holders are included whether beneficiaries identifiable or not, as in the case of the English companies.

(2) Subsidiaries are not excluded if they are not subsidiary to corporations already listed. In the manufacturing and other groups only three and two corporations respectively were involved and it was not worth while altering the original official figures given in T.N.E.C., Monograph 29, pp. 609, 610.

‡ Including non-voting common stocks, 126 corporations totalled 132 issues.

§ Among these 14 companies, the 20 largest shareholders hold 30–39 per cent of votes in 6, 40–49 per cent in 8.

[1] Within manufacturing the main differences are that the American list contains iron and steel and oil, the British, brewing; within other than manufacturing, the American list contains mines and communications, the British, newspapers and shipping. For total of 82, not 85, see Table Vc, note *.

percentage of common voting stock, owned in both cases by the largest twenty shareholders, whether the beneficiaries were identifiable or not.[1] If the proportion of 0–10 per cent and 10–20 per cent held by the largest twenty owners be bracketed the degree of concentration of shares in the ownership of the twenty largest holders in the two countries is fairly comparable. The main differences appear to be that more English companies have a concentration so low that the twenty largest owners hold less than 10 per cent of shares, and at the other extreme that more English companies have a concentration so high that the twenty largest owners hold 50 per cent or over. The latter difference has on average the more weight. While in half the American corporations the twenty largest shareholders hold no more than 28 per cent of the voting common stock and in half more than that, this 'median point' is at about 40 per cent of the shares among the English companies.

Twenty, a conventional committee size, was taken somewhat arbitrarily as a number that might form the nucleus of government, but the government of a company or corporation might be in the hands of more or of fewer shareholders. The hypothesis of a government based on *more* than twenty large shareholders is the less likely in the light of the actual structure of the twenty largest holdings. If these holdings are ranked in order of their size, the sizes appear, in the bulk of the large companies, to taper off rapidly at first and then more slowly. The typical pattern in large companies and corporations can be measured most easily by calculating a 'median' large company with proportions of the capital for each of the twenty largest shareholdings and number of directors and directors' holdings, etc., such that the number of companies with higher and with lower values is the same. In this median large company the slope of the taper can be seen, from Table VD, to be in both countries first sharp and then long drawn-out. The largest shareholding averages for all companies (as measured by the median) 10·3 per cent of voting shares in Britain, 6·0 per cent of common stock issues in America, but the fifth holding in size has tapered down sharply to 1·1 per cent in Britain and 1·27 per cent in America. From the 5th to the 20th holding the rate of decrease is slower. Instead of the holding decreasing four ranks down (from 1st to 5th) to a fifth or even a tenth, it decreases the further fifteen ranks down in Britain from 1·1 to 0·27, i.e. to a quarter; and in America from 1·27 to 0·41,

---

[1] For the difficulties presented by nominees, banks and trusts, etc., holding for unidentified beneficiaries, see Florence, *Statistical Journal*, 1947, Part I, pp. 1–26. Many nominees and brokers hold for a great number of small beneficiaries and (if we knew which) should be omitted from the list of large holders. The American shares are taken at stock market values, December 1937, the English at nominal value. This difference does not seem greatly to affect the *distribution* of shareholding. See Parkinson, op. cit., Chapter 7, where both methods of valuation were tried.

TABLE VD

PERCENTAGE OF SHARES HELD BY REPRESENTATIVE LARGEST HOLDERS IN 82
LARGEST BRITISH AND 126 LARGEST AMERICAN INDUSTRIAL COMPANIES

Largest share-holdings	Percentage of common stock held in American corporations 1937–9			Percentage of voting stock held in British companies 1936		
	Lower quartile (1)	Median (2)	Upper quartile (3)	Lower quartile (4)	Median (5)	Upper quartile (6)
1st	2·7	6·0	16·0	3·6	10·3	23·6
2nd	1·4	2·56	5·3	1·7	3·0	7·7
3rd	1·1	1·84	3·5	1·2	1·85	5·0
4th	0·92	1·56	2·33	0·9	1·3	3·0
5th	0·80	1·27	1·90	0·6	1·1	2·1
10th	0·50	0·71	0·92	0·3	0·6	0·8
15th	0·39	0·50	0·65	0·2	0·3	0·5
20th	0·33	0·41	0·54	0·2	0·27	0·4
Approx. sum of *all* 20 largest share-holdings		22·7*			25·0*	

* Including estimate of 6th to 9th, 11th to 14th and 16th to 19th largest shares.

i.e. only to a third.[1] It is like a race in which the runner coming in first is far ahead of his rivals, the second, though a 'bad second', also pretty far ahead of the rest, but as the rest come in they more and more tend to 'bunch'. The quicker, and richer in shares, the fewer; the slower, and less rich in shares, the more the 'bodies'.

Toward the end of the list of twenty largest holdings, say from the tenth onward, the average (median) percentage held of all shares becomes remarkably similar comparing one large company with another, as the range between the quartiles shows, in spite of the differences in their size and circumstances. The narrower range of the 10th, 15th or 20th holdings as between the different companies is shown

---

[1] In the large American corporations the taper of holdings among the twenty largest shareholders is not so steep partly because of the different method of looking for them. In my analysis of English shareholding I ranked shareholders by the total of votes they possessed whether their shares were ordinary or common, or were preferred with free (not contingent) voting rights. This I still consider the correct practice to discover aggregate voting power. The T.N.E.C., however, separated common stocks from preference and gives the proportion of common stock issues held even though some issues had no votes and the proportion of preference stock held even though in most of these issues the voting is contingent, e.g. on the preference dividend not being paid.

by the distance between the quartiles.[1] In sporting terms, one can fairly safely prophesy (and bet on) the proportionate size of the 10th, 15th and 20th holding, but not so easily prophesy the size of the 1st or 5th.

The practical import of this more or less stereotyped pattern of large shareholdings,[2] is to stress the power conferred by ownership of a few large 'blocs' of shares, fewer even than twenty. Taking the average (i.e. median) of large American companies, the largest and second largest shareholders with a total of 8·56 per cent of voting common stock have more votes than the 3rd, 4th, 5th, 10th, 15th and 20th largest shareholders put together, owning between them only 1·84+1·56+ 1·27+0·71+0·50+0·41 of shares, namely 6·29 per cent. In the British companies the disproportion is still greater. The largest shareholder, in the (median) average large company can outvote the 2nd, 3rd, 4th, 5th, 10th, 15th and 20th largest shareholders, by 10·3 to 8·43. Clearly he who holds the largest share, or the two, three, four or five who own the largest shareholdings, can in most large companies be an important power among the twenty largest shareholders.[3]

The quartiles given in Table VD are useful also in indicating the extent to which companies and corporations have a greater or lesser inequality among holdings and vary from the pattern. A quarter of the American corporations, for instance, had a largest holding of less than 2·7 per cent of the total common stock, but another quarter had a largest holding of over 16 per cent of the total. Among this 25 per cent about 7 per cent of the corporations had a single shareholder with over half of the common stock and were thus legally subsidiaries, but the

---

[1] When items are ranked in order of their values, lowest first, the MEDIAN is the value of the midmost item, the lower and upper QUARTILE the value of the item one quarter and three quarters along the ranks. Half the values will fall in the interquartile range between the two quartiles. Constancy or dispersion is measured by half the interquartile range in relation to the median. This coefficient of dispersion is for the 20th share $\frac{\frac{1}{2}(0\cdot2)}{0\cdot28} < \frac{1}{3}$ in the English companies, $\frac{\frac{1}{2}(0\cdot21)}{0\cdot41} = \frac{1}{4}$ in the American corporations; but for the largest share it is $\frac{\frac{1}{2}(20)}{10\cdot3} \doteqdot 1$ in the English companies and $\frac{\frac{1}{2}(13\cdot3)}{6\cdot0} = 1\cdot1$ in the American corporations.

[2] In conformity, possibly, with Zipf's Law. See G. K. Zipf, *Human Behaviour and the Principle of Least Effort*, 1949.

[3] The pioneer work of Berle and Means in assigning the larger American corporations to control through private ownership, through ownership of a majority or a strong minority of the shares or purely through management, was based, in the case of industrial corporations, mainly on the proportion of voting shares held by the largest single or the largest two or three shareholders. The steep taper from the largest to the next largest shareholder justifies to some extent this concentration of attention on the very few largest shareholders, but the conclusion that control purely by management was becoming the predominant type was somewhat coloured by the omission of the next to very largest shareholders among the largest twenty.

remaining 18 per cent of all corporations possibly may have been virtually controlled by one shareholder. This possibility is made more probable by finding that in most of them the largest holder was a trust or corporation, not a person. Even if considerably less than a half the votes are held by the largest one, or two or twenty holders (still a tiny fraction of the ten to twenty thousand shareholders normal to such companies) they can be important within the company as a whole. In judging their influence, it must be taken into account whether they are real or corporative persons.

The importance of the largest shareholders in the affairs of a corporation or a company certainly depends on their type as well as the amount of their holdings. Shareholders generally were, in the previous section, shown not all to be *named* individual persons but also banks, trusts, insurance companies, other industrial or commercial companies and nominees. The same institutional holders are found among the *largest twenty* holdings, and the T.N.E.C. (Monograph 29) published tables averaging the percentage of all shares held by the various kinds of large holders. Among the twenty largest shareholders individual persons held, in America in 1937, the most shares (10·67 per cent of the common stock in manufacturing, 5·25 per cent in 'other' corporations), with 'banks, brokers, beneficiaries not disclosed' second (5·0 per cent in manufacturing, 3·3 per cent in other). Corporations parent and subsidiary (1·31 per cent in manufacturing, 5·25 per cent in other) and other non-financial corporations (2·75 per cent and 0·81 per cent respectively) appear next most important as holders of the twenty largest shares in large corporations. Their importance appears less than might have been supposed with all the talk about holding companies, but it must be recalled that in America there are legal restrictions on holding companies and that subsidiaries of corporations already on the list were omitted (as in England) from the 200 largest corporations.[1] In English companies, named persons also appeared the most frequent type among the twenty largest shareholders, over half, in fact; followed next in frequency by banker's nominees (about a sixth) and by companies and trusts (each about a twelfth of the largest 20 holders).

Since making these British-American comparisons for 1936–9 I undertook a comparison of structure in 1936 and 1951 for all the 98 'very large' English industrial and commercial companies and also the 11 very large brewery companies. 'Very large' comprised all companies with over £3m. nominal capital in 1951. The object of the exercise was

---

[1] The proportions held by the twenty largest shareholders of various types among the common stock of American public utility corporations was quite a different story—4·98 per cent was held by other corporations and *30·97 per cent held by parent* and subsidiary corporations. Among the 'other' (mostly commercial) corporations it is the telephone industry that accounts for the bulk of holdings by corporations.

not only to find the seat of government but to trace the trend over time. As the companies were split up according to the nature of the industry and some smaller companies were sampled, it was possible also to correlate their structure and policy with their size and type of work.

The statistical picture of the distributions of holdings of various kinds in the larger companies and corporations is now complete enough to allow some knowledgeable speculation on the extent of 'leadership by ownership'. Proceeding thus from the known to the unknown there is certainly evidence for believing that the managerial revolution has not proceeded as universally as is sometimes thought (or stated without thought) and that leadership and the ultimate decision on top policy may remain in many companies or corporations with the larger capitalist shareholders.

Since there may be a conflict of interest between the shareholders owning the capital and the management, it is important to ascertain in which companies the one or the other tends to decide policy. The economists' model of a profitmaximizing entrepreneur carried over to the modern corporation assumes continued shareholder control. The case for the existence of such a type of quasi-entrepreneur government in companies or corporations rests on five shareholding points of fact. The first two points have already been set forth in detail, the others will be discussed shortly.

(1) The highly unequal distribution and concentration of shareholding as a whole so that, on average in large companies, twenty shareholders out of some ten to twenty thousand hold, in America and Britain, nearly a third of voting shares.

(2) The highly unequal distribution *among these twenty* largest shareholdings and particularly the size, on average, of the largest holding.

(3) The family and other connections that can often be traced between many of the twenty largest shareholders, making them a coherent group.

(4) The nature of the largest shareholders which in many companies are themselves companies.

(5) The fact that many of the large shareholders are often directors; or if these shareholders are companies, that the directors of these shareholding companies are often directors of the company whose shares are held.

Bearing in mind these five points I analysed more in detail the 98 largest English companies in 1951 than the 85 largest in 1936, of which 82 had normal voting. Measurable tests were capital gearing (the proportion of debentures to ordinary shares),[1] and vote gearing (the

---

[1] The text has the English wording; the American would be their capital 'leverage, that is, the proportion of bonds to common stock'.

proportion of non-voting to voting shares) as well as concentration of voting shares in a few hands, and the directors' shareholding. The conclusion was that for 27 of the 98 companies, control was probably concentrated among the larger shareholders. Since ownership of the capital was in these companies important for control, I published the name of each of their 20 largest shareholders.[1]

The analysis of control in large companies has recently been continued in America by Larner and Chevalier. Larner has looked back at Means' analysis of the 200 largest non-financial corporations in 1929 and contrasted a similar analysis of the 200 largest in 1963. He used the same tests as Means for classifying into types of control except for lowering the ownership requirement for the 'controlling group' of shareholders from 20 per cent to 10 per cent of the shares. In spite of this modification in favour of shareholders' control, Larner considered[2] that instead of the $32\frac{1}{2}$ per cent of large companies classified as management-controlled in 1929, 80 per cent could be so described in 1963. Fourteen per cent of companies were probably controlled by a minority of shareholders, 4 per cent by a majority and 2 per cent by two or more minority interests. A most significant finding was that control by management spread consistently from larger to smaller companies. Subdividing the 200 largest companies into five groups of 40 each, according to their size, both in 1929 and 1963, control by management has spread consistently from larger to smaller. In 1929 the number out of 40 so ruled were (largest companies first) 27, 21, $15\frac{1}{2}$, $15\frac{1}{2}$, $9\frac{1}{2}$; in 1963 the companies management-ruled were, in all sub-divisions, as high as between 33 and 37.

Chevalier[3] goes even further in modifying the shareholding requirements for control. He quotes the T.N.E.C. study as concluding that a shareholder of less than 10 per cent can assume a controlling position if the remaining shares are widely dispersed, and he considered 5 per cent of stock held by a control group 'represented by the board of directors' sufficient. By this criterion and by consulting the financial press he arrives at a much lower estimate of the speed of the managerial revolution than Larner. He assigns 51 per cent of the 200 largest companies to management control and 40 per cent to control by a minority of shareholders. This difference between Chevalier's assignment and Larner's is mainly due to the significance Chevalier attaches

[1] *Ownership, Control and Success of Large Companies*, pp. 222–65. This publication is possible in Britain which has an official register of shareholders open to the public, but secrecy still seems to surround the ownership of the industrial corporation in the United States, in spite of the importance of that institution, socially and economically.

[2] 'Ownership and Control in the 200 largest Non-financial Corporations 1929 and 1963', *American Economic Review*, September 1966.

[3] *La Structure financière de l'industrie Américaine*, Paris (Cujas) 1970.

to families and commercial banks in the control group and to pension and other trust funds even if they only hold 5 per cent of shares. Even if it holds less than 5 per cent a family may exert a dominant influence through holding chairmanship and interlocking directorship. He considers that a control group may well divest itself of all shares unnecessary for its control if a higher return can be got elsewhere on investment. However, it should be noticed that even Chevalier's 51 per cent of companies under management control in 1965–6, though low compared to Larner's estimate, is larger than Berle and Means' estimate in 1938. The change may not be a managerial revolution and would be more suitably named a managerial evolution.

Though quasi-entrepreneur situations still exist, the trend seems on balance, certainly, to be toward a managerial evolution increasing with the years and developing faster the larger the company. My 1951 analysis was coupled (see pp. 227–8) to the analysis in 1936 of the same largest English companies i.e. 'very large' companies with (in 1951) over £3m. nominal capital. Comparison was possible for 93 of the 98 companies and led to four main conclusions.

(A) Between the two years companies where large holdings of the capital fell outnumbered considerably companies where they rose. Between 1936 and 1951 the percentage of the total of shares held by the largest single holder rose in 29 out of the 93, fell in 59 and stayed the same in the remaining companies; the percentage held by the 20 largest shareholders rose in 20 but fell in 70 companies. This net fall in concentration of capital holdings and in the controlling power of the largest owners applied to all types of holders, personal, nominee or company.

(B) The trend toward divorce of control from ownership was evident, too, in comparing the average for the two years. In 1936 the average proportion of the total votes held by the 20 largest shareholders was 30 per cent; by 1951 it was 19 per cent. The (median) average held by the single largest shareholder fell from 10·3 per cent to 6·3 per cent. The proportion of voting shares held by the directors in the very large companies fell from 2·8 per cent to 1·5 per cent, and among the very large companies the average number of directors among the 20 largest shareholders fell from 2·0 in 1936 to 1·4 in 1951. At the other end of the scale the average per company of directors holding no more than minimum share qualification rose from 2·3 to 2·7.[1]

(C) The size of the company also affects the extent of divorce of control from ownership. The larger the companies the more they exhibit divorce. Besides the 'very large' companies of over £3m. nominal capital, a sample was analysed in 1951 of medium large and smaller large companies respectively with £1–3m. and with a quarter to £1m. nominal capital. The smaller the company the more the proportion of

[1] Op. cit., pp. 102–4.

capital that was found to be held by the board of directors. It was 2·1 per cent for the medium and 2·9 per cent for the smaller large companies as against the 1·5 per cent for the very large. The proportion of directors among the 20 largest shareholders was 21 per cent for the medium and 30 per cent for the smaller as against 16 per cent for the very large companies. The proportion of companies with at least some directors holding more than the minimum qualifying share was 47 per cent for both smaller and medium as against 27 per cent for the very large.

(D) The nature of the work affects the form of government and policy. Engineering companies had distinctly larger boards and more directors interlocking with other non-financial companies, and showed signs of a wider prevalence of divorce between ownership and control in a low proportion of shares held by directors, and few directors among the 20 largest shareholders. The vote-concentration also was particularly low in the very large and medium-large engineering companies though not in the smaller large companies i.e. those with less than £1m. nominal capital. Engineering companies (particularly the larger) practised a high ploughback of profit.

The 11 very large brewery companies, also analysed in 1951, averaged higher capital and vote gearing (or 'leverage'), high vote-concentration and small boards and little interlocking of directors, higher share-owning by directors and other signs of more 'marriage' of ownership and control. In contrast to engineering, brewing companies, particularly the very large, are relatively liberal in dividend distribution.

This contrast may probably be explained ergologically by certain facts of the market and technical situation. The engineering group pre-eminently:

(a) makes producers' not consumers' goods and renders services to other industries;

(b) requires scientifically trained directors even though they hold few shares;

(c) is a growing industry requiring reinvestment of capital.

On the other hand, brewing pre-eminently:

(a) is a consumer industry;

(b) has marketable assets suitable for use as security, especially public houses and their sites;

(c) is fairly stationary, in the sense of both not growing and not being subject to much fluctuation.

Some writers, notably Parkinson in England, have written as though control of a full majority of shares were necessary to secure leadership. His discovery in the thirty British companies he analysed in 1942 that 90·9 per cent of holdings were very small and contained only 29·4 per cent of the capital, that 0·2 per cent of holdings were very large and contained 30·6 per cent of the capital and that 8·9 per cent were in the middle and contained 40 per cent, leads him to speak of the middle-sized shares as 'the pivotal holding' in the largest British companies.[1] He is thinking, as he admits, of the Parliamentary or Congressional parallel where leadership with this distribution of votes would certainly rest on the middle-sized group holding the balance of power. But the real power situation in a company or corporation, as previous sections have expounded it, is surely quite different. The bulk of the shareholders, middle-sized as well as small, are of such a quantity and quality that they cannot and do not form a coherent party. Most of them do not vote and, if and when they do, their votes are as likely to go one way as another—to be scattered indifferently.[2] In this situation the 'resolute' person or a small coherent 'resolute' group of persons determined on a certain policy or certain key appointments such as that of directors can win even with a concentration of a minority of voting shares as low as, say, 10 per cent. This is the situation presented by the five summary points of fact just enumerated. Points one and two stress the considerable concentration of voting power on a few persons, the remaining persons being many; point three stresses the frequent coherence of the few; points four and five the likelihood, since directors or industrial organizations are involved, of a conscious determination in policy (or in appointments to top posts) being connected with the concentration in ownership of shares.

The probabilities resulting from assuming such a situation of a resolute minority and an indifferent majority have been subjected to mathematical analysis by Penrose.[3]

In a committee of three people one member will obtain the decision of his choice—that is to say, he will be on the winning side in 75 per cent of the votings, if the other two members vote in a random manner. In a committee of five, the chance that one member will obtain the decision he wishes will be 11/16. . . .

If a committee or electorate consists of two sections, a 'resolute' bloc and an 'indifferent' random voting group, a small 'resolute' group of people, who always vote together can exercise a surprisingly powerful control over the whole committee. Thus, three resolute votes can control a committee of twenty-three to the same extent that one vote can control a committee of three. Furthermore, a bloc of twenty-three could control, again to the same extent, an electorate of over 1,000. . . . These blocs have about a 75 per cent chance of carrying the decision in their respective electorates, but, by increasing the size of the resolute bloc, any specified degree of control can be obtained.

---

[1] *Ownership of Industry*, 1951, p. 96.

[2] If there is any bias it will, thanks to the officially sent proxy forms, be in favour of the official policy or nominations.

[3] 'Elementary Statistics of Majority Voting', *Statistical Journal*, 1946, Part I, pp. 53–4.

Blocs three times as great as those mentioned would carry the decisions they desired in nearly 96 per cent of the situations encountered.

Thus in a company or corporation with a 1,000 voting shares (and only on the margin of 'large') a resolute bloc with 20×3 votes or $6 \cdot 0$ per cent could, with this 96 per cent probability, carry the decisions they desired.

The important statistical fact which emerges from this discussion is the very high degree of control exercised by a comparatively small resolute group when the indifferent population is very numerous. The same degrees of control are obtained in two populations by blocs proportional in sizes to the square roots of the respective population numbers.

It is obvious that the successful control of voting by a small minority depends on the indifference of the remainder of the electorate.

It is admitted in law that one company holding more than 50 per cent of the voting shares of another company controls that company as a subsidiary. Given the actual share-structure and shareholder attitude of the typical company or corporation, it now appears that one or a few coherent holdings amounting to 40 per cent or 30 per cent or even 20 per cent or 10 per cent of total voting shares might give the owners virtual control and form a virtual holding company. But who precisely are those possibly controlling holders and how do they cohere? As far as allowed by nominee and other holdings where the true beneficiary is not identifiable[1] analysis of the large British companies and American corporations brings out several types of interests dominating by virtue of ownership of shares. The more clear-cut of these dominating types are (1) the single personal holder, (2) the family group, and (3) another or other companies.

(1) The single person controlling by virtue of his preponderant holding is the old entrepreneur under a new guise—an owner-manager taking risks, entirely or mostly with his own money. There are only a few examples either in American or British large companies of this, the prevailing type of industrial government a hundred years ago. In America the T.N.E.C. Monograph 29 tells us (p. 928) that Henry Ford held in 1938 $55 \cdot 21$ per cent of the voting common stock of the Ford Motor Company and in both America and England such entrepreneur control can occasionally be traced indirectly through trusts, or personal holding companies, holding a majority or near majority of shares—trusts in which in turn one person holds a majority of votes.

(2) Family control through large shareholdings is more frequent than personal control. Three out of the 20 English companies analysed in the published pilot enquiry[2] had among their 20 largest shareholdings

---

[1] See *Statistical Journal*, 1947, Part I, pp. 1–27.
[2] Op cit., p. 7.

11·6 per cent, 21·4 per cent and 42·6 per cent of all voting shares (and some directorships) in the hands of the members of one or two families. Tate & Lyle Ltd, for instance, the company with the 42·6 per cent, had in 1935 six Tates among the 20 largest shareholders, holding between them 27·4 per cent of all voting shares and six directorships, and had three Lyles holding between them 15·2 per cent of all voting shares and two directorships. Subsequent analysis found many more such apparently family-controlled companies, particularly in breweries.

In America the T.N.E.C. Monograph draws special attention to the high proportion of the holdings of three families in several companies. Members of the Du Pont family held in 1937 directly or indirectly through trusts, holding companies or foundations, 11·51 per cent of equity securities in the U.S. Rubber Co., and 38·48 per cent in E. I. Du Pont de Nemours. Similarly, directly or indirectly the Rockefeller family held 11·36 per cent of the voting stocks of Standard Oil of Indiana, 12·32 per cent in Standard Oil of California, 13·51 per cent in Standard Oil of New Jersey, and 19·52 per cent in the Ohio Oil Co. Members of the Mellon family held, similarly, 10·13 per cent of the equity securities in Pullman, 29·68 per cent of the Aluminum Co., 37·52 per cent of the Pittsburgh Coal Co., and 42·28 per cent of Koppers United. Other American families can be found with a high proportion of common stock in a single large company. There were eight Firestones appearing by name among the 20 largest shareholders of the Firestone Tyre and Rubber Co. and either directly or through trustees or holding companies they owned between them a third of the common voting stock.[1] An almost equally high concentration of shares in one family was found in S. S. Kresge Co. Ltd, S. H. Kress and Co. and the Cudahy Packing Coporation.

(3) Company law in Britain and, with some exceptions, in America, allows one company to hold the shares of another and this permission has been freely seized and built upon. Where company Y holds more than 50 per cent of the voting shares of company Z it is known as a holding company, and textbooks describe the theoretical possibilities of building up or 'pyramiding' control by piling holding company on holding company. Company Y is presented as formed to hold (just over) 50 per cent of the voting shares of company Z, and company X to hold (just over) 50 per cent of the voting shares of company Y, and company W to hold (just over) 50 per cent of the voting shares of X. A relatively poor but able enterpriser holding, on his own, 50 per cent of voting shares in the super-holding company W will thus control twice his own shares in W itself, four times his own shares in holding company X, eight times his own shares in subsidiary company Y and sixteen times

[1] T.N.E.C., Monograph 29, pp. 117–31.

his own shares in sub-subsidiary company Z.[1] This effect, it is pointed out, will be still greater if sub-subsidiary, subsidiary, holding, and super-holding companies all have non-voting preference shares and bonds or debentures, as is usually the custom.

It is not so often pointed out, however, that our able enterpriser and (with himself as centre) his concentric holding and super-holding companies may attain virtual control on less than 50 per cent holdings of voting shares, resulting in a still more economical and concentrative pyramiding of control. These logical possibilities are realized in practice though not usually exploited to extremes. Both in Britain and America the majority of the large companies are in fact holding as well as operating companies; quite a number are merely holding companies; and sometimes a large company is a subsidiary—occasionally a subsidiary of a smaller company. Comparatively few large companies are neither holding nor subsidiary. Many cases of chains or hierarchies with super-holding companies, or trusts (where a single person holds the predominant share) can also be found notably in British newspaper publishing and drapery and other stores, and in American public utilities; and even, in both countries, some circular holding, when company A holds shares in B, B holds shares in A.

Control by a holding company is found straddling over a number of companies, sometimes as a means of integrating their transactions; more often it is focused on a single very large company and can be seen as a further extension of the trend toward large-scale operation with a concentrated government. Production has been shown to be concentrated and increasingly concentrated in large plants, measured by volume of product, several of these large plants concentrated in the ownership of (larger) firms and these firms co-ordinated in large associations, combines or mergers. Within these combines and mergers, joint stock company in form, further concentration puts government in the hands of one or a few shareholders. These key holdings need not be so very large, thanks to the cumulative effect of (i) 'high gearing' of capital structure so that the ordinary shares are a small proportion of total (ordinary preference and debenture) capital; (ii) differentiation of voting power even among the ordinary shares; (iii) the possibility of companies holding shares in other companies. Further, 51 per cent of the votes is not in fact necessary to obtain control, and the virtual controlling ownership of shares might be concentrated upon 30 per cent, 20 per cent or even 10 per cent of the voting shares.

Thus, on top of large physical plant and larger legally recognized firms come still larger areas of *de facto* control by a few individual

---

[1] This pyramiding is not in fact used as much as text books would suggest, owing mainly to the nuisance of having to consider the minority shareholders.

interests owning comparatively little capital. The joint stock firm or corporation and the combination movement between firms, sets the stage whereon the concentration of power has almost unlimited possibilities. How far the possibilities are exploited is still a matter for research and theoretical speculation. Besides the entrepreneur, family and holding company control through ownership of shares, a further type of control appears to be exercised not by one 'holding' company but by several companies holding large blocs of shares and often having representatives on the board of directors. In one of the British companies of my 1936 survey, the Amalgamated Metal Corporation, seven of the 13 largest shareholders were companies and owned between them 26·9 per cent of the voting power, four of them having one of their own directors on the board. In another British company similarly surveyed,[1] Imperial Smelting Corporation, eight companies appeared among the twelve largest shareholders and owned between them 20 per cent of the voting power, five of them had one to three of their (own) directors on the board. Some half-dozen examples of such companies apparently subsidiary to several companies were found in the 1936 list of the 85 largest British industrial companies. Other examples were two pre-nationalization railway companies holding large blocs of capital in omnibus companies operating in their region. This arrangement for several 'fingers in the pie' may be a useful device to co-ordinate companies whose technical activities were interdependent—or a device for any one participating company to exercise a veto on the subsidiary or the co-holding company.

A final test of a controlling group within a company or corporation is how far members of the small group of large shareholders are also directors. No tendency appears for the 20 largest shareholders to have more directors among them in the large English companies where they held a higher proportion of shares; though about a quarter of the large companies had both a higher-than-average proportion held by the 20 largest holders and also some directors among the 20. Such a director-cum-bloc-holder group where shareholding concentration is reinforced by directorships may fairly definitely assign the company concerned to government by ownership. Among the large American corporations there is many a famous case of directorships reinforcing ownership, often minority ownerships. Gordon gives as a 'case-study' the Du Pont ownership and (direct or indirect) directorships in General Motors and U.S. Rubber; he considers (op. cit., p. 167) that 'the clearest cases of active leadership by a minority interest occur in those corporations in which one or more senior executives are themselves important members of the minority group'. In a number of British companies, directors are among the 20 largest shareholders or represent them,

---

[1] Florence, *Statistical Journal*, 1947, Part I, pp. 1–16.

without those 20 having a particularly large 'bloc' of holdings. Here we are at the negative end of the scale of concentration, where the 20 largest shareholders own relatively little, and where there appears to be no dominating 'interest'.

Outstanding examples of little concentration of shareholding, in England, 1951, were Liebigs with no single shareholding of over 0·5 per cent; Harrods Stores, Courtauld and United Molasses with none over 0·7 per cent. In 1936 10 and in 1951 21 of the largest 94 and 98 industrial and commercial companies had not a single share holder with 2 per cent or more of the voting. In America, 1937–9, American Telephone and Telegraph and Swift and Co. had no shareholding over 0·63 per cent and 0·98 per cent of the stock. In 24 of the common stock issues of the large manufacturing and other American corporations no single shareholder held more than 2 per cent; and as Table Vc shows, in 31 per cent of the issues the 20 largest shareholders held less than 20 per cent of the stock.

Further tests of whether marriage continues happily or whether ownership is divorced from management, can be found by comparing the shareholders and directors of one company and others. If shareholders hold shares only in one company and directors hold directorships only in one company it is a sign that their interests are concentrated there, and that they are more likely to devote their thought and energies to the management or at least to the control of the management of that company. In point of fact the shares are usually widely scattered and the larger the company the wider the scatter. Later it will be demonstrated (Table VE) that the directors of the larger company hold more directorships than the directors in smaller companies.

This situation seems at first sight contrary to logic, since it might be expected that the direction of larger companies would involve greater responsibility, time and energy, and thus be less frequently multiplied, than the direction of smaller companies.

Part of the explanation of this paradox fits in with our assumption that plural directorships are a sign of divorce of control from ownership. The control of larger companies is more divorced from ownership and their directors are not tied down to directing only where they own substantial capital, but can pay attention, promiscuously, to one company after another.[1]

A man who holds several directorships in companies can obviously not own the capital of all of them, or even the minimum to give some control, unless they are very small or he is fabulously rich. Moreover, in a company privately owned the owner-manager is likely to be chary of admitting persons on the Board who have outside interests.[2]

The small and medium investors who practise multiple shareholding do so to spread risks and clearly not to obtain control over

[1] Florence, op. cit., pp. 6, 8.
[2] Op. cit., p. 14.

management. But what about the large shareholdings that have been found in individual companies? Have their owners spread risks and do they hold equally large holdings in other reputable companies? In some cases, notably the very large British insurance companies such as the Prudential, and American brokerage houses, we do find the same names reappearing among the 20 largest shareholdings of the large companies. But names of large individual, personal, shareholders and non-financial company shareholders do not thus reappear. As far as our evidence goes both in Britain and America (though more evidence is needed) most of the large shareholders have large holdings only in one large company and thus concentrate rather than spread their risks. Why? The answer that suggests itself is for control either of their own interests or the interests of a family or some other group and thus for a continued marriage of large bloc ownership and government.

Between the two extremes of marriage of ownership and management, and their divorce through a scattering of share-ownership, there is, among large companies at least, a continuous gradation. There are, to extend the analogy, degrees of union certain and uncertain, and the attempt of the T.N.E.C. to assign all their 200 corporations either to some family or corporate interest group or to no dominant interest group, according as that family or other group owns a proportion of shares even below 10 per cent, is probably too definite. It is more judicious to admit a marginal twilight area, say below 10 per cent ownership, where the interest group may or may not be truly joined to management. Accordingly, I have redesigned the T.N.E.C. method[1] of tabulation in Table VE to bring together and total the more certain assignments and to leave less certain, marginal assignments, literally in the margin. Eleven corporations are marginal because of small ownership by an interest group, 7 not in cols. (1) to (3) in doubt of *any* such group—a total 18 out of the 126 American manufacturing and other corporations, leaving 108 fairly certain.[2] A surprising number of these fairly certain assignments go in America to a dominant family group, in the first three columns, 31 to a single, 24 to two or more families, accounting for 25 per cent and 19 per cent of all the large manufacturing and other corporations.

The marginal twilight zone should perhaps be extended further. As Gordon says,[3] the T.N.E.C. monograph employed very 'mechanical' criteria for their assignment. 'It is certain that, in many companies, which the authors classed as under ownership control, the minority

---

[1] T.N.E.C., Monograph 29, p. 14.

[2] Even so, where two or more families or two or more corporate interests have between them a fair proportion of shares it is not certain that they will work together and further evidence is required such as intermarriage, joint holdings, joint trusts, etc.

[3] *Business Leadership in the Large Corporation*, 1945, p. 166.

TABLE VE

ASSIGNMENT OF 126 LARGEST AMERICAN INDUSTRIAL CORPORATIONS TO
DOMINANT, NO DOMINANT INTEREST GROUP, OR MARGINAL CASES, 1939

Intensity of dominance	Majority ownership (1)	Pre-dominant minority (30–50%) (2)	Sub-stantial minority (10–30%) (3)	Small minority ownership (marginal) (4)	Total (5)
DOMINANT INTEREST GROUP					
Single family	7	12	12	6	37
Two or more families	4	6	14	5	29
Family and corporate	0	1	5	0	6
Single corporate	5	3	1	0	9
Two or more corporate	0	1	2	0	3
MARGINAL CASES				7 ⎫	
NO DOMINANT INTEREST				⎬ 42	
(Executive control)				35 ⎭	
Total	16	23	34	11	126

group did not exercise control in the sense that it made or actively influenced broad policies. It may or may not *have had the power* to do so' (Gordon's italics). He instances the Standard Oil companies in which the Rockefeller family and Rockefeller-endowed institutions had owned in recent years 10 to 20 per cent of the voting stock. 'There is no indication that in recent years the Rockefeller interests have interfered directly in operating or financial policies'. . . though 'in 1929 John D. Rockefeller, Jr., interposed to oust the head of Standard Oil company of Indiana' (pp. 181–2). Like a supposedly extinct volcano, the large bloc-holder may sporadically erupt.

The effectiveness of family control is likely to depend not only on the proportion of shares owned but by whom they are owned and how ownership was acquired. If the large bloc of shares were bought, control was probably intended, if the shares were inherited by a great number of scions less control is likely unless a family trust or personal holding company is formed. In that case it depends who runs the trust. It is safest to declare many companies marginal in their assignment, including those where the twenty largest holders, though holding over 20 per cent of voting shares are, many of them, not immediately identifiable, e.g. nominees or trusts. Briefly put, the assignment of corporations and companies was as follows in the two countries:

	American, 1937–9	British, 1936
Dominant ownership interest	73 (58%)	48 (58%)
Marginal cases	18 (15%)	27 (33%)
No dominant ownership of interest	34 (27%)	7 (9%)
	125	82

Judging from the comparatively low proportion of companies with no discernible dominance of ownership interest, proclamation of any

TABLE Vf

ASSIGNMENT OF 82 LARGEST BRITISH INDUSTRIAL COMPANIES TO DOMINANT, NO DOMINANT INTEREST GROUP, OR MARGINAL CASES*

Intensity of dominance →	Twenty largest shareholders with 20% of votes or more				Ditto with less than 20%		Total
	One shareholder with 50%+ (1)	One shareholder with 20–50% next with less than 10% (2)	Less concentrated dominance (3)	Some large holders not identified (marginal) (4)	(5)		(6)
DOMINANT INTEREST							
Personal and family connections	4	6	13	—	—		23
Company or financial institution	9	6	10	—	—		25
MARGINAL CASES							
Twenty largest hldrs with over 20%				16		}	27
with 10–19·9% of votes					11		
NO DOMINANT INTEREST							
Ditto with less than 10% of votes (Executive control?)						7	7
Total	13	12	23	16	11	7	82
		48		27			

* In 1936. Iron and steel companies omitted.

complete managerial revolution should perhaps, then, have been postponed! Assignment of British companies is given in Table Vf. The method used allows comparison with the American assignments of Table Ve as far as grouping by Dominant or No dominant interest, and the type of dominant interest. In England dominant families seem relatively less frequent, but dominant quasi-holding companies more frequent; and on the whole there appears to be more dominance by shareholding interests than in America. But the columns indicating intensity of dominance (the more intense the fewer the holders and the higher their percentage of shares) are labelled differently in the English assignment for the sake of greater statistical objectivity and of closer 'keying in' with previous tables, especially Vc. The test is retained whether the total voting power of the 20 largest holders is above or below 20 per cent of all votes, and 7 and 11 companies listed in Table Vc with the largest twenty shareholders holding 0–9·9 per cent and 10–19·9 per cent reappear in Table Vf. Companies where 20 hold 20 per cent or above are subdivided according to the relative voting power of the largest share. The first column where the largest share has 50 per cent or more of the votes is roughly equivalent to the first column of the American table (Ve) for single family or single corporations; seemingly 50 per cent company domination, i.e. a legal holding company was more frequent in England.[1] This possibly is a compensation for the larger absolute asset size of single American corporations. When large assets or capitals are to be brought under unified control British companies buy dominating shares in companies, American companies deterred perhaps by anti-trust laws merge or buy up the assets (not the shares) of other companies.

Forty-one or 33 per cent of the large American corporations and 11+7 or 23 per cent of the large British companies had probably (marginally), or fairly certainly, no dominant interest group, as far as shareholding analysis could show. But this does not mean that the resources of statistical research into the real seat of government are exhausted. It means only that the search must turn from the distribution of shareholding to the directors and executives of these companies and corporations.

§ 4. GOVERNMENT BY DIRECTOR OR EXECUTIVE

If companies are not really governed by their nominal controllers, the body of shareholders as a whole, and many are not closely enough held to be governed by a few very large shareholders, where does the real seat of government lie? Who else decides high policy, makes top appointments and organizes and co-ordinates generally? The remaining possibilities within the structure of a company are the board of directors jointly, or some leading individual members or member of the board, or the executive jointly, or some member or members of the executive. There are also possibilities of control from outside the company structure.

---

[1] The same rule was applied in England as in America that to avoid double counting subsidiaries of companies or corporations already on the list were excluded from that list. In five English companies the holding company was foreign, in three cases, American (Woolworths, Fords and Oceanic Steam Navigation), and in two, Scotch (Dewar-Buchanan and Cannon Brewery).

The size of boards varies on the whole with the size of the company. In the largest American industrial corporation Gordon found[1] in three cases out of four that the board numbered between 9 and 16. In the largest British industrial and commercial company with over three million pounds capital the boards are smaller, the bulk numbering 6 to 12 members with an average of 9. From a sample of the smaller British companies as detailed below (p. 244), still fewer directors appeared as the average.

The legal position of the board, already described (p. 209) is roughly similar in both countries. The board of directors is supposed to act as a link between the management and the shareholders (who entrust their powers to the board) and to exercise a general though intermittent supervision. The board of directors unlike the management is not in continuous session and does not deal with day-to-day problems; as its title implies it orders continuation or change in the 'direction' of the ship of business from time to time. A director is legally supposed to act with some degree of skill (though no more than to be expected of his knowledge and experience) honestly and diligently with reasonable care (though no more than an ordinary man might be expected to take in the circumstances on his own behalf). The chief actual functions of directors may be summed up, for both countries, as selecting the executive officers, policy making, checking up on results and asking discerning questions. These functions are equivalent to those of top government, but to judge from the legal requirement the board of directors need not pursue these functions with the intensity to be expected of real leaders.

Considerable thought and systematic observation have been devoted in America to this question, how far directors as a whole really lead. For large companies Gordon's answer is distinctly in the negative.

The board's approval function is more important than its initiating activities. But even with respect to approval, many boards in large companies are almost completely passive. . . . For the majority of the corporations studied, the available evidence strongly suggests that ratification of management proposals by the board is largely a formality.[2]

In the smaller American corporations the boards seem to have little more influence,[3] and it is probable that the American designation of

[1] Gordon, *Business Leadership in the Large Corporation*, p. 117.

[2] Op. cit., p. 131.

[3] Mace in his *Board of Directors in Small Corporations* concludes (p. 87) 'that the typical small corporation board of directors was largely a vestigial legal organ which included merely subservient and docile appointees of the owner-manager'. Here though no figures of assets are given, the small corporation seems to refer exclusively to organizations so small that the manager can own the shares. The board of directors may well be more powerful in the corporations of a size between those entrepreneur-ruled firms and the largest corporations here studied in detail.

the top manager as the president (a practice almost unknown in Britain) denotes real power. The president is *ipso facto* a director, like the British managing director, and often he is chairman of the board as well or, if there is a separate chairman, more dominant than the chairman. He, or possibly vice-presidents and other full-time officers of the company who are also directors are likely to be the leaders, where no very large shareholders appear. Leadership may be exercised jointly in harmony or through compromise by these executives—a fact often formally recognized in the executive committee that is often set up. American boards differ widely in the proportion of full-time officers they include. Gordon reviewing 84 large industrial corporations found 17 with a quarter or less of the board composed of officers, 37 with a quarter to a half, 20 with a half to three-quarters and 10 where full-time officers composed three-quarters or more of the board. Clearly if the board of directors is merely, or largely, a meeting of officers, it may be only a co-ordinating organ for policies already decided upon by the president or other executives.

The part in government of one or a few persons is more likely to be one of positive initiation rather than the mere power and influence or ultimate control of a formal board and we may certainly speak here of 'leaders'.[1] If they are top executive officers their initiative takes effect directly; if non-executive directors, indirectly and often informally, as in a *'pro-bouleutic'* chat or caucus over the table at lunch with the top executive. To reach the springs of industrial policy it is important to look in any company for the type of persons who may have this kind of dominant initiative, and to distinguish them from types who fairly certainly will not. The likely situation is parallel to that found among shareholders. Some, but certainly not all shareholders, may be dominant in a company; similarly some but not all directors may affect policy and organization. Only a few shareholders and not necessarily all directors actually affect the policy of a firm. On the other hand, some non-directors among managers and technicians may be doing so.

In the course of deciding upon a general policy of a large and complex organization (including the state government) several stages can be distinguished in the procedure. In my *Statistical Method in Economics and Political Science*[2] I identified (1) investigation, (2) initiation and drafting, (3) debate, (4) final decision and possibly later (5) revision. In the first two of these stages persons on the 'rungs' of the hierarchy just below the top are likely to participate and some individuals (particularly the technical experts) possibly even to dominate. But the final debating and decision in the industrial company is normally reserved for the board of directors.

[1] See Gordon, 1945, op. cit., pp. 135, 188.
[2] Pp. 416, 418.

In the past academic views on the structure and activities of the board of directors have been ill-informed, partly due to insufficient empirical enquiry and partly due to concentration of attention on the boards of large banking, insurance and the now defunct railway companies, many of them swollen with 'big name', guinea-pig, directors. In fact, even in very large manufacturing and commercial companies with, in 1951, over £3m. nominal capital the board of directors was found to number on average only nine.[1] In the medium large companies with nominal capital between £1m. and £3m. the average was seven and in smaller large companies with capital between a quarter and one million the average was five. Probably in most large companies a majority of directors are full-time executives and certainly not layman in business, whatever the opinions to the contrary. R. H. Tawney wrote:[2]

As to nine-tenths of the problems confronting an industry, nine-tenths of existing directors are themselves laymen. If they are sensible, they act on expert advice, and such advice can be weighed by a trade union official with not less intelligence than by the titled pluralists who inspire—so it is alleged—confidence in shareholders, and amusement or consternation in everyone else.

And even Alfred Marshall, writing in 1920, seemed to regard the directors' function as mainly watching the work of the higher officials of a company.

The situation may have been different in Marshall's time but today few directors are content with weighing or watching. Their work is what their name implies—'directing'. The *Concise Oxford Dictionary* gives senses of this word as 'control, govern the movements of; order person to do a thing to be done'.

Within the board the relations differ somewhat in Britain and America particularly regarding the powers of the top individual.

In keeping each with their own form of national government—presidential or cabinet—American companies appear more one-man led (i.e. monarchical), British more committee- or cabinet-led. In fact in describing the top governor of British companies I have been tempted to use the term 'prime-manager'.[3] American company directors have, however, somewhat more independence than the U.S. president's cabinet ministers appointed by himself, and I have extended the use of the expression 'prime-manager', as the nearest political analogue to the position of top manager in the larger companies of either country. Where a large supply of capital must be drawn from the inexpert or

---

[1] *Ownership, Control and Success of Large Companies*, Sweet and Maxwell, 1961, p. 84.
[2] *Equality*, Allen & Unwin, 1929, p. 267.
[3] Florence, *Economics and Sociology of Industry, 1969*, pp. 142–5.

'sucker' public, a director may be appointed solely for his drawing power. Reputation for honour and honesty is for this purpose more important than actual efficiency, and in Britain the mere possession of a title or 'handle to one's name' may apparently take the place of experience or even of competence to watch the interest of the investing 'sucker'. According to another authority,[1] there were, in 1932, 654 English peers not distinguished before their elevation to the peerage as captains of industry or as active members of city firms, or in other ways known as *executive* members of industrial undertakings. These 654 peers held between them 562 directorates, giving a ratio of 1 directorate to every 1·16 peers. A 'spot' sample of 463 British companies of all sizes in 1936[2] disclosed 172 directorships held by a title, forming over 8 per cent of all directorships. Titled directors were particularly frequent in the largest companies; among the sample companies in 1936 with over £500,000 capital they numbered almost 15 per cent of all directors; indeed 48 per cent of all these large companies had some titled director on its board, and in the iron, coal and steel section all the sample companies of this size had this distinction. At a rough estimate almost half the titled directors inherited their title or acquired it by prowess in the fighting services or sport and not in business and can be considered as probably guinea-pigs. Titles are particularly thick on the boards of British insurance companies where presumably the insured as well as the investing public wants to be assured of honourable, if not noble, treatment. One well-known insurance company had in 1937 among sixteen directors, three knights, one baron, one marquis, one earl and two dukes. But titles are less frequent on the boards of manufacturing companies, which are relatively small.

Age as well as title seems to inspire confidence in the investing public. At any rate, the age-structure of British directors given by Miller and Campbell[3] showed the remarkable proportion of 57 per cent over sixty (the age when civil servants retire) and 42 per cent over sixty-five, the age when university professors retired. Adverse comment was recognized by the English Company Law Amendment Act of 1948 which made seventy the normal retiring age for directors.

In America titles are not available as a test of respectability and honour but 'big names' are, and though more difficult to test, this quality in directors as well as their age (presuming experience and survival by fitness) appears to be recognized as useful for drawing and holding capital.

Individual directors who are not full-time officers are likely to make

[1] Samuel, *Shareholders' Money*, p. 114.
[2] By Siviter and Baldamus at the University of Birmingham. See *Statistical Journal*, 1947, p. 12. Data from Stock Exchange Year Book.
[3] *Financial Democracy*, 1933, p. 98.

their views felt and really to direct only, in fact, if they have strong personality, wide experience and recognized skill and knowledge as professional men, or if they are interlocking directors. In a survey of 500 corporations, large and small, the National Industrial Conference Board listed the frequency of reasons given (in answer to a questionnaire) for appointing 1,868 individual directors of American manufacturing companies.[1] These reasons fall naturally into groups and the groups may be ranked in order of their percentage of frequency.

1st	Knowledge of technical details of business		527	
	Executive officer		30	33·9%
	Retired or former official of company		78	
2nd	Important stockholder		170	
	Represents important stockholdings		238	24·4%
	Represents banks or financial interest		49	
3rd	Sound executive judgment		350	18·7%
4th	Specialized counsel and knowledge	Financial	99	
		Marketing	45	
		Legal	116	18·0%
		External business	57	
		Labour relations	8	
		Foreign markets	11	
5th	Represents	customers or brings business	29	3·0%
		allied manufacturing or commercial interests	27	
	Other reasons		34	2·0%
	Total		1,868	100·0%

Knowledge of details of the business itself, the most frequent type of reason, is, as Gordon suggests, probably synonymous with executive officer; shareholding and financial interests is next in importance; then sound executive judgment; then specialized counsel by some expert or professional man; and finally representatives to bring business. This reason is likely, according to Gordon, to have been soft-pedalled by the companies answering the question and may be more important then the figures indicate.

Whether or not a director has 'sound executive judgment' is hardly subject to outside objective test, but the other groups of reasons for appointing non-executive directors given in answer to the questionnaire are to some extent verifiable. The importance of shareholding and financial interests of directors in the company itself will be checked first; then: (2) the representation by non-executive directors of financial interests outside the company, then (3) the possession of specialized knowledge justifying advice being sought, then (4) connections with other business, and finally (5) a reputation for judgment and general business experience or both.

[1] Gordon, op. cit., p. 127.

(1) Companies have already been described where directors have between them large holdings of the shares and where the classical entrepreneur or family business owner-manager is simply reclothed in corporate garments. But at the other end of the scale, and this is the more frequent case, there are corporations and companies where directors hold practically no shares at all.

The first conclusion to be reached is, in fact, that there is a wide diversity among corporations and companies justifying the distinction, built upon later (Chapter VII, § 4) between the capital-owning entrepreneur type of leadership and the purely executive or management leadership. The second conclusion is that direct proof of entrepreneur leadership based on *the shareholdings of officers and directors* can be established only for a small minority of the large companies or corporations. The hypothesis of extensive control by ownership must be proved mainly from the concentration of shareholding (whether holders were directors or not) already discussed. These two conclusions are so important that the evidence must be given in some detail.

Gordon[1] has graded large American industrial corporations according to the percentages of stock owned by the total of their officers and directors.

DISTRIBUTION OF 115 LARGE INDUSTRIAL CORPORATIONS BY PERCENTAGE OF VOTING STOCK OWNED BY ALL OFFICERS AND DIRECTORS, 1939

	0–1% (1)	*1–5%* (2)	*5–10%* (3)	*Over 10%* (4)	*Median percentage of shares owned* (5)
All officers	66	29	7	13	0·81%
Non-officer directors	44	36	16	19	2·33%
Total officers and directors	23	42	17	33	3·49%

The total of officers and directors are seen to have owned, between them, *less than* 5 per cent of voting stock in the majority of corporations, namely (23+42 =) 65 out of the 115; and the officers alone (but including officer directors) own *less than* 1 per cent in a similar majority of 66.

When individual directors and officers are considered separately the diversity in ownership of shares in the corporations they serve was still more striking. This ownership was more unequally distributed among directors and officers than among the shareholders of the average large company. Executive officers who are not directors have generally a

---

[1] Op. cit., p. 27.

smaller share in shares than directors—in fact on the average of the large corporations only about one-thirteenth as much.[1]

In British companies analysis has been possible only of the shares of directors, whether these directors were also full-time executives or not. It was found, similarly to America, that in most companies the board only held a small fraction of the total voting shares. In the 'median large company' (the average of industrial companies with, in 1936, £3m. nominal capital or over) the board as a whole held, in 1937, £62,139 or 1¼ per cent of the issued capital of slightly over £5m. The directors averaged nine, so the average director held about £7,000 or ⅐th per cent of nominal value of shares. But the 'average' director is by no means typical and the individual directors' holdings varied widely between companies. At one end of the range, two-fifths of the largest companies had at least three directors holding only the minimum qualification (as low, on average, as £1,000) and *just under half the companies had no director among the largest twenty shareholders*. On the other hand, in a quarter of the companies every director held more than the minimum share qualification, and in two-fifths at least two directors were among their 20 largest shareholders—which may indicate an approximation to owner-manager leadership or 'entrepreneurship by commismission'. Midway between these opposite cases is that where only one director has a large holding and may in consequence possess an individual influence, not necessarily identical with that of the management or the boards as a whole. Of the 80 largest British industrial companies, analysed in 1935,[2] there were eleven with one director, but no other, among the 20 largest shareholders, and in these companies this director's position might well be one of real power and leadership.

The picture of leadership by director in Britain is thus variegated. The situation in the larger companies hardly supports D. H. Robertson's generalization that 'the directors are probably not merely paid officials but themselves substantial shareholders'[3] any more than it wholly supports the thesis of a managerial revolution.

---

[1] Judging from the 200 largest non-financial (which include the 115 industrial) corporations, just over one-quarter (26·5 per cent) of the 3,511 positions as officers and directors have each less than 0·01 per cent of all shares, 70·2 per cent have each less than 0·1 per cent (at the other extreme five 'positions' have each more than half the shares). 699 officers who were *not* directors held 780,053 shares or only 1,100 apiece; but 987 officer-directors held each 14,000 apiece and 1,825 non-officer directors 12,000 apiece. T.N.E.C., Monograph 29, p. 63 (illustrated by Lorenz curve) and p. 359.

[2] By H. M. Davis at the University of Birmingham. See *Sociological Review*, XXXI, p. 19.

[3] *Control of Industry*, 1923, Chapter VI, § 2. If merely minimum share qualification for directors are taken, the 'spot' sample (see p. 245) of industrial and commercial companies of *all* sizes showed in 1936 that for 97 per cent of companies, the board as a whole need not hold more than 5 per cent of the capital, and for 62 per cent of companies not more than 1 per cent.

(2) More definite in consequences is the *representation of banks or financial interests*, though little study has been made of this in Britain. In America, hunting out possible money trusts, Wall Street influence and so on, has been the constant care of Congressional committees, and the power of financial interests in industry is well documented.

Gordon gives five or six types of opportunity for a financial house or investment bank to obtain a permanent or semi-permanent part in the government of an industrial corporation. This part does not mean full control but perhaps a veto-power or negative control generally, with positive initiative on financial policy. The opportunities arise when owners of a closely held corporation wish to transfer their shareholdings to a wider public (often corresponding in Britain to the transition from a private to a public company); when an industrial corporation wishes to expand beyond its own means of financing expansion; when corporations merge and a new consolidated company is 'promoted'; when corporations face financial difficulties and have to reorganize; and when, due to the death or retirement of a strong executive, boards of directors seek advice as to the succession or other matters from banks. On these occasions industrial companies may have to deal exclusively with investment banks such as J. P. Morgan or Kuhn Loeb, and a more or less permanent liaison may mean control, by the financial interest, at least of financial policy. When promoting a consolidation or merger, for instance, financial interests are likely to enter into a considerable amount of decision-making. They may determine the conditions for bringing the companies together and for issuing new securities, and they may also choose (or participate in choosing) the directors and chief executive who are to head the new company. Out of the merger is likely to evolve a relationship between the company and bankers which gives the latter a continuing voice in financial affairs and the right to head future underwriting and selling syndicates for the company's securities.

Apart from these occasions of transition, expansion, promotion, reorganization, and the succession, financial houses may just buy a controlling interest through shares in holding and super-holding companies—devices already explained. The policy pursued by directors representing finance, and especially the promoter, may (as outlined later, pp. 350–1) be quite distinct from that of other types of director and as a copious literature attests[1] may run quite counter to the interests of shareholders or of the nation as a whole. The power of the financier and promoter in large American corporations seems, on the whole, however, to be decreasing in the face of the growing power of the executive shortly to be described. Since 1933 fewer opportunities

---

[1] E.g. Lowenthal, *The Investor Pays*, 1933; Ripley, *Main Street and Wall Street*, 1929; Allen, *Lords of Creation*, 1935.

have been presented for financial houses to establish direct participation in the government of corporations, but financiers have perhaps acquired rather more participation indirectly by representing family and other trusts with large shareholdings.[1]

(3) Appointment to a directorship for specialized knowledge may occasionally lead a man to transcend his original function of giving counsel and advice and to have a dominant initiative in the government of the business. Specialized knowledge useful to business which the normal businessman cannot supply, includes knowledge of the law, of accountancy, of technology and sometimes of economics. The sample of 463 British companies of all sizes[2] in 1936 traced among directors at least 127 accountants, 58 lawyers, and 88 men with some technical qualifications. The proportion of the accountants and technicians among the directors, though not the lawyers, increased with the size of the company. For companies with capital below £100,000 technical men numbered 2·6 per cent, accountants 3·2 per cent of all directors, roughly 11 and 14 per hundred companies. For companies with capital between £100,000 and £500,000 technical men numbered 4·7 per cent, accountants 5·0 per cent of all directors, roughly 23 and 25 per hundred companies. While for large companies with capital above £500,000 technical men numbered 4·2 per cent, accountants 7·6 per cent of all directors, roughly 29 and 53 per hundred companies.

(4) The most obvious objective test of a director having connections in other businesses (allied or not) is whether he is also a director of other companies—a multiple or pluralist director. The practice of multiple directorships is as prevalent in Britain as America. The British *Directory of Directors* lists men with as many as 60 directorships to their name, and the sample of 463 British companies of all sizes[3] showed that in 1936 58 per cent of all directors were directors of more than one company and that the larger the company the greater the proportion of these pluralist directors. In the largest class of companies with over half a million pounds capital, 75 per cent of directors held more than one directorship. This tendency for the larger the company the more directorships per director was found by Taussig and Joslyn to be true also of America.[4] Table VG sets the findings in the two countries side by side. In both, the percentage of directors with over ten directorships is seen to be larger for the larger companies and the percentage with one to five directorships to be smaller for the large companies. In these large companies the percentages are remarkably similar for both countries. In the very largest companies 70, 17, 13 in Britain

---

[1] Gordon, op. cit., p. 214.
[2] See footnote 2 above, p. 245.
[3] Ibid.
[4] *American Business Leaders*, 1932, appendix D.

respectively held five or less, six to ten, and over ten directorships; the corresponding percentages were 72·5, 17·5 and 10 in America. For the

TABLE VG

MULTIPLE DIRECTORSHIPS IN AMERICAN AND BRITISH COMPANIES OF VARIOUS SIZES

No. of companies in which directorships held*	Percentage of directors with stated number of directorships at each grade of company size							
	American sample† 1932					British sample‡ 1936		
	E (smallest) (1)	D (2)	C (3)	B (4)	A (largest) (5)	Small (6)	Medium (7)	Large (8)
One to five	95·3	94·6	92·6	85·8	72·5	88	86	70
Six to ten	3·9	5·0	6·7	10·8	17·5	8	11	17
Over ten	0·8	0·4	0·7	3·4	10·0	4	3	13
All directors (actual no.)	100·0	100·0	100·0	100·0	100·0	100 (634)	100 (910)	100 (623)

* The American data is classified as less than five, 5 to 9, 10 or over, *in addition to* the company in which directorship or office held.

† Sizes in terms of millions of dollars of gross income: size E less than half, D half up to one, C one up to five, B five up to fifty, A fifty and over.

‡ Company size in terms of a hundred thousand pounds of capital (Ordinary and Preference Shares issued): small less than one, medium one to five, large over five.

next largest companies, the percentages were in Britain 86, 11, 3, in America 85·8, 10·8 and 3·4.

(5) A director may be asked to join the board of several companies because of a reputation for shrewdness and 'sound executive judgment' or because of the very fact of his general experience of business, or both. He is then an adviser to leaders rather than a leader. This case is more often found in Britain than America; indeed proposals for the transatlantic transplanting of the British practice of 'professional directors' grafted with a new element of responsibility for advice has aroused considerable interest in America.[1]

'Allied manufacturing or commercial interests' is a reason for multiple directorships more easy to verify. The multiple director who is so frequent (and so multiple) in the larger British and American companies is often called an interlocking director and his function appears largely to lock together various interests, to form a community of interests, or, as the National Industrial Conference Board questionnaire puts it he 'represents customers or brings business', or 'represents allied manufacturing or commercial interest'. In this capacity the plural

[1] Hurff, *Social Aspects of Enterprise in the Large Corporation*, 1950, p. 108.

director may be dominant in the government of a company, particularly the smaller associated company of an interlocked group; or he may be just a connecting link with outlook similar to the dominant leaders. The various interests he leads or conducts can be grouped on the usual logical and technical lines as vertically, laterally and diagonally related. British brewery companies for instance interlock directors with the companies owning hotels where their product is consumed—a vertical relation; or companies making electrical equipment interlock directors with electrical power companies whom their product serves—a diagonal relation. Further interesting and logical interlocking is found in the directorships of banks and the insurance companies[1] who have the funds to lend the banks, and in the directorships of shipping and marine insurance. In Britain (but not in America where it has been declared illegal under the Clayton Act) there is also considerable interlocking among directors of companies making the same product—a direct sign of absence of competition between them.

Interlocking directors often merely reinforce other arrangements for combination or association; a holding company will, for instance, appoint one or more of its directors to subsidiaries. Interlocking directors may, on the other hand, be the main tie between several companies dominating between them a large integrated area. After intensive research into interlocking directors in the metal industries of the British midlands, Beesley[2] found that in 1948 more than one third of the workers in these industries were employed within one group of companies thus interlocked, giving the large firms in the group great power over the development of competing processes and products.

American, though not British, authorities appear to be agreed that where shareholding is not concentrated in a family, or otherwise connected group, the real government of most large companies or corporations will lie not with directors, together or severally, but with what Americans call the 'executive'. The difference in the American and British view and the words that are used may well be due to differences in the existing facts of the two countries, rather than in the author's ideology. The differences are that American corporations have a president (and large corporations usually several vice-presidents) where British companies only know a managing director, or even only a general manager not on the board. This, it is suggested, is not just a difference in names. The British chairman of the board is more powerful *vis-à-vis* the general manager even if as managing director he sits on the board, than most American chairmen of the board

---

[1] In America the largest life insurance companies interlocked with 780 corporations, including 145 banks and a hundred other insurance companies. See Lynch, *The Concentration of Economic Power*, 1946. p. 287.

[2] Ph.D. thesis, 1951, University of Birmingham.

vis-à-vis the president. British authors do not have to use the word 'executive' because manager includes all the full-time top British executive officers that exist; but to include presidents another, wider, word must be found in America, and 'executive' serves. Undoubtedly president and vice-president are not merely empty, vainglorious titles. They mark a more monarchical, less aristocratic, form of constitution in America—and unlimited monarchy at that—than in Britain. Committee government marked by the supremacy of the cabinet in her political government distinguishes the actual working of British institutions, and in her larger business organizations the committee called the board of directors has probably more power than in large American businesses, when compared with the power of manager or executives. Britain may be said to have cabinet government in business as well as politics; and we may well call the top manager the prime manager.

It is perhaps, only a matter of degree, and in both countries the real leadership of many large businesses will be found among executives and managers, particularly presidents and director-managers who do not interlock in their directorships too widely. In many, probably most, large American companies there is a powerful committee in the shape of a small group of top full-time executives meeting frequently, usually known as the executive or finance committee,[1] which may act much like the executive committees of the board found in large British companies. The behaviour and policies of such leading executives or director-managers either singly or in small committees will not be uniform, however, and will depend largely on their upbringing, training and experience as will be argued in Chapter VII. Four sub-types will there be distinguished: the executive who has worked his way up the business itself, or has transferred from another business, the executive with technical training, and the trained administrator.

§ 5. INTERESTS, PERSONALITIES AND COMPANY POLICIES

The discussion of the preceding sections as to who possesses actual sovereignty in the capitalist company or corporation is far from being just academic. Within each company or corporation there are different interests, those of the ordinary shareholders, of the preference shareholders, of the bond or debenture holders, possibly of financiers and investment bankers; not to speak of the interests of the managers and directors collectively and individually. These interests may often conflict. Some may strive for a maximum profit either by a high margin per unit of output or by a high turnover, others for a lower profit if only it is steady and secure. When it comes to distributing the profit some

[1] Gordon, op. cit., p. 138.

interests will prefer a stable dividend from year to year; some will prefer a high dividend when possible, others a high re-investment; some will look to the present, others to future appreciation. Or policy may be determined not so much by interests as by a personal bent in a top-manager—a bent, say, toward experiment and heavy investment in gadgets, or a bent for building not machines but empires. A strong personality with initiative and persuasive powers in discussion can often obtain a decision. Here it is important to reiterate the several stages that occur in coming to a decision: initiation, discussion, in or off the board (including getting the advice of consulting experts, canvassing, caucus meetings); and formulating the final resolution (including a possible veto[1]). At any of these stages one personality or interest may predominate, but that predominance may not finally prevail. It is often 'touch and go', and a fine balance of forces. Within many boards of directors, for instance, there is a fairly regular alignment into opposing parties. If these are nearly equal in voting power a personality will count, though in the long run he will probably have to secure backing from some large shareholders.

Enough has been said to demonstrate that there is no single answer to the question of who rules the modern corporation or company. Unfortunately, writers have hitherto taken up one side or the other without any wide evidence or indeed any evidence from accurate tests as to who is in control. Economists now either honourably confess the need for enlightenment[2] or start by leaving the question open as to who is top policy maker, though most of them subsequently assume the more or less extinct owner-manager-technician entrepreneur, paid by profit, to be the man.[3] This assumption was attacked over thirty years ago as a mere 'certified article of economic doctrine', by Thorstein Veblen who considered the economists' 'captains of industry' fell under the changing circumstances 'to second rank, became lieutenants who presently more and more lost standing as being irresponsible, fanciful project-makers'. To G. D. H. Cole, too,[4] 'it looks as if the investor, who provides the money, is destined to become all-important, and the man of enterprise, no longer able to exercise a purely personal control, to be reduced to the status of manservant to the corporate body of investors'. Burnham, however, thinking like Marx in terms of historical sequences, considered we are now at the stage where the managers will be the

[1] See above, p. 176. The parallel stages in the process of state legislating are political agitation, introducing and reading a bill, committee stage, and final passage as an Act.

[2] E.g. Cairncross, *Introduction to Economics*, 1944, p. 89.

[3] E.g. Benham, *Economics*, 1938, contrast pp. 8, 165, 166, 179. See below, Chapter VII, § 3.

[4] *Absentee Ownership*, 1924, pp. 107–9; *Studies in Capital and Investment*, 1935, p. 57.

next ruling class.[1] The truth seems to be that for the last fifty years both in America and Britain some companies have been manager-led, others large-investor-led and in yet others there is a compromise. Indeed the continuing strength of capitalism may lie in this very variety and balance of power allowing the fittest for the given circumstances to dominate.

The policy that emerges may be the result of one interest or one personality predominating or may be a compromise between interests, between personalities or between interests and personalities. But whatever or whoever lies behind a policy, both in Britain and America, enquiry into the facts of balance sheets and profit allocations finds in the same industry and at the same time a measurably wide 'variance' between the policies of apparently similarly situated companies. Bliss[2] for instance, averaging the years 1913–21 for each corporation, found the ratio of total dividend distributed to total profit ranged for 18 American machine-making corporations from 2·2 per cent to 101·0 per cent and for 11 American automobile makers, averaging the years 1916–31, from 17·4 per cent to 850·0 per cent.[3] The policy of ploughing back profit into the business may be decided upon for several different reasons, many of which, also, can be measured. It may be for a physical re-investment in fixed capital or in inventories (or stocks), or it may be to build up a liquid reserve to ensure stable payment of dividends through bad times, or to strengthen the credit position generally. If the undistributed profit is not physically reinvested the familiar financial ratio of current assets to liabilities will tend to rise—and here again a wide variance has been found in firms apparently similarly situated in the same industry at the same time. In 14 American shoe firms, for instance, Paton[4] found current assets varying during the same years from just over twice to over ten times their liabilities, and in 17 cotton firms varying from just over one to over ten.

Preference for liquidity and intensity of investment are also policies where measurable evidence of differences can be found in the balance sheets, the profit and loss and the profit appropriation accounts of different companies. In the same industry and the same period companies show the widest variation in the proportion of assets in fixed plant, in stock (or 'inventory'), and in liquid marketable investment or cash; and in the rates of depreciation charged. Hillman found in the same British industry 'concerns working with labour intensive methods

---

[1] *The Managerial Revolution*, 1942, p. 69. For criticism of both Veblen's and Burnham's predictions see my *Economics and Sociology of Industry*, 1969, pp. 33–4.
[2] See Buehler, *The Undistributed Profits Tax*, 1937, p. 68.
[3] One corporation apparently paid out in dividend eight times its profit for the year.
[4] W. A. Paton, *Corporate Profits as Shown by Audit Reports*, 1935, p. 95.

of production (smaller ratio of fixed assets) and some concerns working with capital intensive methods of production (high ratio of fixed assets)'.[1] If, as for many American corporations, the total output and sales turnover is disclosed, differences in policy could be measured more satisfactorily in the 'operating ratios' such as sales or output total to fixed assets. These measures have been used more or less successfully, as tests of general efficiency, or of the phase of the trade cycle. Success has perhaps been less, rather than more,[2] but the problem here at issue is not the comparative efficiency of firms or the technological requirements of whole industries[3] and the necessities of coping with the cycle, but is the problem of the different free and deliberate policies of companies, similarly situated, adopted by different types of personality and interest.

More sensational evidence of differences in company policies arising from the dominance of a particular interest comes to light if the law of the land is broken. This occurs most often when a dominant financial interest has interests in other companies as well and may, by its policy, sacrifice one company for another; or may 'get out from under' altogether by selling its shares the moment some short-run policy has manipulated a rise in share-values—letting the devil take the hindmost of the other interests.

Has the policy of a risk-*taking* government of an industrial company divorced from the risk-*bearing* ordinary shareholders, in fact become more risky? The evidence of the long-run trend in bankruptcies would say no. Most economists think that, on the contrary, there is a danger of stagnation, of too much prudence and caution. A financial interest may take risks at the expense of the other shareholders in order to make a big profit by buying and selling of shares; but where an executive or big shareholders, who are not financiers, have top rule there is no motive for taking undue risks.[4] If, as seems the case, the financier-led (and often financier left and abandoned) companies are now not frequent either in Britain or America and the large shareholders stay with the company and do not spread their risks in other companies; then it is they who are the risk-bearers. In fact the golden rule of capitalism, enunciated earlier (§ 1), if limited to the large shareholders is often not so far beside the mark. In those companies where the larger shareholders concentrate their shares and rule, it then remains true that they both take

---

[1] *Depreciation Policy*. Manchester School. 1938, No. 1.

[2] For instance a high operating ratio of sales to value of fixed property widely advocated as a test of efficiency and economy of resources, might also be due to an unprogressive policy of low mechanization and investment, or to a 'sound' but too drastic policy of depreciating values.

[3] Dealt with in Chapter I, § 2.

[4] Unless salaries are made dependent on profit. See below, p. 338.

and bear the risks. The small and medium shareholder spreading his risks does, however, neither.

Conclusions need not stop short at the general statement that because the government of capitalist companies is of various sorts, autocratic, plutocratic, aristocratic, bureaucratic, technocratic, different policies follow. It can probably be established that particular sizes of company as well as particular industries are correlated with particular types of government and policy. The evidence seems to support Lord Keynes,[1] for instance, when he writes of very large companies:

A point arrives in the growth of a big institution—particularly a big railway or big public utility enterprise, but also a big bank or big insurance company—at which the owners of the capital, i.e. the shareholders, are almost entirely dissociated from the management, with the result that the direct personal interest of the latter in the making of great profit becomes quite secondary. When this stage is reached, the general stability and reputation of the institution are more considered by the management than the maximum of profit for the shareholders. The shareholders must be satisfied by conventionally adequate dividends; but once this is secured, the direct interest of the management often consists in avoiding criticism from the public and from the customers of the concern.

Statistical enquiry into the allocation of profit of large industrial English companies (mostly manager-, not shareholder-controlled) in 1948–51 supports Keynes' view. Allocation between dividends to shareholders and plough-back could follow three principles (a) some fixed proportion between them, (b) some fixed rate of dividend on shares or (c) a fixed rate of reinvestment on assets. The actual policy was found to be a compromise between principles (a) and (b). Analysis showed that not the assets but the shareholders had priority and that assets were the residuary legatee. The nearest fit to the facts appeared to be for companies to distribute to shareholders just over 1 per cent of assets, whatever their profits; and for companies making higher profits to allow their shareholders in addition only about a fifth share of the profits. This policy resulted in a certain stability of dividend, but violently fluctuating plough-back. Allocation to reserves and consequent investment thus seems to depend almost wholly on the opportunity offered by the amount of the profit of the preceding period.[2]

Again, there seems some evidence that particular industries like the publication of newspapers have companies where through super-holding and subsidiary companies power is concentrated in one or a few large shareholders. On the other hand, companies in the brewing and food industries, at least in Britain, are frequently family governed.

[1] *The End of Laissez Faire*, 1926, p. 42.
[2] Florence, *Ownership, Control and Success of Large Companies*, p. 187. See also 'Factors in Dividend Policy', *Statistical Journal*, Vol. 122, pp. 77–98.

The policies of the large industrial companies or corporations, especially if they are in a monopolistic position, may be of vital importance to the national economy. If Keynes' theories are accepted, a company bent on 'sound finance' setting aside vast sums to liquid reserves would be far from helping full employment; or another company bent on ploughing back profits into its own industry might end by over-producing certain products in relation to the demand for others —might, in short, be misdirecting national resources. As Hurff remarks the money market 'stands as a well-established instrument for the capital requirements of expansion' and may be a better guide to national investment needs than the executive of a corporation.[1]

The executive members of the board, the inside directors, will ordinarily conceive, develop, and formulate expansion projects. In the course of such gestation, a complex of personal motives and personal identification inevitably becomes interwoven with the project. This must cloud and subordinate an objective 'profits' basis of judgment. The cravings for distinction and business prestige are wrapped up with growth, since the internal incentives and rewards of the organization are increased with size. These also include the motive to enlarge the rewards and satisfactions available to subordinates which may spring purely from devotion to their interests or be mingled with the enjoyment of power to bestow benefits. Aside from increased intangible rewards, growth in size may lead to larger compensation both for general executives and subordinates. Few of us indeed can discriminate among our brain children as well as an outsider.

But the divergence of large-company from national policy must not be taken for granted. The super-companies ruled by financiers or interlocking directors unfair, as they often are, to the shareholders of a particular company may often indeed be of national benefit in redirecting resources from one of their companies to another and in selecting what industries to finance. In short, the financier and multiple director may occasionally have that enlightened self-interest and even be the instrument of the invisible hand, classically sanctified.

---

[1] *The Social Aspects of Enterprise in the Large Corporations*, 1950, p. 90.

CHAPTER VI

NATIONALIZATION, CO-OPERATION AND STATE CONTROL

§ 1. WHY ALTERNATIVES TO THE CAPITALIST GOVERNMENT OF INDUSTRY?

CAPITALIST production was, even in its nineteenth-century heyday, criticized on certain counts by a long line of philosophers, idealists and even political economists, by no means Socialist— Carlyle, for instance, and Ruskin, Mill[1] and Henry Sidgwick.[2] These ideological counts against capitalism can be summed up as its commercialism in supplying only wants for which the individual consumer could pay—his demands—rather than his wants not backed financially, and his (and the nation's) needs. The rich man's fancies and luxuries were found supplied prior to the poor man's barest wants. Even if wealth were equally distributed, with no rich or poor, popular *wants*, such as alcohol or gaming or tasty foods obtained might get priority over less unpopular *needs* such as education or plain but healthy fare. Cakes and ale may be preferred to butter and bread.

For this sort of ideology even the most capitalist of societies has supplemented capitalist industry by other systems for supplying goods and services. In America, for instance, and to a less extent in Britain,[3] the provision of education is almost entirely removed from capitalist control. The reason for this exemption from commercial principles and for running schools and universities at a loss is that education is considered a need, a 'must', which should be supplied to all children and adolescents, whether their parents are prepared to pay or not. Similar reasoning in Britain and America removes from capitalist control quasi-educational institutions like museums, art-galleries, public libraries, and also recreation parks and provisions for public health and safety. Until recently hospitals were governed and financed by public authorities perhaps to a greater proportion in America than Britain.[4] But the main British hospitals, supported until then by charity, were, in 1949, taken into the National Health Scheme.

---

[1] *Principles of Political Economy*, 1849, V, xi, §§ 8–16.

[2] *Principles of Political Economy*, 1887, pp. 401–13.

[3] A larger proportion of British than American schools charge fees to cover costs, including the so-called public schools and the preparatory schools preparing for them.

[4] In his *American Notes*, Chapter III, Dickens pays tribute to that welfare state, Massachusetts.

For other activities meeting people's needs rather than demands, the state may finance and govern *in conjunction* with capitalists. Housing is the leading case in Britain; most housebuilding is now subsidized and controlled by public authorities though executed by private capitalist builders and rent is charged, but not sufficient fully to cover costs.

Besides the ideological argument from need (what a man needs as against what he wants is largely ethical and a matter of opinion) there is a further and more tangible argument for not charging commercial prices, due to the physical difficulties of collection. Road building and maintenance is here the leading case. Two hundred and even a hundred years ago, Britain and America used the commercial procedure on the turnpike roads and bridges. The state or a company built a road and at suitable intervals erected a turnpike where traffic was halted and made to pay for the stretch covered. For bridges the procedure was still more obvious—no pay, no crossing—and survives in certain British and American vehicular tunnels. But under most modern conditions a traffic hold-up every so often to pay charges would, particularly in busy city streets, bring transport to an end. Commercialism must be abandoned for the sake of commerce.[1]

A further tangible argument against charging prices is the difficulty of individual assessment, a difficulty, which (among other reasons too philosophical to enter upon here) takes defence and police activities, sewerage and lighthouses, out of the capitalist pay-as-you-use field and into the free-out-of-tax domain.

When discussing the reasons for nationalization of industries and services one practical question should therefore be put first. Can the industry or service be made to pay its own way by charging prices? If the answer be No, full capitalist government is out. Capitalist industry works for at least a normal profit and if no profit is anticipated, capitalism unaided by other methods is not interested; at least some part of the cost must come either from private charity raised by inducement or from state taxation—raised coercively.

Though capitalism is thus limited to profitable enterprise, the state is not. The state may grant the whole cost and charge nothing, or grant part of the cost by a subsidy and a nominal price, or expect to break even without profit (with or without interest charge), or charge normal or even, for the sake of relieving taxation, excessive profits.[2] The question

---

[1] Long stretches of motor road built without egress are now bringing back conditions for collecting charges, as on the American turnpikes.

[2] In France and other European countries the state often takes over an industry such as salt production and the making of matches and cigarettes for the very reason that a monopoly profit can accrue to the state for relief of taxation. In Britain the post office has similarly been used as a milch cow. For a fourfold grading from the full trading or pricing to the tax-and-grant system, and for a classification of indus-

precisely what industries or activities are not to pay their way and are to be subsidized to various degrees with their costs wholly or partially granted out of taxation, is a question not mainly of structure or government but of social and political philosophy or administrative convenience. Though further considered (§ 5A), this question will not be answered in detail.

We turn to industries providing goods and services to be fully paid for by charging a price commercially; and ask the question, familiar in the structural approach, *who* shall do this trading in what industries, as well as why and how?

It is in this field of trading where prices are to be charged that controversy rages today in western countries. Considerable sections of industry have been nationalized in Norway, Sweden and France as well as Britain. The British Labour Party once summed up its reasons for allocation of industries to the nationalized or public ownership 'sector' in three principles.[1]

Public ownership is a means of ensuring that monopolies do not exploit the public. Private monopolists have too much power over the happiness and destinies of their fellow men. Where monopoly is inevitable there should be public ownership.

Public ownership is a means for controlling the basic industries and services on which the economic life and welfare of the community depend. Control cannot be safely left in the hands of groups of private owners not answerable to the community.

Public ownership is a way of dealing with industries in which inefficiency persists and where the private owners lack either the will or the capacity to make improvements.

To the first criterion for nationalization, that in certain industries no price can be charged, we may thus add a second and third in assigning industries to a government alternative to capitalism. Two of the three are primary aims, namely, no monopolistic exploitation or limitation of the consumer by producer, and no autocracy over basic services; the remaining, fourth, criterion, no inefficiency, is a question of means not ends.

The monopoly criterion may be viewed as an extension of the criticism of capitalism already advanced that the price charged will more than cover costs, for it asks whether revenue from prices may not considerably exceed costs, thus exploiting and limiting the consumer. The

[1] *Labour and the New Society:* a statement of the policy and principles of British Democratic Socialism, p. 20, 1950.

---

tries and services according to the degree of state subsidy or profit, see Florence, 1929, pp. 371–5 and 458–63.

resultant profit, more than is required to attract the necessary enterprise or risk-bearing capital, may build up a class of excess profit makers or 'profiteers' with too much economic power over the community. The possibility of profiteering arises where the monopolistic or oligopolistic conditions are present that were discussed in Chapter III.

The risk of these conditions occurring came with the large-scale phase of capitalism and did not worry nineteenth-century philosophers or economists; but in the twentieth century it is perfectly orthodox to attack capitalism, as many U.S. congressional committees have done, on the score of exploitation, monopoly profit and concentration of wealth. There is, however, no orthodox remedy. If the consumer or supplier is thought to be exploited, and it is not possible to modify monopolists' practices by the remedy of state regulation, and if the industry is only efficient when run as a monopoly, then, many argue, the state must itself operate the monopoly and will normally do so without excessive profiteering or exploitation of the consumer. State government is thus to be looked for in industries where large-scale operation on the largest possible scale (i.e. monopoly) is most efficient.

Besides commercialism and exploitation there is the third primary count on which capitalism is criticized, particularly if it is large-scale, namely that it is autocratic. Employed in large-scale plants and firms, workers feel little identity with employers[1] and even the legal owners of the share capital of a large firm do not in fact, as already explained, participate in the firm's policy and organization. Democrats who follow Thomas Jefferson and the English liberal tradition and believe that power and responsibility should be diffused, as among competing independent farmers, do not object to small-scale capitalism where power is distributed among a great number of petty bourgeois entrepreneurs. But they may well look for modification or alternatives to the large-scale capitalism of modern industry. One such modification is trade union participation in control of industrial relations. Large-scale capitalism has of late years been associated with widespread trade union organization in America, as in Britain.

Collective bargaining between trade union and managers (or collective association of employers in an industry) has to some extent meant participation or diffused power—a 'pluralism' in industrial government. This policy in which the state government does not in the first instance interfere I have characterized as *laissez collectives faire*.[2] Its decisions— the terms of the bargain—are in most industries, negative, of the 'thou shalt not pay wages lower than . . . or work hours longer than . . .' variety.

---

[1] See below, Chapter VII, § 1.
[2] *Industry and the State*, 1957, pp. 89, 163.

Autocracy is not confined to large-scale capitalism but may occur in any large scale organization, nationalized or even co-operative; trade unions have indeed been formed and been active in these alternative types of government. British and American trade unionism, and workers' action generally, will therefore be discussed in the next chapter (VII § 1) under labour relations in the larger industrial organizations.[1]

To the indictment of large-scale industry as working against the old diffusion of rule among small entrepreneurs and workers employed in small groups, in short, against more diffused government by the people, one may add that capitalism is normally autocratic and against government for the people in putting private above public interests. With basic industries in large-scale capitalist control, the whole national economy may, it is held, be twisted to serve sectional and immediate ends. This attitude is peculiarly evident in the British Iron and Steel Acts both of 1951 and 1967 when the Labour government separated the basic iron and steel processes of iron smelting and steel rolling from the superstructure of engineering and assembly processes and nationalized only the former. It was held that without nationalization certain social costs which do not affect the profits of the capitalist individual or corporation are ignored and that in a basic industry where these costs are widespread the common man, and the future man too, tend to be neglected. There may, for instance, be restriction of output and consequent unemployment in the basic and the superstructural industries and also get-rich-quick exploitation of natural resources.

The primary principles on which large-scale capitalist government of industry has been criticized, commercialism, exploitation and autocracy, have been recently joined (particularly since the much publicized non-capitalist industrialization of Russia) by a further argument. This argument does not raise matters of final 'ends' but is the question of the efficiency *with which ends are carried out*. The efficiency of any action must always be a secondary consideration since its value depends on the action itself; an efficient is presumably *less* desirable than an inefficient burglar. Granted that capitalist industry does supply some needs as well as wants and demands and not always autocratically or at too great a profit or limitation of the consumer, it is contended that some other form of industrial government might have supplied the same needs, wants and demands more effectively or cheaply.

Efficiency or effective performance here includes stability and avoidance of industrial depression; and also progress in production

---

[1] Interfering pressure may indeed be in the opposite direction as Beacham and Cunningham put it (*Economics of Industrial Organization*, 1970, p. 224) 'the largest representing bodies such as the Confederation of British Industries and the Trades Union Congress, have their main *raison d'être* in the collective pressure which they can exert on the government'.

particularly in the application of science and technology. The argument already put forward for the free supply of roads and bridges was essentially of this nature; it was grounded on the inefficiency of holding up traffic and the administrative impossibility of collecting the price of roadmaking from individual consumers.

Systems of industry exist presumably for man and if we are consciously to plan, should be set up for the generality of men, 'for use and not for profit'. The purposes or aims, the why, of industry in terms of the foregoing discussion may, for later application (e.g. pp. 291ff.) be formally set forth and amplified:

(i) Satisfaction of man's needs, wants and spontaneous demands (in that order of priority) rather than his artificially stimulated demands. For short, the slogan runs, 'needs first'.

(ii) Where it is demands that are supplied at a price, fullest satisfaction of consumers at lowest margin of profit. No limitation of consumer's choice nor his exploitation above cost. In short, consumer's sovereignty.

(iii) Maximum spread of participation and satisfaction (present and future) of the people by the people for the people. Co-ordinated use and direction of resources in the interest of the nation as a whole. The criteria, in short, of democracy.

(iv) Efficiency measured in minimum cost per given output. Prices should reflect not only lowest margin of profit (as in (ii))—but lowest margin over lowest possible cost. This business criterion should include stability and progress, a continuous growth of real income per head.

These criteria are not all economic. In his *Wealth and Welfare* (the original edition of *Economics of Welfare*), Pigou argues that *economic* welfare is likely to be 'augmented' if causes are introduced which (1) make for an increase in the aggregate size of the national product, (2) make for an increase in the absolute share of relatively poor groups, (3) diminish the variability through time of the product.[1] The national product is the annual flow of those goods and services that can be brought easily into relation with a money measure—'everything that people buy with money income'; and Pigou's first two sets of causes of economic welfare—increasing, and evenly-distributed product—correspond roughly to my criterion of consumers' sovereignty in the satisfaction of his demands, to the equality test of democracy and to the minimum economic cost and progress components of the efficiency criteria. Pigou's criteria of diminishing variability corresponds to the stability aspect of efficiency. *Economic* welfare does not, however, consider the 'needs-first' criteria nor social costs, nor the 'for and by the people' test of democracy—these fall into what Pigou calls general

---

[1] Op. cit., p. 16.

or total welfare, of which economic welfare is but a 'part of a part'.[1]

Similarly J. A. Hobson pointed out that economics is only a specialized science showing[2]

that certain acts of individual or national policy make for an increase of marketable wealth. To convert this 'is' into a 'must', and to urge this discovery as a sufficient ground for individual or national conduct, without taking into due account other effects upon public welfare which may or must arise from this commercially profitable policy, is evidently unjustifiable. For when a person or a nation is considering what line of conduct to pursue, . . . he must take for his criterion of conduct the wider standard of wealth which identifies it with welfare. The advice which the mere economist may offer to the statesman must therefore always be adjusted or corrected by reference to this larger conception of the public good.

Modern economists often claim too much for their special science and so confuse and blur the useful and fundamental distinction between economic and general welfare made by both the orthodox Pigou and the, in other respects, heretical Hobson. I make no apology for following in their footsteps and speaking their language in looking beyond purely economic criteria.

Criticism should be constructive, and the practical alternatives will now be put forward to capitalist government. One such alternative has already been declared essential in certain cases, namely government of industries unable or unwilling to charge a commercial price by the state, which can finance them through taxation. In default of charity, state government of industry is the only alternative wherever a commercial procedure is not possible or desired. Where the objection is not against covering cost but only against supposedly excess profit or autocracy, further proposed alternatives to capitalism are, in theory, government by consumers or by workers. Workers' government in *industrial* enterprises survives only as an aspiration except in the limited functions of joint consultation in personnel administration and labour relations and in a few scattered producers' association workshops. Workers' control in *agriculture* appears as producers' co-operation and producers' associations of farmers for certain limited purposes, especially buying and selling. But consumers' control for *all* purposes, through co-operative societies on the Rochdale plan, is in Britain a going concern and in many activities, notably retailing, wholesaling and manufacture of consumers' goods, very much so.

Study and comparison of practical alternatives to capitalism are

---

[1] Economic welfare includes only those parts (op. cit., pp. 9–11) 'that enter easily into relation with the measuring rod of money' and of those parts covers only satisfactions of actual desires—whether 'ethically superior' or else like 'gambling, excitement' and 'excessive indulgence in stimulants', 'ethically inferior'.

[2] *The Science of Wealth*, 1911, pp. 15–16.

much simplified by our exclusion of industries and services planned not to pay their way; and are simplified too by the distinction between industrial structure and government. There is little difference in the structure of capitalist or of otherwise governed industry. State- and consumer-governed factories and units of control must answer the question of efficient size, location and integration in much the same way as capitalist-governed factories and firms. The thesis we have persistently maintained is that these questions of structure are determined mainly on technological and not ideological or sociological grounds. But the structure once determined will certainly in its turn help to determine the form of government. Large-scale organization, as will be seen, is more associated with nationalization than small-scale.

By this time it should be evident that there is some logical and ergological ground for a mixed nationalized, co-operative, capitalist economy such as Britain's today.

§ 2. BRITAIN'S MIXED ECONOMY

Industries, used in the widest sense to cover all economic activities, are so different in their technical and structural conditions that the existence of different forms of industrial government need not be surprising. Table VIA lists all the orders of industry recognized in Table IA (distinguishing several types of service) and covers the total occupied population. Roughly characterizing their technical and structural peculiarities by means of standard symbols, the table assigns specific industries or enterprises within each order to different columns according to whether their government was in the recent past, or is, at present,[1] small-capitalist, large-capitalist, consumer-co-operative or nationalized (including municipalized). It can be seen at a glance how mixed the British economy is and precisely which parts are of capitalist complexion, and why.

The answer to the why of industrial government lies largely in the various structural, technical and market characters of different industries. The symbols for these characters are letters so arranged that those occurring earlier in the alphabet refer to characters of demand for the industry's products and services, and letters occurring later in the alphabet refer to characters of supply. M and Q, in the middle of the alphabet, denoting the need and fact of monopoly and need and lack of capital equipment are due to both demand and supply conditions.

Demand conditions:
  B. Basic to the industrial economy, mainly early-stage producers' (capital) goods or services to production.

[1] As of 1970.

C. Common service to the community—goods and services deman-
ded by the bulk of consumers.
E. Education need.
F. Conservation for possible future demand.
G. Other reasons for gratis grant (not E or H).
H. Health need.

Demand and supply conditions:
M. Need, likelihood or fact, of monopoly.
Q. Need (and lack) of large capital equipment.

Supply conditions:
R. Routine management.
S. Large sized plant or firms typical.
X. Need for (scientific) experts.
Y. Integrated with existing co-operative or nationalized activities,
e.g. defence.
Z. Existing (e.g. company) government inefficient or high in cost.

These characteristics might in many cases have been expressed in the
opposite way. Most of them are measurable along a scale of quantities
between two 'qualitative' poles.[1] A high degree of routine management
is roughly equivalent to a low degree of risk and of need for constant
adjustment. Thus risk and routine need not be separately mentioned.
They are the negative and positive poles or qualities of the same
character. Routine is chosen as the characteristic quality since it is
routine that tends positively to condition nationalization, while risk
and the need to adjust to changing circumstances condition it negatively.

Some textbooks take these conditions one by one and purport to list
under each condition the industries illustrating its influence upon their
government. This is an unsatisfactory presentation since the industries
that may be ripe for nationalization are those that have many more
than one characteristic condition and it is the very aggregate and weight
of favouring conditions that push the industry into the nationalization
column. Thus coal is basic to the economy, is in common use and
important to conserve in the future; its production requires costly capital
equipment and though fairly routine, requires experts to locate large
seams—a formidable array of conditions, B.C.F.Q.R.S.X. Railway
transport and the supply of electricity sport about as many letters; and
here even America, in spite of laissez-faire doctrines, has had to introduce (see § 7) measures of state control.

Are the characteristics (given these letters in Table VIA), which seem
to be associated in the actual event with the nationalizing of industries,

[1] For terminology used here see Florence, 1929, Chapter V.

TABLE VIa
THE MIXED ECONOMY OF BRITAIN, 1971

Order of Industry	Relevant Economic and Technical Characteristics*	Government by			
		Small Capitalist (Entrepreneur, Partnership, Private Co.)	Large Capitalist (Joint Stock Co.)*	State (Nationalized, Municipal, etc.)*	Consumers' Co-operatives
EXTRACTION: Agriculture	F.	Farmers		Forestry Commission Overseas Food Corporation (Q) Colonial Development Corporation (Q)	
Mining and Oil Wells	B.C.F.Q.R.S.X.	—	Coal to 1947 (Z)	1947—National Coal Board	
MANUFACTURE: Process		e.g. Sawmills	e.g. Paper, Textiles, Iron and Steel to 1951	Iron and Steel Corpn (B) (Q) (S), 1951–5, 1967–	Co-operative Wholesale Societies, C.W.S. and Scottish C.W.S.
Assembly		e.g. Baking, Printing	e.g. Motors, Engineering	—	Consumers' Final Goods (C) (R) (Y)
Repairs and Servicing		e.g. Shoes, Garages	—	Arsenals (Y), H.M. Stationery Office (Y)	Laundries

268

PUBLIC UTILITIES: Gas	C.M.Q.R.S.Z.	—	Some Joint Stock Cos. 1949 (Z)	Some Municipal to 1948–9 (Z) Area Gas Boards and Council from 1948–9
Electricity	B.C.M.R.Q.S.	—	Some Joint Stock Cos. to 1948	British Electricity Authority and Area Boards from 1948–9
Water	C.M.R.X.	—	Some Joint Stock Cos.	Some Municipal Some Representative Water Boards
BUILDING:	H.	House Building (state subsidized)	Contractors	'Direct Labour' occasionally
COMMUNICATION:	B.C.E.M.R.S.	—	—	Post Office Board (Posts, Telegraph and Telephone (Q)) Cables and Wireless Board (Q)
TRANSPORT General	B.C.Y.	—	—	Local Passenger Transport Authorities National Freight Authority Transport Holding Co. Building and Maintenance of Roads Some Municipal Buses Passenger Transport Authority
Road	B.C.Y.	Goods Haulage	Passenger Buses	

269

TABLE VIA—continued

THE MIXED ECONOMY OF BRITAIN, 1971

Order of Industry	Relevant Economic and Technical Characteristics*	Government by			Consumers' Co-operatives
		Small Capitalist (Entrepreneur, Partnership, Private Co.)	Large Capitalist (Joint Stock Co.)*	State (Nationalized and Municipal, etc.)*	
TRANSPORT—cont. Rail	B.C.M.Q. R.S.Y. M.Y.	—	1919-48 'The Big' Four (Z) Railway Co. Ownership	British Railway Boards	—
Canals, Docks and Harbours		—		Suez Canal Shares until 1956 Representative Harbour Boards to 1949 Docks and Inland Waterways Executive from 1949	—
Shipping	Y.	Tramps	Shipping Lines (some subsidized) Subsidized to 1947	—	
Air	Q.S.X.	—		1947—B.O.A.C., B.E.A.	
DISTRIBUTION: Wholesale	R.S.	—	Wholesale and Export Houses	Bulk Buying, e.g. Raw Timber (Y) Raw Cotton Commission	C.W.S., S.C.W.S.
Retail Trades		Independent shop-keepers	Chain Stores, Department Stores		(C) Local Co-operative Societies

	R.S.	C.R.S.	The 'Big Three'	(Central) Bank of England (B)	Co-operative
FINANCE: Banking	—	—		(Central) Bank of England (B)	Co-operative Bank
Insurance	—	—	Fire, Burglary, 'Industrial Life' (Z)	National Insurance against Unemployment, Sickness, Funeral, 1949	Co-operative Insurance
PERSONAL SERVICES: Health	(H)	Doctors	—	Hospitals, National Health Scheme	
Education	(E)	Private Schools	—	Grants to Universities, Local Education Authorities, Museums, Libraries	Co-operative Colleges Education Committees
Recreation	(H) (E)	Entertainment	—	British Broadcasting Corporation, City Orchestras, City or National Parks	Co-operative Guilds Clubs
Other		Professions, Law, Accounting, etc.	—	Police and Defence (G)	

* B. Basic to production.
C. Common consumer use.
E. Needed for education.
F. Conservation for future.

G. Gratis supply (other needs).
H. Needed for health.
M. Fact, likelihood or necessity of monopoly.

Q. Need but lack of large capital equipment.
R. Routine management.
S. Large size more efficient.

X. Need for scientific experts.
Y. Integrated or co-ordinated.
Z. Inefficient or high cost in fact.

really logical determinants of nationalization? The logic associating nationalization with several of these characters has already been discussed. Capitalist production is not possible (Chapter VI, § 1) where, for the sake of the community, education (E), health (H) and other commodities (G) must be granted free (owing to the difficulties of assessment and collection costs) out of taxes and cannot be covered by charging a price. Monopolies (M) if they cannot be regulated may (Chapter III, § 6–7) be thought best operated by the state. If the state must have control and supervision of the economy (and this will be argued further in § 7), it may be simplest for the state directly to govern certain basic (B) industries. If private enterprise (particularly the small capitalist) discounts the future too steeply, the state may have to safeguard the interest of future (F) generations. And if an industry is closely integrated (Y) with a main industry already state-governed it may be worth nationalization. The logic of these last two arguments is admitted even in the laissez-faire American economy where conservation of resources is federal and state policy; and where large printing offices, arsenals and shipyards are run by the federal government as integrated respectively with its reports and congressional records, and its military and naval programme. A group of American economists[1] comments on this integration of joint demands under the state.

The controversial importance of this sort of production is that it occurs in fields already occupied by private enterprises and therefore represents an obvious form of government competition. A report to the House of Representatives[2] stated that there were some 225 lines of industrial activity in which government agencies competed with private sources of supply.

Such government competition (as in electrical power, an integrated by-product of Tennessee Valley irrigation) has also been advocated as a 'yardstick' for measuring and judging capitalist costs and prices.

Five characteristics not yet discussed as logical conditions for nationalizing industries are the routine nature of administration (R), the need for investment in capital equipment (Q) and for experts (X), large size (S) and the inefficiency (Z) of the existing capitalist government. These five characteristics are logically connected. Many industries are routine, requiring *expertise* not *enterprise*—not go-getters but expert scientists advising a large-sized firm or plant using heavy capital equipment. If the equipment, the expertise and the large-scale is not forthcoming its firms and plants are likely to be *inefficient*. British coal mining 1919–47 certainly exhibited this 'syndrome'[3] of characteristics;

[1] Lyon, Abramson *et al.*, *Government and Economic Life*, Brookings Institution, 1940, p. 1138.
[2] 72 Cong. 2 Sess. Government Competition with Private Enterprise H. Rep., 1985 (1933), commonly known as the Shannon Report.
[3] See Reid Report (Cmd. 6610), 1945.

possibly also the 'Big Four' British railways 1919–39; and certainly many gas undertakings.[1] The more fundamental of these five associated characteristics are routine management and heavy equipment.

Routine operation was given by Adam Smith and quoted earlier (Chapter V, § 1) as a reason why trades such as banking, insurance, canal-building and water supply might be 'possible for a joint-stock company to carry on successfully'. The wheel has turned a little further. It is now nationalization that is advocated as a suitable government for most of these trades, while the joint stock company is to govern trades needing enterprise and a *lack* of routine. This is not so illogical and topsy-turvy as it sounds. The small capitalist entrepreneur, the large capitalist joint stock company and nationalization (in consecutive columns of Table VIA) form a series of governments less and less able so adjust themselves to situations out of the ordinary routine. But the superior efficiency of the large-scale plant and firm with its ample capital has in many industries made the small capitalist out of the question and the alternatives shift along one column. The practical question is now joint stock company *or* nationalization and of the two the company, so the logic runs, is the lesser evil as far as adjustability goes.

Where nationalization is superior to the company is now exactly where the company proved superior to the small capitalist namely in raising capital and investing in equipment. The dominance of this technical need for capital in an age of applied science has been a logical trend running throughout the argument of this book and since the First World War the need for capital has often, paradoxically enough, told against capitalism. British capitalist coal-mining was starved of equipment during the inter-war period and large-scale investment to the tune of 635 million pounds proposed in the Coal Board's plan of 1950 was not conceivable till after nationalization.

The same high capital cost of original lay-out occurs in 'octopoid' industry such as electricity supply. Under a company regime new capital is forthcoming only when large enough profits have been earned in the past or expected in the future to make (*a*) companies able to reinvest sufficiently and (*b*) persons and other companies willing to subscribe to new issues.[2] Once an industry's profits fall a vicious circle is set up whereby low profit and expectation of low profits result in low investment and low investment in still lower profits. Thus, in specific British industries capitalism has been displaced not because it sweated the worker or exploited the consumer, as foretold by some prophets,

---

[1] See Ministry of Fuel and Power, Report on the Gas Industry 1945, Cmd. 6699, pp. 16 and 17. 603 gas undertakings out of a total of 959 were below the size which could economically support the necessary technical development, seldom reach 75 per cent efficiency and may operate at efficiencies as low as 60 per cent.

[2] See below, pp. 326–36.

but because capitalism failed any longer to attract the commodity on which it originally gained power—capital.[1]

One character, with the symbol C, remains, that of common use. This character is found supported by several others (such as M or S) in all nationalized industries except road transport;[2] the logic of its otherwise unsupported association with nationalization is somewhat doubtful, though clearer in its association with consumers' co-operation, where the consumer is the 'common man'. Road transport need not be large-scale (except perhaps for passengers) and requires little capital (use of roads being granted without direct price charge) or expertise. Its nationalization has been justified by the logic of integration (Y) or 'co-ordination' with the other forms of transport now nationalized rather than by common service. Common service is important only when monopoly threatens, since a monopolized service for the many (particularly where it serves industry generally as does electric power) is logically more serious than a monopolized luxury for the few.

Analysis and interpretation of the actual spread of nationalization in terms of these demand and supply characteristics points the way to future developments—they forecast events as scientific enquiry should. Further industries, including manufacturing industries, which the Labour party may claim as 'ripe' for nationalization may thus be foretold. In programmes put before party conferences the supply of water, cement manufacture, sugar manufacture and industrial insurance all figure as 'ripe'.[3] On my interpretation water is probably C.F.G.M.Q.R.X., cement B.M., sugar M.Q.R., insurance is C.G.R. and, above all, owing to the greater predictability of the law of large numbers, S and X, i.e. it is less costly with greater size and actuaries 'know-how'. It is also claimed that in capitalist hands industrial life insurance is (Z) unnecessarily costly in its method of door-to-door collection.[4]

The attribution of demand and supply characteristics to industries in relation to nationalization must of course be well attested. Many of them were pointed out by impartial official enquiries prior to nationalization. The technical advisory committee on coal-mining, chaired by Sir Charles Reid, reported in 1945 on the diseconomies of small size and dispersed ownership, the perpetual state of financial embarrassment of firms, and yet their need for more mechanical equipment in haulage and loading and for the prior remodelling of the underground roads. And

---

[1] It was, in particular, British capital that originally financed not only Britain's own railways and public utilities but South and North America's as well. Continental European capital for railways was, even at the outset, found by the state.

[2] There is some logic, therefore, in its fluctuation between nationalization and denationalization.

[3] *Labour believes in Britain*, April 1949.

[4] See Beveridge Report on the Social Services, 1944, pp. 277–86.

there was plenty of official evidence on the relative inefficiency of the British coal industry measured in output per manshift. Between 1913 and 1936 there was 'an increase of productivity per manshift . . . as the International Labour Office Committee pointed out, of at least 117 per cent in Holland; of 81 per cent in the Ruhr; of 73 per cent in Poland; of 50–1 per cent in Belgium and Czechoslovakia; of 22–5 per cent in the United States bituminous industry, and in France; and of 10 per cent in Great Britain'.[1]

On the gas industry, a finely blended committee chaired by Sir Geoffrey Heyworth and consisting of a business executive (Sir Geoffrey himself), an accountant, an engineer, a scientist and a trade union leader, took local monopoly for granted and reported[2] in favour of nationalization (or rather regionalization) on the grounds, amongst others, of size, low technical efficiency of many existing units and need of co-ordinated research and expert technical advice and skill. The committee found it possible to make a reasonably reliable forecast of the trend of demand, which suggested that sound routine management using market research is more to the point here than brilliant risk-taking enterprise.

Labour Party programmes put forward other reasons for nationalization side by side with the supply and demand characteristics I have lettered, for instance, 'great influence on employment levels' or 'suffering from very bad industrial relations'. It does not appear that any of the industries that have been nationalized had these characteristics, apart from being basic to the economy or being generally inefficient. The remedy here will be discussed under state planning and supervision (§ 6), or specifically, under labour relations.[3]

Consumers' co-operation does not, any more than capitalism, supply goods and services gratis, and its commercial trading occupies but a small space in Britain's mixed economy as a whole; but that space is significant in distribution. Unlike state government, co-operation does not monopolize industries and its scope must therefore be measured in the relative proportion it has actually secured of any given trade.

The local co-operative societies employed in 1962 about 11 per cent of all retailers as will be seen (p. 301) when testing performance. The highest proportion sold co-operatively are goods (C) in the commonest use and in standard, almost stereotyped demand, such as milk, bread, coal. In wholesaling, however, the English Co-operative Wholesale Society and the Scottish society employed 13,625 in 1962—only 2½ per cent of all wholesale employees—though the percentage is higher for

---

[1] Court, *Coal*, H.M.S.O., 1951, pp. 25–6.
[2] Ministry of Fuel and Power, Report on the Gas Industry, 1945, Cmd. 6699, see especially pars. 4, 86–8, 165–71, 197–209, 231(4).
[3] See below, pp. 317–26.

food only. In manufacture the retail and wholesale co-operative societies are limited in market to the integrated co-operative retail outlets and employed 99,000 in 1935, 103,000 in 1949. This was not much over 1 per cent of all workers in British manufacture though the percentage was considerably higher in consumers' finished goods such as clothing, tobacco and food. Judging from its proportion of national wages and salaries, co-operative production rated at the Census of 1963 even less than 1 per cent.[1]

Besides the character of common use, co-operation is favoured relatively to its capitalist competitors by the large scale (S) of parts of its production organization. The English Co-operative Wholesale Society employed 39,835 workers in 1962 in production—a size that put it among the thirty largest capitalist manufacturing firms; but it owned many of them small, over a hundred plants, and engaged, like a conglomerate, in a wide variety of industries.

In 1962 the London retail society employed 4,074 workers in *production* and services, the Birmingham society 1,779 and Royal Arsenal 1,327; but no other society employed above 1,000 in production. In *distribution*, too, several co-operative societies retail on a large scale through a great number of branch shops in their allotted territory. The London society concentrating in northern London had, in 1962, 13,636 distributive employees, Birmingham 6,038, Royal Arsenal, concentrating in London south of the Thames, 5,904. But no other society topped 5,000 workers in distribution and the majority had less than 200 employees scattered among a few branches whilst many societies may have only one shop.

The Gaitskell Commission[2] advocated amalgamation of retail societies for greater efficiency. Dividing co-operative societies into five ranges of sizes of membership, the Commission found (p. 87) that in the course of 1948–55 a regular trend could be traced for a higher percentage of the largest societies to grow faster than the smaller. Of the largest societies 58 per cent grew more than the average of all societies, 45·3 per cent of the next largest, 44·3 per cent of the next, 41·7 per cent of the next to smallest, and only 33·5 per cent of the smallest societies grew more than average. If large enough, co-operative societies may indeed combine the advantages of national chain-stores with the advantages of their branches being concentrated in one concentrated territory. One reason indeed why consumer co-operation has flourished in Britain and not in America is that the British movement 'got in on the ground floor' in developing chain-stores, well before the British large-capitalist retailer.

A review was made for 1950 of all economic activities, including

[1] Annual Abstract of Statistics, 1969, pp. 144, 348.
[2] Independent Commission, p. 241.

276

central and local government but excluding military forces. The private segment of the British economy employed 77·5 per cent of total occupied man-power (including in this segment 1·7 per cent in co-operative societies). Of the remainder 5·1 per cent were in central government, 6·4 per cent in local government and 11·0 per cent in public undertakings (which in 1945 employed only 0·7 per cent of total occupied man-power). Taking manufacturing and building only, capitalism still retained, in 1950, as much as 95·0 per cent, co-operative societies controlled 1·0 per cent and the public segment 4·0 per cent of British occupied man-power.[1]

In 1969 the mixture was mainly as before. Since 1951 the iron and steel industry was nationalized, then denationalized, then renationalized, and about 300,000 workers must be added to the nationalized segment. The number employed in education, mostly public, has risen by 770,000, in postal services and telephones by 145,000, in gas and electricity by 55,000, in air transport by 35,000, in local and central government by 50,000—a total of *1,355,000*. On the other hand we must subtract workers in (nationalized) coal mining, diminished by 330,000 and in railways diminished by 250,000, leaving a net rise of *775,000*.[2] The total in civil employment rose from 21,993,000 in 1950 to 24,893,000 in 1969—an addition of 2,900,000. The net addition to the nationalized segment of 775,000 was thus 28 per cent—fairly close to the 1950 position where it formed 22·5 per cent of the total employed.

§ 3. THE GOVERNMENT OF NATIONALIZED INDUSTRIES

Unlike capitalist government the state can grant goods and services to the consumer out of taxation without charging a price. This was the relation of the state to the consumer in its original transactions of administering justice, policing, defence or road-building; and though it is not the relation to consumers in industries more recently nationalized, this old external non-trading relation to the consumer has inevitably put its mark on the internal relations of government discussed in Chapter IV. One such mark will be the tight central control necessary where the consumer is getting services free at the taxpayer's expense. In contrast the yardstick of trading results, showing how money spent comes back, makes delegation an eminently practical proposition.[3]

In 1933 I wrote:[4] 'Nationalization does not solve all problems of industrial organization out of hand and ensure our all living happily

---

[1] Ridley, 'The extent of the Public Sector of the Economy in Recent Years', *Statistical Journal*, Part II, 1951.
[2] Annual Abstracts of Statistics, Section VI, 1954, V, 1969.
[3] See Renold in *Large-Scale Organization*, ed. Milward, 1950, p. 211.
[4] Florence, 1933, p. 152.

ever after, as some Socialists seem to imagine, but raises the relations of employment, investment and management as problems of vital public interest.' Today, after many years' experience of nationalized industries, socialists are beginning to realize the vitality of these problems of internal organization. This does not necessarily mean that nationalization was a mistake; but that nationalizers must learn to know and respect the technical and economic characteristics of the industries they propose to nationalize, and to know and respect the political science of large-scale organization with which they propose to effect the nationalization.

In most of the industries recently nationalized the internal relations of government must be adapted to procedures where prices are charged and charged at such a level that, to quote a typical nationalization Act,[1] 'revenues shall not be less than sufficient for meeting all outgoings properly chargeable to revenue account on an average of good and bad years'. The organization that operates this 'sufficient revenue' procedure is in Britain today known generally as the public corporation.

The trend in the form of government of the industries already nationalized is unmistakable: a flight away from government by department of state on the old Post Office model; away from municipal organization; and away from mixed boards of representatives—all toward the public corporation with its board or executive or commission.

The reasons why Britain never repeated the state-department type of organization and indeed has now turned over Post Office activities to a corporation are at least five. First, the Minister in charge, e.g. the postmaster-general, was and always is changing, even during the period of office of any one party. Second, there was (and is) continual questioning in Parliament on petty details of day-to-day middle or low level management. As one consequence the top executives of the department have had to be skilled in apologetics and the writing of Ministers' answers, but not necessarily able in the real business of running the Post Office. Third, the civil service selected, conditioned and organized for a different purpose than 'running' an industry, stood fast, too deliberative, conventional and 'bureaucratic'. 'Initiative counts for nothing against the meticulous observance of regulations which are both made and applied by those who know nothing of the daily detailed exigencies of practical work.'[2] Fourth, even if the department showed some initiative, say in capital development, the Treasury might impose its traditional veto. A fifth and final reason for the flight from departmental government is that any profits from the business are liable to be used for the

[1] Coal Industry Nationalization Act, 1 (4) (C).
[2] Salter, *The Political Quarterly*, April–June 1950, pp. 209–17.

relief of general taxation instead of for reduction of prices. In the years 1946–8 for instance, the general surplus on British Post Office undertakings averaged nearly £22 million, but no reduction was made in postage rates, and telephone and telegraph rates were increased.

The main reason for the flight from municipal government of industry is not the inefficiency of British municipal managements (which as well as being fundamentally democratic have often proved most enterprising and efficient) but the insufficient size of many of the areas covered for economy and development. On the last page of his Fabian edition of the *Common-Sense of Municipal Trading*, published in 1908, Bernard Shaw thought 'a relimitation of the areas and reconstitution of the units of local government is the most pressing requirement made by municipal trade upon our constructive statesmanship. We will no doubt ignore the existing deadlock as long as we can.' 'We' did; and for economy's sake the small British local government units had finally to be by-passed. Points made by the Heyworth report on the gas industry put it concisely:

The main objects which grouping into larger units can be expected to promote are (1) some further reduction of production costs, . . . (3) further economy in capital charges . . . (4) more intensive study of distribution problems (large groupings would permit a higher level of technical skill, facilitating the planning of development on the best possible long term projections of future demand) . . . (5) further concentration on sales policy . . . (6) greater concentration on development of 'fringe' and rural areas . . . and (8) expansion of research and its application.[1]

The main reason for the flight from representative boards is that such boards are liable to become debating societies particularly for airing grievances of the several parties represented, rather than bodies making final decisions on policy and organization. It is mainly for this reason that, in spite of ideology and propaganda, no nationalized industry has direct representatives of the labour it employs on its governing board.[2] But this does not mean that through trade unions or their political vote, labour does not exert strong pressure to maintain employment, keep out foreign labour or keep up traditional trade practices.

The public corporation on a national scale, independent of criticism in Parliament on day-to-day management, and with independent finance, emerges, then, as almost the exclusive pattern for the government of British nationalized industries and is worth describing in some detail. Some variations in the pattern occur, largely due to the previous relation

---

[1] H.M.S.O., Cmd. 6699, p. 39.
[2] This policy of workers' control was explicitly opposed by Mr Herbert Morrison in his *Socialization of Transport*, published in 1931 with reference to the Bill for a London Transport Board which he was then steering through Parliament.

of the state to the industry—railways, air and road transport, and public utilities were all regulated in one way or another before their nationalization as they are in America today; but the main difference lies in the degree of centralization or federation.

The Iron and Steel Corporation is the most federal if not frankly *confederate*; the Coal Board, according to the Act of 1946, the most centralized in pattern, though subsequently 9 divisional boards and 48 area managements were created. In order of most centralized first, the series ran Coal Board, Transport Commission, Electricity Authority, Gas Council and Iron and Steel Corporation. The Electricity Authority has four of the area chairmen serving in rotation on its Board. The Gas Council, which apart from chairman and deputy chairman, is composed of the twelve subsidiary area board chairmen, did little more than co-ordinate and deal with research and general terms of employment. Now (1970) for ergological reasons to be given shortly it does far more. The Iron and Steel Corporation was originally merely a Holding Company, holding all the shares of 96 original Iron and Steel Joint Stock Companies.

These degrees of federation are also the degrees to which the smaller component of organization are given some autonomy as separate firms. The federal consitution of these nationalized industries are in fact an attempt to reach the optimum size of firm which was discussed in Chapter II—in this case to reach down to the optimum from an all-out national size. The new public corporations measured in any units—labour, capital or output—are of a size almost unprecedented in any capitalist firms, British or American. The largest British capitalist firms in manufacture are probably Unilever and Imperial Chemical Industries and both have developed federal constitutions. But the National Coal Board, originally amalgamating 800 different undertakings with over 1,000 pits in 25 coalfields, appeared, according to the *Fortune* magazine directory for 1965 as the third largest industrial company outside the United States in point of assets and then employed over 500,000—a greater number than any American company except General Motors.

Evidence was adduced in Chapter II that there are economies in larger sizes of organization and more than some economists allow. But it does not follow that a sudden jump from a medium size of firm to a size say over 400,000 will also see a jump up in efficiency. Sheer lack of experience of such mammoth concerns would argue the opposite. Federalization of the public corporations has, for this reason, reduced the average size of the operating unit.

The degree of federalism and the size and power of the subsidiary units depend partly on the time of the Act (the Labour government of 1945–50 became more and more conscious of the disadvantages of suddenly creating mammoth nation-wide units with consequent remote control[1]) but partly too on the technical characteristics of the industry itself. The effect of type of work on organization is nowhere more clearly seen than in the centralization of the nationalized gas industry consequent upon the exploitation of North Sea natural gas discussed later. In my first edition (1953) I wrote 'there is no technical possibility of a national grid for gas as there is for electricity and hence little need for a nation-wide government, gas had in effect been regionalized not nationalized.' But today, on the contrary, there is a national system of pipe lines for the transmission of the newly discovered natural gas, and the gas supply will be as centrally administered as electricity. Additional reasons for larger scale organization are the increased capital intensity due to the construction and operation of a national grid and the need for aggressive marketing, if all the natural gas is to be sold that has been contracted to be bought at a bulk price from the producers.

The actual territorial regions into which the nation is in fact divided for the production of gas, coal and electricity and for transport, depend on such technical, economic and administrative considerations as the existing facilities and, to quote the Heyworth report on gas,[2] as 'ability to support the type of administration' proposed; ability to 'command resources sufficient to give an effective challenge to' any competing industries; 'easy contact . . . between headquarters and all parts of the Region'. Furthermore 'any large commercial centre should lie wholly within one region', . . . and 'the boundaries should be drawn so as to create the minimum of inter-Regional problems', to which the statement on the Electricity supply areas (Cmd. 7007) may be added that 'boundaries of Areas should run through lightly populated districts and thus avoid difficulties which arise when populated areas receive supplies from more than one source'. Boundaries were not based on historical and traditional frontiers; Wales, for instance, was split in two for electricity supply, and the northern half joined to Merseyside.

The number of regions varies for the different federalized national industries from six to fourteen. If they averaged just a little smaller and were sixteen in number the average population of each of these sixteen regions would be that of the average population (about four million) of the forty-eight continental states of the American Union. It may be more than a coincidence that the recent federalization of British industry has produced *ad hoc* units of the size of American states. This size may, indeed, form a convenient administrative unit. Regions similar to that of the nationalized industries have appeared also in the decentralization of British government ministries such as the departments of Employment and Productivity, and Trade and Industry.

[1] Chester, The *Political Quarterly*, April–June 1950, pp. 122–34.
[2] Op. cit., p. 42.

Charting the direction of the rule relation within the public corporation, we must place the appropriate minister above the commission, council or board, with its subsidiary boards (which may, as in the Steel Corporation, be functional rather than regional). For he appoints the members of the board, and in the words of the 1946 Act setting up the Coal Board,

(1) The Minister may after consultation with the Board, give to the Board directions of a general character as to the exercise and performance by the Board of their functions in relation to matters appearing to the Minister to affect the national interest, and the Board shall give effect to any such directions. (2) In framing programmes of reorganization or development involving substantial outlay on capital account, the Board shall act on lines settled from time to time with the approval of the Minister. (3) In the exercise and performance of their functions as to training, education and research, the Board shall act on lines settled as aforesaid.

Finally

(4) the Board must provide the Minister with information; and facilities for the verification of information.

The Minister, in turn, is publicly accountable to Parliament and is necessarily succeeded by another Minister when the party in power changes. Parliament by statute creates the upper organization, in some cases as far down as the regional or functional boards; the regional boards of the gas industry are statutory, though the divisional boards of the coal industry are not. Besides the democratic principle of giving the elected representative of the people final control over 'their' enterprises, the Cabinet, Ministers, and Parliament will presumably co-ordinate the several nationalized industries in the interests of industry and the nation as a whole, linking them up, if that is necessary, with national policy. Ministers are explicitly required by all the Nationalization Acts to issue general directions 'in matters which appear to the Minister to affect the national interest'.

But the Minister should not be continually 'breathing down' the board's neck in day-to-day management and Minister and board should not be continually 'looking over their shoulders' in fear of Parliamentary questions. Accordingly, the Acts which have nationalized industries have excluded day-by-day management by confining Ministers to giving 'directions of a general character'. The difficulty is to draw the exact line between general principles and directives and day-to-day particular orders. In fact there is no absolute line; a command can only be relatively more general or more particular than another.

Though Parliament is bound to be involved if there is a 'row', rather like shareholders' meetings when a company is on the rocks, a board and managers also need as much freedom as possible for *general* policy, if it is really to be enterprising and dynamic. No amount of outside control or criticism will make an inefficient into an enterprising manager or board. An industrial organization requires a dynamo and an engine as well as a steering wheel and a brake. While the middle and lower organization is much like that charted in Table IVB the top of the nationalized organization chart falls, then, into the following pattern:

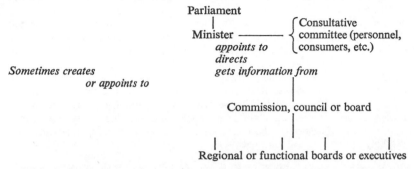

The consultative committees or councils of consumers and others are usually to 'notify' or 'make' their conclusions or report to the Minister who consults the board rather than direct to the board. Their effectiveness will be considered later (§ 5) in discussing how far nationalization satisfies the criteria of low price and democracy.

The *de jure*, paper, pattern of relations between the board (commission or council) of the corporation, Minister and Parliament will not necessarily prove the real *de facto* pattern. Mr Ernest Davies, M.P. (before he became a member of the Labour government), put the influence and power of Ministers, uncontrolled by Parliament, rather high,[1] and this in fact is the way relations have been developing.

Consultation between Minister and board is fully provided for prior to ministerial action. This ensures that the boards are informed of what is expected of them and eliminates the necessity for ministerial direction. In practice, consultation has been the chief way in which Ministers have exercised their influence over the boards; but how it is exercised is shrouded in mystery. There is little doubt that the Minister of Fuel and Power, for instance, is in close and frequent consultation with the industries for which he is responsible, coal, electricity and gas. Such consultation is behind closed doors and the results may be seen in the functionings of the corporation, but no more is known about it. The great disadvantage of such private consultation is that it releases the Minister from the responsibility of answering to Parliament for his actions. If Parliament is unaware of the nature and results of ministerial influence, it cannot question ministerial action. Ministers can only be held to account for matters for which they have responsibility. By refraining from exercising their directional powers over the board and

[1] W. A. Robson (ed.), *Problems of Nationalized Industry*, 1952, pp. 110–12.

preferring to influence them through consultation, they escape responsibility. Ministers can then come to Parliament and decline to reply to questions on the grounds that their responsibility is non-existent. When they come before Parliament, Ministers draw a curtain over the board's activities and stand before it with sealed lips. They may thereby fulfil the letter of the statutes, but not their spirit.

There is little question but that Parliament intended that Ministers should be answerable to Parliament in a general way for the activities of the public corporation, and not that they should admit such responsibility only when they have given specific directions to the boards. . . . Rightly or wrongly, the giving of directions has been regarded as a reflection on a board's competence. Not only have Ministers been reluctant to give them, but boards have complied with ministerial wishes even against their own judgment rather than be directed. This is known to have been the case with the Electricity Authority, when the Minister favoured implementation of the Clow Report, which recommended differential tariffs for winter and summer to reduce winter consumption. No doubt there are many similar instances which are not publicly known.

Without detailed enquiry it is as hard to locate the precise seat of top rule in nationalized, as in capitalist government. Top authority, in fact deciding policy and organization, might sometimes be Parliament; Ministers generally; the appropriate Minister; the board as a whole; the chairman; or some other member or members of the board or any two or more of these men or bodies of men. Where the industry is subsidized by the State as in forestry and civil aviation and transport generally the state (Parliament or minister) may logically be expected perhaps to have more power.

The Select Committee on the Nationalized Industries reporting in 1968 thought that when ministerial policy involved a public corporation in departing from the commercial principle (laid down in the original Act) of sufficient revenue to cover costs, in favour of the principle of public interest, the Treasury (i.e. the taxpayer) should pay for the cost of that departure.[1] Ministerial policy has, for instance, often tried to benefit employees in the form of higher wages in declining industries, such as railways or coal-mining. The policy of the Transport Commission and its Railway Executive for limiting wage increases was based on recommendations of official courts of enquiry, but it was overridden in 1951 at Ministerial level (the Minister of Labour seems to have been more important than the Minister of Transport). An opposite policy of considerably increased wages was adopted at the expense of the consumer paying higher fares.

In short, for the nationalized railways the main signs of policy-making seem to have come from the Minister (or rather 'a' Minister)

---

[1] R. Kelf-Cohen, *Twenty Years of Nationalization*, p. 194.

and mainly as a result of the trade union threat of a widespread strike. A realist might perhaps conclude that here it is the powerful industrial union which should be charted at the top of the tree of command. Since it is common and basic services that have been nationalized, the danger of a strike to national life and to the election prospect of the state government cannot be minimized; so that trade unions, at least in times of full employment, are certainly in a position of considerable policy-making power.

The overruling of public corporations by ministerial policy on the question of wages was itself overruled in 1968–70 by the Prices and Incomes Board. Stabilizing incomes helped public corporations pursue the policy of making ends meet by keeping costs down. On the other hand the Board hindered the policy by stabilizing prices.

The existence of possible powers behind the throne can only be indicated. Except in times of crisis the top power on the throne is certainly supposed to be the public corporation represented by its boards, councils or commissions and especially their chairman. What manner of men were appointed by the various Ministers? Robson's prophecy almost twenty years ago was shrewd:

One must accept the probability that for some time to come most boards will be composed of such elements as (a) a person with previous experience of the industry under commercial ownership—usually a high executive; (b) an ex-trade union officer of standing; (c) a former civil servant of exceptional ability; (d) a leading financial expert or accountant; (e) an engineer or scientist —with an occasional retired general or air marshal thrown in. There is nothing inherently wrong in these categories so long as they are not exclusive or applied in a conventional way. We want men rather than categories. The trouble is that Ministers have too rarely shown themselves willing or able to back their own judgment, when it means taking a risk, rather than to appoint men almost *ex officio*. All too often they have been disposed to play for safety, to select men whose careers lay behind them, to choose reassuring names which would inspire confidence rather than to seek men with the promise of creative ability and dynamic energy.[1]

The actual process of transforming the capitalist government of any industry into a nationalized government is simpler if the capitalist government is of joint stock company variety. The shareholders are bought out either (as were the shareholders of British coal mines) at a specific valuation by accountants, or more simply still (as were the railway, gas, electricity supply and iron and steel shareholders) at the London stock exchange prices of their shares on a given date or series of

[1] W. A. Robson (ed.), *Problems of Nationalized Industry*, pp. 96–7. Statistics of occupational and educational background are presented by Smith and Chester, *British Journal of Sociology*, December 1951, p. 286. See also below, Chapter VII, § 4, pp. 343–59, for analysis of different types of full-time executive.

dates. In place of ordinary or preference shares, or of bonds and debentures, they receive an equivalent face-value of government stock bearing, it is true, a lower rate of interest even than the debentures or bonds,
but guaranteed by the state; security of a fixed money income is given
in exchange for an income higher on average but uncertain in its
incidence. Whether or not shareholders get a bad or good bargain
depends mainly on the valuation put on their shares by the valuers or
the highly competitive stock exchange. There is reason to believe,
after the event, that British Railway shareholders got a good bargain.
The stock exchange was in 1945–8 too optimistic about the ability of
the British railway companies to compete against road transport without
great changes in their outlook, organization and method. But, apart
from stock exchange miscalculation (which might be too high or too
low), there was compulsion to sell at a stock exchange price of which
the owner of the capital had not in fact availed himself voluntarily, and
it was argued that, other things equal, an owner should be paid more if
coerced. Some leaders of his (then) Majesty's (then) Opposition went
so far as to speak of the 'Iron and St*eal*' Bill.[1]

Almost the only case where the displaced capitalist enterprises were
not joint stock companies was the road transport of goods. Here
nationalization does bring about a revolution. The genuine entrepreneur
owner-manager, perhaps of one truck or small fleet of trucks, either
leaves the industry or is turned into a salaried official with certain loss
of independence and probable loss of incentive.

In general, however, nationalization has in Britain been nationalization of large joint stock companies, where capitalism takes a form not
so very different in practice from state organization,[2] and of industries
where, moreover, the state was, in the years of war and the aftermath
of war, already in strong overall control—a control to which we shall
recur in the last section of this chapter.

§ 4. GOVERNMENT BY CONSUMERS' CO-OPERATION

The present relation of consumers' co-operative societies to their
customers has its '1066' in 1844. At that date the Rochdale 'pioneers'
adopted the plan of charging market prices and distributing any profits

---

[1] Oliver Lyttelton, moving the rejection of the Bill, House of Commons, 1950.
[2] It is worth recalling the words of Mill in his *Principles of Political Economy*,
written in 1848 (V, xi, § 11): 'Whatever, if left to spontaneous agency, can only be
done by joint-stock associations, will often be as well, and sometimes better done,
as far as the actual work is concerned, by the state. Government management is,
indeed, proverbially jobbing, careless and ineffective; but so likewise has generally
been joint-stock management. . . . Against the security afforded by meetings of
shareholders (in a joint stock company), and by their individual inspection and

they made as dividends to their members in proportion to the amount of their purchases. The main alternative had been to charge prices just sufficient to cover cost, like the nationalized industries today. But co-operatives were liable to be too optimistic in estimating their revenue and had no 'buffer' like the taxpayer to fall back on in case of a deficit. Hence the only safe finance was to budget for a surplus of revenue over costs and to distribute profits back to consumers *after* the profit had been secured. Though co-operative prices are much the same as capitalist any surplus made goes not to the owner or lender of the capital, but to the consumer and in proportion to his purchases. Co-operative members have to put up some capital (usually a minimum of a pound a head) and often put up more (up to £500 in shares and if more than that, in loans), but they are paid on this capital a low rate of fixed interest, not a dividend varying with profit.

The relation of local co-operative societies one with another is normally agreement not to compete. The country has come to be mapped out into distinct though often odd-shaped areas belonging to one particular society—somewhat like the territories which male birds defend. These areas in which a society may have one or a great number of scattered stores are an historical growth depending on the relative strength of neighbouring societies in the past and thus vary greatly in size as well as shape.[1] Sometimes societies divide up one city. Birmingham, for instance, has two societies splitting the city along an east–west frontier, but each society has a large rural hinterland. Sometimes, again, the frontiers of particular societies zigzag in and out and the areas fit like a jigsaw puzzle. While the costs of competition are thus avoided, the areas are certainly not fitted for octopoid industries requiring piped or wired tentacles issuing from a logical centre like gas or electricity distribution, and often are not even economical for distribution by vehicle and hand.

The constitutional relations internal to a co-operative retail society show two characteristic features: meetings usually every quarter or half-year which are open to all members with decisions made by a majority of heads, not of shares; and election, by all members on this equal footing, of a managing committee or board. At the general meeting, like joint stock company shareholders' meetings, only a small minority

---

[1] Carr-Saunders, Florence and Peers, *Consumers' Co-operation in Great Britain,* 1942, maps, pp. 68–73. This work will be repeatedly cited in the following pages.

---

enquiries, may be placed the greater publicity and more active discussion and comment, to be expected in free countries with regard to affairs in which the general government takes part. The defects, therefore, of government management, do not seem to be necessarily much greater, if necessarily greater at all, than those of management by joint stock.'

287

of the total membership attends—or indeed, considering the numbers often involved, could attend in any one building. But, partly because the meetings are in the members' own locality, the quality of the people attending is different. There is normally, in co-operative societies, unlike joint stock companies

a small active minority of the membership—usually about 2 per cent—who focus [a] general pressure of opinion and who influence the management committee through the constitutional channels of democratic control—that is, through the election of the committee and the members' meeting. This nucleus of keen members who make it their concern to supervise the society's activities, marks off consumers' co-operative undertakings from other forms of democratically controlled industry,[1]

such as a municipal or nationalized industrial undertaking. Co-operative societies print very full details of their transactions and 'some of the members are willing to take pains over examining trading accounts and the other routine business of a co-operative society, mainly because they believe that in so doing they are furthering a social purpose beyond themselves or their society'. The management committee meet only in their spare time—a further evidence of ideological co-operative keenness —but usually appoint full-time officials. The 'anatomy' of co-operative retail government thus follows the pattern:

Quarterly meetings of members *voting by heads for*

|

Spare-time management committee (with sub-commitees)
appointing

|

Full-time officials (monarchy or diarchy)

The large size of some co-operative societies explains to some extent, as already said, co-operative success in retail trading. But the majority of co-operative retail societies are small though by amalgamation the proportion is falling. In 1935 there were, at one end of the scale, 6 co-operative societies[2] and later, in 1946, 8 societies with above 100,000 members; at the other end, 583 in 1935 and 424 in 1946 with less than 2,000. By 1958 and 1968, 18 and 25 societies had over 100,000; 206 and 100 societies less than 2,000 members. In consequence the total number of retail societies is falling (in 1935 the total was 1,096, in 1968, 641)[3] but the average membership of a society is rising. In 1968 43 per cent of the membership was in the 25 societies with over 100,000 members.

[1] Op. cit., p. 290.
[2] Op. cit., p. 62.
[3] *Co-operative Statistics Review*, published by the Co-operative Union, 1968, p. 4.

The diversity in size-structure involves diversity in government of the retail societies. Apart from mere village societies of under a thousand members there appear from the facts to be two normal associations of size with constitution. Associated with the larger societies of over 10,000 members or so is a monarchical type of government where a single top official, usually called a managing secretary, may either be just a secretary to the society and its board, or though still strictly a *constitutional* monarch, may be a real managing director, delegating secretarial routine. Associated with the smaller societies of from 1,000–10,000 members, is a 'diarchical' constitutional government, where a secretary, in charge of accounting and registering members, shareholdings and purchases, and a manager in charge of actual trading, have equal status and are co-ordinated by the management committee itself, thus increasing the power of the committee.

In both constitutions top responsibility for policy seems to lie with the management committee, which usually appoints the secretary and manager, and is elected by the whole membership of the society. A committee-man's tenure of office is 'on paper' usually two years; but he is normally re-eligible and there is in practice

a considerable continuity of tenure. In some societies it seems to be assumed that the only cause which can lead to a member leaving the committee is death. An obvious result of this is that the average age of committee members is distinctly high, members of eighty or more being not unknown.[1]

The committees usually number 6 to 20 but are split up into subcommittees. In the smaller societies one sub-committee usually deals with trading, another with maintenance of buildings. In larger societies there are several trading committees (e.g. for grocery, drapery) and a finance sub-committee; and much detailed supervision and management is done in these sub-committees. A considerable amount of committee work is thus laid on officials and unpaid laymen 'drawn in the main from the skilled artisan class and especially from industries in which there is a high degree of Trade Union organization'.[2] In the large Birmingham society, for instance, an enquiry in 1937 found that

thirteen members of the management committee give about two and a half hours per week to committee work, and the five members of the finance subcommittee a similar period in addition once a fortnight. The secretary and assistant secretary are present at the meetings of the full committee, and four minute clerks attend the sub-committees, which meet fortnightly; the departmental managers will also attend their sub-committees for a short time.[3]

[1] Op. cit., p. 87.
[2] Op. cit., p. 87.
[3] Op. cit., p. 99.

Discussion, in fact, is liable to take the place of specialist skill and research.

For example, some of the largest retail societies have no publicity departments; window dressing is left to the unguided enthusiasm of the assistants of each branch; there is no attempt at market research.[1]

A further result of sectionalized sub-committee management is that 'the balance or lack of balance in the development of the society depends very much on the strength of personality of members of the various sub-committees'.[2]

The whole co-operative organization for trading is based on the broad bottom of the autonomous local retail societies. The national organization is not imposed or delegated from above, as in nationalized industries, but built up by federation from below. There are federal societies for particular local activities (baking, laundry, dairies) but the main sources of production are the English Co-operative Wholesale Society—the C.W.S.—and the Scottish S.C.W.S. The relation of the retail to the wholesale societies is the same as that of individual members to their retail societies. A dividend is declared on the purchases of each retail society, and delegates of the retail societies meet to discuss and elect the management of the wholesale societies just as individual members discuss and elect the retail society management. Voting, however, is not equal for each retail society but weighted according to the purchases of the retail society. Large societies thus have more weight than small, much like large shareholders in the joint stock company.[3]

The management committee of the wholesale society consists not, as in retail societies, of unpaid laymen but of full-time paid directors—originally 28 in number in the C.W.S., 12 in the S.C.W.S. As in the large retail societies these directors form sub-committees for specific departments, but they tend to exceed the usual function of direction. 'An examination of the matters upon which a manager has to obtain the prior sanction of the board indicates that the directors of the C.W.S. concern themselves not only with direction but also with higher management.'[4] Here indeed is a practice not usually found either in capitalist or state industry, the *election* of full-time *managers*. Capitalist directors may be full-time managers and are, nominally at least, elected by the shareholders' meeting. But they are proposed as directors normally because they are managers, not *vice versa*, elected as directors and *ipso facto* becoming managers.

Whether in retailing, wholesaling or manufacture, elected members of committees or boards exercising the top functions of government

[1] Op. cit., p. 305.
[2] Ibid.
[3] Op. cit., p. 274, and footnote.
[4] Op. cit., p. 308.

TABLE VIB

APPLICATION OF CRITERIA TO ALTERNATIVE INDUSTRIAL GOVERNMENTS:
ASSIGNMENT OF MARKS FOR PERFORMANCE

Criteria	Government by				State control planning and supervision of industry (Chap. VI, § 7)
	Small-size capitalism	Large-size capitalism	Consumers' co-operation	Nationalization	
(Philosophic) Individual needs and welfare first	0 Demands only	0 Demands only. Large advertizing to stimulate demand	$\frac{1}{2}$ Demands only, but spontaneous	1 Can grant needed goods and services free below cost or at low profit	Social Security, subsidized insurance benefits, food, houses, health service
(Economic) Consumer sovereignty. Satisfaction of demand	2 Competition 'normal profits'	1 Risk of monopoly exploitation, restriction of output	1 Rebate on prices. Competition with potential capitalist monopolies	0 Risk of bureaucratic overriding of consumer	Control or dissolution of monopoly
(Political) Democracy, national interest, equality and social justice	1 Some diffusion of authority. Exploitation of labour	0 Risk of misdirection of national resources	2 Vote by heads at keen meetings. Workers can be members	1 Popular representation but only remote. Nationalization of resources. Long-run investment	Creation and maintenance of collective bargaining. 'Fair shares'. Priorities and rationing. Regional equalization. Long-run conservation
(Business) Efficiency, current product	0 High cost of small-scale organization	2 Large-scale economies	1 Low costs of capital and land. 'Cheap' administration	1 Largest scale economies	Standardization of products. Rationalization of industries; development councils. Credit facilities for small firms
Stability	0 Trade cycles	0 Trade cycles	$\frac{1}{2}$ (Not in fluctuating industries)	1 Stable employment policy	Relief of unemployment. Price ceilings. Investment policy. Deficit financing
Progress (Growth and investment)	2 Enterprise	2 Finance and research. Resources for large-scale investment. Risk of monopoly obstruction	0 Low rate of physical investment	1 Use of experts and research. Little enterprise. Resources for large-scale investment	Scientific research. Patent law. National planning.

are likely to be inexpert and cautious. In fact their top rule is in some measure shared by co-operative members. Though initiation of policy is normally the work of the management, meetings of members often demonstrate a real discussion and power of veto, and subsequently a real supervision of the management's actions both in retail and in federal societies.

The general meeting of a retail society makes public and brings into relief the significant issues which are before the society at any time. The discussion of these issues has an important psychological influence on the management, which is by this means rendered more keenly aware of the will of the membership. By promoting discussion between the management and the rank and file, the general meeting enhances the solidarity of the society as a whole. The meeting, however, is but a focus; the discussion and criticism would be less significant but for the fact that they are continued in the Guilds and other voluntary organizations and among the general membership. The careful reporting of general meetings in the local pages of the *Wheatsheaf*, and very frequently in the local press, does much to aid the wider participation of the members. In federal societies, including the wholesale societies, the general meeting becomes less a means of expression for a wider membership and more a focus for criticism and an opportunity for the ventilation of the society's affairs. While the effectiveness of this democratic supervision will vary somewhat with the type of society and the nature of the area served, the existing checks are usually adequate to restrain the administration from any line of policy seriously detrimental to the interests of the members.[1]

§ 5. PERFORMANCE. THE TESTS OF MEETING NEEDS, CONSUMERS' SOVEREIGNTY AND DEMOCRACY

The alternative forms of government found in American and particularly in British industry today must now be tested by the criteria of what industry is for, its aim, summed up in section 1. How successful is each alternative in performance? Comparative success means that the actual policy and results of any one alternative form of government satisfy the criteria better than the actual policy and results of other forms. The primary criteria are: needs before demands; sovereignty and no exploitation or restriction of the consumer; and, in the widest sense, democracy. The fourth criterion is economic efficiency including low cost of current production, stability, and progress. These four criteria—roughly speaking, those of the philosopher, the economist, the political scientist and the business man, are listed in the first column of Table VIc and the policy or results of the four forms of industrial government relevant to these criteria are entered opposite each of them and evaluated.[2]

---

[1] Op. cit., p. 292. *Wheatsheaf* is now *Home Magazine*.

[2] These three specific elements in business efficiency (or, to speak more generally, in 'effectiveness') lend themselves more easily to quantitative evaluation than an all-

(A) *The test of meeting needs*

Relevant to the philosophers' 'needs first' it must be repeated that capitalist and co-operative organization only provide needs that are also demands for which the consumer can pay. With fewer people in poverty (as in Britain and America) and a greater equality of incomes, needs approximate more closely to demands and capitalism thus caters more closely to needs such as that for food. Nevertheless, it will still be the state that provides the bulk of the less obvious material needs. Since the first Health and Unemployment Insurance Act of 1911, Britain is considered gradually to have become a 'welfare state'. This phrase means that a large part of state activities is in fact devoted to meeting needs such as education, health services, security and insurance benefits, and that these needs get a certain priority over less needed individual *demands*. One accompaniment, if not a result, has been improved physique, particularly among children, a fall in infant and general death rates and a closing of the gap between the working-age death rates of richer and poorer—all in spite of the set-back to national wealth caused by two world wars. Recently the growing pollution of air and water by uncontrolled industry and its products has pointed to state intervention on the score of health, not to mention amenity.

Large-scale capitalism sometimes goes one better (or is it worse?) than merely catering for individual demand. It may and does stimulate artificial demands by the high pressure salesmanship and advertising described in Chapter III. A patent medicine swallowed simply as a reaction to brilliant publicity is not likely to satisfy a sick consumer's real want and demand to get well any more than his need. Co-operative societies spend but little on advertising, and though they do not meet undemanded *needs*, they produce for spontaneous demands based on genuine wants, rather than for demands erected artificially by pushing and puffing their wares. State government of industries, even when a price is charged fully covering costs, is not likely to stimulate the demand price artificially, either.

Sometimes when a need (for instance, for education) forms an element in demands, a price can be charged to cover costs though with less profit than when a demand of the same sort has less of the need element. The state may then step in to ensure that the demand embodying the greater need does not lose priority. A case in point is the education element that may be supplied by radio broadcasting and television. Here the performance of the (nationalized) British Broadcasting Corporation can be compared with capitalist enterprise in America.

---

embracing economic 'welfare'. Stability in performance is probably the least important of the three and is given, like the philosophical criterion, a range of marks 0–1, instead of 0–2.

Revenue sufficient to cover costs is, under nationalization, obtained by an annual licence per instrument. Under American capitalist broadcasting, revenue is obtained solely from advertisers paying for time. No doubt the American procedure pays best and the producers get a bigger rate of profit. But advertisers paying the piper, literally call the tune. And what a tune! Nationalized broadcasting was introduced into Britain by a Conservative government in 1926 and has been repeatedly investigated by officially appointed but independent committees. The Sykes committee of 1923, the Crawford committee of 1925, and the Ullswater committee of 1935 were finally succeeded by the committee presided over by Lord Beveridge, reporting in 1951 and by Sir R. Pilkington reporting in 1962. After lengthy consideration of evidence on the American commercial system of sponsored programmes —some fifty-five pages of the final report are devoted to it—the Beveridge committee of eleven, though differing in many other respects, decided, with only one dissentient, against this form of private capitalist enterprise. Even the dissentient fully accepted 'the necessity for one public service system, one of the functions of which would be to cater for minorities'.[1] The committee found less objection to the proportion of time the consumer had to listen to advertising than the sponsoring of the *bulk* of all listening time by advertisers.

We reject any suggestion that broadcasting in Britain should become financially dependent on sponsoring as it is wholly in the United States, and largely in Canada and Australia. Sponsoring carried to this point puts the control of broadcasting ultimately in the hands of people whose interest is not broadcasting but the selling of some other goods and services or the propagation of particular ideas. If the people of any country want broadcasting they must be prepared to pay for it as listeners or viewers; they must not ask for it for nothing as an accompaniment of advertising some other commodity.[2]

(B) *The test of consumer sovereignty*
Some economists make consumer sovereignty the main criterion, often forgetful that they are only speaking of the sovereignty of an individual demand backed by ability to pay. But undoubtedly, if it does not necessarily come first among the criteria of a nation's industry, consumer's sovereignty is one of the most important. How do capitalists (small and large in size), nationalized and co-operative industry, compare in satisfying the consumer's demands in quantity, quality and price now and in the future?

The record of the two capitalist alternatives can be briefly summed up since much of the argument has already (Chapters II and III) appeared in detail. Small-size capitalism by competition forces prices

[1] Report, p. 205.
[2] Op. cit., p. 49–50.

down close to the cost of production, but owing to the small-scale operation usually found in small plants those costs may be high. Competition between small entrepreneurs gives the consumer a wide choice of products but all varieties may suffer by the small capitalist's limited resources; he may not, for instance, have a research or design staff. The larger capitalist, thanks to the economies of large-scale operation possible to him, may have low costs; but if there are only a few large producers in an industry an oligopolistic situation may allow a large margin of profit almost to offset the low costs in the price to the consumer. Though the range of choice to the consumer is limited, the quality of the goods within the range may be high owing to specialized research and design. The large producer tends, however, to increase his costs by advertising extensively so as to create a monopolistic private goodwill and a market of his own. This may raise prices to the consumer for goods he is artificially 'made' to want. The tendency for large capitalist firms to generate a monopolistic situation discussed in Chapter III may not only raise price to the consumer and mislead him, but may result in restriction of supply so that some workers are unemployed and some consumers completely unsatisfied.

Turning to the alternative of industry governed by consumers' co-operation, evidence was put forward in 1938 by Carr-Saunders, Florence and Peers, that while prices to the consumer might sometimes be higher than capitalist market prices, when dividends on purchases were subtracted they were in the net result lower. Since then owing largely to the competition from the multiple chain-stores the consumer has looked more at prices and less at dividends.[1] The co-operative societies have avoided charging above the market though this has involved lowering dividend rates. The average rate of dividend on purchases was in 1935 about 1s. 10d. in the £, but fell in 1949 to 1s. 4½d., in 1957 to 1s. 0¾d. and in 1962 to 10¼d. The rates have always varied widely from society to society and region to region. In 1962 it was 1s. 3¼d. in the £ in Scotland, 6d. in the south western region.

In spite of the lower than market prices after subtraction of dividend, co-operative retail sales do not seem to have grown relatively to total national retail sales. In 1956 the Gaitskell Independent Commission quoted 11·1 per cent as the co-operative proportion,[2] but by 1961 the proportion was 10·3 per cent and between then and 1966 official index numbers indicate that while retail sales generally rose in value by 25 per cent, co-operative sales only rose by 6·0 per cent.[3] *Production* by consumers' co-operative societies of goods for sale in their retail shops

---

[1] *Co-operative Independent Commission Report*, 1958, pp. 27–30.
[2] Op. cit., p. 4.
[3] Annual Abstract of Statistics, 1967, p. 322. See also my *Atlas of Economic Structure and Policies*, Fig. 24.

seems to have fallen even more severely than retail sales. The number employed, adumbrated earlier (p. 276), tells the tale over the decade 1958–68.

Thousands employed in	1958	1968
Co-operative retail societies	272·8	203·1
Co-operative wholesale societies production and services	51·5	34·7

When co-operative retail sales are analysed by commodities, as the Gaitskell committee analysed them for 1955, it appears from the co-operative shares of national totals that they were particularly successful in milk (a 34·2 per cent share), coal (a 14·9 per cent share) and bread and flour confectionery (a 14·6 per cent share). They were least successful in household durables (a 7·6 per cent share), in clothing and footwear (a 6·1 per cent share), in chocolate and sugar confectionery and ice-cream (a 2·4 per cent share). The type of work, again, seems to determine what form of organization operates or, conversely, the form of organization determines what type of work is performed. Co-operative organization seems to specialize in uniform common daily needs, and relatively to fail where durable goods with pretensions to design require able and imaginative management. With rising standards of living and a wider, 'choosier' clientèle, design of goods—and of shops—needs more attention.

A further set of figures brings out the wider extent and perhaps greater choosiness of the potential co-operative clientele. The low proportion of co-operative compared to total national sales is in strong contrast to the proportion of co-operative members compared to the total number of families in the nation—a proportion becoming higher every year. There were in round numbers 7,500,000 members of co-operative consumers' societies in 1935, and 10,200,000 in 1948 and 12,800,000 in 1968. Allowing for the occasional occurrence of more than one member per household and of membership of a single person in more than one society, probably over a half of the nation's households in 1935 and nearer two-thirds in 1948 and well over two-thirds in 1968, contained co-operative members. Two-thirds of the nation's households buying co-operatively only a tenth of the type of goods offered in co-operative shops means that the average co-operative member chooses to make only a small proportion of her purchases in her 'own' shop.

Accepting co-operative prices minus dividend as lower than competitors', co-operative consumers, able and apparently willing to compare co-operative with other channels, thus cannot be altogether satisfied with the service, or the quality of the goods sold, in co-operative shops. Service is somewhat difficult to compare objectively,[1] but since a proportion of co-operative sales are co-operative products and co-operative products are not sold at all in non-co-operative shops attention may be directed to co-operative productions. The causes of failure to keep up co-operative production, let alone increase it, may be sought perhaps in the quality of the product as judged by the taste of the consumer—even the co-operative consumer! The department of Commerce of the University of Birmingham organized in 1936 a panel of consumers who were asked to judge thirteen products of the co-operative wholesale society and thirteen similar products of capitalist forms selling for the same price on the same market. The pairs of similar products were chosen as the only products without makers' identification marks. These products were three varieties of biscuit, two of jam, one of margarine, cheese, tea, cocoa, malted milk cocoa, canned peaches, canned pears and a soap powder. When they had duly tasted (or used) these products the panel as a whole were in favour of more of the non-co-operative than co-operative products.[2] There were only four products where a majority preferred the co-operative alternative and nine where a majority (in two cases a large majority) preferred the non-co-operative product. Breaking down the panel into groups of different class, this preference for non-co-operative products was strongest in the lower income groups. In the largest of these groups the majority preferred ten of the non-co-operative products and only three of the co-operative alternatives. A middle-class majority voted for the co-operative product in the case of six, and for the non-co-operative product in the case of seven articles. Majorities even among co-operative enthusiasts of the Women's Guild preferred, out of the thirteen choices, six non-co-operative alternatives with six co-operative—with voting tied on one product.

The limits of production by consumers' co-operation to satisfy consumer demand should not perhaps be judged merely by its record in Britain. Owing partly to the strong defence measures of the private monopolist and partly to unenterprising leadership and a constitution ill-thought out, the chief co-operative producer, the 'C.W.S.', has not fought in the interests of the consumer the monopolies and near-monopolies that appear to exist in such household articles as matches, sugar, or electric fittings. Nor has the British consumer movement as a whole tried to educate the consumer, as might have been expected, in

[1] Consumers' reactions were canvassed in 1937, see Carr-Saunders, Florence and Peers, op. cit., pp. 382–93.
[2] Carr-Saunders, Florence and Peers, 1935, op. cit., pp. 449–51. The panel was not large, sixty households with an average of 1·6 informants per household, and the co-operative societies were advised to repeat and amplify the experiment, but no results have been reported.

food values and other 'values for money'. Consumer research has been left to the independent Consumers' Association.

Infraction of consumer's sovereignty and bureaucratic indifference to his demand has been one of the main results expected and recorded of nationalization by some economists.[1] Often, however, there is some confusion between events resulting from state government of a particular industry, which is here under discussion, and events resulting from the overall planning control and supervision by the state to be discussed shortly. Most industries and services hitherto taken over by the state had previously been ruled by large-scale and often monopolistic capitalism, and the consumer has only suffered in sovereignty in so far as a public monopoly excludes more potential substitutes, and is more directly enforcible than a private monopoly, which may have some potential competition in the offing. To safeguard consumer interests nationalized industries have, as already described, set up consumers' councils to advise the Minister or the board. The actual influence these councils exercise is doubtful. They were designed as a place of last resort to be appealed to after the consumer, who felt himself aggrieved over supposed poor service or injustice, had complained stage by stage, first to his particular supplier and, if still not satisfied, to any local supervising official (e.g. the local fuel overseers) who might exist. Further grievances sometimes arise over such an official's high-hatting! Experience is that few private consumers appeal at all to the councils, and that those that do, jump the preliminary stages.

Members of the councils are all nominated, and therefore in a weaker position than if elected by constituents. Councils are relatively strong where members, however indirectly, represent the consumers and not the ministry or the public corporation, and the consumers are organized, like the traders using transport or the industrialists at the next stage of production (e.g. metal firms using iron, steel or coal). Councils are relatively weak wherever the consumers represented are unorganized or occasional (like air passengers). The coal set-up has in fact two consumers' councils, the domestic and the industrial, and the latter has proved the stronger or at least the less weak. The more strongly entrenched *industrial* consumer has, also, other ways of exerting pressure than through consumer councils. His associations or chambers of commerce can get up meetings of protest and can send deputations to Ministers—can, in fact, 'lobby'. It is not his grievances that want more publicity and 'pressure' behind them but those of the private consumer—who is not organized to elect representatives. Apart from their structure the function of the consumers' councils is misconceived.

[1] E.g. Von Mises, *Bureaucracy*, 1945.

It is doubtful how far any council of people unpaid and busy in other matters and with little paid staff can possibly enter into all the necessary details of private grievances and technical adjustment. A consumer council can advise on general matters of price and quantity, quality (e.g. dirt in the coal) and distribution of goods, and can usefully participate in discussion of new plans. For adjudication of grievances, however, a quasi-legal tribunal is more logical though time-consuming.

Originally the advocates of nationalization thought that since in Britain the common man appoints Parliament which appoints the cabinet, which includes the Minister who is responsible for the government of a nationalized industry, it followed that the interests of the common man would be met both as a worker and as a consumer. This chain of logic has not held and after nationalization workers certainly remain just as much, if not more, organized in trade unions. They exert plenty of pressure to raise wages, while keeping traditional trade practices, thus forcing up prices. It is only fair that a corresponding pressure be organized to keep down prices on behalf of the consumer. In short, nationalization is only remotely democratic and cannot do without organization to safeguard either workers' or consumers' interests. It is time to discuss this criterion of democracy.

(C) *The test of democracy*
How have the alternative forms of industrial government behaved on the score of democracy—government by and for the people—now and in the future? Small-size capitalism with its diffusion of rule among many entrepreneurs is, we have said, more democratic than large-scale capitalism with rule concentrated among boards of directors and a few general managers, and if it were not for the parallel development of large-size trade unionism, large-size capitalism would in fact be highly autocratic. But all large organization tends to be undemocratic in the sense of presenting impersonal, remote control, away from and not by the people. This result is shared by nationalized industries.

Among the arguments advanced for nationalization by British trade unions and members of the Labour party was the democratic possibilities of workers' control or at least of better industrial relations and morale. It was thought that workers would be more satisfied and energetic if they knew they were not working for the profit of the 'B—— capitalist'. Experience of nationalization has in this respect been, so far, disappointing. Grievances, absenteeism and strikes, official or unofficial (and without strike pay), have continued to be frequent. The worker's morale apparently suffers as much from relations with a remote bureaucracy not 'exploiting' him for profit as it does from relations, though close, with a capitalist. Some exceptions to this disappointing experience can be found in the nationalized public utilities.

In the electrical supply industry, for instance, an agreement was drawn up in 1963 between the Electricity Council and the Electrical trades union giving all workers staff status and reducing hours of work, particularly overtime.[1]

Of the four possible forms of government, consumers' co-operation which, in its retail organization, is often small-scale, is the most closely democratic in the sense that the ruling group is immediately sensitive to the consumers it represents and that the workers are by no means unrepresented. A co-operative shop assistant or clerk can be a member of his society and thus join in discussions of the conditions and terms of his own employment and vote for the management committee. In some societies he even sits on the committee.

The criterion of democracy points to government *for* the people as well as *by* the people. In this respect large-scale capitalism with its tendency to monopoly has been criticized from all sides, by Jeffersonian democrats and Adam Smithian political economists as well as by socialists. Clearly consumers' co-operation in the small area within which it operates cannot prevent the misdirection of national resources; and it is only by controlling the basic industries that nationalization can contribute to a balanced economy and a direction for the benefit of the whole body politic. Even so balance and direction are more easily achieved by overall state planning and supervision than by state operation—nationalization—of particular industries. The obvious occasions when capitalism is admitted to fail in national direction for the people is during war, threat of war or the aftermath of war. In Britain in 1914–19 and 1939–45, and America in 1917–19 and 1941–5 the state had to intervene to direct resources into war production and away from lines possibly more profitable to capital; but this state intervention took the form not of nationalization but of state control, described later, over price, production and consumption—public planning and supervision of private production, not direct public production.

Apart from war emergencies, state intervention is also required, as pointed out already, to safeguard the interest of the people in the future. Where particular industries are concerned either with long deferred profit like forestry, or with too high an immediate profit like oil, nationalization may well meet the democratic criterion more simply than capitalist government supervised by the state. Other things equal it is simpler to have one organization than two—one to act and the other to watch that it acts in the required direction.

Care for the interests of the whole people at a future time is paralleled logically with care for the interests of the body of people who live in places where costs are naturally high. The outstanding example is the

[1] R. Kelf-Cohen, *Twenty Years of Nationalization*, p. 257.

rural population who, owing to the high cost of supply where density of population is low, may under capitalism have to pay more for electricity, gas, telephone installation or piped water supply than the city dwellers. Often the common man in the country may not, owing to their unprofitability, get these utilities *at all*. The urbanite and sub-urbanite in America and Britain does not always appreciate that the benefits of 'progress' have not reached many of his country countrymen.

The distribution of prices per unit showed that in Britain before nationalization, inhabitants of large towns (i.e. county and other boroughs) tended to pay less per unit for their gas and electricity, than those in the less densely populated urban districts.[1] Taking the rate of a 1s. 0d. per therm as a standard price for gas in 1944–5, 66 per cent of county boroughs and 41 per cent of other (mostly smaller) boroughs had prices below this, but only 36 per cent of low density urban districts enjoyed these lower prices. Under nationalized operation such as that of the American or British Post Office, the same priced stamps take letters to and from rural areas as between city areas, though rural collection and delivery is far more costly per letter.

§ 6. ECONOMIC PERFORMANCE: THE TESTS OF EFFICIENCY, STABILITY AND PROGRESS

Efficiency is a means to philosophic, economic and political ends, already discussed. It can be measured for single operations or single product industries by productivity or output per man with some allowance for differences in mechanization and capital 'inputs'. But changes in circumstances may often mask the differential effect. Thus output of coal per man was higher and absenteeism lower in 1949 under nationalization than in 1945 before nationalization, but the difference may not have been the result of nationalization—*post hoc* is not necessarily *propter hoc*. In fact productivity was rising and absenteeism falling in all British industries at the time, and the gradual 'settling down' of labour and organization after the war had probably more effect than nationalization.

Most manufacturing industries and firms have a diversified mixed production which prevents the use of physical productivity as a test of their efficiency. To the capitalist, efficiency is normally measured by profit or at least the avoidance of loss. Profit is the difference, it may be repeated, between total revenue (or gross sales) and total costs. Provided the value of sales are not high because of unnecessarily high prices, because, in short, of exploitation of the consumer; or costs low because of exploitation of the worker, the margin of profit or loss is a useful overall test of comparative efficiency for all forms of industrial

[1] Glaisyer *et al.*, *County Town*, 1946, p. 176.

government *that charge a market price*. Since profits is a word with a long history and with deep implications in economic theory which are irrelevant here (and is anyway inclined to stink in certain nostrils) the difference of revenue and cost might be called surplus as by the co-operative societies or just the revenue over costs 'balance'. More important than the question of its name is that of the amount as well as the rate of profit. A high rate of profit on a small output may be less 'efficient' than a high total amount of profit due to a medium or low rate on a large output.

Profits obtained by monopolies or near monopolies exploiting the consumer have already been considered. Here it is profits, surplus or balance obtained by low costs that will be under discussion. Cost tends usually to be lower, we have found (Chapter II, §§ 2–3), where scale of production and the size of plant and firm, favouring large-scale 'operation', are large. The larger-scale capitalist and the larger nation-alized organizations thus have, other things equal, an advantage over the small capitalist.

As between large-scale capitalism and large-scale, if not larger-scale, nationalization, the edge in efficiency depends mainly on whether the industry is of a nature requiring routine or enterprising manage-ment. In America, state and federal appointments are still apparently thought of as liable to graft, bribery, corruption, nepotism, and patronage. This would have appeared self-evident to an eighteenth-century or even early nineteenth-century Englishman, but is quite beside the mark in twentieth-century Britain. Since the middle of the nineteenth century, appointments to the civil service have been by examination; and though sometimes tempted by outsiders, and particu-larly rank outsiders,[1] the British civil servant has proved himself honest and honourable. It is not on the score of dishonesty or lack of intelligence that the British official can be considered inefficient, but rather in his lack of enterprise or, if he is enterprising in early life, be-cause of the frustration bureaucracy imposes on his original enterprise.[2] The ex-administrators in positions of top rule in British nationalized industries are not of the old entrepreneur nor yet of the executive radical replanner types, but are rather experienced in policies of fair compro-mise, in co-ordination and in the supervision of day to day or month to month routine. The notion of efficiency here widens from current balancing of revenue with costs at maximum level of production, to include the test of progress that will be taken up shortly.

Co-operative retailing even though small-scale is found to have

[1] See the report of the Lynskey Tribunal and of the Committee on Intermediaries, H.M.S.O. 1950, Cmd. 7904.
[2] See Sir Arthur Salter in *Problems of Nationalized Industry*, 1952 (ed. Robson), pp. 228–38.

comparatively low costs per unit of sale in rents, advertising and finance due to the loyalty of the customers in seeking out co-operative shops, even if not at main street corners, short-circuiting high pressure salesmanship, and providing sufficient capital (in the form of loans, dividends left on deposit and shares) at a low fixed interest.[1] Co-operative government also *appears* economical in administrative cost; the salaries paid for the management of an equivalent volume of business are on a much lower level than under capitalism and nationalization. But this policy, traditional and ideological in origin, of greater equality in salaries and wages is in the event probably the reverse of efficient. Managers not only unenterprising but inexpert are (in two senses) 'secured'.

This fact peeps out in the brand-names with which the manufactures of the Scottish and English co-operative wholesale societies are baptized. Scottish 'Cogent' cigarettes suggest too rational and dry an argument for relaxation; English Jayce (J.C.) cigarettes, named by and after the factory manager, suggest nothing in particular unless blasphemy. 'Territorial' sauce has an earthy savour; 'I and U' shoes bring to mind being in debt; while 'Federal' bicycles suggest a certain lack of unity. 'Lokreel' tinned goods insinuates something that looks real but is not. These may be personal subjective judgments but, after all, the consumer *is* a person and one very subject to suggestion. The invention of brand-names requires a knowledge of consumers' psychological reactions which managers of works (to whom the societies leave the decision) do not necessarily possess;[2] an administration aiming purely for market efficiency would delegate branding to market and psychological experts.

Though low paid per unit of time, co-operative administration, at least in manufacture, cannot be assumed more immediately efficient than capitalist in cost per output. The implication for progress will be considered later. But it remains true that co-operative trading is comparatively efficient on the score of obtaining land and capital cheap, and of low advertising costs.

By the test of *stability* the record of small scale capitalist industry is not satisfactory. The nineteenth and twentieth centuries, and possibly the eighteenth too, were subject to trade cycles, punctuated by periodic financial crises and industrial depressions culminating almost in a breakdown in 1929–33, when industrial output halved in the United States. So powerful was the impression made even in Britain where the drop in output was less severe, that most current and subsequent schemes for state planning took high and stable employment as the

---

[1] See Carr-Saunders, Florence and Peers, op. cit., pp. 362–82.

[2] The psychological build-up of trade-marks and advertisements was pointed out early enough in Graham Wallas' *Human Nature in Politics*, 1916, pp. 88–90.

main purpose of regulating or superseding capitalism.[1] There is always a question whether the instability of the economy in these centuries of the predominance of small-scale capitalism was due to capitalism or to the monetary policy of the state, or to the unavoidable implications of technological progress. Speculations on the causes, cure and prevention of trade fluctuations fill many a bookshelf and the nationalization of British basic industries was announced explicitly as undertaken to avoid instability in the economy. Neither the state nor consumers' co-operation have, hitherto, governed fluctuating industries such as the manufacture of durable capital goods, or at least not for a sufficient period, to be able to judge from results. In any case, if we believe the Keynesian thesis officially adopted by Britain in the White Paper on the Full Employment Policy issued by the Churchill coalition government in 1944, stability can be secured by state planning, control and supervision without the nationalization of particular industries. Mere state control of capitalism cannot, however, initiate progress.

Progress, and growth generally with or without periodic depressions, is a test of performance which small and large capitalism have met in a high degree. Under the capitalist regime output increased at a pace probably never experienced before in world history. The progress under small-firm capitalism in Britain before 1870 resulted in a high rate of increase in population with a slight increase in the standards of living of the masses. In the years since 1870, capitalism in Britain and America has been associated with a lower rate of population increase but with a faster rise of manufacturing output per worker per hour than in the earlier years of capitalism.[2]

Colin Clark gives the real product of manufacturing per man-hour as rising in Britain in the thirty-four years from 1873 to 1907[3] by 48 per cent and rising in America in the twenty-eight years from 1879 to 1907 by 69 per cent. In the next thirty-one years, from 1907 to 1938, the rise was 163 per cent in America and 100 per cent in Britain.[4] The pace apparently quickened in both countries and in the latter period the rises were equivalent to 3·1 per cent and 2·3 per cent year by year cumulatively. After the disturbance of the war of 1939–45 this sort of pace was resumed. Contrary to general opinion, official index numbers show the year to year increases of productivity per man-hour in manufacturing between 1948 and 1968 to have averaged much the same in the British economy (mixed by then) and the American at 2·7 to 3·0 per cent.

[1] E.g. Barbara Wootton, *Plan or No Plan*, 1934. Keynes and Henderson, *Can Lloyd George Do It?* 1929.

[2] *Long-Term Economic Growth*, U.S. Department of Commerce, 1966, pp. 190–1.

[3] Data is for 1870–6 and 1904–10 respectively, of which 1873 and 1907 are the mid-most years. *The Conditions of Economic Progress*, 1951, pp. 266, 269.

[4] In 1935–8 Rostas calculated the American man-hour productivity level as between two and three times the British. See below, p. 321, footnote.

In both countries the rate of progress is seldom at a constant pace year by year but the trend is fairly persistently upward. Accompanying this increase in manufacturing productivity per worker but at a lower rate went an increase in real income per head and the average standard of living. This rising standard is reflected in falling general and infant death rates and a sharp drop in the proportion of families below the primary poverty line.[1]

The increase in productivity and income per head occurred with a continuing rise in numbers of heads, so that the economies can be considered to have made for growth in two dimensions. Population grew but industrial progress developed faster and industry was not only able to support that growth but to support the growing numbers at a higher standard of living.[2]

This progress in industrial production, in population and in standards of living is associated with the step by step adoption by capitalist industry of technical inventions instead of sticking to traditional

[1] Rowntree, *Poverty and Progress*, 1939; Florence, *Labour*, 1948, Chapter XIV.

[2] This reference to the relation of progress to population is made necessary owing to the inferences unfortunately drawn by a number of economic textbooks and monographs. In his *Trends in Output and Employment*, Stigler speaks (National Bureau of Economic Research, 1947, p. 56) of the 'scientific fate' of the Malthusian doctrine which he enunciates as 'the theory that the mass of mankind in advanced countries could live well only if the population did not tend to grow rapidly'. Malthus's actual wording of his own thesis (Edition 2, Book I, Chapters I and II) was that population has 'a constant tendency to increase beyond the means of subsistence', and 'invariably increases where the means of subsistence increase, unless prevented by some very powerful and obvious checks'. Checks to population he classified as positive, e.g. death from famine and disease, and preventive.

Stigler considers Malthus's theory 'wrong in at least some respects even in the early decades (population grew at a large, relatively constant geometrical rate in England), and it was wrong in all important respects by the middle of the (nineteenth) century'. For some obscure reason Malthus's essay, if read at all, is read only in the first not the subsequent editions, when the preventive check, originally examined in England, was fitted into the main argument. Writing after the returns of the Census of 1811 had shown a greatly accelerated rate of progress in England, Malthus considered that, so far from confuting him, they 'furnished another striking instance of this readiness with which population starts forward, under almost any weight when the resources of a country are rapidly increased'. Where the means of subsistence greatly increased as in Britain 1760–1850 and America 1899–1939, population, according to, and not in spite of, Malthus, will be enabled greatly to increase. Whether the increase is right up to the means of subsistence, or short of it (thus allowing higher standards of living), depends on whether positive or preventive checks are at work. For at least three quarters of the world the checks remain positive as they did almost everywhere in Malthus's time. For western civilization the checks are of the type Malthus named preventive, and social progress can follow from technical industrial progress. In what sense has Malthus's theory suffered any scientific fate except (see my *Overpopulation, Theory and Statistics*, 1926) verification? Incidentally Malthus was no mere theoretician, as Stigler appears to suggest, but subjected his hypotheses to twenty-two chapters of inductive research on the 'less civilized parts of the world', 'past times', and 'the different states of modern Europe'.

305

routines. In short, capitalism, pure or mixed, has proved a form of industrial government revolutionary in its policy, and the phrase 'industrial revolution' first used in France is in this sense apt—a phrase which has justly caught on.[1] In the small scale phase of capitalism, one entrepreneur in any industry would, by his competition and cutting of costs and prices, force new techniques on his rivals or bankrupt them but he might not be able to finance the costly equipment required. In the later phase several of the larger corporations or joint stock companies have engaged in research to improve their techniques. Provided their policy was not monopolistic and restrictive of output (or of new equipment) in order to obtain higher profit margins (or extended use of old capital assets), they have tended progressively to lower real costs.

Nationalized industries are on the largest possible scale, a nation-wide monopoly in fact. Their top controllers we have surmised will not deliberately restrict output or raise price to obtain monopoly profit. But they may not readily abandon old equipment, and are not likely to be particularly enterprising even in the current running of industry.

The government of a maximum-sized public monopoly certainly requires more, for progress, than honest routine management with some aptitude for day-to-day or month-to-month adjustment to meet daily and monthly problems and crises. Progress requires long-run plans and the taking of certain risks. The constitution of some of the nationalized industries allow for a planning body, or a director as differentiated from the other executives. For efficiency and progress such a body or person should be devoted to general long-term policy and the reorganization and re-equipment to achieve it, and should not be involved in specialized current departmental duties.

The Gas Council has a planning director. Gas supply, based originally on the coal-using town gasworks, is one of the nationalized industries which has in recent years faced scientific innovation. Besides two minor developments, the use of naphtha and the importation of liquefied natural gas from Algeria, two major developments have offered the chance of considerable progress: the use of oil in place of coal for gas generation and the supply of the natural gas found under the North Sea. The nationalized gas industry adopted these new techniques fairly rapidly and since 1962 a remarkable upturn has occurred in its sales. Between 1956 and 1961 total sales were static—2,590 million therms was the amount in both years. But in each year starting in 1962 therms sold have mounted steadily—2,723, 2,894, 2,998, 3,310, 3,629 million. To reduce cost by quantity purchase the Gas Council has contracted to buy sufficient natural gas from the exploratory companies to abolish all their 'gasworks'; and this planning probably will necessitate a great expansion in markets, domestic and industrial.

[1] Usher, *Industrial History of England*, 1921, p. 249.

The most familiar case of planning in a British nationalized industry comes not from production or public utilities, in which we are primarily interested, but from the railways. Dr (now Lord) Beeching was charged in 1960 by the Minister of Transport with planning and carrying out measures of efficiency and economy, in the face of competition from motor buses, private motor cars and air transport. The strategy which might end in reducing the losses had to be a sort of rearguard action; and much railway track and many stations were planned to be abandoned particularly in rural areas, owing to paucity of custom.

Probably only a nationalized monopoly could select rationally what to close and what to keep. Certainly when compared to the somewhat chaotic situation in America where many railroad companies appear deliberately to discourage passengers, it is not plausible to lay inefficiency entirely at the door of nationalization. The British railway plan of rationalizing the passenger trade is to concentrate on service between the centres of large cities that are not too far apart. The railways usually have unimpeded access to these centres, thus saving time compared to air service with only suburban airfield facilities, or compared to road transport, public or private, forced to travel through congested streets.

Considerable objective evidence has been published, however, which shows that consumers' co-operation is not particularly progressive or planful. Co-operative societies have not been pioneers in starting new lines of products or in opening up new forms of organization such as fixed price bazaars of Woolworth type, or large supermarkets for which a 'common man' market was found by capitalist enterprise, to be eminently suited. Co-operative lack of enterprise and slow growth, and poor performance generally, has been attributed to (a) low capital investment, (b) the quality of management initiative and (c) much small-scale organization.

Over and above these three factors the probability should be considered that maximizing dividends on sales is a weak incentive for growth. A high margin on sales can, after all, be obtained by restricting sales to those where the costs are lowest, for instance where no overtime need be paid or no additional sales force hired.[1]

(A) A general quantitative test of enterprise and progress in production lies in the fixed capital an organization is prepared physically to invest at risk. Here the balance sheets of the manufacturing co-operative wholesale societies compared to capitalist firms showed in 1936 (at a time of considerable unemployment) a high liquidity preference and a correspondingly low preference for fixed capital, that boded ill, and, in the event, has turned out ill for the expansion and progress of their

[1] See my article on co-operatives in the *International Encyclopedia of the Social Sciences*, New York, 1966.

industries. In their huge holdings of government stock the co-operative manufacturing societies were found comparable to the capitalist joint stock banks, with their large holdings in easily marketable securities, rather than to capitalist manufacturers. Admittedly, co-operative societies must hold reserves to meet their members' claims, but the banking standards of liquidity adopted betrays over-cautiousness in expanding the means of production—particularly when, as already mentioned, many private monopolies in consumers' goods remained unchallenged. The Independent Commission (pp. 135ff.) also showed capital investment to be weak and weakening, in the low proportion of surplus ploughed back. Societies can no longer rely, in view of the relatively low interest they pay, on the old rate of accretions to members' capital.

(B) The management procedure of the British co-operative societies raises in an acute form the possible clashes between principles of democracy, or of supposed democracy, and principles of progress and enterprise. A democratic society with equality of opportunity and status, where the ablest can get to the top and business is not looked down upon, is likely to be proved industrially more efficient than an aristocratic society such as eighteenth-century England, where positions are filled by patronage and nepotism and no one 'who is anyone' engages in trade.

On the other hand, popular elections and mass-quizzing of managers; appointment by seniority and promotion from below and not by attainments; little sacking and no really high salaries (compared with capitalist counterparts), though acclaimed as democratic, do not result in enterprise. The wholesale societies' full-time directors are elected, and few, if any, managers (apart from technical experts) are appointed from outside the co-operative ranks. Since these ranks are recruited, in the first place, from school children between 15 and 17 who have failed to get awards or scholarships to the university, it follows that co-operative management tends to be 'inbred', and inbred from the less intelligent part of the population. Inbreeding is in itself a source of stagnation since it prevents the interchange of new ideas and tends to create a little world of self-satisfied club-members; but co-operative inbreeding of managers is positively dysgenic. No sufficiently high salaries are offered at top grades; so that wherever some intelligent school-child does by accident fall through the rungs of the scholarship ladder, misses education after sixteen and is thus acceptable as a co-operative employee, 'he'[1] is liable to be attracted away to capitalist or state employment.

---

[1] 'He', since the wholesale co-operatives have few if any women among their managers or even directors.

(C) A dilemma familiar also in local government is that the most democratic societies are small but they are probably less efficient. 'Potentially active public opinion', to avoid domination by a clique or sectional interest, requires 'that the public for which the society caters should have a measure of group consciousness and civic sense. . . . There is, in fact, an optimum size for retail societies in relation to effective democratic supervision, as well as the more familiar optimum which is related to technical, managerial and financial factors.'[1] The optimum size for democracy is likely to be much smaller than the optimum for these economic factors—perhaps a society under 2,000 operating in one, not a series of towns. But this is not the size of societies which is increasing. Must co-operative democracy be sacrificed to efficiency?

§ 7. SUMMARY: OVERALL STATE PLANNING AND CONTROL

The many considerations that enter into the comparison of alternative forms of industrial government—meeting of needs, consumers' sovereignty, democracy, current efficiency, stability and progress or, at least, growth—can best be pulled together by returning to Table VIB and noting the marks tentatively assigned there to each alternative government under each of the six criteria. Tentative is the operative word, and these marks, based on the preceding discussion, are added merely to 'point up' the argument. More experience has yet to be gathered of the working of the nationalized industries and the experience of all the alternatives has yet to be far more systematically measured, analysed and interpreted.

Tentatively pointed and marked up, the argument embracing all criteria adds up to the sum of five marks for government of industries by small-scale capitalism and five by large-scale capitalism, five by consumers' co-operation and five by nationalization. A nicely balanced condition but, to follow one of the main themes of this book, the total of marks would vary with the type of work engaged upon, such as Table VIA gives in detail. Needs, for instance, can only be granted free where the activity is nationalized and financed out of taxation. The very significance of a mixed economy is to be able to fit the form of government to the job in hand.

Practical economists and the business community may, indeed, regard the philosophic and political criteria as overweighted or as too imponderable altogether for putting into the scales. Adding only the marks awarded the more measurable and ponderable economic and business considerations included in Pigou's *Economic Welfare*, in the 2nd, 4th, 5th and 6th rows of Table VIc, the sum is four for government

[1] Carr-Saunders, Florence and Peers, op. cit., p. 291.

of manufacturing industries by small-scale, five by large-scale capitalism, two and a half by consumer co-operation, three by nationalization.

This book does not purport to deal with the whole economy of the two nations but only with the structure and government of their industries. Consequently the task of comparing alternative governments for industry may be completed in the last column of Table VIB with only a very brief reminder that the state government, even though it does not nationalize a single industry, may yet plan, control and supervise the whole or parts of the industrial structure.[1]

Planning is perhaps best defined in broad outline by first pointing to its opposite, the market mechanism, whereby, to quote Adam Smith, 'every individual ... neither intends to promote the public interest, nor knows how much he is promoting it. ... He intends only his own gain; and ... is in this ... led by an invisible hand to promote an end which was no part of his intention.'[2] By contrast, national planning is an intention to promote the public interest by the more or less visible hand of the state. In its fully-fledged form it is an acknowledgment of intentions embodied in pre-arranged tasks, based on knowledge of existing conditions and controlled or carried out by an organized structure.[3]

Even in the hey-day of laissez-faire the behaviour of individuals in pursuit of their private gain on the market was not left entirely uncontrolled and unplanned. The hand of the state, though in action, was then almost invisible, however, and tried to control by inducing individuals to behave in certain ways rather than to coerce or prohibit. Such state control as was used was exercised, both in Britain and America, on the general economy mainly by monetary and banking policy acting through devices such as bank rates; and on parts of the economy by indirect taxation. Monetary incentives or deterrents to enterprise and investment were usually intended to stabilize the economy and revive it in time of financial crisis and trade slump. Today, state planning is more visible and often coercive. Indirect taxation of luxuries has been much increased and also subsidies granted on the necessaries to life and efficiency. The devices and means adopted are not confined to incentives and deterrents in the hope that certain quantitative results will thereby be achieved, but consist in the direct setting up of quantitative rations, allocations, targets, quotas and specific price floors and ceilings enforced by cards, licences, permits issued by visible persons in authority.

[1] In *Industry and the State* (1957) I attempt an all-round view of the various contacts in the United Kingdom of the state-government with industry.
[2] *Wealth of Nations*, 1776, Book IV, Chapter II.
[3] See Baykov, *Soviet Economic System*, 1946, Chapter XX (on general planning). His words 'aim' and 'machinery' are equivalent to our 'intention' and 'structure'.

In Britain contrary to much of received opinion, there has been no fully fledged long-run plan. In spite of books published with titles such as the *Pleasures of Planning* or the *Road to Serfdom*, or *Ordeal by Planning*,[1] there has been little idea or ideology, for instance, of planning consumption generally, though (as indicated in Chapter III) this might considerably reduce costs of production and distribution. There have been specific measures of planning at moments of crisis to achieve limited ends. These measures are particularly likely to annoy and exasperate the busy intellectual class from which authors and letter-writers to the press are drawn, as taxpayers, queuers-up, form-fillers or frustrated men of private enterprise—and also to dismay them, perhaps, as social and moral philosophers. Undoubtedly there is a risk of under the counter dealings and of contact-men, five-per-centers and 'spivs', as described officially by the Lynskey Tribunal and the Report on Intermediaries.[2]

These measures of control, however, only deflect the British economy at certain points. In some years an annual economic survey was published giving the actual total expenditure of private persons or corporations and of the state for various purposes (particularly for capital re-investment), and setting tasks and targets for the following year. These targets were not very far from the actual past expenditures and their purpose was mainly just to keep the economy alive—'viable' —through an emergency by securing, for instance, dollars for the import of food and raw materials without which Britain would literally starve. British planning is thus, on the whole, marginal and defensive in its aim, not fundamental, progressive or aggressive.

Positive plans for the distribution of industries into the Development Areas (introduced by the coalition government in 1945[3]) and for the establishment of New Towns to decentralize congested cities and conurbations such as London are apparent exceptions. But even these plans though resulting directly in physical investment aim at stability or equality of employment or prevention of increasing congestion, rather than progress towards new fields of endeavour or a new social organization. And among the methods of British planning, coercion is not much used. Except during and immediately after the war, there was no direction of labour and until recently and only temporarily, no national wages policy dictated by the state. Commands to the employers and capitalist have, like the ten commandments, been negative, often merely hortative, of the thou shalt not (or please, sir, don't) order, rather than of the positive, raucous thou shalt. It is 'control' of private rather than planning of public action.

---

[1] By Horobin, Hayek, Jewkes respectively.
[2] H.M.S.O., 1950, Cmd. 7904.
[3] Distribution of Industry Act, 1945.

In America there is considerably less official talk even of limited and specific state planning and control, but over the last forty years not much less *practice* of it than in Britain. Both World Wars hit the British economy harder than the American and entailed stronger measures of state planning and control in 1914–21 and 1939–51, but the economic blizzard of 1929–34 hit America harder and entailed stronger state planning and control there and then. Writing in 1939 Lyon and Abramson in their *Government and Economic Life*[1] analysed (to quote the first section of their last chapter, p. 1,263) 'a long, intricate and shifting maze which is the relationship of government to economic life'. In the first volume they deal with overall 'governmental implementation and regulation of private enterprise as it has been applied generally to a wide range of industrial and commercial life' in America. Quite apart from the problems of labour, successive chapters deal with the role of the state in creating business corporations, bankrupting and re-organizing them, in providing a monetary mechanism, patent rights, standards, research projects and methods of disseminating knowledge; and in trying to maintain business competition as by the Federal Trade Commission. The second volume deals with state action in America for limited areas of economic life or limited time periods and occasions. Successive chapters cite, in various areas, tariff policy, the considerable regulation and supervision of public utilities and transport by the Interstate Commerce Commission, and the protection of agriculture, bituminous coal, oil and natural gas, and foods and drugs. Under 'Government on some occasions' two chapters describe the National Recovery administration of 1933 and war relationships. Finally, three chapters describe the American Government as a producer of final goods and services (admittedly less developed than in Britain) and as an agent of public relief and of social security.

As a regulator, controller and supervisor of otherwise private enterprise public authority, national or state, seems no less prevalent in America than in Britain. Most of the objectives of British and American public control of industry are the same as those already considered in the criteria for evaluating capitalism, co-operation and nationalization, and a final column can be conveniently added to Table VIB. Apposite to the criterion of individuals' needs before less-needed demands, are subsidized schemes of social security, giving individual persons money benefits at times of need, or as in Britain paying medical fees for health services and subsidizing food prices. Apposite to consumer sovereignty are policies to curb or 'bust' trusts and monopolies—policies more developed in America than in Britain.

But since 1948, and more particularly since 1956, the United

[1] Brookings Institution, 1939.

Kingdom has to some degree followed the United States, at least in curbing possible monopolies and outlawing restrictive practices (through agreements or cartel-type associations) by means of Regulatory Commissions as entered in the left hand column of Table IIIA. While in 1948 an Act of Parliament set up a Monopolies and Restrictive Practices Commission to discover the nature and scope of restrictive practices, an Act of 1956 called for registration of all such agreements and the scrutiny of individual industries by an independent judicial court. In this scrutiny considerable attention is paid to the degree of oligopoly and concentration in the industry. The law laid down certain 'gateways' through which agreements could escape condemnation. The more successful of these pleas were that the agreement defended against a predominant buyer or seller, or offered 'a specific and substantial advantage'. After the judicial court's severe handling of agreements in some industries during the first few years, many other industries voluntarily abandoned their agreements as likely to prove hopeless cases.

In 1956 the Monopolies Commission was retained to investigate single firm monopolies (as against agreements between several firms) and in 1965 the Monopolies and Mergers Act allowed the Board of Trade to stop proposed mergers and break up existing monopolies on the Commission's recommendation. The mergers liable to investigation were not only those threatening monopoly but any involving a take-over of over £5m. of assets. Yet, at the same time the government was encouraging mergers in certain industries. The dilemma of inefficient small-scale competition or large-scale monopoly referred to earlier thus raises its head in the political arena. But the state's position is logical in preferring larger scale monopolists to smaller scale oligopolists if E. A. G. Robinson's conclusion is accepted.[1]

That a group of oligopolists, each assuming that he wishes to retain his share of the market and each assuming that all the others will cut prices if necessary, to retain their shares will reach a price almost indistinguishable from that of a straight monopoly, and because they are smaller and, in some cases, on that account less efficient, a price that may well be higher than that of a unified monopoly.

Relevant to democracy in the sense of participation in industrial government *by* the people are the attempts of the state to create a structure of collective bargaining where employers and employed will have equal power, as for instance the British Joint Industrial 'Whitley' Councils. If necessary the state may participate in negotiations to maintain and keep alive the bargaining at the various stages of the procedure. The state, for instance, may, by 'conciliation', initiate

---

[1] *Scottish Journal of Political Economy*, June 1967.

discussion, may mediate in discussion between the parties, or may, at the final stage, offer to arbitrate.[1]

Relevant to democracy in the sense of government *for* the people *as a whole* are the overall state controls to safeguard the whole community and give its various classes 'fair shares' in times of war or at the crises of the aftermath of war or of post-war reconstruction, or, as in the America of 1933, to weather an economic or financial blizzard. On such occasions there is a New Deal or a Siege Economy in which the state must cope with a failure of demand, or a failure of supplies, by licensing, rationing, allocation of materials. Under capitalism without these controls or any system of priorities, the strong incentive of profit often during the crisis pulls in the direction opposed to the nation's interest. Scarce key supplies such as steel needed for armaments or the post-war construction of factories and workers' houses may be more 'profitably' used in building greyhound racing tracks or luxury hotels to rake in spare earnings and profits. It may be immediately profitable to waste natural resources and, short of nationalizing forests or oil resources or parkland, the state, looking to the future, may control their full use. State control is called in, democratically, to equalize variations in place as well as time; industries are licensed to build in depressed areas and refused licences (and materials) in full-employment areas; encouraged by financial aid in rural, discouraged in congested city or suburban areas. This physical planning includes the British trading estates and independent factories in development areas (under the Distribution of Industry Act passed by Mr Churchill's coalition government in 1945) and the New Towns with industries beyond the Green Belt round London and, lately, beyond most of the provincial conurbations' Green Belts.

Capitalism has a poor record on *stability* and many writers, as already said, have confined planning to devices against unemployment. The weight of planning organizations actually devoted to this aspect of efficiency is therefore not surprising. Since Keynes wrote his *General Theory of Employment* in 1935 the state plan almost universally adopted is that of investment in public works, or encouraging investment in private works with its budgetary counterpart of deficit finance. Public works was a policy in Roosevelt's New Deal without the theoretical foundation since supplied. No serious increase in unemployment has threatened from 1938 to 1971 for testing the full application of the theory. Instead of unemployment there has in Britain and America been the opposite cause of instability—inflation. Here the tools of state control are savings campaigns, price freezing or price-ceilings, budget surpluses, adopted in America, and, in addition in Britain subsidies to keep down the cost of food (or at least its official index), wages as well as price

[1] Florence, *Labour*, 1949, pp. 192–6.

freezings and the adjusting of investment. Public or private works will, according to the principle of the 'multiplier', not only increase earnings of the workers directly engaged, and the demand for materials, but will increase the earnings of workers on these materials, and their earnings will in turn create further demands for food, clothing and other consumer goods; and the opposite, it is held, will happen by a divisor principle. To deflate and reduce money incomes and demands chasing goods, it has been proposed that inessential investment be cut down.[1] There is this difference, however, that much new investment will be investment in more efficient machines—cutting down investment, even when deemed inessential, will thus risk flying in the face of progress and competing when armed with obsolete and worn-out equipment.

It would be a mistake to suppose that the state limits its control of capitalist efficiency to attempts at stabilization. Both the American and British governments have attempted to make capitalism currently more efficient. The state proffers help to the smaller capitalist, where, as we shall find (Chapter VII, § 2) there is a weak spot, by sponsoring organizations that will lend him capital for long or middle terms—organizations such as the American Reconstruction Finance Corporation (which has many other types of clients) or the more specialized British Industrial and Commercial Finance Corporation. The state also cajoles capitalists to standardize their products (and thus to produce on a larger scale), and otherwise to 'rationalize' itself. The success of ex-President Hoover in his standardization drive has already been mentioned (p. 95); and in Britain during the war of 1939–45 the government had, by remission of purchase tax, encouraged standardized utility clothing and furniture which the manufacturer can produce economically on a large scale. The reports of the working parties appointed by Sir Stafford Cripps, when President of the Board of Trade, had in several industries resulted in Development Councils, under the Industrial Organization Act of 1947.

These councils have not as a whole proved as useful as hoped to efficiency or progress. Most of them were soon abandoned mainly owing to opposition from small-scale producers who resented nonproducers on the council and the compulsory levy they had to pay. Some of their activities, however, have been assumed by the 'little Neddies'—the economic development committees—for the separate industries.

Finally, state-government may in theory plan and supervise *progress*. Here again the focus of action is the rate of investment, for by reason of the multiplier production can be quickly hastened as well as stabilized in this way. Technical progress is, in Russia, one of the main purposes of state planning, but in Britain and America the state confines its contribution toward general economic progress mainly to encouraging and

[1] Harrod, *John Maynard Keynes*, 1951, p. 462.

organizing technical and biological enquiry. This is particularly the case in agriculture where the prevailing small-scale capitalism fails to yield the necessary funds for research.

In short, indirect overall action is undertaken by the state to induce or coerce the existing free enterprise, price and profit system toward the main objectives aimed at (though not necessarily achieved) by *direct* nationalization; meeting needs, curbing exploitation, safeguarding the whole community at a crisis and even stimulating efficiency, stability and progress. But coercion and inducement must in the last analysis be addressed to persons and in a final chapter we will attempt realistic analysis as it affects the actual persons taking part in production.

CHAPTER VII

THE STIMULUS TO LABOUR, INVESTMENT AND ENTERPRISE

§ 1. LABOUR RELATIONS IN THE LARGER PLANT AND FIRM

WHATEVER the nature of the top-level government of industry, capitalist, nationalized or co-operative, the general trend determined by the logic of technical progress is toward large-scale operation, the large firm or unit of government and control through a hierarchy of line, functional or staff officials remote from labour at the working base of the pyramid. Labour, the middle management, and even the top level in these huge management pyramids are, however, human. Labour has been considered as a 'human factor' almost *ad nauseam*. We are familiar with the distinction between the financial or pecuniary incentive of the wage and the non-pecuniary incentives such as love of work, desire for recognition and other impulses, dispositions or attitudes dignified, in the quite recent past, with the name of instincts. The relative strength of these incentives in forwarding efficiency, and of the transpecuniary incentive of what the wage will buy have been sufficiently canvassed.[1] To what in 1924 I called the cash-nexus, the hobby-nexus and the fame-nexus[2] must, however, be added, as I suggested in 1933,[3] the crucial personal relationships of the worker to his employer and his fellow workers and neighbours generally. Elton Mayo and his associates are responsible for the acceptance of the importance of what may be called the group or gang-nexus.

The stimulus most directly affected by the large-scale organization and remote control of modern industry described earlier is clearly that of the social relation of employer and employee. The incentive to work, that is, the willingness of the worker to increase or even maintain output at lowest cost is checked at the outset as soon as he finds himself divided off, 'alienated', as a mere employee, from ownership of the products of his labour. The hard work of the peasant proprietor who is independent and his own employer and who makes his own profit grubbing up his probably ill-situated and infertile patch of ground is a commonplace; and it is held true as a general rule that the more a mere employee loses personal contact with the ownership the more indifferent he will become to the efficiency of the industrial organization and the more he

---

[1] See Florence, *Labour*, pp. 98ff.
[2] *Economics of Fatigue and Unrest*, p. 73.
[3] See Florence, 1933, p. 155.

will stick to habits, customs and conventions and resist the innovations characteristic of modern industry. Even if he is induced to adapt himself to a new technique by a higher pecuniary payment, psychological 'unrest' (now called low 'morale') will supervene and rob that new technique of much of its superior efficiency. The employee's sense of fraternity and social equality with his employer and the sense of his own dignity and self-respect tend to be lost as the size of the group enlarges and subdivides; he *identifies* himself less and less with the interests of the firm.

In the plant or organization, such as a small house-building firm employing less than 5 persons, the employer is, like the medieval master-craftsman, working side by side with his employees; he is a co-worker and 'mate' and all may identify themselves with the business. In the plant employing 6 to 20 labourers, the employer may not actually work with his sleeves rolled up among his mates—he is more in the position of a supervisor; but at the same time he probably knows all his employees by their first names, is on familiar terms with them and there is a certain give and take. In the next biggest size distinguished in Chapter I, the plant employing from 21 to 50 men, the group is no longer the size of any 'team' known to sport and the team-spirit is difficult to keep up. The employer may be designated by the American term 'boss', or the British 'gaffer'. He has become a sort of army sergeant, discipline takes the place of community of interests, and more stress must be laid on the pecuniary incentive of the wage. At the next largest size of plant, where 51 to 100 persons are employed in a smallish factory, the employer may possibly have attained a different social class and may be compared to a lieutenant in the army. The incentive to efficiency of the feeling of 'being in the same boat' is lost, and the ordinary employee can no longer regard his own interests in the business as identical with his employer's.

There are by now probably three ranks, since a sergeant grade of foremen comes between the officer-employer and his men.[1] The employer, though possibly regarded as a friend and knowing every employee by his family (if not his first) name, is looked upon as someone not themselves. At best, paternalism and its corollary loyalty, now takes the place of camaraderie and identity of interests; mechanical devices such as 'clocking in' to ensure punctuality at the work are usually imposed and 'tabs' kept on behaviour in the works by output and idle-time records.

Thus the incentive of identification of oneself with the firm and a feeling that one partly 'owns the place' or at least has a stake in the enterprise fades out as the plant or firm gets larger. Where, in a medium-sized plant, 100 to 250 men are employed, the number of an army company under a 'captain', a man appears to be a commodity merely placed

[1] Chapter IV, § 3.

in a factory to ensure proper flow of work. The progress of mechanization and power transmission will possibly demand submission to a
routine of multiple shifts in which he shares one machine, as Box and
Cox did their lodgings, with another worker. Box—and Cox—may, and
do, resist this loss of a sense of property by blaming all mechanical
breakdowns on Cox—or Box—and refusing to take any responsibility
for breakages, waste material or quality and quantity of output.

It is still possible, however, for paternalism to subsist and the 'united
family' feeling to flourish. It was perhaps of this size of plant that
Mr Baldwin spoke so eloquently as Prime Minister in the House of
Commons in March 1925.

I worked for many years in an industrial business and had under me what
was then considered a large number of men. . . . When I was first in business
I was probably working under a system that was already passing. . . . It was
a place where I had known from childhood every man on the ground, where I
was able to talk to men, not only about troubles in the works, but troubles
at home, where strikes and lock-outs were unknown, and where the fathers
and grandfathers of the men had worked and their sons went automatically
into the business. It was also a place where nobody ever got the sack, and
where we had a natural sympathy for those who were less concerned in
efficiency than this generation is. There was a large number of old gentlemen
who used to spend the day sitting on the handle of a wheelbarrow and
smoking their pipes. Oddly enough, it was not an inefficient community.

Where more than 500 are employed, the 'major' or 'colonel' at the
head of the plant, if he is at all logical, will be sitting in an office, have
several sub-managers under him and will have to spend a great deal of
time remote from the shops occupied with files and clerks working out
plans. Though there may still be a certain *esprit de corps*, red-tape and
bureaucracy creep in. The employer's withdrawal will set him off as a
person apart and most traces of a busy united family will have disappeared from the plant. The employer may not even recognize his
employees by sight but merely have a vague feeling that he has seen that
face before somewhere. The process of depersonalization may well be
complete and the social atmosphere of institutionalism in full blast. The
same efficiency of labour may be obtained, but only at an increased cost
in supervisory staff, complicated accounting methods, precise wage-
systems, liberal welfare provisions, checks and balances, scheduling and
routine. Direct access of the individual employee to the employer has
usually to be abandoned, and the two can only meet through employees'
delegates and representatives.

Finally, in the large plant containing more than 1,000 persons, a
towering hierarchy of supervisors, works managers and general managers will, as pictured in Table IVB, rise above the individual employees,
who may not even know their employer by sight. He may in fact have

his office at some commercial centre miles away from the plant, and through departmentalization the employees may have completely lost touch with one another. The incentive of an *esprit de corps* has gone for the plant as a whole, and the worker feels no longer a member of a team but a mere cog in a huge machine, a mere check number filed away in the records.

The *direct* effect on a man's morale and his 'team-spirit' of this mere matter of size is sometimes quite tangible. The organization is not *his* organization and unless he is afraid of dismissal and unemployment he cares little for any *dis*organization due to his leaving at a moment's notice or absenting himself without any notice. But high morale does not always imply a high level of efficiency, and the theory that a large size of plant or firm results in higher absenteeism and labour turnover certainly requires further evidence in proof.[1]

It is, however, in the more *indirect* effects upon efficiency that the increase in the size of firms demanded by economic logic finds its greatest obstacles. An atmosphere is created in which it is difficult for labour to make the necessary logical adjustments for the sake of general industrial efficiency. It is natural for 'employees' who feel they are not identified with the organization for production and are just 'hired and fired' like raw material, to form organizations of their own in the shape of trade unions or just to be members of the unorganized groups or gangs studied by Elton Mayo, or even just to act unconsciously in unison. The trade practices which the unions defend, if need be by striking, are difficult to adjust to any new requirement of technical efficiency. But it is not necessary for any specific conscious organization to inculcate inertia. I have found evidence of deliberate restriction of output both in Britain and America even where trade unionism was excluded.[2]

To use expensive capital equipment more efficiently it was said (p. 167) to be logical to work *it* long hours, and this can be done without causing fatigue among the human workers by working *them* short shifts.[3] This shift system, while reducing labour's working hours, involves not only the sharing of machines mentioned above, but also social and family readjustments of which the labourer may not see the point, unless his interest is more closely identified with the firm's efficiency. He may not see the point for instance of disturbing family habits by working sometimes in the morning, sometimes in the afternoon, his sons or daughters being perhaps on the reverse shift and thus duplicating the service of meals. Unless there are very potent incentives to the contrary, the inertia of custom and convention will prove the stronger force.

---

[1] See Florence, *Economics and Sociology of Industry*, 1969, pp. 117–20.
[2] *Economics of Fatigue and Unrest*, 1924, p. 263.
[3] See Florence, *Labour*, pp. 62–4.

This is only one instance of the lack of adjustment to technological possibilities which is part of the indifference to efficiency engendered in labour by the large plant and firm. To stimulate greater efficiency, where identification of labour with the firm is lacking, the relative strength must be canvassed of various forms of incentive or nexus. Large organization raises labour problems, but they are not insoluble.

The difficulties of management do not necessarily increase with the size of plant or firm if political science, discussed earlier (Chapter IV), or psychology is brought in. Piece-rate payment, the appeal to economic man, is the obvious stimulus in place of identification, but difficulties can also be overcome by allowing greater participation of labour and autonomy of smaller groups within the larger organization.

It is significant that a consistent correlation has been found in British industry as a whole between size of plant and proportion of workers on piece-rates. The proportion rises quite steeply with size. It was in 1961 found to be 13 per cent for plants employing 1–24, 24 per cent, 39 per cent and 49 per cent for plants employing successively larger numbers— up to 56 per cent on piece-wages for plants employing 1,000 or more.

This correlation is not necessarily to be interpreted as direct cause and effect. Large plants allow of large-scale operation, large-scale operation of piece-rates; but the fact remains that large plants can and do provide a pecuniary incentive to labour that may compensate for the loss of identification, and their 'alienation', but it is not always realized what a big difference the change from time to piece-rates can make in productivity performance, particularly on the monotonous work so frequent in mass production. Among 88 workers with records of the same operations before and after the change, unaccompanied by any other changes in several British factories, 50 increased their output 67 per cent and over, and another 29 over 34 per cent. All the workers were interviewed and few complained of fatigue.[1] Difficulties arise, however, in setting piece-rates that will be thought fair as between one job and another. The difficulty can often be avoided by consulting workers' representatives beforehand.

The cash nexus or pecuniary incentive of the wage, and, more important, the *trans*pecuniary incentive provided by what can be bought *through* the wage, is undoubtedly still stronger in America than in Britain, and largely accounts (together with greater mechanization of operations and material handling and perhaps more efficient management) for the higher productivity per man in American factories.[2] In

---

[1] Davison, Florence, Gray and Ross, *Productivity and Economic Incentives*, 1958.
[2] Given by L. Rostas for 1935–9 as 211–24 per cent higher for physical output per worker and 273–92 per cent higher per man-hour. *International Labour Review*, September 1948, p. 297. See Chapter I, § 2, for correlation with mechanization.

America the worker both wants more strongly what money can buy and connects money with his productivity. He, or if not he, his wife, sees clearly what can be bought with his earnings. As a comment on the report of one Anglo-American productivity team put it,[1] members of the team

look behind the operative and see standing there, imperiously commanding, the figure of the American woman. They picture him as valiantly responding to the trumpet call to battle sounded by his wife . . . they quote from a works magazine an article which has as its title 'Endless Desire for New Things Lifts Living Standards'. Indeed, it is just that determination to have a new car every so often, a modern home equipped with every up-to-date amenity and gadget and, generally, a share in the good things of life, which inspires the extra effort which the worker over there thinks is worth while.

Less could be done with cash, and less status was attributed to cash in Britain even before the two World Wars. It was always possible to be an impoverished gentleman, or conversely a rich cad, bounder, or 'outsider'. The British class system did not depend entirely on the possession of wealth. Since the two World Wars, the rationing and scarcities of goods, the theory of 'fair shares', and progressive taxation have still further limited the purchasing power of British money earnings, and the welfare state the uses of money. It is now almost impossible in Britain for parents to *buy* a university education for children, only the children themselves can get it by their examination efficiency. In America there is, on the other hand, a strong (transpecuniary) incentive on the parent toward earning a university education for his children.

It was quite a surprise (surprisingly enough!) to most of the visiting British productivity teams, which included managers and trade union leaders, that the American worker realizes the connection between his output and earnings. The British workers, at least the rank and file, apparently still think the *main* source of earnings to be squeezing profits by aggressive trade union policy. There must, of course, be an alert trade union to ensure that the wage-earner gets his fair share of higher productivity. But the American worker realizes more clearly that no amount of trade union activity is going to get much more for him, if productivity per worker does not rise and he seems less liable to sudden unofficial strikes which he terms 'wild cat'.[2]

American trade unions are in fact stronger in their powers of

---

[1] *Birmingham Chamber of Commerce Journal*, July 1950, p. 615. The Internal Combustion Engines team is that referred to.

[2] The average of days lost in strikes per worker is normally higher in America than in Britain but the damage inflicted upon the economy in uncertainty, dislocation of production and distraction of management is perhaps more nearly proportionate to the *number* of strikes, particularly when unforeseen, and wildcat (i.e. unofficial) than to their duration.

discipline over their members and, where large plants prevail, are organized on a plant rather than a local craft basis. The principle is one plant one union. American trade unions were recognized by employers much later on the whole than British trade unions and were organized with the help of government legislation, in particular the Wagner Act of 1935. In consequence perhaps, American trade unions are more suited to modern industrial organization and to the needs of the economy generally.

Even in America, however, the cash-nexus is not a sufficient stimulus to labour efficiency; and most large employers in America, as well as Britain, have instituted labour or personnel managers to negotiate with trade union or other representatives of labour and to specialize in welfare and industrial relations. This specialization has often produced human and stimulating relations with labour, and even identification such as occur naturally in the small firm, and thus the atmosphere, the fog, of remote control is dispelled and not merely circumvented by high wages and high-geared wage systems.

Both in Britain and America large firms are moving toward the greater participation of labour in government. This does not mean giving workers top control, as advocated by syndicalists, but the exercise of capitalist, nationalized or co-operative government 'as part of a plural society embracing many participating interests whose expectation must receive a measure of satisfaction if it is to remain an effective operational unit'.[1] Chester Barnard's 'two way communication'[2] between management and trade unions is certainly a minimum requirement, command being met by a contributory 'reply'.

To detail various methods of securing labour's reply is not in order here. Some procedures stress making the purpose of a job more intelligible.[3] Others attempt to reverse the trend toward large-scale remote control. Dubreuil for instance seizes upon the possibility

of dividing up the business to show that there is in it a means of reducing the business to the range of the visual field of the average workman. If the outlook of the ordinary man cannot include the whole of the business and simultaneously perceive the place which he proportionately occupies, it is incontestable that this vision will become much easier for him if its limits are contracted to the narrower range of a 'department'.[4]

This indeed was the view of the political scientist in the democratic Greek city state. In order that all citizens should take their share in government Aristotle thought their number should be no more than

[1] N. Ross, Constructive Conflict, 1969, p. 34.
[2] See above, p. 202.
[3] See Florence, Labour, pp. 88–100.
[4] Business and Science, the Sylvan Press, 1931, p. 95. See also International Labour Review, 1951, pp. 285–302.

could be reached by one voice. Breaking up a large factory into autonomous small, often 'face-to-face', groups and avoiding centralization by departmental budgets and a federal constitution will not only delegate responsibility and thus relieve top government (see Chapter IV, § 2) but will facilitate comprehension by labour of economic and management problems.

In the relations between labour and employer there are two alternative methods of facing the march of technical progress. The employer may introduce technically needed changes without consulting labour, changes which labour may then fight to the last ditch. Scientific management, Bedaux systems, dilution of labour will thus be opposed by craft traditions and customary rates of output, until all the technical possibilities of increased production of wealth will be lost in that last ditch. Or a policy of 'informed joint control'[1] may be initiated in all workshop matters that are directly in the workers' 'visual field' or 'area of concern'. The scientific investigation of human efficiency can then be undertaken under the auspices of both parties, employers and trade unions, and in conditions that will ensure not only impartiality but the legislative enactment of the policy scientifically recommended. Such democratic factory legislation, like the constitution and laws of a state, can then be openly recorded in books of rules for the guidance of the executive managers and of any adjudicators in case of dispute.[2]

Investigation of the social relations and other conditions stimulating productivity in any job has proved fruitful; but industrial psychologists and students of labour relations generally have tended to neglect the conditions making mobility easier from job to job according as the national need arose. Adam Smith and Alfred Marshall were exercised by this problem but insufficient attention has been paid, for instance, to the fascination that *respectability* and *sociability* appear to offer to the average man or woman. It is apparently highly respectable, at least in Britain, to keep hands clean and to be able to wear, while at work, a white collar and Sunday clothes. A clerk or a sales assistant can, at desk or counter, wear the black coat or the art-silk frock that manual operatives have to reserve for Sundays. Hence in spite of the additional time and money spent in education and the monotonous and sedentary nature of the work, there is no lack of applicants for these gentlemanly and lady-like distributive and clerical occupations which have a good name. But the attractive power of sociability, the gang-nexus, is perhaps still greater than the name-nexus.

Large-scale organization, though it has reduced the incentive of equality, fraternity and personal contact of employer and employee, has enormously increased sociability as between employees. In a large

---

[1] Florence, *Economics of Fatigue and Unrest*, 1924, pp. 122–4.
[2] See Lord Brown, *Exploration in Management*, 1960.

factory men and women can find plenty of fellow-workers of their own age and status with the same interests and outlook. Though some of these associates may prove unwelcome, as Marshall[1] somewhat gloomily suggests, the more they are together, the greater chance of finding congenial company. Working girls in particular have always appeared to find in the large factory a release from the isolation, the conventional restraints and the petty irritations of home and family life.[2] The large factory thus offers attractions and often recruits more easily than the small.

The process of moving or transferring people can be effected only by making them *able* as well as willing to move. Mobility, like work itself, has to be *con*duced as well as *in*duced. The movement of British workers toward industry has to be induced by relatively higher net advantages, including wages, than elsewhere, and conduced above all by healthy housing in its neighbourhood. Moreover, persons may be willing to move and be attracted to other occupations, but disabled from moving, not by the physical difficulties but by social obstacles. Social stratification, particularly in England, makes it hard for the children of manual workers to move into the professions.[3] Conditions non-conducive to movements between occupations are thus of very wide scope and must be given a place beside the other negative conditions—the non-inducives to move and the non-conducives and non-inducives to work.

The need for new incentives appropriate to the new organization of industrial society with its large plants and firms and its remote control broadens out into a need for four sorts of stimulus. In a free industrial society we may rule out coercives to work or move except fear of unemployment, and the direction of labour in the quasi-military organizations of war-time industry. For full efficiency in a free society, conditions must be such that labour is willing and able to work efficiently, and willing and able to move wherever more efficient work offers. There must be incentives to induce willingness to work, 'attractives' to induce willingness to move, and conducives to enable persons also both to work and to move. These necessary requirements for the full co-operation of labour and, indeed, of *all* agents of production may be tabulated in a model for convenient reference.

This analysis of stimuli which economists and psychologists have pursued furthest in the case of labour, may be applied equally fruitfully to the two other agents of importance to modern industry, namely to the private investor and to the top manager, director or entrepreneur. For

---

[1] *Principles of Economics*, Book IV. § 2.
[2] Graham Wallas, *The Great Society*, 1914, pp. 341ff.
[3] See further discussion below, § 6.

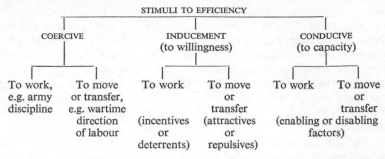

each agent the effective working of a large organization demands the presence and ready availability of these stimuli. Capital investment and the government of enterprises must, no less than labour, have incentives and attractives to induce willingness, and conducives to enable them to act efficiently, and to move into the most efficient employments.

Indeed the economist has been accustomed to speak of the 'supply price' of capital and enterprise as freely as he has of the supply price of labour and the demand price for commodities. But he has only sketched out the framework or 'model' without trying to discover very scientifically what are the precise stimuli, incentives, attractives and conducives to work and mobility to which labour, capital, or enterprise react. The following analysis is thus an attempt to fill in the boxes prepared by the economist but usually left empty of all but a few illustrations consonant to his theory; and we shall follow the economist in carrying over the psychological analysis to the investment of private capital and the government of enterprises, even though the psychologist has done but little work here.

If industrial organization is to be rationalized to act efficiently, i.e. to maximize production with the minimum of cost, it is essential to ensure, not only of labour but of all agents of production, that the structure and forms of government set up will not cut across inducements and conducives to efficient work, movement and adjustment. If they do, the checks to efficiency that will appear as reactions in human behaviour may well prove insurmountable, or surmountable only at an excessive cost. The logic of industrial structure and government must ultimately, in short, be judged by the stimuli and checks now under discussion.

§ 2. THE STIMULUS TO INVEST: THE OUTSIDE INVESTOR

To paraphrase what was said of labour, full efficiency in a free society requires conditions to be such that *capital is willing and able to be invested efficiently, and willing and able to move wherever more efficient investment offers.* But this phrasing would be imputing a personality to capital dangerously near to the superstitions of anthropomorphism and the idolatrous worship of such patriotic emblems as Britannia, or the flag. Capital is not a person and whatever the stimuli addressed to capital, whatever the form of its supply prices, they must be stimuli and prices affecting the behaviour of those persons in whose power lies the investment of capital.

This insistence on the who, and not just the why and how of the matter (an essential part of the structural approach), soon discloses the existence of quite different sorts of persons in the capitalist system who have it in their power to control the supply of capital to an industry. Broadly speaking, there are four categories: private 'men of property', or institutions outside the industry, who are merely potential owners of the capital; the top ruler or executive (director or manager) within the industry who determines policy in the use of other people's property; the entrepreneur within the industry who both owns property and determines how it is to be used; and the financiers, issue houses, banks and brokers who act as middlemen between outside sources and industrialists.[1]

The pecuniary inducement (incentive or attractive) to bring about an efficient use of capital bears a different name according as it is addressed to one or other of these types of investor, and they play a different role in the three components of investment: saving, financing, and physical investment or outlay.[2] The outside man of property or institution finances industry out of savings by buying stocks and shares called 'securities'. The inducement is the expected rate of dividend on the shares (or more accurately, the yield on their market price) when compared to the rate of interest, together with some estimate of capital appreciation in the fairly immediate future. This outside shareholding investor does not invest physically (in the Keynes sense) at all. The executive is paid chiefly by salary or fee, and it is he and his co-directors who makes decisions about the physical investment of company savings. The owner-entrepreneur provides all the components of investment, saving his own money, deciding how much of it to spend on his industry and what to spend it on. He is paid in the form of a profit.[3] The stimulus

---

[1] For a brief summary of the role played by British banks and brokers in the issue and loan of capital, see Beacham, *Economics of Industrial Organization*, 1969, pp. 65–76.

[2] Keynes has acclimatized us to use 'investment' for the physical component, that of spending funds on equipment and stocks; but the word is still commonly used for the transference of savings into industrial finance by buying securities. When even so high an authority as Schumpeter was liable to be confused (see *Economic Journal*, March 1951, review by Joan Robinson, p. 141), it is best always to specify which of the three components of investment is meant.

[3] It has been repeatedly pointed out (e.g. Florence, 1929, pp. 256–7; Cole, *Economic Tracts for the Times*, 1932, 231–87) that unnecessary confusion has

or failure of stimulus to induce efficient behaviour on the part of the entrepreneur, the financier and the executive will be considered in § 3. The present section deals with the reactions of the actual or potential outside investor and the investment component particularly involved is the financing of industry through the purchase of industrial securities. The analysis of stimuli that was applied to labour is also applicable here. Incentives to *willingness* in investing will be considered first, then conducives to *ability* to invest; then incentives and conducives to *move or transfer* investment into one particular industry or another.

(1) The incentive required to overcome his unwillingness to invest must be judged against the outside investor's attitude and propensities. In Britain the industrial revolution occurred earlier than in America and wealth inherited from that period created an important class of *rentiers* living mainly from the proceeds of 'unearned' income—often the share-holding denizens already mentioned of the 'home counties' and other purely residential districts. The behaviour of these heirs of fortune and other private investors who look for steady incomes is often marked by 'business shyness' and timidity in handling their investments.[1] The chief drawback to industrial securities from the private individual investor's point of view are that they are not secure—in fact a better name for them might be insecurities. They are attended by varying degrees of pecuniary risk and uncertainty according to the period and terms of the stock. Thus in Britain, at least, obstacles appear to arise in the provision of the cheap long-term investment of risk capital required for industrial efficiency. They are the potential private investor's desire for security and his insistence upon being paid handsomely for bearing the uncertain risks of a type repulsive to him. Before this apparent unwillingness of the outside investor and the consequent high supply price of risk capital is assumed, however, more basic research is required on the composition of the investing and potentially investing public and on the various attitudes displayed— starting out perhaps from the varying rates of share turnover already (Chapter V, § 2) indicated.

[1] See Chapter V, § 2, p. 214.

---

been engendered by trying to identify each of these names of payments with a stimulus for some specific function in the organization of industry. While interest is said to be paid purely 'for' abstinence or waiting, profit is said by some to be paid 'for' taking and bearing risks, by others it is identified with payment for enterprise or earnings of management. The truth is that each name arose to describe events at different stages in the evolution of industrial institutions. Profits may usefully describe a form of payment occurring where entrepreneurs manage, own and risk capital, but in the more recently developed institution of the joint stock company with its payments in the form of debenture interest, dividends, fees and salaries, nobody gets a payment to which 'profit' can specifically refer.

In the corporation or joint stock company the majority of ordinary shareholders have little real control over policy.[1] Once the shareholder has invested, the risks are borne but not taken by him—they are not of his choosing. This feeling of helplessness adds to his demands for compensation. Moreover, the procedure of the joint stock company or corporation and the possibility of escape via the stock exchange deprive the investor of any non-pecuniary incentive in identification with the business. The ownership of a few shares in a company which can at any moment be exchanged though possibly at some loss for the shares of another company and which are held with shares in many other companies, will hardly offer much of the old sense of property or stake-in-the business type of incentive.[2] Apart from the freedom to escape by way of sale of shares on the stock exchange (a conducive rather than an incentive), the only important non-pecuniary incentive which, acting as a counterweight, can lighten the pecuniary load of interest or dividend which industry must offer to obtain finance, is the gambling instinct.

The instinct to speculate does not appear to be strong among the main body of persons holding or likely to hold investments, at any rate in Britain. Those who wish to risk money do so in Britain in horse-racing, the dog tracks and football pools, not in industrial investments. When buying shares few retired professional men, or widows and other heiresses, or trustees, or the investment trusts in which they all seek for security, want to gamble. Most of them have the *rentier* psychology and wish to play safe. They invest to obtain a definite annual income or a fixed sum at a definite date (depending on such transpecuniary considerations as provision for old age or education of children) and probably do not like the thought of a slight chance of heavy loss even though there be a big chance of moderate gains.[3] Private owners of property or trustees will therefore prefer hoarding in the form of savings deposits at the bank or investing in stock as secure as government loans or industrial debentures. They have, as Keynes put it, a liquidity preference. The incentive to overcome this preference, and to induce the bearing of uncertain risks by purchasing ordinary industrial shares must therefore be strong. Proprietors, divorced from personal contact with large-scale industry, become as indifferent as labour to its needs, and a relatively high rate of yield, varying from

[1] See Chapter IV, § 9.

[2] Many American corporations now feel the need to cultivate their shareholders by a conscious policy of good relations, showing a close affinity with the labour relations programme discussed in the previous section (see National Industrial Conference Board, *Stockholder Relations*, 1950). An odd need as between officers and the proprietors of the firm who, legally, appoint them (Chapter V, § 2), which forms a measure of the status of the proprietors!

[3] For the theory and statistics of this presumption see Florence, 1929, Chapter VIII.

firm to firm[1] must be offered to make outsiders willing to participate in the necessary risks and uncertainties.

In America potential investors, or at least a large section of them, appear to have an attitude and incentives very different from those of the rentier, who looks to steady (unearned) income over a long period. The attitude is much more that of the gambler looking to a profit margin from quick resale of shares or of a speculator in the sense, to use Keynes' definition[2] of one 'forecasting the psychology of the market' rather than 'forecasting the prospective yield of assets over their whole life'. The difference is important enough to have drawn comment from two leading British economists, Keynes and Salter.

Even outside the field of finance, Americans are apt to be unduly interested in discovering what average opinion believes average opinion to be; and this national weakness finds its nemesis in the stock market. It is rare, one is told, for an American to invest, as many Englishmen still do, 'for income'; and he will not readily purchase an investment except in the hope of capital appreciation. This is only another way of saying that, when he purchases an investment, the American is attaching his hopes, not so much to its prospective yield, as to a favourable change in the conventional basis of valuation, i.e. that he is, in the above sense, a speculator. Speculators may do no harm as bubbles on a steady stream of enterprise. But the position is serious when enterprise becomes the bubble on a whirlpool of speculation. When the capital development of a country becomes a by-product of the activities of a casino, the job is likely to be ill-done. The measure of success attained by Wall Street, regarded as an institution of which the proper social purpose is to direct new investment into the most profitable channels in terms of future yield, cannot be claimed as one of the outstanding triumphs of *laissez-faire* capitalism.'[3]

America, more than any other great country, has a mass psychology which is subject to moods and impulses of a range and intensity not known elsewhere.

These conditions account for the scale of the speculative boom of 1929. In actual folly it has often been more than equalled. Nothing in recent years, for example, has touched the wild frenzy of the South Sea Bubble in England. But in range and in volume, and consequently in its far-reaching results, the 1929 speculation has had no equal or rival in economic history. Never before in the history of the world has there been a public, to be numbered not by hundreds of thousands but by tens of millions, with both the will to speculate and the financial facilities to enable them to do so. It is a new and terrifying phenomenon. . . .

When a speculator bases his operation, not on a judgment of economic realities, but on a guess as to what other speculators will do tomorrow; when,

[1] Highest rates usually for the smaller and less well-known firms, see Chapter II above, but both higher than for state enterprise. See Sharp, *Economic Journal*, December, 1951, pp. 804–11.

[2] Keynes, *The General Theory of Employment*, 1935, p. 158.

[3] Keynes, op. cit., p. 159.

for example, he 'bulls' shares not because he thinks they are undervalued but because, although he knows there must some time be a crash, he guesses that others will first overvalue them more, and he hopes to get in and out again before the crash comes . . . the trough of the waves is deepened, not smoothed out, the storm is both increased in intensity and prolonged. Speculation based on economic realities may be beneficial, but 'speculation on speculation' is definitely injurious. And when this happens on a vast scale the results may be widespread and disastrous.[1]

Americans might have done better for *stability* had they concentrated, like the English, on race-course speculation—on playing the horses rather than the capital market. But they might not then have achieved their high rate of *progress* in capital formation.

(2) The extent to which the man of private property will carry uncertainty-bearing investment does not indeed depend solely on the incentives affecting his willingness. As in the case of the labour supply there is also the factor of capacity to be considered. The main 'conducive' to invest is savings, and this depends on a man's liquid assets, his total income and the proportion of total income that he saves. The two latter are connected in Keynes' assumption of the 'propensity to consume', which relates community consumption or savings to the level of total individual incomes.[2] For the single individual anything that limits his total income, such as increased taxation or a reduction of salary or business dividends without changing the propensity to consume, decreases his capacity (though not necessarily his willingness) to invest. In joint stock companies ownership is divorced from government and from the authority which invests, in the sense of turning savings into physical instruments. Persons who save or have inherited savings or property are not identical with those who finance or physically invest in industry. Nevertheless, that part of investment which depends upon personal savings must come out of the difference between the totality of persons' incomes and expenditures. They may devote more (or less) savings to hoarding and less (or more) to holding

[1] Salter, *Recovery*, 1932, pp. 36–8.

[2] Statistics comparing families at different income levels certainly show that the poorer families save less, and proportionately less, than richer families; below a certain level they do not save at all and in fact may on average be borrowing, i.e. dissaving. Saving and oversaving by the rich is a corollary of Engel's Law mentioned in Chapter III and was adduced by J. A. Hobson as early as 1889 when relating trade depressions to the unequal distribution of wealth. But Engel-type statistics are not a verification of Keynes' propensity to consume which refers to the same people at different times, not to different sets of people at the same time. Statistical proof of the proposition that the proportion consumed falls significantly as the same people's income rises is still incomplete. See Paradiso, *Retail Sales and Consumer Incomes*, Survey of Current Business, October 1944; Moulton, *Controlling Factors in Economic Developments*, 1949, pp. 125–38.

industrial securities, but in proportion as their savings diminish they must do less of the two together.

The proportion of income saved is not necessarily, and perhaps not usually, determined consciously but may be the indirect though inevitable result of the standard of living adopted. If the standard of living and spending is fixed in physical volume—the same tonnage of food, acreage of clothes, mileage of travel, being bought year by year—then a rise in retail prices or the price of personal services will, with a given total money income diminish automatically the income saved, because more money income must be spent on the same fixed standard. If standards of living rise and the national product does not, if more is spent by the investing class on conspicuous consumption to 'keep up with the Jones's' either at home or abroad, or if more is spent on children's education to spread the old or adopt a new level of gentility, then saving and the fund out of which securities might have been bought and/or held is depleted. To obtain funds industry will be driven to seek capital elsewhere than from the private property owner; the capital needed will have to come from reinvestment, from a 'ploughing back', of the income of businesses controlled by entrepreneurs or executives. But if re-investment is into the same industry 'ossification' is a threat. Ossification points to the need for movement from industry to industry as no less important for capital than for labour.

In the first stage of capitalist society a business man used his own property to make a profit; in the second stage he induced others to lend him theirs by hope of large dividends; now a third stage is being reached. Here the stimulus necessary for success in overcoming private owners' inertia and unwillingness to risk their property may be too high in cost to obtain the quantities of capital that are necessary for modern industrial technique. Recourse is had to a veiled levy on capitalist dividends through investment of retained profits by boards of directors; or to modification of private capitalism through state direction of investment; or to its complete abandonment as in some British industries, in favour of nationalization and central state finance.

A complicated mechanism has been built up in the shape of the stock exchange, brokerage and issue houses, highly conducive to the *mobility* of investment between old issues of capital, and conducive in a less degree to the guidance of investment into new industrial issues. But though the outside investor is thus enabled easily to mobilize, transfer and direct his capital, it has been found increasingly difficult to attract it into the channels most likely to be efficient and to increase national income. Here the obstacles to efficient organization are not only the investors' ignorance, business shyness and speculative rashness mentioned already, but the strong economic incentive offered to the company promoter's private purposes. Either the investor is ignorant but does not know it, in which case he falls an easy prey to the optimistic and boastful prospectuses whereby the promoter can obtain funds for inefficient investment—and is called a sucker or a gull for his pains; or he is ignorant and knows it, in which case he is either overcautious and dare not transfer, or else so 'spread his risks' by so-called scientific investment that his capital is invested in inefficient as well as efficient directions.

On this point the British 'Macmillan' committee (of which Keynes was a member) was most explicit.[1]

It is all-important to the community that its savings should be invested in the most fruitful and generally useful enterprises offering at home. Yet, in general, the individual investor can hardly be supposed to have himself knowledge of much value either as to the profitable character or the security of what is offered to him. How easily he can be misled in times of speculative fever by glittering—even tawdry—appearances is proved by the experience of 1928.

The way to overcome this incapacity in the human (investor) factor lies in education for investment—correlative with education for management—and a more strict company or corporation law so that education would have some acknowledged discipline to impart.

Education for investment cannot of course be a professional training confined to a few specialists in college or university but must be undertaken, as it already is to a limited extent, through newspapers, journals and broadcasting honestly reporting the facts, criticizing existing practices, raising public opinion standards—above all by teaching the public to ask the right questions. Propaganda analysis and the psychology of mass communication have advanced far enough to form a scientific basis for 'debunking the sucker' willing to invest but incapable of investing profitably to himself or the nation.

While educating the investing public to be more capable of analysing and interpreting the relevant facts, the facts themselves must be better analysed and better recorded. Secrecy and *mystique* still befog and bedevil the acts and policies of the broker's trade. Conducives to more efficient investment are, in short, the teaching of the potential investor, and things easier and clearer to teach.

At present the sources of knowledge available to dispel the ignorance and fear of the prospective investor, and thus to make him capable of directing his resources and purchasing the securities of any one industry or firm, rather than another, are roughly four:

(1) His own personal knowledge of the 'inside story' of a business firm;
(2) A general knowledge of the economic situation;

[1] Report of Committee on Finance and Industry, 1931, Cmd. 3897, p. 166.

(3) Professional advice of an expert such as a bank-manager or stock-broker is supposed to be; and finally

(4) Knowledge based on published accounts of the firm's prospects or position.

The third source of information, if honest, usually tends to play safe and to foster the policy of distribution of risks. The second source of information may be dismissed as available only to a select minority. The first source of information, though it may move some investment into more 'fruitful and generally useful enterprises', is likely to move as much out as it moves in. As the Report of the Liberal Industrial Enquiry[1] put it:

The actual proprietors of a concern are frequently at a serious disadvantage with 'outsiders' who can obtain access to 'inside' information, with the result that they may part with their property for less than its real value, owing to their ignorance of the actual facts. At the same time, knowledge by the public that there is such a thing as valuable 'inside' information often puts them at the mercy of alleged 'inside' information which is only intended to deceive, and of market tips which are part of a scheme of manipulation;

or else it may frighten those who realize that they have no such 'inside dope' into avoiding industrial risks altogether.

As to the fourth source of information, in regular published statements, prospectuses often become sheer advertising 'stunts' liable to give a false impression, while balance sheets or income and expenditure accounts issued to the shareholders, convey inadequate information. There is little public knowledge of who are the largest shareholders or how the large shareholdings are changing ownership; nor, though more easily available, of what classes of shares and their voting rights the capital structure of any company consists.

In accounting and reporting on holdings, American practice since the stock exchange crash of 1929 and the subsequent 'New Deal' may serve as an example to Britain of the possibilities in state regulation of the companies and corporations which, after all, the state itself creates. The Securities and Exchange Act of 1934 set up a securities and exchange commission of five men to be appointed by the president with the advice and consent of the senate. This commission supervises both the issue of new securities and the ownership, government and market 'behaviour' of old securities.

New securities must be registered by the issuing house in considerable detail and with time for the commission to verify statements before the securities can be put on the market. Once a corporation is a going concern, the commission makes public month by month the ownership of shares forming over ten per cent of any issue and of all

[1] *Britain's Industrial Future*, 1928, p. 86.

shares owned by any directors or principal officers, thus effectively disclosing any dealings of these 'insiders'. Directors' individual remuneration is also disclosed. The commission further assists intelligent corporation government by insisting that shareholders whose proxies are asked for are given detailed information about the agenda to be voted on.

The British Companies Acts require for public companies a register of all shareholders for public inspection, but otherwise do not go so far as the American legislation. Only the total, not the individual, remuneration of directors need be given, and though recommended by the Cohen committee on which the Act was based, nothing was done to disclose the real beneficiary owner of shares, large or small. The device of nominees is still legal and still prevents the possible buyer of shares in a company from knowing who his fellow shareholders would be, and thus continues to restrict his capacity for efficient investment.

It still remains doubtful how far the men of property even of average intelligence and education can react intelligently to tables of figures and lists of shareholders, however truthfully and logically analysed. Investments are, we know, by reason of inheritance and spreading risks, diffused to such an extent that if a person is an investor in one large company he is probably an investor in at least half a dozen others,[1] and he cannot enter into the subtleties and avoid the pitfalls of all the accounts and figures of all of them. What is ultimately necessary to conduce to efficient direction and movement of capital is some reliable authority to interpret industrial accounts. The Macmillan committee recommended, in fact, that 'relations between finance and industry should be so developed that issuing institutions of first-class strength and repute should vouch to the investor more normally and more fully for the intrinsic soundness of the issues made'.[2]

The position of an outside investor, without education, expert guidance or economic knowledge, was indeed well epitomized in the British Liberal Industrial Inquiry Report of 1928.[3]

It is hardly an exaggeration to say that half the business of successful investment today in industrial shares consists in getting hold, in one way or another, of private information not available to the general body of shareholders or investors. The honest financier spends his time in getting hold of true information to which he is not entitled, and the less honest in spreading false information for which, under the cover of general darkness, he can obtain credence.

To sum up. With all this ignorance and chicanery the supply price

---

[1] See above, p. 216.
[2] Op. cit., p. 168.
[3] *Britain's Industrial Future*, p. 85.

of efficient investment from sources outside the firm is likely to be high. If there is an efficient outlet, it will have to make itself evident in extremely high yields before it can attract the prospective investor, or else dividends will have to be stable and enterprise limited by safety-first principles. Even then, it is found necessary for the attraction of funds that prominent names be found on the prospectus. In Britain guinea-pig, and in America big name, directors are often paid high fees without returning much in administrative efficiency. They are commonly said to be appointed to attract investment and 'to make a good impression; to give the impression of an honest and straight-forward board of high standing'.[1] But, since guinea-pigs like most directors are appointed through co-option by existing directors, the motive of social advancement by mixing with peers or baronets or 'big names' cannot be excluded. Anyway, whatever the motive for their selection as directors, these guinea-pigs do not exercise, in fact, very much intelligence in the use of capital.

An alternative to the investment of capital from private savings was found to be the growing reinvestment of profits within the business. But this presents the dilemma of ossification when it is a question of the movement and redistribution of capital. It may be a mistake for a firm, however efficient and profitable within the bounds of any one line of product, to reinvest its profit in the same line of production but equally so to use its profit to develop other lines by lateral or vertical expansion. The one policy may lead to overproduction at the ruling price of the original line, the other to the small-scale conglomerate operation of numerous lines and consequent distraction of management.

The obstacles to the provision of industrial capital logically and economically from the private investor have proved so formidable in recent years that the participation of the state has been proposed at various points. If the ignorance of the majority of investors is too great to be overcome by education or by legal insistence on publication of more detailed accounts, and their timidity not assuaged by sponsorship from more expert and responsible issue houses; then the possible stimuli to efficient investment from outside offered by free enterprise capitalism must be declared inadequate. The conclusion must then be drawn that it is not possible to raise the standards of professional con-duct of the financial community to correspond with the importance of their fiduciary trust. The state government may have to appoint directors who would combine vigilance on behalf of the national and the investors' interests with business intelligence, or there may have to be state investment control, not to speak of nationalization of specific industries financed by guaranteed fixed interest stocks.

[1] Evidence before the Greene Committee, Samuel, *Shareholders' Money*, 1933, p. 121.

§ 3. THE STIMULUS TO LARGE-SCALE ENTERPRISE

Besides labour and invested capital the third agent in the modern organization of production is that variously described as the entrepreneur, the management, the administration, the higher or top control, or business leadership. The reason for this plethora of names is partly that they refer to different phases in industrial development, and in Chapter IV it was agreed to drop the word 'entrepreneur' except for the phase where top control is combined in one person with management and ownership of all or most of the capital. The more modern phase, where ownership and management are divorced, though it has been developing in practice for the last fifty years, has not yet engraved itself upon the economist's mind, or, for that matter, upon the popular imagination, and no single word has been coined that satisfactorily fits the actual situation. Apart from the confusion in definition already pointed out, administrator conveys too much the bureaucrat without enterprise, and manager too little of the rule-making, almost legislative, powers involved in large-scale organizations. Reluctantly, we denoted the comprehensive powers involved as top government or top rule; the persons involved as business leaders or prime managers.

Whatever the name used, the important work this third agent is called upon to perform in modern large-scale industry can be summed up from Chapter IV as decisions on general policy and strategy, involving enterprise on what to make, at what price and in what quantities and by what combination of factors including capital investment; and contingent decisions in internal organization, in top appointments and co-ordination.

What motives and incentives stimulate business leaders toward efficiency in this industrial government?

If all the forms of *pecuniary* incentives were listed in order of their strength, the schedule might plausibly be drawn up as follows:

(1) Profit. The remainder after subtraction of expenses from receipts.
(2) Commission on value of goods sold. Discriminating fees varying with values involved.
(3) Tips.
(4) Progressive piece-wage.
(5) Straight piece-wage. Standard fees per transaction.
(6) Degressive piece-wage.
(7) Time wages, short term—day or weekly wage.
(8) Time wages, long term—monthly, quarterly, annual salary, annual fees.

The position of tips in this order is perhaps somewhat arbitrary— the theory of tipping has yet to be written—but there can be no doubt that among the more usual pecuniary incentives, profits are likely to be the strongest, and time wages and long-term salaries the weakest in their direct results on efficiency. Profits, the remainder when costs have been subtracted from total gross receipts, may be negative and turn to loss. They differ from piece-wages in increasing or decreasing not at some settled ratio to the amount produced, but at an ever accelerating or slackening rate, and it does not require a long mathematical formula to show that the slightest rise in output and receipts may mean a manifolding of profit. Suppose a manufacturer of shoes can get £2 for each pair, and starts making 100 pairs for gross receipts of £200, with fixed expenses of £100 for time wages and overhead, variable expenses of £80 for materials and piece wages, and consequent £20 profit. If he increases the amount produced by 10 per cent to 110 pairs for gross receipts of £220, his profit will be £220 minus variable cost of £88 and the fixed cost £100, i.e. £32. In short, a 10 per cent increase in output means a 60 per cent increase in profit, from £20 to £32!

The gradual change over from payment in the form of profit to an 'entrepreneur' toward payment by salary (i.e. time wages on long terms) to a general manager or annual fees to a director, is thus likely to have some effect on keen management and enterprising government. Here indeed were two reasons already given (p. 77) for the survival of small-scale organization. Every capitalist firm works for a profit, but obviously the smaller and therefore the more numerous the firms producing any given aggregate of goods or services, the more are the points at which calculations of the personal profitability of any venture are made. Further, this calculation may not, in the case of the fewer but larger firms, be so closely tied up with policy as in the case of the smaller firms that are usually controlled by an entrepreneur. The salaried general manager of a joint stock company may be expected usually to play safe. If when taking risks he is successful, the additional profit does not accrue to him; if unsuccessful, his job and salary may be in jeopardy. This hypothesis will be followed up when considering, in the next section, specific types of industrial leader.

This damping effect of payment by salary has been recognized and attempts made to remedy it in the recent policy of many American and some English firms. They have initiated schemes for sharing profits with their salaried managers and salesmen offering, for instance, favourable options to buy shares as distinct from schemes for a general profit sharing with all or the bulk of employees.[1] Fees to directors are sometimes also made to vary with the net receipts or with the dividends distributed. Such 'bonus' schemes reached a peak in America in 1929, but since the depression remained less popular.[2]

[1] See Marquand, *Dynamics of Industrial Combination*, 1931, p. 159.
[2] Gordon, *Industrial Leadership in the Large Corporation*, 1945, pp. 284–93.

Some readers may protest that this sordid calculation of financial interest, though applicable to routine workers and suitable to the chapter devoted to labour, is not admissible in the analysis of incentives to efficient administration. That realist, Adam Smith, was, however, of a very different opinion and was not prepared to exclude even his own profession. In some univerisities

the teacher is prohibited from receiving any honorary or fee from his pupils, and his salary constitutes the whole of the revenue which he derives from his office. His interest is, in this case, set as directly in opposition to his duty as it is possible to set it. It is the interest of every man to live as much at his ease as he can; and if his emoluments are to be precisely the same, whether he does or does not perform some very laborious duty, it is certainly his interest, at least as interest is vulgarly understood, either to neglect it altogether, or, if he is subject to some authority which will not suffer him to do this, to perform it in as careless and slovenly a manner as that authority will permit. If he is naturally active and a lover of labour, it is his interest to employ that activity in any way from which he can derive some advantage rather than in the performance of his duty, from which he can derive none.[1]

But, Adam Smith proceeds,

if the authority to which he is subject resides not so much in the body corporate, of which he is a member, as in some other extraneous persons, in the bishop of the diocese, for example, in the governor of the province, or, perhaps, in some minister of state, it is not, indeed, in this case, very likely that he will be suffered to neglect his duty altogether.

We are not here interested in bishops or governors of provinces so much as in employers and business leaders. But Adam Smith's reference to superior authority is obviously just as applicable. If a time wage or salary fails in incentive the superior authority (if there is one) can dismiss his inefficient subordinate; or alternatively he can provide the incentive of promotion into a higher wage or salary grade. The quasi-pecuniary incentives of dismissal or promotion may therefore act as substitutes for direct pecuniary incentives to efficiency; but only if there is a superior authority and if that authority has the capacity and willingness to discover the efficient and inefficient and the capacity and willingness to promote and dismiss them according to their efficiency.

In the joint stock company or corporation there is normally a superior authority to the manager vested in the board of directors; but that authority is greatly influenced by the opinion of the management itself. Though the directors and the higher management may dismiss or retard, as they promote, the middle and junior management, it will be more difficult for the directors to dismiss the higher management. How far the dismissal policy is no respecter of persons and

---

[1] *Wealth of Nations*, Book V, Ch. I, Part III, Art. II.

promotion a matter of merit depends on the appointing capacity of types of business leader, to be discussed shortly. Here it may be pointed out in anticipation that if leaders are obtained 'democratically' by promotion on merit from the junior staff then there will be a corresponding attraction of ambitious men to the staff and incentive for them to work efficiently. Every foreman or clerk will feel that he carries a director's baton in his knapsack. But if, as is so often the case in family businesses, nepotism prevails and promotion goes to a scion of the family on the so-called 'stud' system, then able subordinates who may have ambitious projects for the efficient development of the firm but who are not members of the family, will feel frustrated at an administration which they can never supersede. Their main hope is inter-marriage, but chances in that direction seldom depend on business ability unless a *mariage de convenance* is arranged. A well-known London city bank, now merged, passed three times to sons-in-law in the course of its 200 years' career. Curiously enough the emblem or 'state flower' of this bank was the marigold.

The analysis of the reactions of labour to various stimuli has, however, taught us to beware of considering pecuniary incentives as of sole importance in making or marring efficiency. Though Adam Smith was undoubtedly right in considering one form of pecuniary payment as a stronger incentive than another, there is the wider question how far pecuniary incentives of any form are strong or weak in comparison with entirely *non-pecuniary* incentives, and how far their strength depends on the *transpecuniary* considerations of what the money can buy. To this wider question the answer must vary according to the type of business leader, entrepreneur or administrator, under discussion. For it is a capital mistake to suppose that there is just one type of businessman and one fixed set of incentives to which he will react; that that type is marked by an insatiable appetite for pecuniary rewards, a machine-like precision and effectiveness, and an inhuman callousness to all non-pecuniary or transpecuniary considerations. This mistake is fostered, partly by the economist's functional rather than structural approach and his neglect of the variety and types of mankind and partly by his 'habit of describing the actions of groups of human beings in the passive voice or in the third person singular, and *neuter* at that'. Thus when price changes are under discussion the usual wording is that 'prices are fixed' or 'are determined', not that so and so decides or would probably decide to change prices.[1]

The head of a large-scale business likely to lead the market remains a human being and his main lines of policy and organization will vary with his individual character, his antecedent environment, the

[1] Florence, 1929, p. 25.

conventions of his social class, and various psychological stimuli to which he is exposed. Like those of labour and the investor, the reactions of the top ruler of a business will depend on his capacity and willingness. People vary greatly in their 'constitutional' willingness and capacity, their zeal and energy, quite apart from incentives, so that great importance attaches to the method of appointing top rulers. But any constitutional willingness of a given level will be affected for better or worse by certain incentives or motives. Talcott Parsons in an article on the motivation of economic activity[1] adds to the money motives of a businessman the powerful incentives of self-respect, recognition by others, pleasure in the work and the affection he inspires in his group. In short, to use somewhat familiar terms, the entrepreneur, the executive or whoever wields top rule in industry are linked to their work, like labour, not only by a cash nexus but by a name, fame, hobby or gang nexus. The policy of a firm will therefore be determined by ordinary human reactions to any given situation, by ordinary human solutions of the problems that are presented.

A realistic analysis must avoid the presumption of an exclusive profit motive, let alone a maximization of profit motive. There may be no motive in the industrial leader, just an abounding energy on behalf of the firm with which he is identified, coupled perhaps with a sense of public duty—a duty nexus. Or if there is a motivation, different motives will stimulate different types of leader to act differently toward different problems.

Five crucial practical problems in 'enterprise' may be picked out as confronting the firm operating or wishing to grow and to operate on a large scale with high capital investment and a specialized expert staff. Three are problems of decision on policy and strategy: whether to innovate larger-scale operations, if necessary by cut-throat competition and thus reduce costs and perhaps price; how far to co-operate or combine with firms, 'rationalizing' division of business; how much profit to re-invest. Two are problems of internal social organization: the problem how to delegate authority, secure co-ordination and stimulate line and expert staff at the lowest overhead cost; and the problem how to appoint and promote keen and capable subordinates. On a successful solution of these problems by a large-scale business leader, whether capitalist, nationalized or co-operative, depend the satisfaction of the consumer, and the efficiency, stability and progress for which industry strives.

The particular solutions that are reached by the government of various firms are to some extent measurable (as already suggested, pp. 255–6) in statistical returns and operating and financial ratios based on balance sheets and trading and profit and loss accounts. These

[1] *Canadian Journal of Economic and Political Science*, 1940, p. 194.

would give, for instance, the proportion of profit reinvested instead of distributed in dividends, and the form and intensity of investment.

Though the solutions adopted and their relative efficiency are amenable to measurement, as well as the various types of governing authority, little attempt has hitherto been made to relate the two statistically. All that will be done here is to put forward certain working hypotheses, such that if a director with technical engineering training is the dominating figure, policy is likely to be progressive and the profit re-invested in capital equipment likely to be high, but if the dominating figure is an accountant the balance sheet is likely to be liquid and business more stable. These hypotheses which can be statistically tested may take the form of a table of marks, 2 if the dominating leader keenly embraces large-scale policy, 1 if not so keen or neutral, 0 if averse.

The success of different types of leader in large-scale operation will, of course, vary according to the industries in which he is engaged and the sort of organization he controls. The true entrepreneur, for instance, is probably more efficient than the administrator without capital of his own, wherever adjustments have constantly to be made. In 'jobbing' manufacture for specific orders or in agriculture or services, as already shown, the small owner-manager survives and flourishes, but not in the more routine rail transport, banking or manufacturing of staple goods. Moreover, the different problems may vary in their importance in different sorts of industries. In decaying industries re-investment for instance may in the long run be an inefficient policy; in others sufficient co-operation and combination of firms may already have been achieved.

The estimate of how the methods of money payment, listed above, from profits through tips to salaries, act or fail to act as incentives to efficiency may have to be severely modified in so far as the businessman is not purely an economic calculator, but a creature of habit, sentiment, emotions and instinct. Clearly, the stronger the non-pecuniary incentives and attractions to enterprise and administration and the greater the satisfactions into which given pecuniary payments can be translated, the cheaper (in pecuniary terms) will be the unit services obtained. Hence, if inefficiency and expense appear, part of the explanation may be sought in insufficient non-pecuniary and transpecuniary inducements, for the administrator must then be paid extra to work 'against the grain'.

Emerging from the forms of capitalism recognized in Chapter V and forms of nationalization and co-operation in Chapter VI, there appear four main types of top governing authority. The first is the old entrepreneur type, governing the firm by virtue of ownership of the capital or some of it. He may be an entrepreneur who has achieved greatness, the head of a family business who is born great, or the large shareholder in a company. The other three types occur where government is divorced from ownership. Final authority may then be in the hands of financiers, or greatness may be thrust upon part-time directors or upon full-time executives. In the first case, where entrepreneur, head of family or big shareholder is the leader the stimulus to efficiency includes that already considered in § 2, namely returns to capital.

§ 4. TYPES OF LEADER IN LARGE-SCALE BUSINESS GOVERNMENT

Social biologists distinguish nature and nurture in determining the character of a man. The types whose likely behaviour is here described are types by virtue less of their nature than of their nurture—the economic circumstances of their upbringing, their education, training and experience, rather than their inborn inherited temperaments. Being business *leaders* these types can all be assumed born with a certain potential ability; they were also born to have varying tempera-ments and 'personalities' and these natural gifts are likely to affect their leadership as much perhaps as their nurture. Natural temperament is not yet, however, successfully measured, while differences in nurture are fairly easily distinguishable objectively. It is worth tracing the likely effects of types of nurture, always bearing in mind the equal importance to business leadership of temperament and personality, qualities not so easily sorted out into ascertainable types.

(I) *The entrepreneur type*

To avoid ambiguity the term entrepreneur has throughout this book been limited to those leaders of an enterprise who own the assets of the firm as well as managing it, or who at least participate substantially in owning and managing. For it is only to this type that economists can refer when they speak of a top control responsible for bearing the financial risk and uncertainty, and being directly stimulated by profits. To call whoever is in top control of a firm 'the entrepreneur', whether he owns any capital or not, is to ask for confusion in this discussion of stimuli and reactions in view of the historical association of the word entrepreneur with the owner-manager. However widely entrepreneur is defined at the outset as whoever (possibly a salaried manager or director) is in control of top policy, readers and sometimes even the author, are likely to slip back into the accustomed groove. They will think exclusively of an *owner-manager* entrepreneur when the psycho-logy of preferences in policy and financial incentives to policy are being discussed later in the text.

The original meaning of entrepreneur, used by the French economists Cantillon and J. B. Say and as already said (p. 197) renewed by Schumpeter, is that of anyone, including promoter or merchant, who

M*   343

takes a risk in bringing together land, labour and capital in various proportions in the hope of selling their product at a profit. English classical economists right up to the writings of Marshall and his elder pupils such as Pigou, MacGregor (and their American contemporaries such as Taussig) hardly make use of the word. In 1920 Henry Clay in his *Economics for the General Reader* wrote only of the *organizer* of production. By 1922, however, the 'entrepreneur' appears fully defined in the 'united' but restricted sense of manager-owner-risker (the sense used in the present book) in Hubert Henderson's *Supply and Demand*.[1] Enterprising business men

perform to a large extent the work of management; they supply capital on what may be a considerable scale; but it is the taking of business risk which is perhaps their most characteristic function. It is the union of these functions which distinguishes them as an essentially different type from the salaried manager. . . . In other languages there is a specific name for the man who combines all these three functions; in French he is called an entrepreneur.

Only since about 1930, mainly under Keynes' lead, have English and American economists professed to broaden out the meaning of entrepreneur to cover whomsoever makes the top policy decisions of the firm especially in investment and the amount of employment. But their professions are only honoured in the breach; and confusion reigns when they ignore salaried executives without capital or benefit of profit (who control such a high proportion of business today) and confine their thinking on incentives and motives to the profit-maker.[2]

[1] 1922 edition, p. 116. Section headed 'the entrepreneur'.

[2] Keynes (*Treatise on Money*, I, p. 159; *General Theory of Employment*, p. 261) takes the entrepreneur to make the crucial decisions about wages to be paid and the amount of employment and investment *and* takes his remuneration to be profit. This identification of employer and policy-maker with profit-taker proves awkward when discussing (*General Theory*, p. 151) the influence of the private investor (who shares in profit but not industrial operation) on the rate of current investment, and Keynes is led to distinguish him from the 'professional entrepreneur'. The results of uncertain definition of the 'who' involved become more glaring in post-Keynesian textbooks. Compare for instance Benham, *Economics* (1938 edition), p. 165: 'We shall use the term "entrepreneur" to mean the person or group of persons controlling the policy of a firm' with p. 175: Profits 'exist because of uncertainty and the consequent risk of business. It is the entrepreneur who bears most of these risks, and his profits will vary with his success in forecasting future changes'. Benham fairly burns his boats (p. 179): 'the behaviour of *all* (his italics) entrepreneurs is determined by the same general principle. They will all endeavour to maximize their profits. There is no "subjective" or "psychological" aspect of the matter. The actions of an entrepreneur are not determined by his own particular scale of preferences but by objective market facts.' Even in the most modern American books written long after Berle and Means had shown that top decisions were, as often as not, made by salaried managers, we find it assumed that top control is in the hands of persons with capital, or borrowed capital. For instance in their *Theory of Investment of the Firm*, 1951, F. A. and Vera Lutz write (p. 42): 'It seems appropriate to suppose that the entrepreneur should aim

(A) *The entrepreneur who has grown with his own business.* This is the type of autocratic business chief made familiar by the classical economists. He has come to the top by a sort of natural selection, surviving because he was the fittest in the struggle—the haggling—between competing businesses. But this haggling is becoming out of date, and he may no longer be the fittest under the new environment of large functional or staff-and-line organization.

His incentive is mainly pecuniary in the form of profits. For this he is willing to work hard so that his output often comes out at a low cost per unit. Slichter enumerates a number of non-pecuniary or quasi-pecuniary incentives, including gambling on one's own ability that make further for a low cost service on the part of independent entrepreneur.

When account is taken of all the men who prefer business ownership because of its greater security, those who prefer it because they are optimists and have great faith in their ability to make money, and those who prefer it because it gives them greater freedom and authority, and those who prefer it because of the prestige which it confers, the probability seems strong that the number of men who become independent business owners is sufficient to reduce the average (pecuniary) return for their services below the wages paid to employees of about the same ability.[1]

There may also be a strong non-pecuniary incentive in rivalry with competitors. Entrepreneurs appear to enjoy the game of competition, they love the secrecy of *private* enterprise and the sense of playing for a side, and they feel more zest in fighting against a rival than in combining with him. It all hangs, perhaps, on the pride of ownership, a petit bourgeois point of view. But after all these men are petits, till by their efforts they become grands bourgeois.

The training and experience of this type will have been chiefly in shrewd dealing and, added to perhaps a somewhat rigid mental equipment, may not conduce to efficiency in managing the internal organization of a large, really grand bourgeois, concern. The entrepreneur may not have powers of co-ordinating the specialized work of managers and expert staff under his command, and he may be a poor judge of ability and use inadequate methods of measuring past performance when appointing or promoting those managers. The probabilities are, however, that the entrepreneur's many contacts with competitors and customers have given him a better working knowledge of human

[1] Slichter, *Modern Economic Society*, 1931, p. 718.

---

at maximizing the rate of return K on his own capital.' They append the footnote (which still ignores corporation structure): 'If he has no capital at all of his own, but has to borrow all that he invests, we may suppose that he wants to maximize V–C for this is his net worth and becomes in a sense his own capital.'

character than powers of co-ordination and that his appointments will be more suitable than his subsequent organization of the work of his appointees. Though wider research in business psychology and history is required marks are assigned hypothetically in Table VII for efficiency in large-scale policies and organization; the self-made entrepreneur may be given 1 out of a possible 2 for appointments, but 0 for co-ordination.

In respect of re-investment of funds the entrepreneur should, considering his limited funds, get moderate marks.[1] There is often a strong instinct for speculating with resources which are (in this case) his own, and the self-made entrepreneur has not been brought up to expensive habits on which to spend the substance of his profits. In respect of expansion of operations on a large-scale basis the entrepreneur type is likely to keep to his established practice and is not prone to think out policies from such first principles as were enumerated in Chapter II.

TABLE VII

COMPARATIVE EFFICIENCY IN LARGE-SCALE OPERATION OF TYPES OF BUSINESS LEADER

Type of leader	Policy of large-scale operation			Organization	
	By large-scale innovation (1)	By co-operation or combination with other firms (rationalization) (2)	By reinvestment of profit in fixed plant (3)	Large-scale co-ordination (4)	Top appointments (5)
I. Entrepreneur or quasi-entrepreneur					
A. Self-made entrepreneur	1	0	1	0	1
B. Family head	0	0	1	2	1
C. Large shareholder(s)	1	1	0 or 2	0	1
II. The financier	0 or 2	0 or 2	0 or 2	0	1
III. The part-time director					
A. Interlocking	1	2	1	0	1
B. Professional	1	1	0	1	2
IV. The executive					
A. Ex-employee	1	1	1	1	1
B. Ex-technician	2	1	2	0	0
C. Trained administrator	1	2	1	2	1
D. Ex-other-business	2	1	1	1	1

[1] For scattered evidence see Lavington, *The English Capital Market*, 1921, pp. 278–80. For a detailed case-history see Best, *Brass Chandelier*, 1940, especially pp. 148–9, 157. This autobiography of a small Birmingham business, to which I wrote an introduction, throws light on many aspects of entrepreneur leadership.

Hence, though he has initiative, the entrepreneur's initiative in propensity to innovation on large-operation lines can only be marked 'one'. When it comes to co-operating with other businesses the love of independence, and the individualism and 'devil take the hindmost' attitude that has helped the entrepreneur to advance in the competitive guerrilla warfare stage of capitalism, will definitely check the development of larger organizations. With his strong sense of ownership the entrepreneur may prefer power over a small organization as compared with a share of power in a large amalgamation where he will no longer have complete freedom to develop and test his own ideas. He gets no marks, therefore, for co-operation.

(B) *The head of the family that founded or owns the business or some scion of the family.* This hereditary, dynastic or aristocratic type of entrepreneur is characteristic of British industry, and though most prevalent in private companies is by no means unusual in public companies.[1] For this man the pecuniary incentive to large-scale expansion though it is in the form of profit, may be weak, since the family are already well-established. The transpecuniary objects are often stability and a conventional standard of life with plenty of leisure and long weekends devoted to sport and other gentlemanly pursuits, rather than making one's way farther up the ladder. The attitude to his business is for many of this type, almost feudal; a certain reasonable amount of annual profit and the handing of the property unimpaired to one's heir are regarded as a right and duty almost on a par with rights of seisin, merchet, tallage, and heriot that were expected by the medieval seigneur or lord of the manor. A minimum degree of innovation is thus likely, only enough perhaps to keep up the property for future generations.

In England, though less so in Scotland, it is regarded as a 'right' by this type of business proprietor that he should send his sons to the same (good old) Public School that he attended and probably to Oxford or Cambridge as well. Previous to a Public School it is also regarded as necessary for a young gentleman to go to a preparatory school. From the age of 10 to 22 each son will be boarding away from home at an expense of three hundred to eight hundred pounds per year. All this must be paid out of the father's profit, not to mention daughters' possible attendance at equally expensive boarding establishments. Clearly the gross standard income required must be at least in the neighbourhood of five to ten thousand pounds per year; but after these 'conventional needs' are satisfied the head of the family may not be ambitious and may often take up a dilettante attitude to business. As economists put it, his demand for income in terms of effort will, after a point, become highly elastic. He will be inclined to relax and

[1] Chapter V, § 3.

only great expectations of profit per unit of effort will induce him to work harder—it may under the Sargant effect[1] even deter him.

In respect of co-ordination of line and staff as also of appointment, heads of a family business are cramped by the restrictions of the family tradition. Logical organization is subject to the family relationship of the persons holding positions as managers or submanagers, or wishing to hold such positions; and there are examples of positions even on the expert staff being given in consideration of family connection rather than 'expertise'. Further, since a family that has held property for two or three generations tends to become aristocratic in outlook, any persons outside the magic family circle who are taken into the control of the business will generally have to be of equally good family and breeding. The selection is thus limited, particularly in England, to gentlemen—school or university friends, perhaps, of the younger scions. On the score of efficiency of appointments for large-operation and expert-staffed businesses, therefore, the family firm cannot be given more than one mark, but on the score of co-ordinating efficiency may perhaps be given two. In spite of illogical divisions of functions such as have been disclosed in a typical family business,[2] it must be recognized that the human beings composing an organization are not mere functionaries, and are themselves illogical. Among the higher ranks and the expert staff the more intimate family or personal relations lubricate ill-fitting parts of the organization, though the mixture of scions, friends, experts and promoted workers may put some sand in the oil. Lower down the ranks foreman or worker may be more successfully co-ordinated and 'handled' by a member of a family he has worked for all his life than by one merely appointed for his reputed efficiency. Jollying a worker along the path of efficiency by a preliminary passing the time of day or by judicious enquiries into the health and progress of his family is a necessary art of the manager or line officer. It is perhaps nowhere better performed than in the family business where the susceptibilities of the personnel are known but respected.

On the important question of re-investment of revenue in the firm, the family business is often restricted because of large holdings of stock that distant cousins, aunts, widows and even children may possess as a result of past inheritance through many generations. It is not felt right to deprive these members of the family—complete 'passengers' though they be—of their expected dividends. It would be 'letting one's people down'—and 'one's people' are not like ordinary shareholding people. Hence dividends are likely to be kept up at the expense of reserves and reinvestment to be only moderate.

[1] See § 5, p. 362.
[2] Chapter IV, § 4.

As to co-operation or amalgamation with other firms the possessive feudal attitude which makes for identification of personal interests with those of the whole firm becomes an obstacle, when efficiency demands co-operation or even amalgamation. With the merger of a family business into a larger rationalized concern no longer possessing the family name this identification goes, and not even loyalty or *esprit de corps* may remain. All that does remain is the sentiment of the gentleman against hard toil and a lack of training in technical or even administrative methods. The standard of life expected 'as of right' then becomes excessive in view of services rendered.

(C) *An owner or owners of a large bloc of shares   A large share-holder* who may be a director or, if not, possesses power behind the throne, has a pecuniary incentive in the form of dividends on his large holding, while he retains it and capital gains when he sells. This should make him, *ex hypothesi*, as willing to further the profitability of the firm by innovation as the original entrepreneur, but he may not have the ability or power to organize large-scale expansion. As large dividend recipients, some shareholders may not be too keen to re-invest instead of distributing the profit,[1] but other large shareholders looking to a far horizon may wish to increase the value of their holding by bold re-investment. A large shareholder is not likely to be particularly anxious for co-operation with other firms but probably won't oppose it tooth and nail. Not working full-time in the firm he will not have much influence on internal co-ordination but in making top appointments he will be free from jealousy and bias and should have sufficient experience to make a good choice. As a working hypothesis the large shareholder leader may be given 0 marks for co-ordination, 0 to 2 for re-investment according to horizon, and 1 each for large-scale innovation, for co-operation with other firms leading to large-scale operation, and for top appointments.

There is always the danger, however, that a large shareholder may not keep his holdings in the company. If he is a director or in-directly has access to private information he may steal a march on his fellow shareholders or future shareholders. As a director once said in evidence,[2] 'I saw the gross and net earnings constantly decreasing ... and I thought to myself there was only one result possible and I decided I wanted to get out.' Getting out means selling his shares and it follows that some person or persons buy them, as a 'sucker'—a nice point in directors' ethics. However large his holding, the large shareholder has only a fraction of the total capital, and may thus act rather differently from the original entrepreneur who owned all or a

[1] During the last century British shareholders may often have seen in the colonies more profitable lines of investment outside than reinvestment inside their company.
[2] Löwenthal, *The Investor Pays*, p. 8.

majority of the capital. He may act more like the professional financier type next described. To keep the stimulus and reaction of the two plutocratic types clear we shall take it that the large shareholders are fairly permanent and have few other interests. It would in fact be difficult for persons really owning any of the twenty largest shares of a company to 'get out' without a big fall in market values. Under the American Securities and Exchange Commission, any sales by a holder above a certain percentage of an issue are made public—a deterrent to transient large shareholding and a warning to 'suckers'!

(II) *The financier*

The financier's incentive is largely pecuniary with a love of power and perhaps prestige added. His money reward does not necessarily depend on his efficiency in large-scale operation; it is usually obtained by differences or margins in the capital value of the shares held by the financier. The pecuniary interest of the financier is to buy shares cheap and sell, or issue, them dear, and his interest in the efficiency of the firm is not likely to be lasting. Even during his holding of the shares it is often window dressing, to attract the investor and to boost the shares, that he strives for, not large-scale efficiency, though this assumes that he intends to hold the shares only a short while. Certain financial houses in America, on the other hand, are known (see Chapter V, § 3) to have had large holdings in certain industrial firms for a long time, and here prestige enters in to foster the efficiency of the firm often by large-scale operations.[1]

The financier's love of power may rest on the ultimate future pecuniary gain he hopes to reap or may be love of power for its own sake. The purchase directly or indirectly through holding and super-holding companies or trusts, of a majority of the shares with voting rights will permit the exercise of control over people and capital that is dear to his soul even though he lose money in the process. What else can explain the losses industrial magnates appear willing to sustain in purchasing control of newspapers that never had much chance of paying, or in integrating quite unrelated industries? Controlling public opinion, having a finger in every pie, King- and cabinet-making and megalomania generally is not confined to feudal barons or modern politicians. Thus for large-scale schemes of innovation the willingness and capacity of the financier may often be readily enlisted, and enlisted relatively cheaply. His inducement in Britain may even be the desire for

---

[1] See Marquand, *The Dynamics of Industrial Combination*, 1931, pp. 118–20. Marquand considers that the modern variety of American financier is more concerned with administrative efficiency. H. G. Wells, in his *Work, Wealth and Happiness of Mankind*, gives short biographies of leading varieties of financier-administrators. See also Allen, *Lords of Creation*, 1935.

national recognition in the form of a baronetcy and subsequent peerage.

Undoubtedly this pursuit of speculative profits, power and public recognition often leads the financier toward a policy of large-scale operation, particularly by association or amalgamation of firms rather than through successful competition. To boost the value of his shares he may, however, pay out the maximum dividends instead of re-investing funds in the business.

Increase in size of organization by combination may often be ill-conceived from the standpoint of large-scale operation. Combination has taken the form of the indiscriminate conglomerate integration found (in Chapter II, § 4) to be of doubtful advantage. Hence it is difficult to 'mark' the efficiency of the financier's policy toward large-scale operation either by innovation, by re-investment or by co-operation. All three must be marked 0 or 2 indicating the ambivalence found in fact. For as Marshall remarks:[1]

There are nearly always some businesses with a greater future before them than is generally known: an able promoter may perceive their capabilities, procure the capital they need, bring them into unison, and push them on their way to success faster than they could otherwise have gone. . . .

There are few who do more to increase the efficiency of labour in creating material wealth than an able and upright company promoter. . . . In strong contrast with him is the promoter, whose ventures are commonly chosen because he thinks he can induce others to believe they have a good chance of success, though he himself suspects they have none; and who is careful to clear out from them before they collapse.

In the making of appointments the financier often plays a particularly important role in putting salaried types of managers in immediate control of the firm as managing directors.[2] Where the financier thus limits his activity, ultimate control is exercised by two types acting together, and the salaried administrator, without capital or without influence with capitalists, may be able to secure at least some control only in this way.

The financier has probably a fair experience and flair for picking efficient men and is tough in dismissing the inefficient; he should get one mark for top appointments, but, as an outsider, will not be helpful in internal co-ordination, and deserves no mark.

(III) *The part-time director*

Though not logically necessary, directors have normally, under a company's articles of association, to hold qualifying shares. In Britain,

---

[1] Marshall, *Industry and Trade*, 1919, II, ix, pp. 329, 331. See also 'The story of the great age of American Finance', told by Allen in his *Lords of Creation* with that quoted subtitle.

[2] See Chapter IV, § 9.

we have seen that the minimum amount is often fixed as low as a £100 share, but in the large industrial companies of over £3 million capital the most frequent minimum was found to be £1,000, the next most frequent £500 and the next £2,000. Companies with these three minima (very low in relation to the total capital) accounted for three-quarters of the large companies. Assuming directors to be economic men, the actual amount of shares held will have some influence on their identification with the interests of the company. In the typical median large company introduced in Chapter V, the total of shares held in their own names by nine directors was, it will be remembered, only 1¼ per cent of all capital. In America the median proportion of common voting stock held by all non-officer directors was found in large industrial corporations to be 2⅓ per cent. The percentages in the two countries are not precisely comparable, but both point to the low stake held by directors in the shares of their companies, though they are supposed to represent shareholders' interests.

The proportion of the total capital of a company that directors hold is not immediately relevant, however, to the strength of the stimulus acting upon them. For any one director the question is whether his own income comes mainly in the form of fees or of dividend from his holdings or possibly from buying and selling stock. In the British median large company with nine directors the *average* holding per director was £7,000, giving at 5 per cent a dividend of £350, at 10 per cent a dividend of £700 a year. A director's annual fee is normally more than this, and in any case an 'average' holding is deceptive. Just over a quarter of the directors had holdings no more than the bare minimum qualification for their company. Among the others, many with shareholding above average, may well in their policy have an economic profit motive not unlike the entrepreneur's. The most frequent reasons, indeed, for appointing directors, given in Chapter V, § 4, merely reinforce the influence of large shareholding or executive officers. Part-time directors may, however, have a specific influence on policy where they are appointed to represent 'special interests' or to provide special knowledge.

Directors of the British 'guinea-pig' type are appointed mainly to attract and reassure small shareholders; but they are not likely to be a ruling power. Two other types of director, however, may be so: (*a*) the interlocking and (*b*) the professional-man director.[1]

(*a*) A 'community of interests' between firms is often built up by appointing the same directors on the boards of the several firms. Both

---

[1] See V § 4 above. Manufacturing companies have smaller boards than insurance companies and the iron and steel and railway companies before nationalization. The average size for the 98 largest industrial and commercial companies in 1951 was nine members. Guinea-pig directors are less frequent and full-time professional directors more frequent.

in America and Britain, as already demonstrated (Chapter V, § 4), a great number of men may hold directorships in several companies, often in the same or linked industries. In that case the ground is laid for closer combination in the future and for large-scale 'rationalization'. The interlocking director thus gets high marks for willingness to co-operate, but he is not likely to be very interested in the internal affairs of any one of the independent companies of which he is director and therefore may not be an efficient co-ordinator.[1]

(b) A director may be appointed for a special or general knowledge that may be helpful to the board. Professional men, such as chartered accountants, solicitors (and in Britain even tax-inspectors and inland revenue officers), whose opinions and ability a firm has learnt to respect, brought on to a board of directors, should lead to greater efficiency in taking advice from the expert staff and their greater co-ordination within the whole organization. But overall co-ordination will not be the professional man's *forte* and one mark is probably the correct rating. Similarly he may have contacts and facilitate co-operation with other firms, though not to the (full mark) extent of rationalization.

Whatever the reasons for putting part-time directors on a board they are paid by fee which, unlike profits, does not vary intimately with administrative efficiency. Moreover, like the financier, they are not continuously at work within the organization and thus tend to strengthen the board of directors rather than the management. They raise points about management at board meetings that may be trivial and fussy, yet they are on the whole likely to give sound advice on large-scale operation by innovation since, seeing the whole wood and not isolated trees, they should override objections, on questions of detail, to the scrapping of small-scale practices. Katona remarks that the influence of the cost accountant on the thinking of business owners and business executives can hardly be overestimated.[2] A professional accountant on the board will presumably intensify this influence. The directions toward which accountancy is likely to influence policy (and rules of thumb) is, to follow Katona, largely determined by stress on liquidity and on the cost of idle overhead capacity. Both considerations are likely to make for caution in ploughing profits back into capital equipment and plant.

(a) and (b) In the problem of the higher appointments the professional director is likely to have a much wider, and the interlocking director a somewhat wider, knowledge of men than most entrepreneurs

---

[1] A distinction must be made between interlocking among otherwise independent firms, the case here considered, and interlocking to strengthen the dependence of constituent firms of a combine. In that case the interlocking director is almost by definition an internal co-ordinator.

[2] *Psychological Analysis of Economic Behaviour*, 1951, p. 233.

or executives who have kept their noses close to the firm's grindstone. One mark may be assigned to part-time directors of both types for large-scale innovation; and one to the interlocking, but none (with his caution) to the professional director for re-investment of profit in plant. For success in making appointments, two marks may be granted to the professional with his wide knowledge of men, and one to the interlocking director.

(IV) *The full-time executive*

Leaders of nationalized and co-operative undertakings can only be of this type. Executives become the leaders in capitalist firms when (and if) the so-called managerial revolution has been accomplished.[1] The part-time director has often some stake in the property and profits of a company and is legally supposed to look after the interests of the shareholders as their trustee; but the executive of a large corporation, who is or is not a director, has on average only a minute share of its stock. He is simply the salaried employee of the company or corporation and has little direct incentive through profits. Yet he does appear to identify himself psychologically with the firm. The owners are to him not 'they' but 'we'. Indeed, company officials who own but a small fraction of the stock sometimes go so far as to consider themselves the proprietors of the business; in a U.S. senate enquiry such officials were compelled to admit that they had never before appreciated the fact that 'they did not actually own the damn company'.[2] This identification means that the executive wants his firm to do well just as (or a little more than) he might want his own football or baseball team to make higher scores than rival teams. But the score is not necessarily measured in rates of profit. Katona[3] tells us that when

top executives of large corporations were asked about their own and their competitors' profits during preceding quarters and years, it was found that they frequently did not have the answers at their finger-tips. When, however, they were asked about their own and their competitors' volume of business, and especially about their own and their competitors' share in the total market, exact answers were quickly forthcoming.

This attitude may account for a further observation—the apparent desire of executives for a 'satisfactory' rather than the maximum profit supposed by theoretical economists.[4] Rather than maximum profit,

---

[1] In his *Managerial Revolution*, 1942, Chapter VII, Burnham refers particularly to technical and production executives as the 'managers'.

[2] Sharp and Fox, *Business Ethics*, 1937, pp. 134–5.

[3] Op. cit., p. 203.

[4] Loc. cit., p. 202. Since I quoted this in my first edition, H. A. Simon has coined the word to 'satisfice' to denote making a decision that meets satisfactory standards rather than discovering and selecting the precisely optimum alternative.

growth often seems to be the main positive goal of the (normally almost shareless) executive, with important consequences for economic theory.[1] A growing firm under his management gives the executive not only prestige but usually an increase in salary. Growth may occur by innovation, by combination and mergers with other firms, or by reinvestment of profit. Different types of executive may prefer different means (as suggested later) but executive leaders can, as a whole, be assigned higher marks (as in the first three columns of Table VII) for policies of large-scale operation than the entrepreneur leaders.

(A) *The employee promoted from the lower ranks of the organization, the ex-foreman or ex-clerk type*   This *quasi-democratic* selection, without much schooling, is almost universal for the top management of the large co-operative wholesale societies and usually produces a man reacting strongly to pecuniary incentive in the form of salary increases, though his average level of monetary requirement and his standard of living is set fairly low. If the business is on a large scale and is expanding, however, his corresponding level of education and adaptability may not conduce to adjustment to new circumstances. He will be inclined to rely on traditions and rule of thumb and will not acquire the methods of government necessary for larger-scale operations; and though well-versed in the minor details of the business and a loyal subordinate he may be narrowly bureaucratic and a poor co-ordinator when in control of a large organization relying upon a specialized staff for expert advice. His general knowledge may be insufficient for weighing the pros and cons of this expert advice, and subconsciously aware of his inferiority he may become a martinet. Rivers[2] has suggested that 'one of the factors that enters into the production of "red-tape" is the activity of a defence-mechanism; that it is a protection adopted in a more or less, usually more rather than less, unwitting manner by those who find themselves confronted with administrative problems to which their powers are not adequate.'

The ex-foreman or ex-clerk is often unable by his antecedents and training to take a wide view and may fail to see possible lines of development and expansion, particularly if he was formerly employed on the production rather than the sales side. He will cling to the separate identity of the firm or society in which he was brought up and be but lukewarm to amalgamations and associations that might have led to a wider efficiency. Thus he must be given only moderate marks for co-ordinating efficiency and willingness to co-operate, and for innovating large-scale operations. As a working member of the firm and not a mere absentee owner, the ex-employee will favour re-investment of funds

---

[1] See R. Marris, *The Economic Theory of Managerial Capitalism*; W. J. Baumol, *Business Behaviour, Value and Growth*.

[2] *Psychology and Politics*, 1923, p. 24.

(though probably in liquid not fixed assets) rather than high dividends and his capacity to judge subordinates may have been developed when a foreman or supervisor. One mark may be given for re-investment of profit and one mark for appointments.

(B) *Technician or other specialist transferred to the work of general administration*   By such a 'technocratic' system of appointment an engineer may, for instance, take charge of a whole engineering business. This type of administrator is becoming more frequent, has been enthusiastically advocated,[1] and certainly supplies men trained to think scientifically and to be keen on their work apart from the salary they obtain. But the ex-technician may be unfamiliar with the work of the specialists in other techniques whom—under a functional or staff-and-line management—he is called upon to co-ordinate, and he may over-emphasize the importance of his own late function as against the other technical divisions (e.g. selling or accountancy) of the large firm's work. This will not conduce to efficient large-scale organization under the system of free production for free consumption which is assumed to continue. The technocrat may make a hobby of some invention of his own, thus providing a non-pecuniary incentive to his work, but such special interests may distract him from the 'core' functions of general government; and when the business is on a large scale, all his time should be needed for generalship. The ex-technician is likely to over-emphasize quality at a high price at the expense of quantity at a low price and be unwilling to expand business on mass-production lines even though the total net revenue of the firm would thereby be increased. He may pride himself on being a craftsman not a quantity merchant, and his supply of effort per unit of pay tends to be inelastic like that of the family head, though due to technical rather than social conventions. He therefore gets no marks for large-scale co-ordinating efficiency but high marks for innovation in large-scale operation.

On the other hand, the technician's mental attitude is likely to be favourable to capital re-investment, for he will see clearly the technical possibilities, and he may not be averse to association and amalgamation with other firms. His knowledge of men is not likely to be great and his judgment of abilities in others somewhat doubtful. For these reasons a high mark is assigned for re-investment, one mark for co-operation, and none for efficiency in appointment.

(C) *The administrator trained specially to administer*   Not one of the six types hitherto listed, it will be noticed, has more than 'picked up' the skill and knowledge necessary for the work of administration. The self-made entrepreneur has learned if at all by experience; the head of the family type is more or less an amateur, while the financier, the part-time director, the ex-foreman and ex-technician, have all either learned

[1] See Veblen, *The Theory of Business Enterprise*, 1904, passim.

trades different from that of administration, or no trade at all. The type of administrator now under consideration regards the work of administration as seriously as that of a profession. A physician undergoes six to ten years' training, a lawyer passes examinations before he is admitted, a teacher attends a training college for two years, a civil service administrator is picked by competitive examination from university graduates of the highest academic attainments. Why should a business administrator not also require selection, education and training? Large-scale operation and organization certainly call for as much mental ability, knowledge, and thought in weighing pros and cons as any of the liberal professions. Learning by experience is required in addition, but this is not less true of the medical practitioner, or the lawyer, or the teacher. It is not suggested that the university graduate who has taken, say, a commerce or economics course should be forthwith appointed general manager. It is not a question of training versus experience; but a choice between training plus experience, and mere experience. The value of a specific university training for business administration is, in America, fairly generally agreed upon.

The ready market for graduates in business in the U.S. is shown by the steady rise in the proportion of executive positions held by graduates. . . . There is mutual appreciation of the fact that what can be taught at an educational establishment is knowledge *about* rather than skill *in* administration. Skill in a practical art calls for learning by doing, but the period of learning is shortened and the skill is acquired more completely if practical training is carried out against a background of knowledge.[1]

Though university education for business was initiated in England by Sir William Ashley in the Faculty of Commerce of the University of Birmingham, as early as 1901, and only two or three American universities anticipated Birmingham, the number of British managers specifically university trained has in the past been disappointing. Caves has indeed commented that 'business as a subject for professional training and the adoption of a professional attitude by its practitioners have lagged in the United Kingdom behind both North America and the Continent'.[2] Recently, however, post-graduate and post-experience schools of management studies have been organized in British universities, many of them designed for training *after* several years of business experience.

Among the trained administrator type must be included men trained by systematic experience in large-scale organizations such as the civil service or trade unions, who may have had a university training (like the

---

[1] *Education for Management*, Anglo-American Council on Productivity, 1951, pp, 14, 15.

[2] Caves (ed.) *Britain's Economic Prospects*, 1968, p. 305.

administrative class of the civil service) or may not. Others may have been accepted by some business firm for the express purpose of training by experience of various positions in the workshops, in selling and finally in management, the object being, not immediate service, but training for ultimate service as a general executive.

What are likely to be the reactions of the trained, experienced, administrator to the problems of large-scale operation; how efficiently will he solve them, and how cheaply can efficient work be obtained from him? Will he, typically, be bureaucratic?

Let us begin with the cost of his services per unit of output. Since he has deliberately chosen administration as a profession and has been trained for efficiency therein, it is likely that the trained administrator will find a certain interest and pleasure in the successful performance of his work. He will not have to be heavily compensated to engage in otherwise repugnant activities. Nor with his view of business administration as a profession will he regard his work as dishonourable, and exact further pecuniary compensation for overlooking honour. On the other hand, the trained administrator will be a salary earner and have the disposition to play safe common to other types of salaried administrators; the chief danger to large-scale innovation is that if he has been trained in the civil service, he may have become a bureaucrat fixed in his habits and rules and conventions. He will not have the incentive of profits to spur him on to additional efforts and new adjustments when these are called for, though university education should give him more versatility than, say, the ex-employee type.

The trained or experienced administrator is likely to be an efficient line and staff co-ordinator for his practical training has introduced him to the work and difficulties of all the specialists now under his command and his theoretical training has familiarized him with 'paper' methods of control. On the other hand, he may be lacking, as already suggested, in fertility of innovation. He may realize the superior efficiency of large-scale operation but not have the drive to carry new schemes through. In making appointments, too, his judgment may be faulty; neither formal university education nor practical training can ensure an accurate valuation of other men. For co-ordination, large-scale innovation and appointments the marks assigned may therefore be 2, 1 and 1 respectively. Considering the problem of co-operation or competition with other businesses, the trained or experienced administrator is not likely to be biased in favour of maintaining the independence of the 'good old firm'; on the contrary there is likely to spring up a sort of camaraderie between all such administrators whatever firms they are administering and temporarily tied up with. The common interests of the whole industry are thus likely to obtain a favourable consideration and schemes of rationalization and combination are unlikely to be radically opposed. The problem of the disposal of gross profit is also quite likely to be decided in favour of a considerable re-investment, since the trained administrator has no more of a purely capitalist proprietary outlook than other salaried administrators. Two marks may therefore be assigned to the trained administrator on the score of co-operation and one for re-investment.

(D) *The executive transferred from another business* Finally, the executive leader within one firm and industry may have been injected from an executive position (and possibly leadership) in another industry or firm. This 'parachuting' has proved in fact the most frequent method used in appointing to the boards of nationalized industries, though not to the chairmanships of boards.[1] As against ex-employees appointed by promotion or seniority up the ranks of the same organization, this sort of appointment brings in new ideas and an all-round view of the whole wood instead of impressions of the separate trees encountered going up the ranks. In making the appointment, moreover, evidence can be used of previous success at the same level of authority. Thus the larger *retail* co-operative societies tend to appoint managers who have already shown success as managers in the smaller societies. The co-operative *wholesale* societies usually appoint as their directors men with some record of office in retail societies but, as already described, appointment is by election and not necessarily based on successful performance in a similar office.

As against appointing trained administrators, transference from other business has the advantage of obtaining men prepared to take the risks of large-scale innovation (if necessary by competition) and who have experience of more than one market, so that this type of leader can be marked 2 on that score. Since he has proved himself a successful business leader, though in another firm, he may receive one mark for the will and capacity to solve the other problems of large-scale operation.

Summary
The total of the marks assigned are in line with the existing situation, and the trend, in large-scale operation. No one type of leader predominates vastly in marks, or in fact; but there is a slight advantage in total marks to the ex-other-businessman, the trained and experienced administrator and the 'good' financier, who get a total of six or seven; and a slight disadvantage in marks to the self-made entrepreneur, the large shareholder, the ex-employee and the ex-technician, who get a total of four; and a large disadvantage to the bad financier who only gets one mark net. These advantages and disadvantages *from the stand-point of large-scale operation* correspond roughly with the actual increase

[1] Acton Society Trust, *The Men on the Boards*, 1951, pp. 5 and 6.

and decrease in the types of leaders as large-scale operation grows. The entrepreneur and the large shareholder(s), for instance, are in both countries less important as leaders than fifty years ago.

It is quite possible for more than one type of leader to be governing a firm and marks for fitness in large-scale operation can be averaged accordingly. The financiers' underwriting of a salaried administrator has already been cited. An ex-technician executive might similarly take the advice of a professional man director and thus supplement his probable deficiencies in choice of top appointments.

§ 5. THE SHORT AND LONG-RUN SUPPLY AND SUPPLY PRICE OF LEADERSHIP

Much quantitative analysis on various models has related the supply and the productivity of labour and of capital with their remuneration or price. The conditions of supply of the third factor of production —the entrepreneur, executive and business leader generally—has until recently received less attention of this sort, though the supply is of the utmost national importance. The analysis applied on pp. 281–2 to labour and capital is equally useful here. Now that the various qualitative types of business leader have been recognized, quantitative questions to ask are what sort of incentives to offer various types of business leaders so that they will be *willing* to do required amounts of work and will be attracted where needed; and how much expenditure is necessary to make them more *able* to work and to move. Their work includes not only tackling the five main problems of large-scale organization already cited but getting efficiency out of the organization and the plant, however large or small. Variations in the productivity of labour are shown mainly by differences in the same job in the same plant or firm between the outputs of different workers.[1] Variations in the efficiency of management and leadership can perhaps be shown by differences in the average output of all workers on similar jobs in different plants and firms *under different management*. Measured in this way, as much variation appears in manager and leader as in labour productivity. British enquiries, particularly the reports of the post-war working parties set up by Sir Stafford Cripps, have shown in industry after industry how wide is the variation in average output per man on the same jobs under different managements. In making utility furniture only, and taking 43 firms of similar size only, employing 50 to 99 workers, and therefore presumably with similar problems in mechanization, output per operative was under 50 per cent of average in two firms and 150 to 299 per cent in four.[2] Again, in the woollen industry, taking one type of cloth, six factories in a single district varied in cost of overcoating from 79 to

[1] E.g. Florence, *Economics of Fatigue and Unrest*, 1924, pp. 221–4.
[2] Working Party Report, H.M.S.O., Furniture, p. 62.

111 per cent of the average; and in four other comparisons between eight to ten different factories in the same districts making the same cloth the variation in average costs for each factory was 90 to 115 per cent, 81 to 117 per cent, 85 to 122 per cent, and 82 to 122 per cent of overall average. A still more thorough enquiry into the British shoe industry showed that working on similar standard shoes, the average man-hours (including indirect labour) varied among twelve factories from a minimum of 3·74 to a maximum of 6·02 per dozen pairs on one operation, from 2·16 to 4·06 on another and from 0·99 to 2·26 on yet another.[1]

Clearly, incentives as well as appropriate selection and training methods may push up considerably the efficiency of some factory managements. These incentives and conducives to management should be as low in cost as possible if the price required for the product is to be kept down and standards of living and competitive position up. This cost or supply price of leadership will combine for nearly all types of leader pecuniary and non-pecuniary elements, *but the greater the non-pecuniary, the less needed are high pecuniary incentives and the cheaper to the nation is business government*;—we may speak here as for the other factors of production of the economical non-economic motives. A standard term of economics, the social science dealing precisely with these quantitative relations of costs and product, of inputs and outputs, may prove useful. Income and price elasticity of demand have, in discussing consumption, been found handy, and in discussing production, supply price is another such tool. The supply price for any amount of a commodity, so runs the concept, is the price (in money or kind) 'required to call forth the exertion necessary for producing that amount' and can be applied to each of the factors necessary for producing a unit of output (such as a yard of cloth),—capital, labour and management.[2]

It is usually assumed by economists that *in the short run*, when available supplies of labour are limited, a higher rate of pay per given exertion will be an incentive for more work to be done by labour and that the pecuniary supply price rises for greater amounts of output. This may not be the case if the labourer has a fixed standard of living and does not wish to increase his total earnings; a higher rate of time wage will then induce him to work less time and a higher rate of piece wage to make fewer pieces.[3] When saving is being discussed this possibility is always admitted by economists, its first statement being

---

[1] British Boot and Shoe and Allied Trades Research Association, Report on Women's Shoes, 1951.

[2] Marshall, *Principles of Economics*, 1910, p. 142, and especially footnote p. 344.

[3] Florence, *Labour*, 1949, pp. 99–100.

attributed to my great-great-uncle, William L. Sargant.[1] If the saver wishes merely to have a fixed income in the future then a higher rate of interest will induce him to save *less* principal. But when it comes to the entrepreneur or administrator no such Sargant effect is admitted. To quote Keynes:[2]

'When the actual rate of entrepreneurs' remuneration exceeds (or falls short of) the normal ... entrepreneurs will ... seek to expand (or curtail) their scale of operations at the existing costs of production.'

Yet certain types of business leader have differently shaped supply-price curves. Some entrepreneurs and family heads have just as much of a fixed income standard in their minds as certain types of labourers or savers; and with increasing rates of pay they may restrict their output and activities in precisely the same way; increased exertions will not be 'called forth' by increased pay.

At the time, early in the nineteenth century, when the English classical economists were laying the foundations of economic theory, the capitalist entrepreneur does seem to have been a regular hustler, at any rate in England, eager to match work with pay. Say, the French economist, was filled with wonder at the intense restless energy of all classes of Englishmen. 'Everybody runs absorbed in his own affairs,' he wrote. 'Those who allow themselves the slightest relaxation in their labours are promptly overtaken by ruin.'

By the middle of the Victorian era, in Ruskin's hey-day, the ideal standard of living of the business man which he described in the town hall of Bradford[3]—presumably to a knowing audience of Yorkshire manufacturers—appears distinctly static and less elastic in response to pecuniary incentive.

Your ideal of human life then is, I think, that it should be passed in a pleasant undulating world, with iron and coal everywhere underneath it. On each pleasant bank of this world is to be a beautiful mansion, with two wings; and stables, and coach-houses; a moderately sized park; a large garden and hot-houses; and pleasant carriage drives through the shrubberies. In this mansion are to live the favoured votaries of the Goddess; the English gentleman, with his gracious wife, and his beautiful family; always able to have the boudoir and the jewels for the wife, and the beautiful ball dresses for the daughters, and hunters for the sons, and a shooting in the Highlands for himself. At the bottom of the bank, is to be the mill; not less than a quarter of a mile long, with a steam engine at each end, and two in the middle, and a chimney three hundred feet high. In this mill are to be in constant employment from eight hundred to a thousand workers, who never drink, never strike, always go to church on Sunday, and always express themselves in

---

[1] Marshall, *Principles of Economics*, IV, vii, § 9.
[2] *A Treatise on Money*, 1930, Vol. I, p. 125.
[3] *The Crown of Wild Olive*, Lecture II, published, 1866.

respectful language. Is not that, broadly, and in the main features, the kind of thing you propose to yourselves? It is very pretty indeed, seen from above.

I do not wish to criticize this ideal, or to blame the businessman for valuing leisure and distributing his time as seems best to him. He is no doubt following as far as in him lies the Greek philosopher's ideal of the good life and, as Ruskin says, it is very pretty. But the implication of his attitude should not be missed by the economist. It is rash to assume, at any rate in England today, that in the short run, before any increased supply of new men can come on the market, greater pecuniary incentives will stimulate every type of existing entrepreneur or business leader to additional work, and that greater output can always be immediately obtained by paying higher supply prices. The static philosophy of the aristocrat and gentleman pervades the twentieth-century British bourgeoisie particularly (as described later, pp. 376–7) through the medium of the English 'public schools'. If, owing to general prosperity or a greater demand for their products, the net revenue of certain firms appears likely to rise, the reaction of certain types of business leaders may be either to pay no attention and stay on the same scale or, aiming at the same revenue, to restrict activities.

The ex-technician type of leader who is keen, like the medieval craftsman, on the limited production of a well-wrought article may be impervious to any economic stimulus in higher income, may continue to 'class' produce rather than 'mass' produce, and may neither increase nor decrease his exertion and the amounts of output. Together with all annual salaried full-time administrators divorced from ownership, he will not tend to be quite so alert to the new possibilities in expanding his work as the classic entrepreneur who would strive to reap all the extra profit of such expansion; for the additional net revenue would not immediately accrue to these salaried executive types but would swell the dividends of the ordinary shareholders. And the shareholders, as was explained in the last chapter, are ignorant of the possibilities of expansion. They are liable to be satisfied, or at least not to protest, when dividends are maintained, in happy ignorance of the fact that their dividend might have been much higher. There is, then, in modern capitalist organization, a distinct likelihood that the pecuniary stimulus may not yield a reaction in enterprise one way or the other. The same absence of reaction to money stimulus may occur under nationalization. The board or the managers of nationalized undertakings are also on a salary and the taxpayer who is likely to suffer by their inefficiency is in some ignorance of the possibilities of tax relief due to incurring smaller losses on operations.

But there is a possibility not just of absence of reaction but of a negative reaction. To call forth more exertion the supply price must be lowered not raised, like the need to lower interest rates to get more saving, observed in the Sargant effect. Some entrepreneurs, particularly of the head-of-the-family business type, and some managers and directors, too, may feel, when their income or the shareholders' income appears likely to rise considerably above a given standard, that they can relax their efforts and spend more of their time in well-earned rest and leisure. They will not be so keen to obtain new business and will be less pushful in their salesmanship, making little effort to cut down prices. Hence their exertions and the extra output for which they are responsible will not expand with expectations of increased remuneration for themselves or the shareholders, but may actually contract.

Under competition this relaxation may not be continued long, but if there is a monopoly or monopolistic conditions where trade associations or agreements can be arranged among like minds[1] in the same industry, then the *downward* supply curve—the higher the income per unit the less the supply—may well get established. This hypothesis, which I have consistently advanced, of occasional negative reaction and not merely a neutral in-action to rising income has met with a storm of denials, but a pronouncement by one of the leading authorities on British industry, speaking as president of the economic section of the British Association, may be quoted in my defence:[2]

Theoretical economic analysis commonly proceeds on the assumption that a business man, when acting rationally, enlarges his output to the point at which his net profits are maximised; but this assumption seems to be refuted by the common observation that the general run of business man is content to stop short of that point. His aim is rather to ensure to himself over a long period an income which enables him to maintain a customary standard.

An entrepreneur or family head can adjust his exertion and working days to please himself; and even a salaried employee may, but need not, do overtime or 'home-work' and above a limit can exert himself as he pleases so long as results (with or without his exertion) are satisfactory.

The taxpayers who under nationalization take the place of the shareholder in bearing risks are not likely to be any more alert to possibilities. The situation in consumers' co-operation is more complex, and directors are judged by the results of single transactions rather than by the aggregate of profit or loss for a whole period. But here again, whenever favourable outside trade conditions exist, the manager or director may exert himself less, for results will be good in any case. Anybody with this form of reaction, seeking a fixed net income will, if really consistent, be stimulated to work harder when taxes on income are increased.

[1] See above, Chapter III, § 6.
[2] Allen, 'Economic Progress, Retrospect and Prospect', *Economic Journal*, September 1950, p. 473.

The question naturally arises which of these three sorts of quantitative reaction to higher pay—positive, neutral, or negative—is the more frequent among the men that ultimately govern industry? A direct answer would involve an analysis of the total output and services of each country according as they were provided under the control of the several types of leader that we have recognized. The plausible hypothesis may be advanced (to be tested) that owing to their selection and training, soon to be described, more British than American business leaders have negative or neutral reactions to increased supply prices or incentives. Research has not proceeded far enough in Britain or America to give even an approximate estimate but some definite statements can be made about the *changes* that have occurred in both countries, in the comparative aggregates of business controlled by men of different reactions.

Most of nineteenth-century business was probably controlled by the self-made entrepreneur working harder when increased rates of remuneration were in sight, but toward the end of that century many of the businesses that had developed earliest had fallen into the hands of the sons or the grandsons of those self-made pioneers. A greater proportion of business became controlled by family heads merely because they were the heads of families. This leadership by inheritance was probably true of the business of banking and large-scale businesses in industries such as iron and steel and coal mining, even though in form they became joint stock companies; and family control continues to prevail in many of the smaller, but old-established industries, such as, in Britain, pottery, clothing and footwear, furniture, printing and publishing[1] and the older branches of engineering. It is possible that the relative decline in British industry between 1880 and 1930 when compared with that of other industrial countries has been due to the large proportion of its output controlled by family heads reacting less keenly to higher profit, and re-investing less of that profit.

The inter-war and post-war era, however, has shown signs of a further transference of control. The importance of the family business in the total national trading is probably waning, and that of the salaried administrator, sometimes influenced by financiers and part-time directors, waxing. The large doses of rationalization quietly swallowed in America and Britain during the depression of 1930–3, involved the pensioning of family veterans, and the passing over of the less promising heirs. With the proportionately increasing volume of business falling into the hands of corporations and joint stock companies and combines of various sorts, less business is likely to be under the control of the self-made entrepreneur and more under various types of executive.

[1] See Florence, *Ownership, Control and Success of Large Companies*, pp. 13–17.

With the increased volume of business nationalized the salaried ex-business man or trained administrator types are likely to gain in importance.

The immediate result is that existing businesses are not so likely to seize their opportunity of expanding the profits during prosperity, or to adjust themselves by contracting during a depression, as in the period when the entrepreneur was the most frequent type of leader. The salaried administrator has probably not the same keenness to increase his shareholders' profits whenever there is the least chance that the remuneration of enterprise may rise, as had the first-generation entrepreneur. On the other hand, compared with the family business era, we may expect less output limitation as the reaction to slack times and higher remuneration.

Salaried executives have the economic advantage of adjustability of supply. Where non-pecuniary motives apply it is possible for their services to be obtained relatively cheaply; and to meet the expectation by financiers and directors of higher return to enterprise, it is possible for more of their kind to be readily called in. These possibilities depend on the two conditions: that the present leaders making top appointments shall not be blind to the efficiency of potential leaders now in subordinate posts; and, a long-run policy shortly to be discussed, that a supply of efficient potential leaders shall be trained in sufficient quantities.

If additional amounts of the pecuniary incentive—the cash nexus—fail, greater enterprise on the part of business leaders may perhaps be stimulated, and stimulated at low cost, by intensifying the 'economical non-economic' incentives so often proposed for labour, such as the name or fame nexus, the sporting nexus, the hobby nexus, the gang nexus. The British, like the Russian government with its Heroes of the Republic, crowns successful business careers with medals, orders and honours such as knighthoods and peerages which give a man fame and a 'handle' to his name, or at least letters after his name.[1] It is also an incentive to most executives or managers if they can acquire fame through publicity on their success story, an incentive more freely offered by the American than the British press. And again there is a certain sporting spirit in business competition and rivalry which stimulates the British as well as the American executive to increased exertion. And

---

[1] American business has, in Galbraith's view (*American Capitalism*, 1952, p. 29), 'evolved a system of procedure hardly less rigorous than that of Victorian England. It is based almost exclusively on corporate assets. In the business peerage the ducal honors belong to the heads of General Motors, Standard Oil of New Jersey, Du Pont and the United States Steel Corporation. The earls, baronets, knights and squires fall in behind in reasonably strict accordance with the assets of their respective firms.' Fame (and power) would, on this thesis, prove a non-pecuniary attractive toward larger organizations.

when business methods are made a matter for mutual discussion between executives (as it frequently is among trained administrators) a certain gang interest may increase effort, or, rather, increase output without effort. A similar economy occurs where business leaders like so many technicians make their work their hobby and, as possible in smaller firms, are their own masters. On the other hand, the status-nexus which, in a large organization, depends so much on the salary scale, is an expensive stimulus. A manager has to be paid a lot just to get more than his colleagues, even though most of it is super-taxed away!

In the long run a higher pecuniary supply price as well as non-pecuniary considerations may attract further supplies of entrepreneurs and executives into the industry, or stimulate existing entrepreneurs and executives in other industries to add goods and services to their line of production. This long-run equilibrium by recruitment and integration assumes an available and mobile supply of brains and resources that depends largely on education and brings into play further parts of our analysis of stimuli: the attractives to become a leader and the conducives to be an able leader. The leaders demanded are only a small fraction of the population and there is probably a fair supply of potential leaders, mute and inglorious, who would react strongly to incentives if they had the chance. This small demand and fair supply should result in a low supply price, if supply were freely available.

Obstructions in the supply of talent is probably stronger in Britain than America. Pecuniary attractives in Britain and especially America appear to be in favour of business and industry as against professions. In America this income differential has the normal *long-run* effect an economist assumes. Many if not most of the ablest personnel are duly attracted into industrial management, and start on a career headed for business leadership. But the economists' assumption of economic man fails to materialize in Britain and, in spite of special pecuniary attractions, much of the ablest youth of Britain avoids entering business management, a fact that may well be one cause for the lower productivity of British compared to American industry. Elsewhere I have set forth British salary scales which show[1] that the incomes, actual and prospective, of the growing numbers of professional administrators in industry compares favourably with those of persons having at least similar abilities in the state civil service, and the legal, academic and medical professions. It should follow, if men were guided chiefly by pecuniary attractives, that industry will secure the highest grade of ability in its administrators. Nor at first sight does any obstacle appear to such attraction on the side of pecuniary inability. The will to enter

[1] Florence, 1933, pp. 233–6. Realistic analysis must add expense accounts to salaries.

or transfer into business administration is not blocked by any apparent need of an elaborate education, or of the cultivation of manners and correct intonation, such as confront the doctor, the lawyer, or the university teacher. In short, the pecuniary 'conducives' enabling a person to become a business leader do not appear out of reach. The self-made entrepreneur has come to the front by outbidding and out-bargaining his rivals, without much educational apparatus or early pecuniary endowment, and the ex-employee type of executive has also been promoted to greatness without owning pecuniary resources.

Nevertheless, some pecuniary obstacles do exist to the free supply of capable business leaders. Even in the course of progress of the self-made entrepreneur and the ex-employee, poverty in early life would probably eliminate all potential business chiefs who did not combine, with the necessary administrative qualifications, an iron constitution able to resist the inroads upon a low diet, of long and arduous hours of work climbing the lower rungs of the ladder. And in the progress of other types of business leader more adapted to large-scale, highly organized industry, the supply of administrative ability still depends largely either on the ownership or control of capital or a relatively expensive education. The supply of family heads available in the future is limited naturally by the number of business families, and their low birth-rate. The financier, and the interlocking director must, by definition, own or control pecuniary resources, or at least have influence; and the ex-technician, the professional man and the trained administrator types of leader must all undergo a long education. At present the high cost of the sort of education that is considered desirable in British salaried executives adds to their salary an institutional rent; this high salary in turn sets up a high conventional standard of living and leisure among executives to which the standards of new accessions must conform. A vicious circle of high costs per unit of effort is thus set up that is probably unnecessary. In relation to their effort salaried men of equal ability are probably obtainable for industry cheaper on the continent of Europe than in Britain; and some attempt to break the vicious circle must be made if competition with foreign businesses is to be more successful. One type of salaried manager—the ex-employee—has, it is true, fairly modest requirements; but it remains to adjust effort and salaries (and expense accounts) of the executives more suited to large-scale industry, the ex-technician and the trained and experienced administrator, as also the part-time director. This adjustment can be effected through the normal demand and supply equilibrium, as already suggested, by attracting and training a larger supply of capable hard-working executives.

In short, difficulties appear in attracting able but impecunious young persons into business due to the lack of pecuniary conducives to mobility out of the poorer strata. There are, too, certain *non-pecuniary* psychological and sociological distractives pulling all young people away from business as a career, such as the dull life and hideous aspect of industrial towns; and certain non-pecuniary factors *disabling* them from becoming leaders, such as the narrow routine to which they may be held instead of being granted varied experienced and some early responsibility.[1] Though a potentially efficient business executive might react successfully to the pecuniary incentives offered him, and be attracted to business and away from other pursuits by the high salary, he might remain merely potential because there were non-pecuniary distractions, and/or because he has not been *enabled* mentally and socially to enter upon a business career, or to work efficiently when he had entered it.

When discussing labour, non-pecuniary deterrents were found largely the result of conventional modes of thought unaffected by education, and disabling factors largely of the physical order. A labourer cannot move from one occupation to another for lack of transport or housing, he cannot work efficiently because of lack of sufficient food or excess of working hours. But in stimulating leadership the nature of the pecuniary deterrents or attractions and the nature of the conducives to entrance and efficient work in a business career are influenced so greatly by education that the matter will be considered next in a separate section.

§ 6. RECRUITMENT AND EDUCATION FOR INDUSTRIAL GOVERNMENT

To have discussed education for management a hundred years ago would have been thought grotesque. Management, as such, hardly existed. There were entrepreneurs, proprietors, partners—businessmen, generally; but management was merely an incident, almost a side-line in the work of those industrialists. To be educated for that side-line was preposterous. You were either born to a great business as the son and heir of a family concern, or you achieved greatness by successful competition against rivals, or you had it thrust upon you by promotion from the ranks of clerks or foremen. You never trained for business as for the law or the church or medicine. In short, management was not a profession.

With the increasing size of firms and their transformation into joint stock companies, a devolution has taken place which has been described in some detail. The functions of capitalist-entrepreneurs are in most firms split, and carried out by the private investor, speculative or gilt-edged; by the trustee-director with a seat on the board but exercising

---

[1] See Bowie, *Education for Business Management*, 1930, especially pp. 126–31.

no continuous supervision; and, finally, by the full-time executive, president or managing-director and his general staff.

It is recruitment and education of the salaried, professional industrial executive that will here be chiefly discussed, since this is the type of leadership, not limited to owners of capital, where supplies can be more readily expanded.

The core of top government in large industrial organizations was found to consist[1] in external general policy and strategy, what to make, how much of it, at what price and with what capital investment, and in internal general organization, including top appointments. The function of the top governors of a large firm may perhaps be summed up in one word as generalship.

The head of a large modern business must not only show initiative in his strategy and policy but must appoint, command, co-ordinate and delegate work to the functional specialists and the captains, majors and even colonels under him. In a large firm there arises (as shown in Table IVB) such a hierarchy of line and staff officers that a captain of industry is really very small fry.

Over and above the qualities required in all leadership of men, this new industrial generalship makes new special calls on human faculties and powers. The job demands, first, the ability and will to control large organizations. A general, if a continually growing organization is not finally to overwhelm him (as economists so gloomily predict), must know how to delegate. But so much has been written in praise of specialization and division of labour since Adam Smith, in the very first pages of the *Wealth of Nations*, pointed to its use in pin-making, that the necessity of re-co-ordinating and organizing the divided parts must now be emphasized. If A makes the head of the pin and B the shaft someone has to see that heads and shafts are produced in equal numbers by a given date at a given place. There must be specialized technicians, accountants, personnel managers, market researchers; the general of industry must be able and willing to organize and co-ordinate the work of these specialists for the final purpose of industry—to produce and sell goods. In a word he must have system.

At the same time the main requirement of the old entrepreneur enterprise still subsists. The new 'general' of industry must have the urge and ability to invent, initiate and command. He must have ideas about possibilites—imagination, for instance, about possible customers, possible wants or tastes in design. He must be decisive and prepared to make quick decisions involving risks and must possess resourcefulness in adapting the means at his disposal to secure the fruits of his imagination. In a word, he must still have enterprise.

Finally, the combination of the new requirements of the large firm

[1] Chapter IV, § 6.

with the old requirements of the owner-manager entrepreneur, set in a new world of science, will involve digestion of statistical records, judging reports and advice from experts, planning ahead in accordance with judgments, and checking up on results. It will require some knowledge of the expert's principles and a scientific frame of mind able to draw inferences by isolating factors and seeing the wood for the trees. The general of industry must have trained intelligence coupled with zest for intellectual work.

In the nineteenth century Ruskin thought that[1]

the tact, foresight, decision, and other mental powers, required for the successful management of a large mercantile concern, if not such as could be compared with those of a great lawyer, general, or divine, would at least match the general conditions of mind required in the subordinate officers of a ship, or of a regiment, or in the curate of a country parish.

This view of the 'mental powers required' still holds the field in some 'mercantile (and manufacturing) concerns' and trained civil service administrators are often surprised by the difficulty the untrained business man finds in applying general principles. He is unable to class individual cases under general headings and thus will bother himself making new decisions about subsidiary details that he should have arrived at almost automatically. Without intelligence and system at the top a *large* firm is not, however, likely to grow, or even to remain large.

Of these three requirements for top industrial government, system and enterprise are particularly important for the chief or directing manager, but intelligence is equally important to his general staff. While the chief may to some extent organize and supply initiative to his subordinates, he cannot supply intelligence and must here be met half-way.

The question must now be faced whether education is able to prepare men for the tasks of large-scale industrial government. Will it give men system, enterprise and intelligence? Will it supply not only ability to organize, initiate and think intelligently but also the willingness, the urge, the zeal to do so?

A person of adequate inborn general intelligence can certainly be taught at school and university to be more systematic and to adjust mind and action more intelligently to changing and changed circumstances. No one advocates putting new-fledged graduates right into positions of business responsibility; but school and university education *plus* some experience is certainly more useful than exposure to experience alone—than mere 'weathering' without training in powers of thought to learn from experience. It is the opinion of educationalists on both sides of the Atlantic that Britain, with its specialized scholarship and degree courses and its rigorous examination system, pushes students

[1] *Unto this Last*, Essay I.

about two academic years ahead of Americans of similar age; but in the past fewer Britons ever reached the universities. Colin Clark[1] gives a table for sixteen countries of the number of university students per thousand population in 1930–2. America ranked top with 7·88, England and Wales bottom with 1·21. England without Wales would have a still lower ratio, Scotland always ranked much higher.

Since the Second World War the English ratio has greatly increased with the founding of many new universities and the conversion to university status of colleges of technology. In 1938–9 there were 15,153 new full-time students admitted to British universities, in 1968–9 there were 59,378—nearly four times as many.[2] But the legacy of under-education will continue to affect the (older) top of the business hierarchy for some time to come.

After schooling and some university education a person can further be trained to know the best techniques in his profession and to know how to improve upon the best. This training in know-how is the main task of the technical college, or of post-graduate training at the university. Here, in professional training for industrial government, America is outstanding. Though almost the first university degree in Commerce was founded in England, at the new University of Birmingham,[3] America has now far outstripped Britain in its university undergraduate and post-graduate schools of business administration, and in the attention devoted by its institutes of technology to problems of management. School and university education can thus supply, in not too long a long-run, intellectually adjustable and mobile recruits for top industrial government. This source of supply is much greater, even proportionately to its greater population, in America than Britain.

What can education do for industrial government besides thus supplying a certain number of recruits provided (in the words of our analysis of stimuli) with 'conducives to enable them to act and to move wherever more efficient employment' offers systematically and intelligently?

An educationalist is naturally inclined to claim too much for what education can do. He should remind himself of what education can *not* do. Men are born unequally gifted with intelligence and in character, and while education can develop what gifts are there and compensate perhaps for the lack of other gifts it can never entirely change this inequality. There are particular distributions of mental abilities just as there is a certain wide scatter of physical characters, and however much he takes thought and lecture courses, a man cannot add more than a certain fraction of a cubit to the stature of his powers. Still less can

---

[1] *The Conditions of Economic Progress*, 1951, p. 480.
[2] Annual Abstract of Statistics, 1938–49, Table 121; 1969, Table 122.
[3] § 4, p. 357 above.

formal education affect temperamental differences. The powers of system and intelligence may be heightened and deepened, but what can education do for the powers of enterprise or even the temperament and *zeal* to be intelligent and systematic required for top industrial government?

This question is usually asked rhetorically and the orator stops not for an answer. But there is an answer, definite, though limited. The educational system can weed out recruits born temperamentally as well as mentally unsuitable for industrial government. Education, too, can supply interests as non-pecuniary attractives and incentives so that young people *with the required inborn powers* will develop; so that they will find their way toward the appropriate work, will be attracted to it and not repelled, and will be induced to perform that work apart from pecuniary incentive with pleasure and without friction.

In citing three powers as particularly required for modern business government—system, enterprise and intelligence—the word powers was used deliberately to cover both abilities and willingness to exert them. What proportion of children that are born are ever likely to have within them the powers—abilities *and* willingness—that are required of top industrial government today?

The required combination of powers I take as somewhat scarce, and assume that perhaps only one child in fifty can ever make an efficient large-scale manager, however successful its education. If that is so, the practical purpose of education from the standpoint of management is to *attract* the one child out of fifty that is born potentially able and willing into management, or at least not to distract it therefrom; and to *develop* that inborn capacity and willingness not only by providing the necessary knowledge and skill conducive to business ability but also non-financial incentives.

Another limit to the effectiveness of formal education must be admitted besides inborn incapacity and unwillingness. A boy or girl does not grow up *only* at school or college, but is subjected to all sorts of home and social influences unconnected, or only incidentally connected, with the educational system. He or she will be affected by the economic conditions of the home. The child of the poor will be cramped in housing and the facilities for studying and developing freely and, possibly, be short even of food; there may be little intellectual stimulus from parents or other relations. Thus, however suitable their education may be for large-scale management, perhaps two-thirds of the poor, born able and willing, may never develop a sufficient basis of physical vitality or of mental interest. In Britain and America, at least three-quarters of the community receive less than half the communities' income and may be called relatively poor. If inborn powers are equally distributed among rich and poor it follows that half (i.e. two-thirds of three-quarters) of our assumed one-in-fifty potential managers may thus be lost. From a 2 per cent of possibles we have already dropped to 1 per cent.

Education has thus to contend against the unequal natural distribution of powers and the unequal economic distribution of opportunities of developing these powers. But even where poverty is not an obstacle, there will be a further psychological set of factors to contend with. Children, we are told by psycho-analysts, discover early (and the earlier the more effectively) that certain things are *not* the thing, and certain deeds *'not* done'. These attitudes will block or twist education and by modifying children's ambitions will attract or distract them in all sorts of ways. Many of these *'don'ts'* may certainly tend against the attraction and development of able and willing top managers required in industry today. Since parents are necessarily a generation behind, sentiments will be inculcated and habits imitated unsuitable to the requirements of the modern age. These parents were influenced by their parents, and those parents by their parents and so back and back into the mists of medieval and ancient history and even pre-history. A mass of traditional lore has thus accumulated profoundly affecting the social outlook and mental attitudes, and forming a set of conventions that may lag centuries behind the needs of the time. This lore will be very different for different cultures.

The American culture is to foreign eyes peculiarly commercial. Business has high prestige and there is a minimum of obstacles to the attractiveness of business as a career. Somewhat different in Scotland, the sociological climate of England is more different still. And since low British labour productivity has been partly attributed to management (see § 1) considerable attention must be given to English education and attitudes to business. From the (often sympathetic) writings of foreign observers we may single out the peculiarity the Germans call the ideal of the gentleman—*das Gentlemanideal*. The ideal of the gentleman appears in many manifestations of English life and manners, but from the standpoint of business as a career it has several particular consequences.

First of all, the old tradition is that a gentleman does not engage in business *at all*. He is above seeking profit and as he does not soil his hands with manual toil so he does not soil his soul with trade. In England traditions die slowly and though this view is now seldom openly expressed as it was a century or so ago, it continues to affect men's behaviour today. In Jane Austen's *Emma* Mr and Mrs Cole 'were very good sort of people, friendly, liberal, and unpretending; but, on the other hand, they were of low origin, in trade, and only moderately genteel'. More than a century ago Ruskin thought that[1]

---

[1] *Unto this Last*, Essay I.

philosophically, it does not, at first sight, appear reasonable that a peaceable and rational person, whose trade is buying and selling, should be held in less honour than an unpeaceable and often irrational person, whose trade is slaying. Nevertheless, the consent of mankind has always, in spite of the philosophers, given precedence to the soldier. . . . Not less is the respect we pay to the lawyer and physician.

Thus a business career failed in Britain to exert the attractive power to which its comparative pecuniary rewards might entitle it because of the non-pecuniary consideration of comparative social disrespect. The superior respectability of the gentleman, who does no work at all, has now enveloped the liberal professions and given them an attraction superior to business as a career.

Secondly, if a gentleman, by sheer necessity, has to enter business, he is inclined to foster the notion that he is doing so as a sportsman—and an amateur sportsman—not a professional. It is not 'the thing' to make business a science and 'a job of work'. It is viewed as a game slightly amusing but nothing to become over-zealous about, or to work week-ends for, and nothing for which to train the intellect.

The ideal of a gentleman [writes M. Siegfried[1]], the foundation of modern British civilization, seems to have contributed to this relaxation of fundamental energy. A gentleman, we must realize, never strives too much; it is not considered the thing. He does nothing too well; he leaves that to the professional and the champion.

Thirdly, the idea of the gentleman implies the existence of men who are definitely *not* gentlemen, and who, though no doubt they may be sympathized with and given a helping hand, are of a different class, and outsiders. If they attempt as 'bounders' to jump the boundary, the privacy of the gentleman must be asserted by various forms of social ostracism and 'cutting'.

Foreign observers, writes Tawney,

come to the conclusion that Englishmen are born with *la mentalité hiérarchique*, and that England, though politically a democracy, is still liable to be plagued, in her social and economic life, by the mischievous ghost of an obsolete tradition of class superiority and class subordination.[2]

The hierarchical character of English society finds . . . expression in the restriction of the sources from which leadership is derived, and in arrangements which make it certain that many of those who direct will rarely, even in childhood, mix freely and spontaneously with those who are directed.[3]

Thanks mainly to the wider intake into higher education this gentleman-ideal is perhaps now weaker but still affects the provision of

[1] *England's Crisis*, 1931, p. 147.
[2] *Equality*, 1931, p. 30.
[3] Op. cit., p. 97.

efficient business leadership. There is no reason to suppose that England, compared with other industrial countries, is not provided at birth with as many persons possessing potentially the three special requisites for large-scale business government—enterprise, intelligence and system. But quite apart from poverty fewer of these potential leaders reach business, or if they reach business act with the enterprise, intelligence and system with which potentially they were born. To take business seriously 'is not done' and a gentleman is a man who does the 'done thing' socially, who holds, as Dr Renier[1] puts it, the 'ritualistic conception of life'.

Now for the next question. Does the English educational system tend to overcome the blocking and diversion of a promising business career by these conventional attitudes and sentiments? On the contrary, much of the system so far from being a corrective of the consequences of the gentleman-ideal seems definitely to be based on that ideal and calculated to clamp it down still harder.

England is different from other Western countries (including Scotland) in that the children of the poor and the children of the rich are usually separated for purposes of education. Normally the poor go to the elementary or primary school, and lower forms of the secondary school till the age of 15, a minority of them proceed further up the secondary school, comprehensive or grammar and a few thence to the older, or, more likely, the London or provincial or newer universities. The rich are, first, either educated at home or go to a private preparatory school. Then nearly all of them proceed to a so-called Public School,[2] whence at least a goodly minority proceed to a university, often Oxford or Cambridge. English education has thus tended to intensify rather than to overcome class segregation and class attitudes. Writing in 1939 Greenwood sums up that the poorer 'elementary school children have not quite half and others have more than three times their proper share of the university population'.[3]

The time has now come to review what has happened to the twenty out of every thousand assumed born in both Britain and America with potential powers for top business government. Fifteen of these were supposed to be born in poor circumstances, of whom ten were handicapped in early life for that very reason. That leaves us five poor and five rich hopefuls. Of the five rich and capable in America, four may

---

[1] *The English, are they Human?*, 1932, Chapter IX.

[2] Here spelled with a large P and S to warn the American reader that they are not public in the sense of free or run by the state, but rather the contrary. As Tawney puts it (*Equality*, p. 96) they are schools 'that the great majority of the public are precluded from entering'. They are boarding schools and the fees are high. The nearest American equivalent is the preparatory school or military academy.

[3] *Statistical Journal*, Part III, 1939, p. 367.

well go into business without question and some will do so highly trained in university graduate schools of Business Administration. In Britain, however, the careers of the rich are subject to many subtle conflicting currents. All the hypothetical five probably went 'through the mill' of the Public Schools, and the schools for very young gentlemen preparatory to them.

These boarding schools attempt to influence temperament and character and largely succeed, through the close contact of the inmates, the system of self-government maintained by prefects, and the importance attached to games. The Public Schools are continually worrying to keep up their 'tone'—rather a monotone indeed—and the most absurd customs are enforced by physical punishment and moral pressure to keep little boys in their place and make them feel how small they are. All this imprints rather the opposite of the powers of enterprise required in business. It puts a premium on adherence to etiquette and the slavish following of tradition, and bars any original ideas and behaviour. It is a Public School ideal to 'play the game', but business inventiveness and competition imply the thinking out of new games, not just play the old games with the old rules. The emphasis placed on games, again, detracts from interest in mental work. No one can gain much popularity by intellectual achievement, and original zest in this direction is usually effectively knocked out of a boy by the time the 'milling' process is over. The prefect plan does form some training ground in system, but it is the power required for the intimate face-to-face supervision of a group of men, not the more abstract powers required in the head of a large firm who must spend most of his time in an office away from the actual scene of operation. At least one of our supposedly qualified richer boys is thus, in Britain, likely to have had his enterprise knocked out and another his intelligence damped down at school. Of the remaining three, one may go out into business with or without a modern university degree and perhaps be a success; and the other two may be taken to have gone up to Oxford or Cambridge. What happens to these undergraduates?

At the universities games are not compulsory, the mental work is more interesting, and there is less discouragement of enterprise. The view that business is relatively dishonourable compared to the 'services' and liberal professions, and that a tradesman is no gentleman, persists, however, at the older universities (as it does to some extent at the Public Schools) and channels the more ambitious boys, not forced by inheritance into some family concern, away from business. Hence while England has perhaps the ablest lawyers and civil servants in the world, her business men are on the average of lower attainments and keenness than their opposite numbers in the United States.[1]

[1] This paragraph gives the substance of a paragraph in my *Logic of Industrial*

What about the careers of the five relatively poor but able children who succeeded in surviving the consequences of poverty early in life?

Of recent years children of relatively poor British parents (thanks mainly to local education authority awards and a highly specialized secondary school education) have been able to reach the university in larger numbers. Whether they attend the older or the newer universities, many are destined to be school teachers or technicians, but a certain proportion of them either take commerce courses with a view to a business career or, qualified as technicians, end up via production management at top level.

The chief circumstance checking the flow of capable working-class boys into business is the difficulty of finding positions that lead anywhere. Such positions, where they do exist, are too often reserved for family connections, or friends of the directors or partners. Usually the young man with initiative and brains, but no connections, has to accept a subordinate routine position from which he has no assurance of being promoted, however efficient he may have proved. It may pay best to leave school for business at sixteen, since any more lucrative or promising position will probably not be obtained by leaving the university at twenty-one. This, as explained earlier, is definitely the position in the consumer's co-operative organization.

Thus it comes about that of the five potential top managers among the British poor, remaining in spite of their poverty, two may be lost by the educational wayside at sixteen (perhaps one will succeed eventually)

Organization (p. 256) written and published in 1933, which came under strong criticism. In 1951, however, the Anglo-American Council on Productivity's team on *Education for Management* pointed out (Report, p. 8) that:

'To be a high industrial executive in America is not only eminently "respectable" but is "socially desirable". It is a prevailing opinion that business attracts the best talent from educational institutions, whereas in Britain there is a strong tendency for the best students to find their way into the Civil Service and the professions generally.'

The importance of sociological attractions *channelling* a country's able children into one profession or another is now, in fact, fairly generally recognized. Sir Raymond Priestley, Vice-Chancellor of the University of Birmingham, wrote in his 1951 report to the University Council (p. 22):

'We [in Birmingham] do not in fact ever receive a fair sample of public school men. But, if this is true, and if it is also true, as I believe it is, that Oxford and Cambridge have a prejudice against developing the applied sciences on the large scale, then this channelling of brains and character to the public schools must aggravate the already difficult problem of producing sufficient engineers of such quality of mind and personality as will enable them to make their way on to the directorates of the great industrial concerns and to see that the best possible use is made of the genius for invention and design that the nation unquestionably possesses. In the present situation too great a proportion of the elite of our youth is likely to pass through the great humanities specialist courses—such as Greats and Modern Greats—and the Cambridge Triposes; either to the Civil Service or to research in pure science.'

while of the three survivors reaching the university, one will probably drift into teaching and another into a purely technical vocation. Is it too much to hope that one of these qualified poor may definitely get the preparation for business management and thus, supplemented by an occasional richer graduate, yield one or two out of a population of a thousand able, willing, and educated for the successful administration of large-scale British enterprise?

The American tradition is that there is no class system in the sense that a boy or girl of poor parents cannot enter a higher income class, and in 'Middletown' citizens 'refrained from the use of "class" language'.[1] Undoubtedly (at least for whites) the education system is in fact more uniform and at secondary or high school and university level is more open to all comers than in Britain. Nevertheless, even in the northern and western states of America there is considerable class immobility. A sample of the residents of San José, California, showed between 60 and 73 per cent of the occupations of sons to be about the same class level as those of their fathers.[2] Joslyn and Taussig[3] showed that of the fathers of a sample of business leaders[4] 56·7 per cent were themselves business men and 13·4 per cent professional men; although of the total occupied married male population only 7·4 per cent and 2·8 per cent were respectively business or professional men. Of the occupied married male population as many as 31·9 per cent were non-skilled labourers and 41·6 per cent farmers, but among the fathers of the business leaders only 2·2 per cent and 8·6 per cent followed these occupations. In short, sons of 'middle class' business and professional men are much more likely to become business leaders than perfect mobility would allow. These American authors found also that nearly a quarter of all partners or owners, over a quarter of all chief executives and over a third of all subordinate executives had influential connections in their present business. Among executives these proportions were greater in smaller than in larger businesses. Possibly there were more family businesses among them.

The differences between Britain and America in the recruitment and training of business leaders thus appear matters of degree, questions of more or less, which no doubt will eventually be measured. From our present limited knowledge it can only be surmised that the mobility which allows business leaders to be recruited from poorer families in substantial proportions is greater in America thanks to the prevailing traditions and philosophy and to wider opportunities for learning both

[1] McIver and Page, *Society*, 1950, p. 375.
[2] Op. cit., p. 368.
[3] *American Business Leaders*, 1932, p. 240.
[4] 8,749, or over half of the names selected as leaders by objective tests from Poor's *Register of Directors*. See Taussig and Joslyn, op. cit., Chapter II.

academic and vocational; and that there is less, if any, deflection of possible recruits from the richer families by reason of odium against business. Opportunities and philosophy are, however, rapidly changing in Britain and traditions breaking down. Possible bourgeois recruits and their parents can no longer afford to prefer the prestige of the professions to the pecuniary attractives of business; and in the future the present extensive award system may carry many more proletarians through the university to the topmost levels of business authority. In short, business will have a wider range of choice and more of the few born capable of it will attain business leadership.

CHAPTER VIII

SUMMARY AND CONCLUSIONS

§ 1. SUMMARY OF FINDINGS

I

(1) Structural analysis of the people engaged in the main orders of industry shows that Britain has a higher proportion than America in manufacture and mining, lower in agriculture. In both countries, however, over half the occupied population are now in services, and until recently an increase of people in services has been the trend.

(2) Between industries the major distinction is whether they provide services or goods and if goods, the technical characteristics of the product and of the material and processes used. Manufacturing industries vary widely in the weight, durability and uniformity of their materials and their product. They differ also in the stage, early or late, at which they occur in the production sequence from the extraction of material to the marketing the product (in which distribution to final consumer is the last stage). Other industries provide service or repair at any or all stages. These ergological differences have profoundly different effects on the location of plants and, through various intensities of mechanization, on the size and scope of plants and firms in different industries. Intensity of investment is also reflected in financial or accounting ratios such as fixed to total assets, annual wages per total capital, or sales per fixed investment.

These ratios as well as the horse-power per worker show a wide range of variation among manufactures, but it was found that the same industry will in both countries usually have a similar technological rank. For instance, though the general level of mechanization is higher in America, any one industry will tend to have the same relative position in degree of mechanization among British and among American industries.

(3) Within an industry the social structure consists of congregations of people in factories or plants, and organizations of peoples in undertakings or firms. The firm, which may own one or several plants, is the unit within which planning, control and government is carried on. In free enterprise capitalism, a firm may choose which transactions it wants to perform. Partly for this reason industries are difficult to define precisely except as the aggregate of certain plants specializing in certain transactions. Practical organizers have come to realize that there are no pre-ordained categories of industry, but industries, groups and orders

381

of industry must be distinguished according to types of production for purposes of administration and collective bargaining. New industries have continually grown up, while others die or merge together.

(4) Measured by workers employed the sizes of plants and firms are, in almost all industries, widely distributed; very small units exist side by side with large. But most industries are marked by a prevailing range of size of plant or firm within which the bulk of their workers are employed. The prevailing size appears surprisingly similar in Britain and America for the same industry. In both countries industries such as iron and steel and motor-cars can be classed as predominantly large-plant; others like clothing, predominantly small-plant. The same size distribution is also found in both countries in industries where the bulk of workers are (like rayon) in largish or (like cotton spinning) in medium sizes of plant, or where, like clothing and tailoring, workers are not concentrated in any typical size of plant. Taking manufactures as a whole the average American plant employs less workers, but only slightly less, than the British. Over recent years the average size of manufacturing plants both in Britain and America has remained stable in the majority of industries when measured by workers employed. But reckoned in volume of output it has increased. This significant difference in reckoning is due to machines continually displacing workers.

The variety in sizes is still wider for firms than plant, and the size larger; a few mammoth firms both in Britain and American employ (usually in a number of factories) a considerable proportion of all the workers in manufactures. The British firm measured in persons employed is on average larger than the American.

(5) The places where different industries occur, and the spatial relations of their plants, one to another, form different patterns with various degrees of localization. According to these location patterns, recognizable by statistical measures, such as the coefficient of localization, industries can be classed as rooted to resources, residentiary (tied to the usually dispersed consumers), swarming, linked (tied to another producer) or footloose. Outstanding examples of each pattern are, respectively, iron and steel, baking, cotton, machine-making and light engineering. The same industries tend to fall into the same classes of pattern in Britain and in America; the patterns persist, and industries do not readily move.

(6) Plants or firms extend the scope of their activities in different directions and to different degrees; they 'integrate' very differently. In Britain and America, some firms and plants confine their work narrowly and specialize, others extend their work vertically over several processes, laterally over several types of product, or diagonally to include services. Studying the structures where a firm integrates several plants,

American research has found that the constituent plants most frequently perform the same activities, next most frequently lateral activities diverging from the same material, then vertically related activities. Wide integration also occurs within a plant; 719 of the plants owned by the fifty largest American manufacturing corporations each made six or more types of products, 153 of their plants making nineteen to a hundred.

II

(1) When the meaning of the words used is made clear, a working hypothesis can be formulated about mechanized manufacturing, where materials and product are more or less transportable. This hypothesis is that large-scale operation, usually involving larger organization, standardization and specialization is of greater efficiency than small-scale, due to the principles of bulk transactions, massed reserves and multiples. Objective measures of this efficiency can be found in survival, growth, productivity, wages for workers, profits and cost per unit.

(2) Examining the hypothesis of large-scale efficiency, the high proportion employed in large firms and plants in many British and American manufactures, and the increase in the proportion employed in large firms are quantitative indications, tested by survival and growth, of superior efficiency. Qualitative arguments have hitherto suffered by a confusion between the different structures to which they referred. There are economic advantages in the large firm with a single plant, in the large firm producing a single article in one or more plants, in the large firm owning several plants each engaged upon different processes and products, and in other structures with large-scale features; but the advantages are not the same.

The profits test of efficiency has been applied to the American large firm regardless of its sub-structure. Results, where different industries were not mixed up, showed on the whole higher rates of profit, or lower rates of loss, on capital in the larger firm and especially greater stability in profits throughout trade fluctuations. The small firm survives by virtue of the difficulty of supervising small scattered plants, the need for a strong profit incentive in coping with nature, and with human nature (especially in customers), and the absence of the need for high capital or for risk-spreading integration. Specialization among firms allows small firms to operate one process or make one product on a large scale. The existence of many small firms is, however, due not to any logic in their fitness for purpose but to a time-lag, or to competitors' inefficiency, —or unwillingness to kill them; the small firms found at any time to exist, may exist only for a short while—their infant death rate has been found high in Britain and America.

(3) The comparative cost-of-production test of efficiency has been applied in several American industries. Some enquiries found that larger or medium-sized plants produced standard products at less cost than smaller plants in the iron and steel, the cement and other manufactures. Larger plants in British and American industries yield higher earnings per man-hour than smaller plants. Statistical enquiry into the characteristics of British and American industries where large plants prevail show that on the whole they are highly mechanized industries. Industries where small plants prevail are on the whole industries where transport costs force proximity to dispersed materials and markets. There is a connection between size of plant and degree of dispersion or localization such that the lower the coefficient of localization of an industry the smaller the prevailing size of its plants tends to be.

In Britain, though less so in America, a secondary trend was disclosed, cutting across this main tendency. Industries where the coefficient of localization is *very* high are also, like industries where it is low, industries where small (or medium) plants prevail. This association of small (or medium) plants with a high localization is explicable on the logical grounds of the external economies of small but specialized plants localized with linked industries in a production centre—a 'concatenation' which provides many of the same economies as the internal economies of a single plant.

(4) Integration is the opposite of specialization and standardization and should logically prove inefficient. But realistic case-studies of actual structure show that integration often enlarges the scale of operation where the various products and processes integrated have common costs; that technical factors such as avoiding reheating of materials, service on the spot, supervision of quality and convenience in distribution through retail stores often make integration economical; and that to avoid risk due to fluctuations and uncertainty in the customer's demand, in competition and in progress, a firm is logical in not concentrating on one product. There is, however, an optimum integration beyond which many firms have 'over-integrated', as evidenced by the thousands of models of the same product which the standardization movement can only try to reduce to perhaps hundreds. Over-integrated firms may, however, survive, if they do, for temporary or incidental reasons.

(5) Several of the industries most highly localized in Britain and America are, in spite of apparent logic, not concentrated near the materials they procure or the markets to which they distribute, but 'swarm' almost anywhere. Their localization is due to the external economies of a pool of skilled labour, of services and of linked industries which specialize in different vertical stages or lateral lines or diagonal services. Large local integrations partly replacing, partly reinforcing

large plant organization are particularly measurable in the industrial conurbations of America and Britain. Dispersion and not localizaton is still required where the costs of procurement and distribution outweigh the economies of large-scale localized production. Some industries are rooted to dispersed, intransportable or heavy materials, others tied, almost like services, to a dispersed market for heavy products. Existing locations cannot all be justified as now logical, but sometimes were determined irrationally at the time the plants were built, or, if rationally then, irrationally for the present, or rationally for private but not for public benefit. National or regional planning is thus often necessary for a logical location in the private and especially in the public interest.

(6) The hypothesis that a large-scale specialized production carried out by large plants and firms is in manufacture logically the most efficient, is subject to modification in practice by reason of technical, distributive and risk factors. The facts often diverge from even this practical logic, a divergence attributable either to a logical producer having to cope with an illogical situation or to his own illogic, or both.

A manufacturer is up against nature and human nature including his own. Nature limits him by reason of scarcity, physical dispersion, intransportability and the variation and discontinuity of supplies and materials. Human nature limits him in the lack of adaptability of consumers and fellow producers to changing circumstances and their resistance to changes in institutions, to standardization and to the applied science of the engineer, though the engineer's plans may be far more efficient and logical than the old customs and traditions.

A producer who is not a manufacturer but an extractor or servicer has to contend more severely still with nature or human nature and, as a whole, extractive industries like agriculture, and the service industries are organized in small units. Large-scale organization appears, however, in mining, insurance, banking, railroads, wholesaling and chain and department stores and public utilities, which suggests the economic logic of the large plant and firm in spite of natural and human obstacles.

III

(1) The consumer has needs, wants and demands; the three are not identical, and the wants and demands of different consumers are very different. In western civilization the consumer is free to demand the products and services he can afford, and the variety and uncertainty of his behaviour limit economical large-scale production and raise middleman's distributive margins.

(2) Some regularity does, however, underlie the consumer's demands owing to the restriction of the poor to the necessities of life and the

conventionality of the middle-class. Producer's demands tend to be logical, though less so than might be expected. The most unpredictable are the demands of the well-to-do consumer who, as Engel's Law implies, spends relatively little on standard foods, fuel and other necessaries and has more individual taste. In America, at least, these less predictable demands are growing.

(3) Unpredictability of demand is particularly awkward where demand must be anticipated and equipment for producing goods planned and laid down beforehand. Small-scale operation is multiplied when rival producers continually devise new designs which may or may not be fit for purpose, and distributors apply high pressure salesmanship.

(4) The would-be large-scale producer of standard designs, looking to the logic underlying consumption, can forecast to some extent from generalizations like Engel's Law about the expenditures of various classes of consumers or from known seasonal, cyclical or secular trends in incomes, or from the linked consumption of goods in joint demand like housing and furniture.

(5) Competition with its uncertainty as to the policy of rival producers brings difficulties in the logical application of market research. If large-scale operation is to be attained, competition must be, to some extent, a knock-out by the fittest, using considerable sales pressure and advertising which may in turn lead to an illogical artificial demand. But if 'bally-hoo' is countered by consumers' research and scepticism, advertising can concentrate demand on well-designed articles which can then be produced economically on a large scale. Monopoly has economies, especially in marketing, over and above those due to the maximum scale operation it makes possible, and competition is particularly expensive and wasteful where there is high fixed overhead cost. Monopoly obtained by combination thus has attractions.

(6) Possible consequences of monopoly are exploitation and restriction of output and employment and a check to the use of new inventions. The conditions enabling monopoly power to be exercised are largely structural, particularly large organizations—unitary firms and federal combines as well as trade associations. In Britain combines, mostly of holding company type as legally recognized, increase the proportion of employment in large organizations; so that half the factory population which was, by 1935, in firms employing five hundred or more was in 1963 in firms of 3,240 or more. The area covered by single systems of interlocking directors was still wider. It is not, however, large organization absolutely, but size of unit relatively to the size of the industry, the 'concentration' in one or a few units, that is relevant to monopoly, and this does not seem to have increased much till quite recently. Monopoly is not necessarily always connected with combination (knock-out competition may be effective) and not all sorts of combines or large units aim at

monopoly. It is therefore important to analyse and disentangle the structure, government and policy of such organizations and their relation to their particular industry, before resorting to state action—often a matter of counter-organization.

(7) High degrees of concentration of workers under the control of a few organizations have been discovered both in Britain and America and show a remarkably similar extent for industry as a whole and similar incidence for particular industries. In both countries, for instance, high concentration is significantly frequent in industries, often small industries, within the chemical and the primary metal group both of them with high capital intensity, and within the assembly group of industries requiring large plants. Thus the pattern of concentration is due largely to the particular industry's inherent technical and distributive supply and demand characteristics, of which state policy must take account if it is to be effective.

IV

(1) The trend toward greater mechanization and larger plants and firms requires that attention be shifted from the higgling of the market to the policy (particularly the investment policy) of large firms and their internal organization. Investment implies, in logic and fact, more fixed costs, and planning to meet trade fluctuations, with an increase in staff, office workers and middle management.

(2) The entrepreneur of classical economics owning, managing and ruling the firm has now to share his rule with a staff of specialized, salaried managers; while ownership, if not abandoned, is shared with partners and 'shareholders'. The difficulties of management do not set a limit to size of organization, as economists assume, if through delegation of powers the middle management lightens the load of top government. The problems involved of internal organization and of procedure for decision-making have been tackled by pioneers in the application of political science to industry like Barnard, Fayol and Urwick.

(3) The load on top management is lightened in hierarchical line structure by rules determining the chain or span of command—rules which are often broken. Inherent sources of inefficiency are failure to get and use information, bureaucracy and lack of expert and specialized skill.

(4) In a functional structure, the load on top management is lightened by rules (likewise often broken) to ensure that the work to be done is sufficiently and economically covered. Functional structure carried out too radically has often cut across the hierarchical rules and led to disunity of command.

(5) The load on large-scale top management is perhaps lightened

most by delegation of expert advice to a specialist staff, and of the necessary planning and co-ordination to a general staff, with co-ordination strengthened by committees. But there has been a lag in introducing this structure logically.

(6) Lightened by delegation, the 'core' load left at the top level of industrial government consists of final decision on policy about what and how much to produce at what price and with what investment, and of decision on internal organization, particularly the creation of new posts, appointment to upper posts and top supervision and co-ordination.

Two questions then arise: who performs this top role of industrial government (the answer differs for capitalist, nationalized and co-operative systems); and what is the stimulus to the governing party to command, and to the governed to co-operate, efficiently?

V

(1) The American corporation and the British joint stock company have increased the extent of their control over industry to a remarkably similar degree as plants, firms and capital invested have become larger. Plants owned by corporations and companies are larger than other plants, and there appears to be a factual and logical connection of deeper investment due to technological progress, with increased incorporation. The legal constitution of the company or corporation is based on the theory that sovereignty, though delegated to the board of directors, should lie with the risk-bearing shareholders.

(2) Shareholders as a body, do not in fact wield the top rule that the law supposes, partly because in many companies voting is restricted to particular classes of share, but mainly because shareholders are too many, transient, ignorant and business shy, or too much engaged on other business. Risk-spreading leads many shareholders to divide their interest between several companies. The distribution of shares in American and British companies is most unequal, more unequal than the distribution of gross incomes in the population as a whole, and gives power to a few holders of large blocs of shares who form a minute fraction of the whole number of shareholders.

(3) Taking the twenty shareholders with the largest holdings as including a group that might conceivably wield top rule, the larger British and American industrial and commercial companies are found to possess similar patterns in the proportion of voting or common shares owned by this number. In both countries the proportion of shares held by the largest, the second, third and fourth largest owners and so on, tapers off first sharply and then slowly, permitting a predominant voice among the twenty largest shareholders to the largest few. The majority of these large shareholders are persons mentioned by name, but

institutions and other companies frequently appear among them. The evidence of an extremely unequal distribution of shares, and the nature, connections and directorships of the largest shareholders taken cumulatively suggest that, in a certain proportion of British and American companies, top rule is in fact still wielded by a few shareholders. This quasi-entrepreneur leadership is particularly evident where large shareholders have family connections or are holding companies

In Britain, 1951, this proportion was probably about a third of all industrial and commercial companies of over £3m. nominal capital; more for the smaller companies. In America the owner-controlled proportion appears to have been declining since 1938. A 'managerial evolution', if not revolution, is apparent.

(4) In companies where no very large shareholdings appear and no coherent group of owners seems in a position to be sovereign, policy is possibly decided by the directors as a whole or, more plausibly, by some particular director or directors. Some directors 'lead' by virtue of their shareholding or by representing banks or other financial interests, especially when they have promoted the company; others lead by virtue of their specialized professional training; and yet others by virtue of business connections indicated by their multiple and interlocking directorships. These types of directors are recognizable and are likely to have a distinct line of policy. In large American, but less so in British companies, the most frequent type of leader is an executive officer such as the president or managing director, and policy is then likely to depend on the relatively unpredictable personality of the executive and on his ascertainable conditioning and training as a promoted employee, a technician, an administrator or an executive transferred from another business. Company policy is thus partly predictable even when the shareholder is divorced from government.

(5) Within large companies there are different interests such as large or small ordinary and preference shareholders, bond-holders, directors; and also personalities that may or may not conflict. No one interest necessarily dominates in capitalist control generally, but one or other probably dominates in particular companies. The different types of domination are to some extent predictable according to industries, and result in measurably different policies: safe, or enterprising and risky; of national benefit or the opposite. An overall restraint is imposed, however, by the type of work upon both the form of organization and upon policies.

VI

(1) Capitalist government of industry has been replaced by public operation or control both in America and Britain when, for reasons of

need or for convenience, no price is to be charged or the price chargeable is insufficient to cover cost. Even when costs can be covered, Britain has nationalized certain industries where large-scale organization involved private monopoly and basic control of the whole economy or where inefficiency appeared under capitalism. Criteria are not entirely economic; to compare alternative industrial governments as a whole, philosophic and political aspects were brought into the account.

(2) The British economy today shows a mixture of small-scale and large-scale capitalist, nationalized and co-operative governments. The actual assignment of an industry to one alternative or another follows fairly logically from its demand or supply characteristics. These are its basic or common service to the community, or the need it meets for education, for conservation of resources or for capital unobtainable under capitalism, or from the routine nature of its business or the risk of monopoly exploitation.

(3) The government of British nationalized industries follows a fairly regular pattern. Instead of direct ministerial operation, a specific public corporation is set up, manned and supervised by a Minister, and charged with covering costs by its prices. Nationalized industries differ, however, in their degree of large-scale central control as against a federation of regional controls—a difference depending largely on technical factors. The Ministers appear to be exercising more top government than contemplated in the paper constitutions; and efforts are being made to democratize nationalized industries by greater Parliamentary control over the Minister and by more effective consumer councils. The process of nationalizing a capitalist industry has been easier, where capitalism is represented by company rather than entrepreneur control.

(4) The organs of government of consumers' co-operative societies are meetings open to all members, and unpaid committees elected by members each with one vote. In the local British retail societies with part-time committee-men, the manager-secretary appointed by the committee has great influence. The elected Board of the manufacturing wholesale societies, where the directors, elected by delegates of the retail societies, work full-time, appears unenterprising and often inexpert in policy.

(5) The criteria of meeting educational and other needs, rather than commercial demands, have been applied to British broadcasting. Consumers' sovereignty is in doubt when artificial demands are built up by advertising and met at a monopolistic price. The prices minus dividend on purchase of co-operative societies are low, but societies, though extending membership, are not growing in terms of goods produced or sold. Consumer councils to counteract the possible bureaucratic indifference to the consumer of nationalized industries were duly set up

but have not been very effective so far, possibly for lack of research staff independent of the administrative bureaucracy. On the democratic test of government by the people all large-scale organization tends to fail, but government for the people, wherever or whenever they live (in rural areas, or in future times) is more easily achieved by large-scale nationalization.

(6) Tests suggested earlier showed the efficiency of large-scale operation. Large capitalist firms seem more efficient than large nationalized or co-operative organizations where enterprise rather than co-ordination is required; but they have not shown stability. The century of large-scale capitalism has been a century of industrial progress; and where, as in western civilization, population has been limited and state or trade union policy has redistributed wealth, it has been a century of social progress too.

(7) Alternative forms of industrial government, tested by the 'performance' criteria of meeting needs, consumer wants, democracy and efficiency, score fairly equally; but co-operation falls behind if democracy is omitted and nationalization if needs are omitted. In Britain and even in a *laissez-faire* regime like that of America, considerable state planning and supervision is in fact practised to overcome shortages in war or defence preparations; also to curb monopoly, to avoid financial instability and trade depressions, to conserve national resources and to encourage efficiency by standardization and progress by research. These objectives are similar to those sought by nationalization.

VII

(1) Identification of labour with the interests of the firm depends largely on the firm's size, the number of ranks in the hierarchy and the remoteness of the control. Without such identification, labour is apt to feel a mere cog in the large-scale industrial machine, and trade practices may check adjustment to large-scale machine techniques, such as shift-working. One of the strongest incentives overcoming, in America, these checks to productivity and also to mobility of labour is 'transpecuniary'. The American worker connects output with earnings and earnings with something to buy 'through' his earnings. Signs of a further 'social' stimulus to production are found if small autonomous groups are organized within the large factory. Any cost-benefit analysis comparing the attractiveness of different occupations must take full account of the importance workers attach to the respectability and sociability of any job they seek.[1]

(2) The analysis, applied to labour, was found applicable to the

[1] A comprehensive model of such possible attractions and deterrents is presented in Fig. 19 of Florence, *Atlas of Economic Structure and Policies.*

supply of capital. It is still persons, the entrepreneur or other 'inside' contributor of capital of the firm or an outside investor, who make decisions to invest in, or finance, a firm. The joint stock company does not provide participation in government and control of policy as the necessary stimulus to overcome the outside man of property's unwillingness to take financial risks; nor, in Britain, is he actuated by the 'gambling instinct'. He spreads and frequently transfers his risks, but still demands a fairly high yield on his capital. The capacity of the outsider to finance industry depends on his savings and they in turn on his assets, his propensity to consume and the relation between his earnings and standards of living.

A national problem is how to stimulate movement of capital into efficient industry, when the outsider is ignorant, subject to herd instinct, and liable, as in the boom of 1928, to invest in meretricious concerns. The failure of the private investor and ossification attributable to re-investment of company funds has, in Britain, fostered nationalization.

(3) *Very* large organization usually involves the displacement of the entrepreneur, managing and owning his own business and remunerated through a profit by fee'd directors and by salaried managers of a corporation and, in Britain, a joint stock company or a nationalized concern. Profits, stronger than any other pecuniary motives, do not normally apply to the top executive. The middle managers have the incentive of promotion and higher salaries unless there is nepotism or the seniority rule. Various non-pecuniary supplement pecuniary motives. Bearing in mind, realistically, that different motives stimulate different types of leaders to act differently toward specific problems, five practical problems can be picked out as important in large-scale operation: large-scale innovation, rational co-operation or combination with other firms, re-investment of capital in fixed plant, internal co-ordination and making the top appointments.

(4) Four main types with some subdivisions can be recognized both among British and American business leaders, each with specific incentives and capacities to solve these problems. One type combines leadership with ownership and is thus an entrepreneur in the original sense of the word (I). The other types are (II) financiers (III) part-time directors and (IV) salaried executives.

(I*a*) The self-made entrepreneur, who is rare in large modern firms, has often failed to adapt himself and his organization to large-scale planning and technique. He re-invests heavily taking big risks in the hope of big profits, but his education and experience and individualist habits are usually not conducive to the successful co-ordination and integration of specialists or to co-operation with other firms. (I*b*) The family entrepreneur may head a smoothly co-ordinated firm but may not always be large-scale minded or co-operate with other firms. He wants business independence and may have the fixed standard of living of the gentleman of leisure and the chance of a higher profit may not necessarily move him to new enterprise and risk-taking. (1c) Real leadership when wielded by a large or a few large controlling shareholders directly or indirectly represented on the board of directors is likely to have a strong influence on policies of capital re-investment or high dividends. The question will be decided according as the large holders want immediate or long-term gains. Large shareholders are not particularly efficient at co-ordination, but will often favour large-scale co-operation with other firms.

(II) The financier's money and power incentives lead to ambitious combinations and mergers between firms which history has shown to be ambivalent in result but often to make strongly for re-investment in fixed plant, rationalization, and large-scale innovation.

(III) The part-time director holds very little capital and thus gets little incentives from profit. He cannot be expected to co-ordinate staff very efficiently. If he is an interlocking director he will certainly promote co-operation between firms; if he is a professional man he will probably show judgment in top appointments and give sound rather than spirited advice on questions of policy.

(IV) The executive leader, whatever his antecedents, is mainly paid by salary and has a less strong pecuniary incentive than the entrepreneur, shareholder or financier paid by profit, but he often identifies himself with the firm and strives at least for a satisfactory output. If before his appointment, he was (a) always an employee of the firm he will probably be particularly keen to re-invest profits in the firm, though probably in liquid rather than fixed assets. He may be too conservative of the old tradition to change to large-scale operation or co-operation with other firms. If he was (b) originally a technician he will be particularly keen to innovate and re-invest profit but probably will not shine at internal co-ordination and top appointments. If he was (c) originally a trained administrator his *forte* will be co-ordination, if he came from (d) other business, he will not be obstructed by the traditions of the firm and should lead toward large-scale innovation. The last two types of executive appeared satisfactory in other requirements of large-scale leadership.

(5) Management, tested by the average productivity of different firms at the same job, appears to differ widely in efficiency. The pecuniary incentive to enterprise and management does not always act positively and the different types of business leader have different supply price curves. It is normally assumed that more pay will call forth more exertion; but some types of leader may remain unaffected, others restrict their activity, and some estimate can be made of trends in the frequency of these several reactions. To get more work out of business

leaders at less cost, non-pecuniary incentives were found important. The long-run supply of business leaders and their price depends on attracting and training young persons; here Britain has lagged behind America. But now in most British universities, much more numerous than in 1945, management studies are offered.

(6) Only a small proportion of children exist in any country with powers for top industrial government and many of these young hopefuls are prevented from developing and exercising their powers either by the poverty of their parents or, particularly in Britain, by the social conventions and institutions such as 'public schools' and the older universities. Here training and codes of behaviour like the 'gentleman-ideal' are ill-suited to large-scale industrial leadership and many promising young people who reach these places are deflected into 'liberal' professions. Till recently only in some modern universities was the same provision made as in America for a training and orientation toward industrial government.

VIII

It is worth bringing together the main dissimilarities and similarities of American and British industry today. The main dissimilarities are in the degree of mechanization and in the strength of the incentives to labour and the attractives and facilities offerred to enterprising and research-minded management, together accounting largely for the higher physical output per head in America. In spite of these differences and others more fundamental, such as differences in size of area, climate, soil and mineral resources, striking similarities were found in the structure and government of industry. Corresponding manufacturing industries had similar patterns of location, integration and prevailing sizes of plant and firm (measured in number of workers) and similar degrees of concentration of output from a few firms. In manufacture *generally* both countries had much the same distribution of sizes of plant and firm, and had similar average staff ratios, and the same trends in these distributions and ratios. Manufacturing, extraction, building, trade, transport and the service orders of industry ranked roughly the same in average size of firm in both countries. This similarity in structure was capped by a striking similarity in the government of the firms. The proportion of business controlled by British joint stock companies and by American corporations was very similar in the corresponding sectors of industry. Company and corporation, the leading form of capitalist government for large firms, had much the same very unequal distribution of shareholdings. Partly as a result, a fairly similar frequency of assignment of the top control was possible either to executives or to one or a few large shareholders who might be persons, a family, or another or other companies or corporations. The holding company device is reinforced in both countries by interlocking directorates.

The inside management relations, and the outside relations of industrial firms with trade unions and consumers were also very similar. The most surprising result of investigation was the similarity in the degrees of concentration of control in the hands of a few firms for the various branches of manufacture, and the similarity of the high concentration of control over the output of certain products. The risk of monopoly or oligopoly in certain similar industries is calling forth policies of investigation or supervision by the public authorities of both countries.

§ 2. SUMMARY OF RESEARCH METHODS

(1) The truth or probability of the findings just summarized depends on the research methods used. These methods were not purely deductive, abstract and analytic, as in the orthodox approach of economic theory, nor yet purely empirical, descriptive and realistic, but integrated theory as a working hypothesis with attempts at inductive statistical generalization based on the observed facts of the situation as a whole. The method may be called *realistic analysis*. Some of the hypotheses advanced have not yet been sufficiently tested by the data, notably the theories of the different reactions to various stimuli of types of industrial leaders; some of the statistical results still cannot be interpreted satisfactorily. Yet a certain interlocking of hypothesis and statistics was achieved by the comparative method and the isolation of factors.[1]

[1] See Florence, 'Patterns in Recent Social Research', *British Journal of Sociology*, September 1950, and Chapter VIII of *Economics and Sociology of Industry*.

Data had to be obtained by observation rather than experiment; and the observed data of human behaviour if measurable at all show a peculiarly wide and skew variation. Statistical measures had to be devised to summarize frequency distributions far from normal. An arithmetic mean size of firm or plant or an arithmetic mean shareholding could not generally be taken as typical, except for *ad hoc* comparisons where data were not otherwise measurable. Special and often indirect indices, like the grading of sizes of plant or the coefficient of localization had to be used to measure the points at issue.

Once the facts and relationships between facts were as far as possible objectively measured, explanation was attempted. The hypotheses used as explanations were drawn from a wide sweep of social sciences—not merely, like the law of increasing returns, from economics, but from political science, psychology and sociology. Integration thus figured largely in the methods used—integration of theory and observation

395

familiar in the natural sciences, and integration of various social sciences with one another and with developments in the applied sciences and technology.

(2) The approaches through the different social sciences had this in common that they began with structural analysis before discussing function. The starting point of each was the fact of measurable, observable societies or bodies of men. Exploration then proceeded comprehensively into the relations, for instance competition or monopoly, or the functions of these structures, particularly the functions of government. We asked *who* before detailing *how* or *why*, and focused attention on the more persistent and pervasive bodies of persons and their characteristics. The main permanent social structures of industry are the plant and the firm and the chief characteristics described and explained are their size and site, and the scope and scale of the industries or operations in which they are engaged.

The structural and statistical approach ensures that every part of the whole situation is comprehensively covered before a generalization is considered proved, and that an author does not rest content with specially picked illustrations of an hypothesis.

(3) The structure of an industry was taken as logical if it resulted in maximum efficiency, given the technical and distributive conditions. Comparing two countries with differing geographical, social and political circumstances, the surprising similarity of the structure of the same industry in both countries, and the wide differences between different industries in the same country, isolated the technical factors and pointed to their importance. They formed the basement,[1] so to speak, under the ground floor of an industry's social structure. Industries were in consequence considered separately, particularly manufacturing industries which are relatively free from the restrictions imposed by natural risks and uncertainties, scattered materials and consumers and supplies and products costly to transport. This analysis supplied some evidence for the main hypothesis of the logical efficiency of large-scale production in large plants, firms or localizations.

(4) When some of the facts appeared to negative this hypothesis, logical on technical grounds, for getting the greatest physical output of goods and services from the least physical input, this 'engineer's' logic was, as a next step, modified by allowing for psychological and sociological factors which are partly reflected in economic values. The consumer follows social tradition and custom and will not adapt his demands to physically efficient production and distribution on a large scale; or he has unpredictable whims and fancies that in a free society increase the producer's risks.

[1] An alternative metaphor to 'hinterland' which I have adopted more recently for the ergological interpretation.

Man as producer also deviates from what appears rational economic behaviour, and the behaviour of worker, investor and industrial leader was studied empirically in a standard frame of reference. Men's external observable reactions to external observable stimuli were traced through their supposed internal willingness in response to incentive and capacity in response to conducives. The apparent irrationality of all three factors of production may be logical behaviour for ends deemed irrational merely by the observer; or may be illogical behaviour whatever the end. Both possibilities can be studied rationally through this frame of reference, and a certain regularity of behaviour found in the apparent irrationality—a regularity which permits, after all, some scientific generalization and prediction.

(5) The structure of industries determined at basement level by technical and physical, and modified at ground-floor level by economic, sociological and psychological factors, appeared at the next level to determine the form of government of industries. The large-sized plants and firms with large capital investment, found prevailing when the industry was free of physical restrictions and on large-scale production were governed rather differently from small plants or firms. A few corporations, joint stock companies or schemes of nationalization are taking the place of many small entrepreneurs. This evolution makes the political science of large organizations more important, in comparison with the economics of perfect competition in a market of large numbers of suppliers. The political science of industry cannot be content with the legal façade but seeks the real seat of power, the real mechanism of government and the real pressures and balances of forces within the actual large-scale structures. Here again much variety was found and resort was necessary to the statistical method to show relative frequencies, degrees of power, and correlations of types of structure with types of function.

(6) The mood of this enquiry has until this point been indicative, not imperative or optative. New policies, structures or forms of government have not been demanded, nor have new ultimate objectives been wished for. Practical considerations were limited to the question how given industrial ends and objectives were to be reached by variously organized bodies of men with maximum efficiency. For instance, types of business leader were evaluated, with a system of marks, in respect of specific requirements for large-scale operations, and alternative forms of industrial government evaluated similarly for specific objectives. These objectives were, however, not narrowed down to the satisfaction of consumers' demand as economists are wont to do, but were widened to include meeting social needs and safeguarding, as far as possible, democracy and stable progress.

This book may fitly end with some practical conclusions that follow from the search for efficiency in attaining these objectives.

§ 3. SOME PRACTICAL CONCLUSIONS

The efficiency kept in view throughout this book has been defined as maximum return, physical, pecuniary or psychological, to an industrial organization or to the nation as a whole at minimum physical, pecuniary or psychological cost, and industrial organization was considered logical in so far as it resulted in this efficiency. Long-period physical efficiency of industry would probably be increased by larger-scale operation, that is, specialization of firms or plants upon one or a few standard commodities produced or sold in large quantities. Many producers and distributors in Britain and America were shown to operate on a small scale; small plants and small firms continue to provide goods and services in unstandardized variety and small quantities. Explanations of this seemingly inefficient organization which have been attempted in this book, suggest some practical steps, particularly in overcoming checks and breaking vicious circles, toward a more efficient and more logical structure.

The distributive system and the margin exacted by middlemen is blamed for high costs and the high prices charged to the consumer. Goods could certainly be obtained cheaper if consumption were planned by authority so that the exact kinds and amounts required were known and standardized. Such a revolution is not a practical proposition in countries which look to the continuance of a system of distribution for free demands rather than for officially determined needs. This system must remain expensive, since the final consumers will buy on a small scale for family use only, and all consumers' demands remain multifarious and unstable. The practical policy for abating this variability is to trace types, find the elasticity and forecast the trend of demand, then design products and fix prices, and output accordingly, charging highly for atypical unstandard demands.

The competition of numerous firms adds greatly to the difficulties of such scientific marketing. New varieties produced on a small scale are continually placed on the market by competitors thus stimulating in a vicious circle further demands for a variety that involves further small-scale operation. Competition and trade fluctuation also makes it difficult to compass a long term policy for an industry as a whole. Reliance for breaking the circle must be placed either upon the emergence, out of competition, of firms operating on a large scale (possibly through advertising of specific products), or upon the combination of firms each eventually specializing in one product. Both courses carry the danger of monopoly, and may thus eventually involve, as at least

a partial solution, the public control of industries, if not their nationalization.

In its internal organization the large-scale, highly capitalized firm
must apply scientific method both to its physical investment and to its
human management and employment relations. The growth of mechanical equipment and investment in fixed capital specialized for one
purpose, which probably involves large plants, demands scientific
accounting as well as industrial psychology. Working short multiple
shifts should, for instance, show lower costs by fuller use of physical
capital equipment and of fixed overhead. While distributing shorter
hours over the labour force, adjustment of habits are called for.

Economists have supposed the efficiency of large-scale firms to be
limited chiefly by the ability of the manager to cope with the volume
of work, but this limitation of size is not necessary if some political
science is applied in the organization of the specialized managers that
large-scale operation permits. Large firms are often inefficient because
they indulge in a wide variety of small-scale operations, and neglect
principles of organization. Both hierarchical organization and functional system may lead to inefficiency in large-scale operation and thus
to its neglect. This check may be overcome by organization of line-and-
staff type. By delegation of powers and the introduction of a general staff
and expert staff advisers, large-scale organization can avoid too great a
concentration of duties while preserving a 'core' of ultimate undelegated
and unspecialized top government. In industry this top government,
apart from questions of internal organization, normally reserves to
itself the policy of what to make and with what investment of capital,
how much to make and at what price. Top rulers change, and the long-
run top questions are who appoints the top ruler, and how.

In the modern large-scale capitalist system corporations and joint
stock companies have displaced the small-scale entrepreneur and care
must be taken that they do not lose the enterprise associated with his
name. If top government of large companies and corporations, usually
wielded by one or a few large shareholders or by one or a few salaried
executives, or both, does not link profit directly with enterprise,
efficiency for the company's purposes is not automatically secured by
a strong pecuniary incentive. Instead, enterprise and efficiency must be
won by the appointment of executives of energy and ability for large-
scale operation, with some strong non-pecuniary incentives. It is an
advantage to the capitalist company when it can draw talent from many
sources.

Though efficient for its own purposes a company may not be ful-
filling national purposes efficiently particularly if it has a monopoly.
Its valuation of returns, costs and efficiency are not always the national
valuation. The British displacement of capitalism by nationalization in

certain types of industries and the corner carved out by consumers' co-operation has an underlying logic applicable, possibly, elsewhere. Even in America, wherever monopoly exploitation threatens, nationalization may be found more effective than the present national and state regulation.

Forms of nationalization can be devised that should preserve both central control over large-scale operations and the enterprise associated with the older, if not the present, capitalism. Semi-independent public corporations, taking the place of control by government departments, engage as efficiently as joint stock companies in industries where orderly routine, technical expertise, provision of capital and conservation of resources are important. Like large-scale operation under any control, efficiency under consumer or state control depends largely upon the selection of the business leaders and upon constant research into organization and methods of management.

Large-scale operation will not in and by itself ensure efficiency. Apart from the insistence of the consumer upon an uncertain multiplicity of goods and services that cannot be produced at low costs by large-scale methods, there are difficulties in adjusting employment, investment, and management relations into the frame of large-scale organization. Men engaged in business as directors, executives and risk-taking investors are, no less than the labourers they employ, human beings, not as is sometimes assumed, hundred per cent efficient mechanisms. They are not continually geared up to the maximum productivity; and certain psychological conditions are required to keep them even to a moderate efficiency. Thus there is a certain loss of stimulus to the human factor connected with large-scale organization itself, and since scale of operation is partly dependent on scale of organization, this may offset the physical advantages of large-scale operation. Psychological as well as organizational checks to a logical scale of operation can, however, be overcome by psychological means, and new incentives and conducives must be applied to stimulate the willingness, and the ability of labour, investors and business leaders.

The loss by labour of all sense of identity with the interests of the firm as the firm grows larger, can be met by the grant of more local autonomy to factory departments and by a policy of informed joint control in the determination of the conditions immediately affecting the workers' life. The weakness of non-pecuniary incentives makes the wage or salary, and especially piece-work payment, of outstanding importance in large-scale industry, but the strength of this inducement depends upon connecting earnings with productivity in the worker's mind and with the outlets for spending them. A flexible, ambitious standard of living and leisure time in which to spend earnings, enhances the 'transpecuniary' incentive of higher wages. Non-pecuniary factors such as the comparative sociability or respectability of an occupation affect the mobility of labour, and industries that require additional men, but lack these attractions in the eyes of labour, must compensate for their net disadvantages by paying higher wages. The state can help toward a flexible economy by providing physical conducives to movement such as cheaper transport and houses.

There are checks to the logical accumulation, distribution, and redistribution of industrial capital in the outside investor's ignorance, and the suspicion of shareholders not in control of company policy. These checks may be partially overcome by the forced publication of more accurate and systematic information in the prospectus and the accounts, and by recording the large beneficial holders in companies, and the transactions of directors and officers. To avoid ossification of industrial structure threatened by companies re-investing their profits in the same industry, more reliance will probably have to be placed in the future upon the knowledge of investors in the market about old and new capital issues, and upon sponsorship by trustworthy issue-houses. Failing these capitalist measures for the supply of capital, there remain the public corporations financed by fixed interest loans and state regulation by investment control.

The wide variation in the average productivity of plants and firms in the same industry, engaged on the same product in the same country, (as also between different countries) shows the practical possibilities of greater efficiency in management; the less productive could, by comparing methods and organization, be pushed up nearer the standard of the more productive. The weakening of the pecuniary stimulus at the very core of industrial government by the substitution in the company or corporation of salaries for profit is a serious check to the keen conduct of large organizations and partially explains the survival of small firms. Incentives to efficient industrial leadership are not, however, all purely pecuniary or non-pecuniary; and transpecuniary stimuli in the uses of profits or salaries must be observed for their effect on the various types of persons actually governing industrial organizations—the owner-manager or entrepreneur, the director and the executive of various experience. Each of these types reacts differently to the vital problems upon whose solution large-scale efficiency depends, such as innovation and large-scale expansion, co-ordinating the several departments and functions of the firm, re-investing capital, in making appointments, and co-operating or combining with other firms. The type of leader must be selected appropriately for the nature of the business, and appropriate incentives offered.

For a long-run expansion of efficient production, larger supplies of business leaders must be obtained in order to break the vicious circle whereby short supplies keep up salary costs, forming, in turn, habits of consumption requiring persistence of those costs. In Britain where able personnel turn away from industry, a business career must be invested with stronger non-pecuniary social and psychological incentives and attractives than are at present attributed to it in educational circles; and an education must be devised that will conduce to administrative efficiency and will stimulate movement of all the potentially efficient into the various branches of business.

The present English educational system has recently undergone thorough readjustment and will soon help more in supplying efficient industrial leaders. Education should lead children out of the rut but it still tends to abandon most of the relatively poor at an early age and to inculcate those who remain at school still deeper in traditional attitudes. Both in America and Britain, training as well as experience are required for maximum efficiency in the government of modern large-scale industry. We must break the vicious circle that stops able men training for business because, as so demonstrably in Britain, business thinks able men need not train. Employers should realize that the standard of workaday efficiency tolerated in the past is not necessarily the future standard required in a more logical industrial organization. Educational institutions should make it possible for the fittest of the new generation, whatever their class, to prepare for the profession of business government, and thus allow inborn ability plus training plus experience to supply leadership for a new, more efficient, more logical industrial order.

INDEX *

Abramson, V. (Lyon and Watkins), 272n, 311
Absentee ownership, 217
Absenteeism, of labour, 175, 299, 301, 320; of shareholders, 219–20; of directors, 245
Accountants, 341, 353
Accounting ratios, 13, 255–6, 341
Acton Society Trust, 359n
Adelman, M., 150n
Adjudication, 3, 176–7, 190, 199–200, 324
'Administered' prices, 150–2
Administration, 3, 177–9
Administrative headquarters, 35
Administrators, 356–60, 366; see also Executives
Adolescent industries, 170; see also Growth
Advertising, expenditure on, 73; consumers' self-protection against, 144; prestige, 143; creates artificial demand, 144, 162, 293; can help standardization, 144, 398; psychology of, 295, 303n
Agriculture, 5, 6, 14, 21, 47, 76n, 88, 105, 114, 207–8, 265, 268–71
Aims, 264, 292–3; see also Amenity; Democracy; Education; Fair shares; Health; Progress; Stability
Air transport, 268–71, 277, 307
Aircraft, 30n, 50, 171
Albu, A., 219
'Alienation', 180, 317, 321
'All-sites-all-sizes law', 84
Allen, F. L., 221n, 249n, 350n
Allen, G. C., 147, 221n, 351, 364n
Allocation of resources, 147, 257
Aluminium rolling, 8
Amalgamation, 288; see also Combines; Mergers; Take-overs
Amending the constitution, 199, 208–11; see also Structuring
Amenity as an aim, 293
American-British comparisons, see British-American comparisons
Anchors and chains industry, 102
Andrews, P.W.S., 75–6, 182
Anglo-American Productivity Teams, 357n, 378n
Apparel Group, see Clothing
Appeals procedure, 180
Appointing function, 176, 179, 198–9, 339 et seq.
Apprenticeship, 172
Aristotle, 323
Arithmetic mean 40; see also Averages
Armstrong, A. (and/) Silberston, 159
Articles of Association, 209
Artificial stone, see Concrete
Ashley, Sir William, vi, 357
Assembly industries, 9, 10, 81–2, 195n, 387

Assets, 72–4; fixed, per person, 150
Associations, see Trade associations
Attractives: to labour 325–6; to business leaders, 366–9, 375–8; to capital, 383
Austen, Jane, 374
Autocracy, 262–3
Automobiles, see Motor and cycle industry; Transport; Vehicles
Autonomy, 174–5, 280; of factory groups, 324, 400
Averages, shortcomings of, 24–6, 39; see also Arithmetic mean; Median

Babbage, C., 61n, 71
Bain, J., ix, 27–30, 127, 150
Baker, J. C., 177
Baking Industry, 10, 39, 47, 108, 126, 382; see also Bread
Balancing of Production, 62, 89–91, 106–8; see also Multiples, Principle of
Baldamus, W., 245n
Baldwin, Lord, 319
Balfour Committee on Industry and Trade, see Committees
Banking, 16, 77, 114–16, 206, 207, 268–71, 310, 327, 385
Barna, T., 150
Barnard, Chester, 177, 183n, 202, 323, 387
Barriers to entry, 148–9, 162
Baumol, W. J., 355
Baykov, A., 310n
Beacham, A. (and Cunningham), 263n, 327n
Bedaux system, 324
Beeching, Lord, 307
Beesley, M., 154–5, 252
Beet sugar, 30, 109
Behaviour, concept of, 180
Behavioural sciences, 180
Bendix, P., 180
Benham, F. C., 254n, 344n
Bennet, A. J., 101
Berle, A. A., 177, 226n, 230
Best, R. D., 346
Beveridge, Lord, 274n, 294
Birmingham, University of, 104n, 155n, 245n, 248n, 252n, 297, 357, 372, 378n
Blair, J. M., 43, 67n, 110, 159
Blast furnaces, 99
Bliss, J. H., 13n, 255
Blue-collar workers, 168
Board of Trade, 313; Engineering Trades Committee (1916–17), 95
Boards of Directors, size of, 229–30, 242, 352n
Bonds, 206
Boots, see Shoes

* Industries are indexed for references in the text but not if occurring only in the statistical tables. Economic sectors (e.g. agriculture, mining) are listed wherever they occur.

INDEX

INDEX